Core Competencies of Relational Psychoanalysis

Core Competencies of Relational Psychoanalysis provides a concise and clearly presented handbook for those who wish to study, practice, and teach the core competencies of Relational Psychoanalysis, offering primary skills in a straightforward and useable format.

Roy E. Barsness offers his own research on technique, and grounds these methods with superb contributions from several master clinicians, expanding the seven core competencies: therapeutic intent; therapeutic stance/attitude; analytic listening/attunement; working within the relational dynamic; the use of patterning and linking; the importance of working through the inevitable enactments and ruptures inherent in the work; and the use of courageous speech through disciplined spontaneity.

In addition, this book presents a history of Relational Psychoanalysis, offers a study on the efficacy of Relational Psychoanalysis, proposes a new relational ethic and attends to the importance of self-care in working within the intensity of such a model. A critique of the model is offered, and issues of race and culture and gender and sexuality are addressed, as well as current research on interpersonal neurobiology and its impact on the development of the model. The reader will find the writings easy to understand and accessible, and immediately applicable within the therapeutic setting. The practical emphasis of this text will also offer non-analytic clinicians a window into the mind of the analyst, while increasing the settings and populations in which this model can be applied and facilitate integration with other therapeutic orientations.

Core Competencies of Relational Psychoanalysis is inspired by Barsness' students; he was motivated to create a primary text that could assist them in understanding the often complex and abstract models of Relational Psychoanalysis. Relevant for graduate students and novice therapists as well as experienced clinicians, supervisors, and professors, this textbook offers a foundational curriculum for the study of Relational Psychoanalysis, presents analytic technique with as clear a frame and purpose as evidence-based models, and serves as a gateway into further study in Relational Psychoanalysis.

Roy E. Barsness is a Professor at the Seattle School of Theology and Psychology, the Brookhaven Institute for Psychoanalysis and Christian Theology, and the Relational Psychoanalysis and Psychotherapy Group, Seattle. He was formerly the Clinical Director at Seattle Pacific University and a Clinical Associate Professor at the University of Washington School of Medicine, Department of Psychiatry. He has been in independent practice for over 25 years.

Relational Perspectives Book Series
Lewis Aron & Adrienne Harris
Series Co-Editors

Steven Kuchuck & Eyal Rozmarin
Associate Editors

The *Relational Perspectives Book Series* (RPBS) publishes books that grow out of or contribute to the relational tradition in contemporary psychoanalysis. The term *relational psychoanalysis* was first used by Jay R. Greenberg and Stephen A. Mitchell in *Object Relations in Psychoanalytic Theory* (Cambridge, MA: Harvard University Press, 1983) to bridge the traditions of interpersonal relations, as developed within interpersonal psychoanalysis and object relations, as developed within contemporary British theory. But, under the seminal work of the late Stephen A. Mitchell, the term *relational psychoanalysis* grew and began to accrue to itself many other influences and developments. Various tributaries—interpersonal psychoanalysis, object relations theory, self psychology, empirical infancy research, and elements of contemporary Freudian and Kleinian thought—flow into this tradition, which understands relational configurations between self and others, both real and fantasied, as the primary subject of psychoanalytic investigation.

We refer to the relational tradition, rather than to a relational school, to highlight that we are identifying a trend, a tendency within contemporary psychoanalysis, not a more formally organized or coherent school or system of beliefs. Our use of the term *relational* signifies a dimension of theory and practice that has become salient across the wide spectrum of contemporary psychoanalysis. Now under the editorial supervision of Lewis Aron and Adrienne Harris, with the assistance of Associate Editors Steven Kuchuck and Eyal Rozmarin, the *Relational Perspectives Book Series* originated in 1990 under the editorial eye of the late Stephen A. Mitchell. Mitchell was the most prolific and influential of the originators of the relational tradition. Committed to dialogue among psychoanalysts, he abhorred the authoritarianism that dictated adherence to a rigid set of beliefs or technical restrictions. He championed open discussion, comparative and integrative approaches, and promoted new voices across the generations.

Included in the *Relational Perspectives Book Series* are authors and works that come from within the relational tradition, and extend and develop that tradition, as well as works that critique relational approaches or compare and contrast it with alternative points of view. The series includes our most distinguished senior psychoanalysts, along with younger contributors who bring fresh vision. A full list of titles in this series is available at https://www.routledge.com/series/LEARPBS.

Core Competencies of Relational Psychoanalysis

A Guide to Practice,
Study, and Research

Edited by Roy E. Barsness

Routledge
Taylor & Francis Group

LONDON AND NEW YORK

First published 2018
by Routledge
2 Park Square, Milton Park, Abingdon, Oxon OX14 4RN

and by Routledge
711 Third Avenue, New York, NY 10017

Routledge is an imprint of the Taylor & Francis Group, an informa business

British Library Cataloguing in Publication Data
A catalogue record for this book is available from the British Library

Library of Congress Cataloging-in-Publication Data
A catalog record for this book has been requested

ISBN: 978-1-138-21836-9 (hbk)
ISBN: 978-1-138-21839-0 (pbk)
ISBN: 978-1-315-43777-4 (ebk)

Typeset in Times New Roman
by Keystroke, Neville Lodge, Tettenhall, Wolverhampton

To my students, with deep gratitude

Contents

Contributors

Lewis Aron, PhD is the Director of the New York University Postdoctoral Program in Psychotherapy and Psychoanalysis. He was President of the Division of Psychoanalysis (39) of the American Psychological Association, founding President of the International Association for Relational Psychoanalysis and Psychotherapy (IARPP), and co-founder and Co-Chair of the Sándor Ferenczi Center at the New School for Social Research. Lewis Aron was one of the founders of and is an Associate Editor of *Psychoanalytic Dialogues*, and is the Series Editor (with Adrienne Harris) of Routledge's *Relational Perspectives Book Series*.

John Thor Cornelius, MD is a psychoanalyst working in Sacramento, California. In addition to his private practice, he is Clinical Faculty at the University of California at Davis, Department of Psychiatry, and is the Instructor of Record for the Introduction to Psychodynamic Psychotherapy course.

Adrienne Harris, PhD is Faculty and Supervisor for the New York University Postdoctoral Program in Psychotherapy and Psychoanalysis, the Psychoanalytic Institute of Northern California, and is co-founder of the Sándor Ferenczi Center at the New School University. She is Series Editor with Lewis Aron of the *Relational Perspectives Book Series*, which has published over 60 volumes. Her publications include: *Rocking the Ship of State: Women and Peace Politics, Gender as Soft Assembly, Storms in Her Head* (with Dimen), *On Women and Hysteria* (with Aron), *The Legacy of Sándor Ferenczi* (with Botticelli), *First Do No Harm: Psychoanalysis, Warmaking and Resistance*, and *The Legacy of Sándor Ferenczi: From Ghost to Ancestor* (with Kuchuck). She is an editor of the new IPA ejournal *Psychoanalysis Today*, and serves on the editorial boards of: *Psychoanalytic Dialogues, Psychoanalytic Perspectives, Studies in Gender and Sexuality,* and the *Journal of the American Psychoanalytic Association.* Her plenary address on Sabina Spielrein was published in a recent issue of the *Journal of American Psychoanalysis.* She writes about gender and development, analytic subjectivity, ghosts, and analysts developing and writing around the period of World War I.

Steven Knoblauch, PhD is an internationally recognized clinician, teacher, and lecturer on psychoanalysis and psychotherapy. He serves as Faculty and Clinical Consultant at the New York University Postdoctoral Program in Psychotherapy and Psychoanalysis, the Institute for the Psychoanalytic Study of Subjectivity, and a number of other training programs in New York City and abroad. He is the author of numerous journal articles and the book *The Musical Edge of Therapeutic Dialogue.* This text has been translated into Japanese. He is also co-author with Beatrice Beebe, Judith Rustin and Dorienne Sorter of *Forms of Intersubjectivity in Infant Research and Adult Treatment.* He is on the editorial boards of *Psychoanalytic Dialogues, Psychoanalytic Perspective,* and the *International Journal of Psychoanalytic Self Psychology.* He also serves on the Board of Directors of the International Association of Relational Psychoanalysis and Psychology. He continues to play saxophone and study Brazilian percussion, integrating these experiences into his teaching and practice.

Steven Kuchuck, LCSW is the Editor-in-Chief of *Psychoanalytic Perspectives,* Associate Editor of Routledge's *Relational Perspectives Book Series,* Board Member, Supervisor, Faculty and Co-Director of Curriculum for the training program in adult psychoanalysis at the National Institute for the Psychotherapies (NIP), Faculty/Supervisor at the NIP National Training Program, the Stephen Mitchell Center for Relational Studies, and other institutes, and serves on the Board of the International Association for Relational Psychoanalysis and Psychotherapy. His writing focuses primarily on the psychoanalyst's subjectivity; most recently, he was a contributor to and editor of the Gradiva Award-winning book *Clinical Implications of the Psychoanalyst's Life Experience: When the Personal Becomes Professional* and *The Legacy of Sándor Ferenczi: From Ghost to Ancestor* (co-edited with Adrienne Harris).

Karen J. Maroda, PhD, ABPP is Assistant Clinical Professor of Psychiatry at the Medical College of Wisconsin, and works in private practice in Milwaukee, Wisconsin. She is the past ethics chair and board member of Division 39 (Psychoanalysis) of the American Psychological Association, and past President of Section III, Women, Gender and Psychoanalysis, of Division 39. She was elected to APA Fellow status in 2012. She is the author of three books: *Psychodynamic Techniques: Working with Emotion in the Therapeutic Relationship*, *The Power of the Countertransference: Innovations in Psychodynamic Technique*, *Seduction, Surrender, and Transformation*, and numerous book reviews and journal articles.

Karol Marshall, PhD, ABPP is a board-certified psychoanalyst and psychologist in Seattle, Washington. She has published numerous articles and reviews on aspects of sexuality in psychoanalysis: *Sex Is Funny That Way, Sexuality, Intimacy and Power: A Review, The Queering of Psychoanalysis: A Review*, and *Beyond Sexuality: A Review.* She has taught and lectured on eros, the transgender experience, and erotic transference, as well as creative writing for psychotherapists.

Nancy McWilliams, PhD teaches at Rutgers University's Graduate School of Applied and Professional Psychology and practices in Flemington, New Jersey. She is the author of *Psychoanalytic Diagnosis, Psychoanalytic Case Formulation* and *Psychoanalytic Psychotherapy*, and Associate Editor of *The Psychodynamic Diagnostic Manual*. She is a former President of Division 39 (Psychoanalysis) of the American Psychological Association.

Jon Mills, Psy.D, PhD, ABPP is a philosopher, psychoanalyst, and clinical psychologist. He is Professor of Psychology and Psychoanalysis at the Adler Graduate Professional School in Toronto, and is the author and/or editor of 17 books on philosophy, psychoanalysis, and psychology. Recipient of many awards for his scholarship, he received the Otto Weininger Memorial Award for lifetime achievement from the Canadian Psychological Association in 2015. He runs a mental health corporation in Ontario, Canada.

Stuart Pizer, PhD, ABPP is a founding board member, Faculty, Supervising and Personal Analyst, and former President of the Massachusetts Institute for Psychoanalysis; Assistant Professor of Psychology (part-time), Department of Psychiatry, Harvard Medical School; Faculty,

Supervising and Personal Analyst at the Institute for Relational Psychoanalysis of Philadelphia, and a past President of the International Association for Relational Psychoanalysis and Psychotherapy. He is an Associate Editor of both *Psychoanalytic Dialogues* and *The Psychoanalytic Quarterly.*

Allan Schore, PhD is on the clinical faculty of the Department of Psychiatry and Biobehavioral Sciences, UCLA David Geffen School of Medicine. He is author of four seminal volumes: *Affect Regulation and the Origin of the Self, Affect Dysregulation and Disorders of the Self, Affect Regulation and the Repair of the Self,* and *The Science of the Art of Psychotherapy,* as well as co-author of *Evolution, Early Experience, and Human Development* and numerous articles and chapters in multiple disciplines, including developmental neuroscience, psychiatry, psychoanalysis, developmental psychology, attachment theory, trauma studies, behavioral biology, clinical psychology, and clinical social work. He is past editor of the acclaimed *Norton Series on Interpersonal Neurobiology,* and a reviewer or on the editorial staff of more than 45 journals across a number of scientific and clinical disciplines. He has received a number of honors for his work, including an Award for Outstanding Contributions to Practice in Trauma Psychology from the Division of Trauma Psychology, the Scientific Award from the Division of Psychoanalysis of the American Psychological Association, and Honorary Membership by the American Psychoanalytic Association.

Daniel Shaw, LCSW is a psychoanalyst in private practice in New York City and in Nyack, New York, and Faculty and Supervisor at the National Institute for the Psychotherapies in New York. His papers have appeared in *Psychoanalytic Inquiry, Contemporary Psychoanalysis,* and *Psycho-analytic Dialogues,* and most recently, his book *Traumatic Narcissism: Relational Systems of Subjugation* was published by Routledge for the *Relational Perspectives Book Series.*

Anita Sorenson, PhD practices, teaches, and writes at the intersections of theology, psychoanalysis and spiritual formation. In addition to her position as Pastor for Spiritual Formation at Pasadena Covenant Church, she has a private practice in psychoanalytic psychotherapy in Pasadena, California.

Brad Strawn, PhD is the Evelyn and Frank Freed Professor for the Integration of Psychology and Theology at Fuller Theological Seminary,

School of Psychology in Pasadena, California. He obtained advanced training in psychoanalytic psychotherapy from the San Diego Psycho-analytic Institute in San Diego, California, and co-edited *Christianity and Psychoanalysis: A New Conversation* (with Earl Bland). In addition to publishing in the area of religion and psychoanalysis, he maintains a private practice in Pasadena.

Steven Tublin, PhD is Training and Supervising Analyst at the William Alanson White Institute, and on the faculty of the New York University Postdoctoral Program in Psychotherapy and Psychoanalysis and the Institute for the Psychoanalytic Study of Subjectivity. He is the author of articles on a number of topics, including contemporary psychoanalytic technique, the use of music and literature in clinical inquiry, and the interface of politics and psychoanalysis. He serves on the editorial board of *Contemporary Psychoanalysis*, and is an associate at Upstart Logic, an organizational consulting firm. He is in private practice in New York.

Pratyusha Tummala-Narra, PhD is an Associate Professor in the Department of Counseling, Developmental and Educational Psychology at Boston College. She is also in independent practice in Cambridge, Massachusetts. She has presented and published on the topics of immi-gration, race, trauma, cultural competence, and psychoanalytic psycho-therapy. She is the author of *Psychoanalytic Theory and Cultural Competence in Psychotherapy.*

Acknowledgments

In a book that focuses on relationships, it seems fitting to begin with a thank you to Marie, Jonathan, and Jordan, the three persons who have loved and surrounded me for the longest period of my life and have challenged me to be a better husband, father, and person. Thank you, and all of my family and friends, who stick with me in spite of me, believe in me, confront me, laugh with me, and now celebrate with me in the completion of this book.

I am particularly grateful to the Co-Editor of the *Relational Perspective Book Series*, Lewis Aron, without whose vision and advocacy, this text would not have come to be. Lewis is a man of extraordinary vision and contribution, and I am humbled that my idea caught his eye and that he saw the value in my efforts for this book. I am also indebted to the *Relational Perspective Book Series'* Associate Editor Steven Kuchuck for his keen insights, helpful edits, and gracious presence, whose guidance in this project has helped immeasurably, and to Adrienne Harris, whose encouraging words in our chance meeting at the Freud Museum in Vienna gave wind to the writing and completion of this book. I am also very grateful to the publisher Routledge and to editor Charles Bath, who has been always patient, kind, and supportive, and also to the project management team at Keystroke including Huw Jones (copyeditor), Sarah Brown (proofreader), Jeremy Complin (indexer) and Maggie Lindsey-Jones (project manager) for their help and guidance during the production process.

Thank you to each contributing author for your generosity and graciousness. You have no idea how much you have come to mean to me, both personally and professionally. Each of you have been excited to contribute to the idea of a text focusing on core fundamentals in relational psychoanalysis and granted me considerable editorial latitude in accomplishing this goal. I have been deeply moved by your kindness and thoughtfulness, and am certain the readers of this text will be forever grateful for your contribution to their professional development.

And special thanks to the research participants who gave freely of their time to reflect upon their work that generated the original data that formed the basis of this book. Their gift now offers the student *Core Competencies in Relational Psychoanalysis*. Without their participation, this project could never have succeeded. I wish to also thank Tim Stanley and Sean Hogan, who spent endless hours assisting me in the coding of the data and asked critical questions that sharpened the accuracy of our findings. Thanks also to Christina Kemp and Chris Paredes for their assistance in conducting the comparative analysis in the review of the International Association for Relational Psychoanalysis and Psychotherapy symposium.

In the past few years, I have had the privilege to be on the faculty of the Brookhaven Institute for Psychoanalysis and Christian Theology. Founded by gifted and wonderful imagineers Lowell and Marie Hoffman, this organization has brought together many like-minded folk, providing a place to deepen our passion for psychoanalysis and theology. In particular, I have had the privilege to work with dear colleagues and friends Earl Bland, Anita Sorenson, and Brad Strawn, teaching, presenting and writing together. What a privilege.

This book is dedicated to all my students from the several institutions that I have had the privilege to teach (Fuller Theological Seminary, Seattle Pacific University, and University of Washington), and in particular the students at the Seattle School of Theology and Psychology, who have inhabited my life these past 13 years. It is students who asked the right questions that motivated the research and the writing of this book. I am also grateful to those who grant me the privilege of supervising and mentoring them, and to my/our patients, who instruct us all in bettering our skills in our service to others. But beyond being students/mentees, I also wish for them to know that they are mentors to me and have been instrumental in my own formation as a person, as a clinician, and as a professor.

With gratitude . . .

Organization of This Text

Part I: Current Research and History of Relational Psychoanalysis

This part covers:

- the research behind the Core Competencies;
- efficacy of the models;
- the history of relational psychoanalysis.

Part II: Core Competencies

This part has been designed to offer the reader four points of entry into learning the Core Competencies:

- one-line "naming" of each Core Competency
- a brief introduction to each Core Competency
- properties of each Core Competency, offering categorical bullet points taken from the qualitative research that describes it;
- an in-depth essay on each Core Competency.

Part III: New Frontiers

This part covers current issues relevant to contemporary practitioners, including:

- relational ethics;
- the brain and psychoanalysis;
- sexuality and gender;

- cultural considerations;
- self-care.

Part IV: A Critique

This part offers the reader a critique and a counter-critique of Relational Psychoanalysis, offering theoretical constructs that will continue to need revision, conversation, thoughtfulness, and thoroughness in order to continue to advance our field.

Part I

Current Research and History of Relational Psychoanalysis

Chapter 1

Core Competencies in Relational Psychoanalysis

A Qualitative Study

Roy E. Barsness

Freud (1912) compared psychoanalysis to the game of chess where "only the opening and closing of the game admit of exhaustive systematic description . . . and that the gap left in between can only be filled in by the zealous study of games fought out by master hands" (p. 342). He says this about rules:

> I bring them forward as recommendations without claiming any unconditional acceptance for them. The exceptional diversity in the mental constellations concerned, the plasticity of all mental processes, and the great number of the determining factors involved prevent the formulation of a stereotyped technique, and also bring it about that a course of action, ordinarily legitimate, may at times be ineffective, while one which is usually erroneous may occasionally lead to the desired end. However, these circumstances do not prevent us from establishing a procedure for the physician which will be found most generally efficient.
>
> (p. 342)

Freud ultimately settled upon the primary techniques of the "ethic of honesty" and "free association", with the primary goal of providing insight through the interpretation of transference, defenses, and resistance, and with the end goal that the ego gain sovereignty over id impulses and superego constrictions.

Though this tradition has been challenged since psychoanalysis began—in particular the role and the authority of the analyst and the intersubjectivity of the analytic work—by such theorists as Theodore Ferenczi, Erich Fromm, Frieda Fromm-Reichmann, Karen Horney, Irwin Singer, Harry

Stack Sullivan, and Clara Thompson, it eventually grew into a movement in the 1980s. In Chapter 3 in this volume, Adrienne Harris effectively charts the evolution of the relational movement and its shift away from a one-person drive theory towards intersubjectivity, mutual influence, and interaction. This re-positioning opened the windows to other traditions "derived from constructivism, critical theory, post-structuralism, feminist philosophy, sociology, linguistics, narrative literary criticism and decon- structionism" (see Mills, Chapter 17 in this volume), arriving at what I call a psychoanalytic ecumenism. This union offers a mixture of the diverse elements from the richness of all of psychoanalytic theory, philosophy, and culture, inviting a new analytic discourse of interactionism and mutual influence extending our practices beyond insight and interpretation.

As one would expect, this new understanding of the self as socially, politically and culturally constructed, muddied analytic technique. Indeed:

> As relational theory has evolved, it has increasingly emphasized multiplicity in the encounter: multiple interpretive frames that might be relevant, multiple self-states from which to speak and to address, and multiple meanings that might plausibly be assigned to the patient's and the dyad's experience. Taken together, these render the notion of a unitary, proper technique, as it has been traditionally understood, problematic.
>
> (Tublin, Chapter 4 in this volume, p. 72)

As relational psychoanalytic theory has reworked historical models through a perspectival lens, the rules for practice have become less clear. As relational theorists turn from insight as the primary order of change to the reworking of early trauma within the therapeutic dyad, new techniques and clinical skills are required. With this in mind, a qualitative research study was conducted to determine fundamental techniques or competencies that can provide a working framework for contemporary analytic practice. This chapter reports the results of that research.

Why Study Psychoanalytic Technique?

The genesis of this study emerged from years of teaching a year-long graduate course in relational psychoanalysis. In addition to this year- long course, students are enrolled in several other courses in systemic, developmental, and object relations theories. They are also involved in an intensive three-year practicum/case conference training program focusing on issues of transference/countertransference, establishing the therapeutic frame, and exploring narrative as well as practices in intervention. However, encountering their first internship and introduced to their first patient, they report feeling like "a deer caught in the headlights." One year, a student raised her hand and with a tenor of lament stated, "I have all this theory, but I don't know what to do." As students were now being exposed to evidenced-based models, some ready to sign on because it was comprehensible and immediately applicable, while the analytic theories remained obscure, inaccessible and the practice of it "squishy," I felt a call to some action. Consequently, I decided to work more intentionally in translating and communicating rich and complicated psychoanalytic theory into how we actually practice.

I began by mapping my own mind as it operates within the clinical hour. In this mapping, I began to see a pattern in how theoretical constructs and psychoanalytic knowledge occurred in actual practice with my patients. The pattern went something like this. The patient would stimulate some thought and/or affect in me, I would begin to consider this stimulus from developmental, early object relations, transferential/countertransferential affective, and cultural perspectives, while considering defensive structures, interpersonal relations, and how the narrative unfolded. I metabolized these relational and affective complexities with questions such as, "What the hell is going on here anyway?" or "What is the feeling or thought trying to express?" Furthermore, I attended, as best I could, to countertransference reactions, understanding them not only as something of my own, but as a stimulus and a means of access to the inner workings and interpersonal world of the patient. I simultaneously imagined ways I could articulate my experience to the patient, mindful of the possible effect it might have upon our relationship. As I had earlier in my practice adopted a particular stance of courageous speech/disciplined spontaneity (see Barsness and Strawn, Chapter 12 in this volume), I was aware that in speaking honestly and openly about what I was experiencing within the analytic relationship, misunderstandings, ruptures, and enactments would befall us. Therefore, I did my best to consider the consequences in expressing my experience, aware of the cost of entering into the "fray" and the effort required in "working through" difficult dynamics. Having mapped my own mind and finding it helpful to me as well as in teaching and supervision,

I decided to advance the study of my own "map" by constructing a qualitative study "mining the minds" of seasoned analytic clinicians.

Prior to launching the study, however, I had to contend with my own reluctance to codify technical principles, easily indentifying with many in the analytic community who view the analytic experience as "unformulated technique," believing that what we do is intuitive, automatic, and organic. Though this may be true, I think it is also true that each analyst has their own internal guidelines—they simply are not articulated. For example, I think we "know" we *listen* in a particular way different from other disciplines and we "know" we *engage* our patients differently. The question is: how do we do this?

Secondly, my draw to psychoanalysis was essentially a spiritual calling. I understand our vocation as an invitation into the sacredness of the human encounter where change and healing occurs by calling to the depth of each person within the encounter. The nature of the human condition, the fluidity of the self and our relationships, is not categorical. So to label, categorize, or define scientifically this unique relationship, I found unsettling.

However, with the echoes of Freud in my mind, "that these circumstances [should not] prevent us from establishing a procedure for the physician which will be found most generally efficient" (Freud, 1912, p. 342), and recalling the value of science as an intellectual and practical effort to systematize and make sense of the world through observation and experiment, I realized there did exist an intellectual and systemized ritual to my work that could be documented. I believed this was true for every analyst, and therefore set out to determine through research a baseline of fundamentals identifying the commonalities in our work. As is true in all research, these standards or Core Competencies are not the final word. However, these findings, I believe, do offer an important foundation that assists in fostering change in our patients' lives, and will hopefully encourage further research and dialogue.

It is also my hope that in building a bridge between theory and practice, understandings of theory will be less compromised. For example, I have found that students/supervisees can be loose cannons, misunderstanding theories such as mutual recognition, intersubjectivity, or disclosure as a means to irresponsibly spout off whatever is on their mind. I have also noted that when interpersonal conflict and entanglements occur within the treatment, rather than working it through, the therapist will often defensively "hide" behind diagnosis or interpretation. Often, if these ruptures are pursued, they are "repaired" by blaming the patient or by offering pseudo-apologies to avoid the ensuing conflict. Therefore, I hope that by having a set of guidelines informing and guiding theory, the integrity of a relational psychoanalysis can be maintained.

The overall purpose of this study is to:

- develop foundational competencies for the study and practice of relational psychoanalysis;
- offer a gateway into the study of relational psychoanalytic theory;
- address the concerns of what Freud (1912) referred to as "therapeutic ambition" and Greenberg (2001) referred to as "psychoanalytic excess," offering a framework as a guide for practice;
- offer analytic "techniques" with as clear a frame and purpose as evidenced-based models.

Method

A qualitative research study was conducted using in-depth interviews of 15 psychoanalysts identified with contemporary theories of relational psychoanalysis. To analyze the data, Grounded Theory Analysis (GTA) was chosen because, much like psychoanalysis, GTA is "emergent, is broadly constructivist and subjective, relying a great deal on hermeneutics while recognizing the importance of scrutiny and careful analysis" (Rober, Elliott, Buysse, Loots, & De Corte, 2008, p. 407). Similar to psychoanalysis, GTA seeks to let the data speak, while recognizing that the researcher and participant co-construct these data and, to some degree, the analysis. In GTA, the researcher repeatedly asks: "What is going on here?" "What are the core issues that are at stake?" "What is trying to be worked out?"

Grounded Theory Analysis was originally developed by Glaser and Strauss in 1967 as a method to assist in developing theory, grounded in data systemically gathered, organized, and analyzed. It is a method that does not assign prior assumptions to what is under study to prove or disprove, but seeks to gain a sense of central themes indicating a particular model or idea constructed from the data, and grounded in the participant's lived experience: "The generated theory explains the preponderance of behavior in a substantive area with the prime mover of this behavior surfacing as the main concern of the primary participants" (Glaser & Holten, 2004, p. 13). In applying GTA, I discovered an uncanny similarity between analyzing the data and how I work with my patients. Concepts such as co-construction, open-mindedness, patterning, and linking are common to both Grounded Theory and psychoanalysis. These methods outlined by Glaser and Strauss (1967), Strauss and Corbin (1998), Glaser and Holten (2004), Charmaz (2006), and L. Belgrave (personal communication, 2015), include:

> simultaneous involvement in data collection and analysis; constructing analytic codes and categories from data, not from preconceived logically deduced hypotheses; using the constant comparative method which involves making comparisons during each stage of development; advancing theory development during each step of data collection and analysis; advancing theory development during each step of data collection and analyses; memo-writing to elaborate categories specify their properties, define relationships between categories and identify groups; sampling geared toward theory construction, not for population representativeness; conducting the literature review after developing an independent analysis.
>
> (Charmaz, 2006, p. 5)

Participants

As qualitative research is suitable for in-depth explorations of a particular subject, the sampling process is expected to go narrow rather than broad. Thus, participants are sought who are in a position to be knowledgeable about the phenomenon under study, whether by expertise, experience, or both. For example, though this study might easily be generalized to other branches of psychoanalysis, it had a specific focus on relational psychoanalysis. Therefore, the participants were limited to:

• those who self-identified as relational psychoanalysts;
• those who had completed full psychoanalytic training at an analytic institute (with the exception of two academic psychologists, who have studied psychoanalysis extensively and are on the faculty of an institute and practice psychoanalysis).

Most had published in psychoanalytic journals. Two were among the founding members of relational psychoanalysis. All had over twenty years of experience.

Sample Size

Because qualitative research seeks depth rather than representation, sample size is determined by how deep one has to drill before no new information is discovered. Therefore, the researcher cannot predict sample size at the outset of the study. A method known as *theoretical saturation* determines when data collection can end. Theoretical sampling has the potential to be limitless, as each interviewee possesses his/her own personal and unique perspective. However, by coding data, assigning categories, and comparing early data to the categories until such time as no new data appears significantly different—that is, until they are fully described, with no holes, are connected through the data, and the researcher has some assurance no new data are needed—sampling can cease. Charmaz (2006) states: "Categories are 'saturated' when gathering fresh data no longer sparks new theoretical insights, nor reveals new properties of these core theoretical categories" (p. 113). Determining theoretical saturation was more reliably determined in this study by having two research assistants assist in the coding of the data. Codes were only included through consensus, and coding ceased when there was concurrence no new codes were emerging.

Sensitizing Concepts

Sensitizing concepts provide a useful yet potentially hazardous tool in Grounded Theory. Sensitizing concepts alert us to issues of importance while presenting a risk when the researcher "knows" the subject under study and can easily default to naming categories within the vernacular of what is being studied. Throughout the analyses, it was incumbent upon me to let go of my theoretical knowledge and to let the data have its way. For example, "enactment" was a common term in every interview, and it would have been easy to allow it to become its own concept without further analysis of it. However, each person had a different way of expressing it, such as "entanglement," "collision," "rupture and repair," or "getting sucked up," and these varying views were then collapsed into broader categories of repetition and working-through, as well as deep listening, affective attunement, and courageous speech. In this rather arduous process of determining codes and categories, I discovered again that having research assistants served as protection against submitting to the lexicon of the discipline when creating nomenclature for the categories.

The assistants were insistent in "keeping me honest" as they asked for clarification and helped expand the data into meaningful categories.

Data Collection

The collection of data was done through personal interview. Each potential interviewee was given the following invitation:

> I am asking you to participate in a research study about how the mind of a relational psychoanalyst functions in the actual therapeutic moment, to discern if there is a set of principles or practices that can serve as guideposts in the practice of our work.
>
> Prior to our interview, reflect upon the previous day at work or a particular patient with whom you are currently working. Consider and perhaps jot down how your mind was/is working and what kind of experiences, thoughts and feelings were/are actively informing your work. Consider the role or function that you play and the position or stance that you hold that you believe facilitates the work. Pay attention to the words you use and why. Consider what you believe is the desired outcome for your patient.
>
> In our interview I will listen and record your reflections, interact with you and facilitate further dialogue and ask questions such as the following:
>
> • What helped you through your day or your work with a patient? What did you do?
> • What ideal/principle/discipline did you want to hold on to but did not? Why?
> • What about your day/work matched your notion of relational psychoanalysis, what did not?
> • What did you hear yourself saying? Is this a common phrase in your work?

Interviews/conversations lasted on average 60 minutes. Each conversation was put in writing and sent to the interviewee for verification and editing. As Grounded Theory Analysis allows for and encourages progressive dialogical conversation, co-edits and verifications were essential to the process to best capture what the interviewee sought to convey.

Data Analysis

The data were initially analyzed through the use of open line coding, resulting in over 1000 codes, each code containing one complete idea from each interviewee. Through the constant comparison method, which incorporates four stages—"comparing incidents applicable to each category; integrating categories and their properties; delimiting the theory; and writing the theory" (Glaser & Strauss, 1967, p. 105)—data were then comared and interpreted across all interviews where particular concepts began to emerge. The entire process, from initial coding to focused coding to the development of a set of categories, required a constant return to the original data in order to refine the data and develop ideas for naming the primary categories. Rober et al. (2008) have noted that in using the constant comparison method, the data results "in a list of categories and subcategories, organized in a hierarchical category structure, where lower order categories are properties or instances of higher-order categories" (p. 409).

Table 1.1 illustrates the hierarchal structure of the subcategories to the core category Therapeutic Intent. The highest order within this hierarchal structure is called a core category; the lower categories demonstrate the properties of the core categories. (Please note: each Core Competency will be displayed in this format at the beginning of Chapters 4–10).

Table 1.1 Coding Example

Competency One: Therapeutic Intent

1.1   An analytic treatment is first established by a clear understanding of the intent or purpose of the analytic endeavor.

    1.1.1   Increased capacity to experience and manage multiple affective states and to enjoy the full range of emotion

    1.1.2   Increased access to multiple aspects of the self without shame

    1.1.3   Ability to comfort and soothe oneself and to be self-reflective

    1.1.4   Ability to accept responsibility

    1.1.5   Ability to tolerate ambiguity and uncertainty

    1.1.6   Ability to be more truthful with oneself

    1.1.7   Ability to think more creatively and openly about one's past rather than to continue to repeat it

    1.1.8   Relief from internal constraints and rigidities that have become problematic

    1.1.9   A more imaginative and creative mind

    1.1.10   Increased capacity to love and to work; self-efficacy

    1.1.11   To engage in more meaningful and redemptive relationships

    1.1.12   Hope

It is important to note that in Grounded Theory Analysis, the researcher seeks to discover one central explanatory concept or core category, which is intended to capture the essence of what has been studied. In fact, this study did arrive at a core category of Love that was representative of the seven competencies. However, such a broad core category required deconstruction, which the seven categories and their subsequent properties provide. Furthermore, the competencies could have ostensibly been grouped under three primary categories (rather than seven), namely: Positioning, Reflecting, and Engaging. However, given the breadth of what occurs in the practice of psychoanalysis, each of the seven competencies reported seemed "core" in its own right and useful in learning the breadth of competencies required in the practice of psychoanalysis—the purpose of this research. Equally important is that by incorporating all seven competencies, a comparison with earlier research on technique was made possible, thus advancing coherence in establishing fundamental competencies for Relational Psychoanalysis.

Results

Précised results of the seven Core Competencies are as follows (an expanded explanation of each Core Competency in the format set out in Table 1.1 will appear at the beginnings of Chapters 4–11).

Core Competencies

Positioning

- Competency One: Therapeutic Intent
- Competency Two: Therapeutic Stance/Attitude

Reflecting

- Competency Three: Deep Listening/Immersion
- Competency Four: Relational Dynamic: The There and Then and the Here and Now
- Competency Five: Patterning and Linking

Engaging

- Competency Six: Repetition and Working Through
- Competency Seven: Courageous Speech/Disciplined Spontaneity

Core Competency

- Love

Comparing Results

To enhance confidence in discoveries from the Grounded Theory Analysis, this study compared the findings to a:

a. literature review of 15 articles where 75 students were assigned to locate practices within theory;
b. review of the 2008 *Symposium on Relational Psychoanalysis* sponsored by the International Association for Relational Psychoanalysis and Psychotherapy;
c. the landmark meta-analyses research conducted by Blagys and Hilsenroth (2000) on defining techniques in psychoanalysis.

Literature Review

As noted earlier, in conducting a Grounded Theory Analysis, data are collected and reviewed prior to a literature review to ensure that it is the data driving the outcome, rather than the literature. Conducting the literature review following the collection of data and the analyses allows the researcher to build and compare properties to the findings and to integrate the findings into the literature.

Seventy-five students were asked to read articles by Altman (2013), Aron (1996), Barsness & Strawn (2014), Bass (2001), Benjamin (2004), Bollas (1987), Davies (2006), Ehrenberg (2010), Fosshage (2011), Harris (2011), Hoffman (2011), Maroda (1998, 2006), Mitchell (1997), Schore (2014), Shedler (2010), Singer (1994), Thompson (2001), and Tublin (2011). Students were given specific instructions to locate practices within theory. Using a frequency analysis, these practices were compared among the readers and then compared to the findings of the Grounded Theory Analysis. The

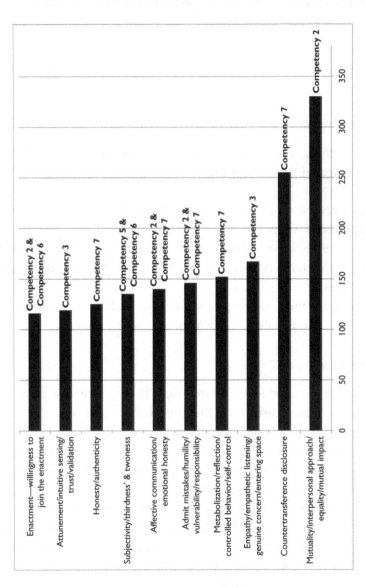

Figure 1.1 Frequency Analysis Comparing Literature Review with Grounded Theory Analysis

analysis produced similar results to the GTA (see Figure 1.1), as noted in the following practices:

- non-authoritarian collaborative stance;
- attention to deep affective states;
- deep listening;
- repetition and working through;
- courageous, honest speech.

Review of the *2008 Symposium on Relational Psychoanalytic Technique*

Along with two research assistants, I reviewed a symposium on technique sponsored by the International Association for Relational Psychoanalysis and Psychotherapy (2008). We each recorded key words referring to technique. Only consensual data were retained. Results were then compared to the Grounded Theory Analysis. Predominant techniques evidenced in the review of the symposium were:

- enactments;
- non-authoritarian stance;
- attending to affect;
- posture of curiosity;
- negotiation;
- linking;
- patterning;
- the use of intuition and countertransference experiences of the analyst.

Each of these techniques is evident in the seven competencies found in the Grounded Theory Analysis. An interesting "tone" evidenced in the GTA study and present in the symposium confirmed the discomfort and ambivalence psychoanalysts experience in establishing "techniques." Technique, from a relational perspective, must be adaptable, flexible, and unscripted and attuned to the idiosyncratic nature of the patient. The analyst must attend to the vicissitudes of each relationship, attending to the affective states that stir into action historical events pressed into the unconscious, where the past is replayed and re-encountered within the therapeutic relationship. Consequently, the work cannot be mechanistic or manualized.

However, it was also evident from both research participants and those in the symposium that they practiced with a particular ear, a particular stance, and a particular form and rhythm that guided them in their work.

Comparing with the Blagys and Hilsenroth Study

Blagys and Hilsenroth (2000) conducted a large meta-analysis by conducting an empirical examination of actual session recordings and transcripts from the PsycLit database identifying empirical studies that compared the process and technique of manualized psychodynamic psychotherapy with that of manualized cognitive behavioral therapy. Techniques "were selected on the basis of both theoretical and empirical evidence of their distinctiveness" (p. 168). Seven features reliably distinguished psychodynamic therapy from other therapies:

1   focus on affect and expression;
2   exploration of attempts to avoid distressing thoughts and feelings;
3   identification of recurring themes and patterns;
4   discussion of past experience (developmental focus);
5   focus on interpersonal relationship;
6   focus on the therapy relationship;
7   exploration of fantasy life.

Their research has been further advanced by research articles evaluating the seven techniques with outcomes (Hilsenroth, Kivlighan, & Slavin-Mulford, 2015; Lehmann, Levy, Hilsenroth, Weinberger, Fuertes, & Diener, 2015; Joseph, Hilsenroth, & Diener, 2014; Stein, Pesale, Slavin, & Hilsenroth, 2010; Hilsenroth, 2007; Caleb, Siefert, Hilsenroth, Weinberger, Blagys, & Ackerman, 2006; Hilsenroth, Defife, Blagys, & Ackerman, 2006).

Their findings have found their way into several General Clinical Methods texts to define contemporary psychoanalytic practices (Prout & Wadkins, 2014; Sperry, 2010; Weiner & Borstein, 2009; Levy & Ablon, 2009; Good, 2006; Connors, 2006; Holmes & Bateman, 2002).

Their research has also been heralded by many relational analysts and offered as a template for relational practices. These include Aron & Starr (2012), McWilliams (2004), and Shedler (2010). Aron and Starr included it as a template in their book *A Psychotherapy for the People*, considering it as "substantial evidence in what constitutes an analytic

Table 1.2 Comparison of the Blagys-Hilsenroth and Barsness Studies

Blagys and Hilsenroth	Barsness
Focus on affect and expression	**Deep Listening/Affective Attunement (Competency Three)** *Properties*: • Pay deep attention to affective states. • Follow affect both within themselves, their patients, and the relationship between themselves. • Recognize that what resonates at the emotional level, not the intellectual level, is what leads to change.
Exploration of attempts to avoid distressing thoughts and feelings	**Deep Listening/Affective Attunement (Competency Three)** *Properties*: • Pay close attention to negative or unwanted emotion (in particular sex and aggression) and discipline themselves to stay with these emotions and to discover with the patient their usefulness in understanding the patient's own negative or unwanted emotions. • Listen beyond content and pay close attention to the words, the affects, and the bodies of their patients to assist in the exploration of incongruities, dissociations, defenses, and connections.
Identification of recurring themes and patterns	**Patterning/Linking (Competency Five)** • Pay close attention to recurring themes and patterns and how they are linked to past with present, dreams and fantasies, here and now, thoughts and affects, and bodily experiences.
Discussion of past experience (developmental focus)	**Relational Dynamic: There and Then and Here and Now (Competency Four)** *Properties*: • Focus on the past experience, particularly early attachment, developmental arrests, and its replication in current living.
Focus on the interpersonal relationship	**Relational Dynamic: There and Then and Here and Now (Competency Four)** *Properties*: • Engage the patient in direct relationship with the analyst, believing that the most powerful work is what emerges between the analytic dyad. **Repetition and Working Through (Competency Six)** *Properties*: • As deep change occurs at the emotional level, the analyst attends to the inevitable conflicts that emerge in the relational dyad.
Focus on the therapy relationship	**Relational Dynamic: There and Then and Here and Now (Competency Four)** **Repetition and Working Through (Competency Six)**
Exploration of fantasy life	**Therapeutic Stance (Competency Two)** *Properties*: • Adhere to Freud's ethic of honesty, holding both themselves and the patient to a commitment reflecting upon all areas of mental life, including, one's fears, shame, guilt, desire, dreams, and fantasy. **Patterning and Linking (Competency Five)** *Properties*: • Dreams and fantasies

therapy" (2012, p. 375). They report that the Blagys and Hilsenroth findings are in fact:

> key aspects of how we work [and] are eminently suited to study and teaching . . . [their findings] match very closely with most analysts clinical self-understandings. They are confirmed by empirical research, providing evidence that this is not just what analytic therapists think they do, but rather, it is what they do.
>
> (Aron & Starr, 2012, pp. 378–379)

Given the significance of this prior research, I conducted a comparative analysis of the Blagys and Hilsenroth study with my own. What I found is that though some of the categories may be labeled slightly differently, the two studies arrive at comparable conclusions. This similitude, I believe, highlights and expands the reach and the goal towards the development of "fundamental practices" in relational psychoanalysis. Table 1.2 is a comparison of the two studies.

Further Advancement in Relational Psychoanalytic Technique

As Blagys and Hilsenroth's (2000) study was a comprehensive review of psychoanalysis in general and the current research focused solely on relational psychoanalysis, specific practices unique to relational psychoanalysis were discovered, and are as follows:

- **Therapeutic intent**: Participants hold to the belief an analytic treatment is first established by having a clear understanding of the intent or outcome of the analytic endeavor.
- **Therapeutic stance/attitude**: Participants hold a unique stance where they are relentlessly curious about the mind/body experience and the dynamic between the patient and the therapist.
- **Courageous speech/disciplined spontaneity**: This particular study reveals that the relational analyst has foregone the myth of the neutral analyst, contending that the analyst must be deeply immersed in the affective, intersubjective field of the analysis and must speak as directly as possible to what is occurring between the patient and the analyst.

- **Therapeutic love**: This study arrived at a core category of Love. Love came to be defined by the very kind of relationship the analyst provides—a relationship that requires of him/herself honesty and risk-taking, where the analyst is willing to resist the urge for self-protection, to surrender certainty, and to engage in the inevitable conflicts, misrecognitions, and ruptures, and to stay in the conflict until it is worked through.

These additional practices seem to be crucial additions to the previous research in advancing teaching, supervision and outcome research.

Conclusion

No two analysts work in the same way, and no two of a given analyst's patients are ever handled in precisely the same manner. This is due to differences in the analyst's theoretical orientation, his professional style, his personality and character, and also his feelings, fantasies, and attitudes, conscious and unconscious, about each of his patients. Consequently, all writings on technique are slanted by the analyst's personal idiosyncrasies. In addition, all detailed writings on technique reveal a good deal of the analyst's intimate and personal goings-on within himself. This tends to make the analyst's own view of what he does unreliable and is apt to lead to some unconscious idealization or denigration of his work . . . . Despite all these qualifications, I believe that a text that attempts to depict what a psychoanalyst actually does, and why, will help to stimulate a full, open, and continuing discussion of psychoanalytic technique.

(Greenson, 1967, pp. xxxvii–xxxviii)

No two analysts work in the same fashion. Given the uniqueness of each relationship and the working through of what happens in that relationship, it must be so. However, practices that guide how we *position* ourselves (therapeutic intent and therapeutic stance), how we *reflect* (deep listening; attending to the there and then/here and now and patterning/linking), and how we *engage* (repetition/working through and courageous speech/disciplined spontaneity) can be universal practices that assist us in our practices.

The data produced in this research are a composite of the richness of experienced analysts as they think and practice within the complexity of the analytic dyad. They provide only broad strokes and are representative only of the relational psychoanalyst. However, through the use of the comparative analysis, this study does add to the theoretical traditions and empirical documentations on technique, expanding the accumulation of research data on this essential topic. Though more research is needed in our field to arrive at any definitive word about technique, this study establishes distinctive competencies, consistent with theory and previous research, that can assist in teaching and supervision as well as in future research between treatment processes and outcomes. Towards that end, I am hopeful that this study will contribute to a foundational curriculum in the study and practice of relational psychoanalysis. I am hopeful that the results will be clear enough to capture imaginations and hearts and serve as an invitation to a life-long commitment in the study of psychoanalytic theory and practice in a very complicated profession.

The remainder of this text grounds the research with the writings of master clinicians, expanding the seven primary competencies. In addition, this book presents a history of relational psychoanalysis, offers a study on the efficacy of relational psychoanalysis, and attends to the self-care of the therapist in working within the intensity of such a model. A critique of the model is offered, issues of race and culture are addressed, and current research on neurobiology and its impact in the development of this model is presented. The reader will find the writings easy to understand and accessible, and find them immediately applicable within the therapeutic setting. It is also hoped that the practical emphasis of this text will also offer non-analytic clinicians a window into the mind of the analyst, will increase the settings and populations in which this model can be applied, and will facilitate integration with other therapeutic orientations.

Convinced that profound and long-lasting change occurs through a deep, authentic encounter with another human, I have sought to compile a text that invites the reader into the practices of a depth psychology that genuinely engages both the therapist and the patient, leading to significant change and transformation within their lives.

References

Altman, N. (2013). Psychoanalysis in and out of the office. *Psychoanalysis, Culture & Society, 18*(2), 128–139.

Aron, L. (1996). *Meeting of the minds*. New York, NY: Analytic Press.

Aron, L. (2008). The question of technique. Retrieved from http://iarpp.net/colloquium.

Aron, L., & Starr, K. (2012). *A psychotherapy for the people*. New York, NY: Routledge.

Barsness, R., & Strawn, B. (2014). Playing our cards face up: The positive power of arousal and disclosure in the therapeutic setting. *Journal of Psychology and Christianity*, *33*, 227–239.

Bass, A. (2001). It takes one to know one; or whose unconscious is it anyway? *Psychoanalytic Dialogues*, *11*, 683–702.

Benjamin, J. (2004). Beyond doer and done to: An intersubjective view of thirdness. *Psychoanalytic Quarterly*, *73*, 5–42.

Blagys, M. D., & Hilsenroth, M. J. (2000). Distinctive features of short-term psychodynamic interpersonal psychotherapy: A review of the comparative psychotherapy process literature. *Clinical Psychology*, *7*, 167–188.

Bollas, C (1987). *The shadow of the object*. New York, NY: Columbia University Press.

Caleb, J., Siefert, C. J., Hilsenroth, M. J., Weinberger, J., Blagys, M. D., & Ackerman, S. J. (2006). The relationship of patient defensive functioning and alliance with therapist technique during short-term psychodynamic psychotherapy. *Clinical Psychology and Psychotherapy*, *13*, 20–33.

Charmaz, K. (2006). *Constructing grounded theory*. Washington, DC: SAGE.

Connors, M. E. (2006). *Symptom-focused dynamic psychotherapy*. Mahwah, NJ: Analytic Press.

Davies, J. M. (2006). The times we sizzle, and the times we sigh: The multiple erotics of arousal, anticipation, and release. *Psychoanalytic Dialogues*, *16*, 665–686.

Ehrenberg, D. B. (2010). Working at the "intimate edge." *Contemporary Psychoanalysis*, *46*, 120–142.

Fosshage, J. L. (2011). The use and impact of the analyst's subjectivity with empathic and other listening/experiencing perspectives. *Psychoanalytic Quarterly*, *4*, 139–159.

Freud, S. (1912). Recommendations to physicians practicing psycho-analysis. In J. Strachey (Ed. & Trans.), *The standard edition of the complete psychological works of Sigmund Freud* (Vol. 31, pp. 342–343). London, England: Hogarth Press.

Glaser, B. G., & Holton, J. (2004). Remodeling grounded theory. *Forum Qualitative Sozialforschung/Forum: Qualitative Social Research*, *5*(2). Retrieved from www.qualitative-research.net/index.php/fqs/article/view/607/1316

Glaser, B. G., & Strauss, A. (1967). *Discovery of grounded theory*. Mill Valley, CA: Sociology Press.

Good, G. E. (2006). *Counseling and psychotherapy essentials: Integrating theories, skills and practices*. New York, NY: W. W. Norton.

Greenberg, J. (2001). The analyst's participation: A new look. *Journal of the American Psychoanalytic Association*, *49*, 359–381.

Greenson, R. (1967). *The technique and practice of psychoanalysis*. Madison, CT: International University Press.

Harris, A. (2011). The relational tradition: Landscape and canon. *Journal of the American Psychoanalytic Association, 59*, 701–734.

Hilsenroth, M. J. (2007). A programmatic study of short-term psychodynamic psychotherapy: Assessment, process, outcome, and training. *Psychotherapy Research, 17*, 31–45.

Hilsenroth, M. J., Defife, J. D., Blagys, M. D., & Ackerman, S. J. (2006). Effects of training in short-term psychodynamic psychotherapy: Changes in graduate clinician technique. *Psychotherapy Research, 16*, 293–305.

Hilsenroth, M. J., Kivlighan, D. M., & Slavin-Mulford, J. (2015). Structured supervision of graduate clinicians in psychodynamic psychotherapy: Alliance and technique. *Journal of Counseling Psychology, 62*, 173–183.

Hoffman, M. (2011). *Toward mutual recognition: Relational Psychoanalysis and the Christian narrative*. New York, NY: Routledge.

Holmes, J., & Bateman, A. (Eds.). (2002). *Integration in psychotherapy: Models and methods*. New York, NY: Oxford University Press.

Joseph, D. M., Hilsenroth, M. J., & Diener, M. J. (2014). Patient participation in psychodynamic psychotherapy: Contributions of alliance and therapist technique. *Journal of Clinical Psychology and Psychotherapy, 21*, 123–131.

Lehmann, M. E., Levy, S. R., Hilsenroth, M. J., Weinberger, J., Fuertes, J., & Diener, M. J. (2015). Evaluating pretreatment patient insight as a factor in early therapeutic technique. *Journal of Psychotherapy Integration, 25*(3), 199–213. doi:10.37/a0039560

Levy, R. A., & Ablon, J. S. (Eds.). (2009). *Handbook of evidence-based psychodynamic psychotherapy: Bridging the gap between science and practice*. New York, NY: Humana Press.

Maroda, K. J. (1998). Enactment: When the patient's and analyst's pasts converge, *Psychoanalytic Psychology, 15*, 517–535.

Maroda, K. J. (2006). *Psychodynamic techniques: Working with emotion in the therapeutic relationship*. New York, NY: Guilford Press.

McWilliams, N. (2014). *Psychoanalytic psychotherapy: A practitioner's guide*. New York, NY: Guilford Press.

Mitchell, S. A. (1997). *Influence and autonomy*. Hillsdale, NJ: Analytic Press.

Prout, T. A., & Wadkins, M. J. (2014). *Essential interviewing and counselling skills: An integrated approach to practice*. New York, NY: Springer.

Rober, P., Elliott, R., Buysse, A., Loots, G., & De Corte, K. (2008). Positioning the therapist's inner conversation: A dialogical model based on a grounded theory analysis of therapist reflections. *Journal of Marital and Family Therapy, 34*, 406–421.

Schore, A. N. (2014). The right brain is dominant in psychotherapy. *Psychotherapy, 3*, 388–397.

Shedler, J. (2010). The efficacy of psychodynamic psychotherapy. *American Psychologist, 2*, 98–109.

Singer, E. (1994). *Key concepts in psychotherapy*. New York, NY: Aronson Press.

Sperry, L. (2010). *Core competencies in counselling and psychotherapy: Becoming a highly competent and effective therapist*. New York, NY: Routledge.

Stein, M. B., Pesale, F. P., Slavin, J. M., & Hilsenroth, M. J. (2010). A training outline for conducting psychotherapy process ratings: An example using therapist technique. *Counseling and Psychotherapy Research, 10*, 50–59.

Strauss, A., & Corbin, J. (1998). *Basics of qualitative research techniques and procedures for developing grounded theory*. London, England: SAGE.

Thompson, M. G. (2001). The enigma of honesty: The fundamental rule of psychoanalysis. *Free Associations, 8*, 390–434.

Tublin, S. (2011). Discipline and freedom in psychoanalytic technique. *Contemporary Psychoanalysis, 47*, 519–545.

Weiner, I. B., & Bornstein, R. F. (2009). *Principles of psychotherapy: Promoting evidence-based psychodynamic practice*. Hoboken, NJ: John Wiley.

Chapter 2

The Case for Psychoanalysis

Exploring the Scientific Evidence

John Thor Cornelius

The goal of this chapter is to use scientific and clinical evidence to develop a reasoned case for the use of psychoanalytic psychotherapy. It was written to address two persistent but common misconceptions that are held by many academics, mental health trainees, and practitioners:

Misconception 1: Psychoanalysis has little to no evidence of effectiveness.

Misconception 2: Cognitive behavioral therapy (CBT) and the prescribing of antidepressants are different from psychoanalysis in that they have high levels of scientific evidence and are 'proven' to be effective.

To address these misconceptions, the chapter will:

1. Review typical claims against psychoanalysis.
2. Present the concepts of scientific significance, effect size, and bias.
3. Explore actual evidence around antidepressant treatment and CBT.
4. Review the evidence supporting psychoanalysis in comparisons to these other treatments.

This process will hopefully accomplish the following goals:

Goal 1: Demonstrate how the evidence supporting psychoanalysis is significant and robust.

Goal 2: Demonstrate how psychoanalysis has the capacity to distinguish itself from other treatment methods in meaningful ways.

The Claims against Psychoanalysis

The misperception of inefficacy regarding psychoanalysis in comparison to CBT and antidepressant medications is increasingly being reported (Shedler, 2012; Driessen et al., 2013; Leichsenring, Klein, & Salzer, 2014; Curtis, 2014; Shedler, 2015). To underscore the extent and pervasiveness of these misperceptions, one needs to look no further than YouTube. In Yale University's "Introduction to Psychology" class, PSC 110, Dr. Paul Bloom, a well-known and respected psychologist and editor of one of the premier psychological journals in the United States, *Brain and Behavioral Sciences*, is openly critical of psychoanalytic theory and technique. Without supporting evidence, he compares psychoanalysis with astrology and encourages the class to join in a chuckling rebuke of the field. He refers to psychoanalysis as "unprovable" and "unscientific" with "very little empirical support," stating: "The claims that psychoanalysis proves itself by its 'tremendous' success in curing mental illness is almost certainly not true. For most, if not all psychological disorders, there are quicker and more reliable treatments" (Bloom, 2009, 40:10 in video). Other claims are made by the Association for Behavioral and Cognitive Therapies, which states: "Dozens of multi-year studies have shown that EBPs [Evidence Based Practices, referring to CBT] can reduce symptoms significantly for many years following the end of psychological treatment—similar evidence for other types of therapies is not available to date" (Association for Behavioral and Cognitive Therapies). Given repeated exposure to these misperceptions, it makes sense that those practicing psychoanalytic therapy are regularly confronted by students, practitioners, and academics who incorrectly assume psychoanalysis is without evidence and largely a waste of time. Unfortunately, it can also leave psychoanalytic practitioners feeling frustrated and disillusioned in the scientific method itself.

How Do We Study Treatment Effectiveness?

To combat these misperceptions, it is important for readers to first have a realistic understanding of the scientific process. Despite an idealized image that science would be unified, logical, and implicitly fair, the process is actually filled with confusion, passion, politics, and debate. The complexity and vociferous nature of scientific disputes can make some people reject the scientific process altogether. However, the fact that individuals and societies make decisions about how to use limited resources based on these debates makes it important that psychoanalytic practitioners are present, knowledgeable, and participating in the scientific process. This includes understanding both the power and limitations of scientific evidence and the ability to critique evidence in a fair, reasonable, and appropriate manner. This is particularly true in the field of mental health, where bias can be both common and unrecognized (Shedler, 2015; Cipriani et al., 2016).

We will now look at three ways scientific evidence is generated: the randomized control trial (RCT), the observational study and the meta-analysis.

The Randomized Control Trial

A randomized control trial is an experiment which aims to test the effectiveness of one or more treatment interventions while trying to minimize bias. The study attempts to find a representative population of test subjects and randomize that population into groups. Sometimes, an intervention group gets actual treatment, and a control group receives a placebo or "treatment as usual" (TAU). In other RCTs, two active treatments are tested against each other. The data are then collected and an evaluation is made to see if there are valid differences between the groups.

Observational Studies

The other common form of study design is the observational study, where subjects are not randomized or acted upon, but simply observed. While non-randomization can theoretically bias a study, research into this issue has found that well-designed observational studies regularly present valuable data that are in keeping with RCT data and are considered a scientifically valid method of research (Anglemyer, Horvath, & Bero, 2014).

Meta-Analyses

Meta-analyses work differently from the above studies in that they do not directly collect data from research subjects. Instead, they integrate data from multiple individual studies using statistical methods. By combining data from multiple studies, the sample size, and thus the predictive power, of the results should increase (Walker, Hernandez, & Kattan, 2008). However, meta-analyses are particularly sensitive to publication bias (see below).

Significance, Effect Size, and Bias

To critique scientific evidence, individuals need to understand significance, effect size, and various forms of bias.

Significance and Effect Size

A fundamental goal of science is to be significant, where conclusions are reasonable, valid, relevant and realistic. However, proving significance is actually a difficult and debatable process. To try to prove significance, RCTs, observational studies, and meta-analyses all regularly use something called the effect size (ES) to measure study results. The ES, expressed in standard deviation units, is a measurement of the difference in results between the groups in the study. For example, if we compared treatments A and B on a depression scale and ended up with an ES of 0.23, it means that patients with treatment A did 0.23 of a standard deviation better than patients with treatment B at that point in time on the scale.

Many people desire a gauge for assessing different effect sizes. While it is important to recognize that small effect sizes are still valid but represent smaller effects, a regularly cited textbook provides the following guide (Cohen, 1988):

Large Effect Size ~ 0.8
Medium Effect Size ~ 0.5
Small Effect Size ~ 0.2

Bias

Bias is defined as any tendency which prevents unprejudiced consideration of a question. However, despite efforts to eliminate bias, it cannot be completely avoided. In addition, one unfair method of dismissing meaningful studies is to exaggerate acceptable bias to unfairly undermine results, or generalize bias found in one study to unfairly discredit larger theories. To strike a fair balance, it is important to detect bias and *reasonably* assess its impact on the topic. Here are some examples of biases.

REPORTING BIAS

It is normal in a discussion of a study to emphasize some parts of a study and not others. However, reporting bias occurs when key information regarding aspects of a scientific study is egregiously ignored to draw a distinctly biased conclusion. An example of this is one author's report of attending scientific meetings where there were repeated claims of "statistically significant results" of CBT in the *Treatment of Depression Collaborative Research Program*, a US National Institute of Mental Health study of manualized treatments. However, an examination of the study revealed that those who received CBT in the study only demonstrated a 1.2-point difference from the control group on the 54-point Hamilton Depression Scale. While it was true that this value was "statistically significant," even the original authors concluded that the result was clinically meaningless (Shedler, 2015). This is an example where the true significance of the study was being hidden through claims of "statistical significance."

CALCULATION BIAS

A fundamental aspect of science is an evaluation of data. While the process can be a benign and necessary part of science, problems were underscored in 2008 when a Freedom of Information Act request revealed that the Food and Drug Administration (FDA) had access to a large amount of data regarding the efficacy of antidepressant medications that were not being released. This included data that were originally part of some studies but were omitted before publication. The re-incorporation of this data back into the studies found that 11 antidepressant studies that had previously conveyed positive results were actually negative (Turner, Matthews, Linardatos, Tell, & Rosenthal, 2008).

PUBLICATION BIAS

Many researchers do not want to publish data that demonstrate a failure of their hypotheses. However, when negative studies are not published, meta-analyses miss crucial bodies of data and the evaluation of the topic becomes statistically skewed. In the FDA example above, the Freedom of Information Act request from the FDA in 2008 also revealed 22 fully negative studies regarding antidepressants that had simply never been published. Combined with the above calculation bias, the two processes decreased the percentage of positive antidepressant studies from 94% to 51% and decreased the calculated effect size of antidepressants in general (Turner et al., 2008). There are also studies detecting publication bias regarding psychological papers in general, but CBT in particular (Cuijpers, Smit, Bohlmeijer, Hollon, & Andersson, 2010).

SELECTION BIAS

This is when groups are selected for studies in ways that do not mimic real-world populations. An examination of the typical selection criteria for antidepressant studies found that 80% of people in the real world diagnosed with depression would not be accepted into current clinical antidepressant trials. The authors point out that this difference between test subjects and real-world populations interferes with those studies' abilities to predict the real-world effectiveness of these drugs (Preskorn, Macaluso, & Trivedi, 2015). Similarly, a study of selection bias noted that 68% of people were excluded from psychotherapy depression studies, possibly interfering with the generalizability of their results as well (Westen, Novotny, & Thompson-Brenner, 2004).

SPONSORSHIP BIAS

Everyone should be aware of the incentives behind research studies. It has been demonstrated that antidepressant studies funded by for-profit pharmaceutical companies are more consistently positive about their drug than studies conducted by competitors or more neutral parties such as federal agencies (Baker, 2003).

Confounding

Confounding is a common problem that occurs when an unaddressed and often unknown variable affects a study's outcome in a way not accounted for within the study. It is a frequent and devastating critique of studies in mental health, where many variables cannot honestly be controlled or accounted for (Pannucci & Wilkins, 2010). The best we can do in these cases is read the study carefully and assess its ability to adequately address this form of bias.

To make assessments, individuals need to be open to results from studies, but also reasonably critical and aware of bias. Do not be too quick to embrace individual studies wholeheartedly. Allow yourself to be challenged, but not overwhelmed by individual study results. Make assessments based on bodies of evidence that develop through time and survive ongoing, reasonable debate.

Evidence Regarding Antidepressants and CBT

Antidepressants

First, some epidemiologic data:

- In the United States, antidepressant use increased by almost 400% between 1988–1994 and 2005–2008 (Pratt, Brody, & Gu, 2011).
- In England, the number of prescriptions had risen from 18 million in 1998 to nearly 43 million in 2010 (Ilyas & Moncrieff, 2012).
- Antidepressants were the third most common prescription drug taken by Americans of all ages in 2005–2008 and the most frequently used by persons aged 18–44 years (Pratt et al., 2011).
- Eleven percent of Americans over 12 years old take antidepressant medication (Pratt et al., 2011).
- More than 60% of Americans taking antidepressant medication have taken it for two years or longer, with 14% having taken the medication for ten years or more (Pratt et al., 2011).
- Despite this, rates of depression rose during this same period. Depression rates for American adults increased from 3.33% to 7.06% between 1991 and 2002 (Compton, 2006).
- Suicide rates in the United States also increased by 24% between 1999 and 2014. This increase was in every race, gender and age group, except black males and in those over age 75. These rates increased even more substantially between 2006 and 2014, implying this problem is worsening and not improving (Curtin, Warner, & Hedegaard, 2016).

Let's take a look at some data regarding antidepressants and see if there is any explanation why, despite the significant use of antidepressants, depression symptoms seem to be increasing.

Antidepressant Efficacy

As stated above, a major re-analysis was done by several researchers after the FDA released its full body of data regarding antidepressants in 2008

(Turner et al., 2008). The meta-analysis that followed included 12,564 patients participating in 74 studies between 1987 and 2004. When the overall effect size was recalculated with all the data, negative and positive, **the effect size of antidepressants was reduced to 0.32** (Turner et al., 2008). For adults, researchers reported that the **antidepressants regularly did not beat placebo except in the most severe cases of depression** (Kirsch, Deacon, Huedo-Medina, Scoboria, Moore, & Johnson, 2008). Another recent meta-analysis of antidepressants for adolescents found that **only one antidepressant out of the 14 tested was able to beat placebo, even in cases of severe depression** (Cipriani et al., 2016).

Depression and Suicidality

Growing data show that antidepressants may actually *increase* suicidal thoughts in some populations (Stone et al., 2009; GlaxoSmithKline, 2006). This led to the FDA placing a black box warning for increased suicidality on antidepressant use for those under 25 years of age (Food and Drug Administration, 2007). The evidence of antidepressants causing increased suicidality in those over age 25 is mixed (Healy, 2000; Fergusson et al., 2005; Stone et al., 2009), and methodological problems in studies around evaluating suicidality and antidepressants were noted in multiple reviews, making it difficult to fairly assess this issue (Fergusson et al., 2005; Gunnell, Saperia, & Ashby, 2005). Given this kind of complexity, it would be wise to follow the advice of recent studies that recommend close monitoring for suicidality upon initiating antidepressants in people of all ages (Coupland, Hill, Morriss, Arthur, Moore, & Hippisley-Cox, 2015).

STAR*D

The Sequenced Treatment Alternatives to Relieve Depression study, or STAR*D, was conducted by the National Institute for Mental Health, involved over 4000 patients at 41 centers across the United States, and had *inclusive* selection criteria to study the real-world depressed population. It used a treatment algorithm that included multiple treatments, pharmacologic agents, *and* CBT. Depressed volunteers worked with doctors to choose their treatments following a treatment algorithm with four basic steps in the treatment. At the end of the study, 68% of patients met criteria for being declared in "full remission" from their depression symptoms.

STAR*D generated a huge amount of data, and over 120 journal articles have been published using the dataset. For many, it is considered the most consequential study of depression treatment to date (Pigott, 2015).

However, given the large penetration of antidepressant usage in the United States cited above and the good rate of remission reported in STAR*D, many would *not* expect the increasing rate of depression found epidemiologically within the United States. So what is going on?

Long-Term Results

A fundamental problem in antidepressant treatment studies was exposed in the long-term monitoring of symptoms in STAR*D, where patients were provided with 12 months of ongoing psychiatric care after the end of the study.

> The long-term results of STAR*D showed a rapid failure of treatment regimens. Depending on treatment group, between 40% and 71% of patients relapsed to major depression by the end of the 12 months. This occurred, on average, within only four months of the end of the study.
>
> (Rush, 2006)

The fact that so many patients in active treatment relapsed within a year of successful remission is a significant and troubling relapse rate, but an effect that has been found in multiple other studies (Vitiello et al., 2010, Hollon et al., 2005; Hansen et al., 2008).

Tachyphylaxis

Supporting the above result is a clinically well-known phenomenon called antidepressant tachyphylaxis (or "poop-out"), which is well documented in the literature (Targum, 2014).

Cognitive Behavioral Therapy

Similar to antidepressants, CBT has an evidence base that is supportive of its use in a number of mental health disorders and has generated meaningful end-of-study effect sizes. For example, those with major depression demonstrated an effect size improvement of 0.82 when compared to a wait list and 0.23 when compared to selective serotonin reuptake inhibitors. Those with generalized anxiety also demonstrated an effect size of 0.82 when compared to a wait list, while those with obsessive compulsive disorder showed an effect size of 1.3 when compared to their pre-CBT state (Butler, Chapman, Forman, & Beck, 2006). Many of the findings were supported by a recent meta-analysis done in 2012 (Hoffmann, Asnaani, Vonk, Sawyer, & Fang, 2012). CBT was also part of Step 2 in the STAR*D trial, where its response and remission rates were comparable with antidepressants (Thase, 2007).

However, while continuing to demonstrate benefit in multiple arenas, emerging evidence has increasingly differentiated what CBT has been able to scientifically and clinically justify and what it has not.

Areas of Limited Evidence and Effectiveness

Even as more recent meta-analyses list areas of strength for CBT, such as the treatment of anxiety disorders, the reports are also listing areas where scientific support for CBT is *not* as strong. This includes noting the increasing controversy regarding the benefit of CBT in contrast to psychoanalytic therapy for the treatment of depression and the limited evidentiary role of CBT in treating bipolar disorder, schizophrenia, and personality disorders (Hoffmann et al., 2012). **Evidence of publication bias has also been found in psychotherapy studies in general, but in CBT studies in particular, where one study estimated the overall efficacy of CBT should be reduced from 0.67 overall to 0.42** (Cuijpers et al., 2010).

Significant Relapse Rates

CBT has a significant number of studies that show that those who receive CBT regularly have a decay of benefit after their treatments end. For example, the long-term relapse rates of CBT from STAR*D are the same as the antidepressants (Rush, 2006). This phenomenon is significant and regular enough that it has been confirmed both in other individual studies and meta-analyses (Hollon et al., 2005; Huber, Zimmermann, Henrich, & Klug, 2012). Here are two particular examples of this:

Britain

A study conducted by a branch of the National Health Service in Britain studied the long-term outcomes and cost-effectiveness of ten different CBT studies that had previously been found positive. They followed the health records of the individuals for two years after they had completed their treatments. Here are excerpts from their study:

> The positive effects of CBT found in the original trials were eroded over longer time periods. No evidence was found for an association between more intensive therapy and more enduring effects of CBT.
>
> (Durham et al., 2005)

> The cost-effectiveness analysis showed no advantages of CBT over non-CBT.
>
> (Durham et al., 2005)

> Psychological therapy services need to recognize that anxiety disorders tend to follow a chronic course and that good outcomes with CBT over the short term are no guarantee of good outcomes over the longer term.
>
> (Durham et al., 2005)

In conclusion, through studying the ten different studies over the long term, they were unable to find *any* evidence of a link between the short-term success with CBT and how the treated patients did over the long term (Durham et al., 2005).

Sweden

The results from the British study are in keeping with the clinical evidence emerging from Sweden. Believing the rhetoric around CBT to be the only "evidence-based" and effective treatment, the government engaged in a massive shift away from offering a plurality of different psychotherapy treatments to a near exclusive use of CBT. A recent talk by Goran Ahlin, a psychiatrist from Sweden, described the closing of psychoanalytic institutes and how authorities only supported certificate training exams for those being trained in CBT (Ahlin, 2015). Between 2008 and 2012, CBT was *the* psychotherapy supported by the government. For example, of those citing mental illness in their national welfare to work program, 90% received CBT. Over the following four years, two separate studies (Jensen et al., 2011; Inspectorate of Social Security, 2012) were done regarding this program. **They showed that those who received CBT did not spend any**

less time in the sick leave program than comparable individuals who did not receive CBT, and a cost analysis showed substantial economic burden due to CBT, without economic benefit (Sandell, R., personal communication, June 2, 2014). Scott Miller, PhD of the Center for Clinical Excellence said this:

> The latest issue of *Socionomen*, the official journal for Swedish social workers, reported the results of the government's two billion Swedish crown investment in CBT. The widespread adoption of the method has had no effect whatsoever on the outcome of people disabled by depression and anxiety.
>
> (Miller, 2012)

The good news is that recently the Swedish government has reevaluated its position and is adopting a more pluralistic approach to allow individuals choice in the types of psychotherapy they receive.

Psychoanalysis

Psychoanalysis Has Significant Studies and Results

In direct contradiction to the claims cited at the beginning of this chapter, there is a significant evidence base supporting the use of psychoanalytic therapy in mental health that is comparable to antidepressant therapy and CBT. One study used five independent reviewers to evaluate the quality of psychoanalytic evidence. The reviewers agreed that 63 studies published between 1977 and 2010 were scientifically valid. They found that psychoanalysis beat an inactive comparator 75% of the time, and equaled other active treatments such as CBT or antidepressants 72% of the time (Gerber et al., 2011). For comparison, antidepressants had 74 studies where only 51% were positive, and the vast majority of these studies were against an inactive placebo (Turner et al., 2008).

End-of-Study Effect Sizes for Psychoanalysis Compare to CBT and are Greater Than Antidepressants

There have been multiple studies and meta-analyses done of psychoanalytic treatments that demonstrate end-of-study data that are directly comparable to CBT and antidepressants. For example, **a meta-analysis by Abbass in 2004 demonstrated end-of-study effect sizes for symptom relief related in those treated with dynamic therapy in the range of 0.59 to 1.08 when compared to a wait list** (Abbass, Hancock, Henderson, & Kisely, 2004). **Another meta-analysis by Maat demonstrated end-of-study effect sizes of 0.94 for severe personality symptoms for those treated with long-term psychoanalytic therapy** (Maat, Jonghe, Schoevers, & Dekker, 2009). The effect sizes of psychoanalysis and CBT are both generally greater than the antidepressant effect size of 0.32 (Turner et al., 2008).

With effect sizes that are directly comparable to that of CBT against similar control groups, and greater than antidepressants, it is actually somewhat confusing as to why CBT and antidepressants could make claims to be more effective than psychoanalysis.

Psychoanalytic Effect Sizes Improve over the Long Term

One difference in the evidence base between CBT, antidepressants, and psychoanalysis is a growing body of literature that finds that those who received psychoanalysis continue to improve long after therapy ends.

Cochrane Library

The Cochrane Library is a large, independent group of researchers and professionals dedicated to evidence-based decision-making in medicine. They publish reviews in all areas of medicine. In 2004, they did a meta-analysis of psychoanalytic therapy evaluating 26 different studies. In addition to the positive end-of-study data presented above, the Cochrane group continued to follow the patients after the official end of treatment for an additional nine months. **What they found was that in every category, the effect sizes continued to increase after the end of the therapy. General symptoms improved from 0.97 to 1.51, somatic symptoms improved from 0.81 to 2.21, depression symptoms improved from 0.59 to 0.98, and anxiety symptoms improved from 1.08 to 1.35. These results demonstrated a tendency for those treated with dynamic therapy to continue to improve after the end of treatment** (Abbass et al., 2004). These data are in direct contrast to the STAR*D data that showed a significant relapse rate after the termination of the STAR*D study (Rush, 2006).

Long-Term versus Short-Term Therapy

A similar study was done comparing short- versus long-term dynamic therapy (50 sessions over a one-year period). Long-term therapy was shown to be more effective (Leichsenring, 2008). **Again, the effect sizes continued to improve 23 months post-treatment.** This result generated significant scrutiny from the scientific community, but the authors produced a follow-up article demonstrating how the results did indeed stand up to careful scientific review (Leichsenring, Abbass, Luyten, Hilsenroth, & Rabung, 2013).

Psychoanalysis versus CBT

A recent head-to-head study from Germany directly compared CBT and psychoanalytic therapy. In contrast to many studies, it used experienced therapists of each modality to conduct the therapies. **The study found that after three years, patients who received CBT began to once again worsen in their Beck Depression Inventory (BDI) scores, while BDI scores of those who received psychoanalytic treatment continued to improve** (Huber et al., 2012).

Psychoanalysis Shows Efficacy Even for Severe Disorders

Another possible difference between other therapies and psychoanalytic therapy is the capacity of psychoanalytic therapy to treat those with severe fundamental struggles that would typically be diagnosed as personality disorders. One study looked at change in severe personality symptoms in longer-term therapy, lasting for at least 150 hours, noting continued improvement in symptoms over time, this time over multiple years (see Figure 2.4) (Maat et al., 2009). **The severe personality symptoms improved from an effect size of 0.94 at the end of the treatment to 1.02 measured 5.2 years *after* the treatment ended** (Maat et al., 2009).

Mentalization Based Therapy

One example of a dynamically oriented treatment is Mentalization Based Therapy (MBT), which was designed to treat those diagnosed with borderline personality disorder. Ongoing monitoring collected long-term data showing that those who received MBT had sustained decreases in suicide attempts, hospitalizations, and ER visits, while there were also increases in school and work participation. **The study also showed that patients had ongoing psychic improvement over time, with 87% of MBT patients no longer meeting criteria for borderline personality disorder at eight years, compared to only 13% of treatment as usual controls** (Bateman & Fonagy, 2008). Additional studies have been conducted looking at applying this therapy to a broader range of severe disorders, including drug-resistant severe depression, eating disorders, and psychosis (Brent, Holt, Keshavan, Seidman, & Fonagy, 2014; Luyten, Fonagy, Lemma, & Target, 2012; Skårderud & Fonagy, 2012).

Conclusion

While cognitive behavioral, antidepressant, and psychoanalytic therapy each have a large and complicated evidence base, the goal of this chapter was to give the readers a basic framework of understanding about scientific and clinical evidence, to help them challenge persistent misperceptions about the relative evidence levels of the different treatments to make a reasoned case for the use of psychoanalysis in the arena of mental health.

Antidepressant medications, though very common and effective for some people, have problems in the areas of low overall efficacy, may actually worsen depression symptoms like suicidality, and have demonstrated significant relapse rates. Cognitive behavioral therapy, while proven helpful in certain disorders, has less evidence regarding severe diagnoses such as bipolar and personality disorders, and also demonstrates significant relapse rates that have translated to a lack of economic and lasting psychological benefits.

Psychoanalytic therapy has a clear and documented evidence base that shows effectiveness on a par with or better than comparable treatments. It also demonstrates a capacity to treat severe and chronic illnesses, such as personality disorders, and has repeatedly demonstrated effect sizes that increase over long periods of time, even after the end of treatment.

No single treatment modality can provide solutions for every person and situation, and different treatments need to be considered for effective management of individual struggles, capacities, and needs. This is especially true given the complicated and ongoing collection of evidence around these treatments. However, the goal of this chapter was to address persistent misperceptions regarding an imagined superiority of antidepressant and

CBT treatment compared to psychoanalysis. It is only through a reasoned and educated understanding of the evidence that these misperceptions can be effectively challenged and proven to be false. As I have shown, psychoanalytic therapies demonstrate both scientific relevance and benefits that positively differentiate them from the other forms of treatment presented here. The increasing recognition of the scientific support for psychoanalysis make it well placed within the assembly of valid treatment options in the field of mental health.

References

Abbass, A., Hancock, J., Henderson, J., & Kisely, S. (2004). Short-term psychodynamic psychotherapies for common mental disorders (protocol). *Cochrane Database of Systematic Reviews, 2.* doi:10.1002/14651858.cd004687.pub2

Ahlin, G. [Challenging the Cognitive Behavioural Therapies: The Overselling of CBT's Evidence Base] (2015, January 17). *Goran Ahlin—the rise and expected fall of CBT in Sweden* [Video file]. Retrieved from https://www.youtube.com/watch?v=2gOrahtKk3w

Anglemyer, A., Horvath, H. T., & Bero, L. (2014). Healthcare outcomes assessed with observational study designs compared with those assessed in randomized trials. *Cochrane Database of Systematic Reviews, 4.* doi:10.1002/14651858.mr000034.pub2

Association for Behavioral and Cognitive Therapies. (n.d.). Retrieved from www.abct.org/Help/?m=mFindHelp&fa=WhatIsEBPpublic

Baker, C. B. (2003). Quantitative analysis of sponsorship bias in economic studies of antidepressants. *British Journal of Psychiatry, 183*(6), 498–506.

Bateman, A., & Fonagy, P. (2008). 8-year follow-up of patients treated for borderline personality disorder: Mentalization-based treatment versus treatment as usual. *American Journal of Psychiatry, 165*(5), 631–638.

Bloom, P. [YaleCourses] (2009, September 30). *3. Foundations: Freud* [Video file]. Retrieved from https://www.youtube.com/watch?v=7emS3ye3cVU

Brent, B., Holt, D., Keshavan, M., Seidman, L., & Fonagy, P. (2014). Mentalization-based treatment for psychosis: Linking an attachment-based model to the psychotherapy for impaired mental state understanding in people with psychotic disorders. *Israel Journal of Psychiatry and Relational Sciences, 51*(1), 17–24.

Butler, A., Chapman, J., Forman, E., & Beck, A. (2006). The empirical status of cognitive-behavioral therapy: A review of meta-analyses. *Clinical Psychology Review, 26*(1), 17–31.

Cipriani, A., et al. (2016). Comparative efficacy and tolerability of antidepressants for major depressive disorder in children and adolescents: A network meta-analysis. *Lancet, 388*(10047), 881–890. http://dx.doi.org/10.1016/S0140-6736(16)30385-3

Cohen, J. (1988). *Statistical power analysis for the behavioral sciences*. Hillsdale, NJ: Lawrence. Erlbaum.

Compton, W. (2006). Changes in the prevalence of major depression and comorbid substance use disorders in the United States between 1991–1992 and 2001–2002. *American Journal of Psychiatry, 163*(12), 2141–2147.

Coupland, C., Hill, T., Morriss, R., Arthur, A., Moore, M., & Hippisley-Cox, J. (2015). Antidepressant use and risk of suicide and attempted suicide or self harm in people aged 20 to 64: Cohort study using a primary care database. *British Medical Journal, 350*(7996). doi:10.1136/bmj.h517

Cuijpers, P., Smit, F., Bohlmeijer, E., Hollon, S. D., & Andersson, G. (2010). Efficacy of cognitive-behavioural therapy and other psychological treatments for adult depression: Meta-analytic study of publication bias. *British Journal of Psychiatry, 196*(3), 173–178.

Curtin, S.C., Warner, M., & Hedegaard, H. (2016). Increase in suicide in the United States, 1999–2014. NCHS Data Brief No. 241. Hyattsville, MD: National Center for Health Statistics. Retrieved from www.cdc.gov/nchs/products/databriefs/db241.htm

Curtis, R. C. (2014). Systematic research supporting psychoanalytic and psychoanalytic treatments. *Contemporary Psychoanalysis, 50*(1–2), 34–42.

Driessen, E., et al. (2013). The efficacy of cognitive-behavioral therapy and psychodynamic therapy in the outpatient treatment of major depression: A randomized clinical trial. *American Journal of Psychiatry, 170*(9), 1041–1050.

Durham, R., et al. (2005). Long-term outcome of cognitive behaviour therapy clinical trials in central Scotland. *Health Technology Assessment, 9*(42), 1–174. doi:10.3310/hta9420

Fergusson, D., et al. (2005). Association between suicide attempts and selective serotonin reuptake inhibitors: systematic review of randomised controlled trials. *British Medical Journal, 330*(7488), 396.

Food and Drug Administration. (2007). *FDA proposes new warnings about suicidal thinking, behavior in young adults who take antidepressant medications* [Press Release]. Retrieved from https://www.fda.gov/NewsEvents/Newsroom/PressAnnouncements/2007/ucm108905.htm

Gerber, A. J., et al. (2011). A quality-based review of randomized controlled trials of psychoanalytic psychotherapy. *American Journal of Psychiatry, 168*(1), 19–28.

GlaxoSmithKline. (2006). *Paroxetine adult suicidality analysis* [Press release]. Retrieved from www.gsk.com/media/paroxetine/briefing_doc.pdf

Gunnell, D., Saperia, J., & Ashby, D. (2005). Selective serotonin reuptake inhibitors (SSRIs) and suicide in adults: Meta-analysis of drug company data from placebo controlled, randomised controlled trials submitted to the MHRA's safety review. *British Medical Journal, 330*(7488), 385.

Hansen, R., et al. (2008). Meta-analysis of major depressive disorder relapse and recurrence with second-generation antidepressants. *Psychiatric Services, 59*(10), 1121–1130.

Healy, D. (2000). Emergence of antidepressant induced suicidality. *Primary Care Psychiatry, 6*(1), 23–28.

Hofmann, S. G., Asnaani, A., Vonk, I. J. J., Sawyer, A. T., & Fang, A. (2012). The efficacy of cognitive behavioral therapy: A review of meta-analyses. *Cognitive Therapy and Research, 36*(5), 427–440.

Hollon, S. D., et al. (2005). Prevention of relapse following cognitive therapy vs medications in moderate to severe depression. *Archives of General Psychiatry, 62*(4), 417–422.

Huber, D., Zimmermann, J., Henrich, G., & Klug, G. (2012). Comparison of cognitive-behaviour therapy with psychoanalytic and psychoanalytic therapy for depressed patients: A three-year follow-up study. *Zeitschrift für Psychosomatische Medizin und Psychotherapie, 58*(3), 299–316.

Ilyas, S., & Moncrieff, J. (2012). Trends in prescriptions and costs of drugs for mental disorders in England, 1998–2010. *British Journal of Psychiatry, 200*(5), 393–398.

Inspectorate of Social Security. (2012). *Rapport 2012:17: Rehabiliteringsgarantin* [Report 2012:17: Rehabilitation guarantee]. Stockholm, Sweden: Inspectorate of Social Security.

Jensen, I., et al. (2011). *En nationell utvärdering av rehabiliteringsgarantins effekter på sjukfrånvaro och hälsa. Slutrapport del I* [A national evaluation of the rehabilitation guarantee effects on sick leave and health. Final report, Part I]. Stockholm, Sweden: Unit of Intervention and Implementation Research, Institute of Environmental Medicine, Karolinska Institutet.

Kirsch, I., Deacon, B. J., Huedo-Medina, T. B., Scoboria, A., Moore, T. J., & Johnson, B. T. (2008). Initial severity and antidepressant benefits: A meta-analysis of data submitted to the food and drug administration. *PLoS Medicine, 5*(2), e45. doi:10.1371/journal.pmed.0050045

Leichsenring, F. (2008). Effectiveness of long-term psychoanalytic psychotherapy. *Journal of the American Medical Association, 300*(13), 1551–1565. doi:10.1001/jama.300.13.1551

Leichsenring, F., Abbass, A., Luyten, P., Hilsenroth, M., & Rabung, S. (2013). The emerging evidence for long-term psychodynamic therapy. *Psychodynamic Psychiatry, 41*(3), 361–384.

Leichsenring, F., Klein, S., & Salzer, S. (2014). The efficacy of psychoanalytic psychotherapy in specific mental disorders: A 2013 update of empirical evidence. *Contemporary Psychoanalysis, 50*(1–2), 89–130.

Luyten, P., Fonagy, P., Lemma, A., & Target, M. (2012). Depression. In A. Bateman, & P. Fonagy (Eds.), *Handbook of mentalizing in mental health practice* (pp. 385–418). Washington, DC: American Psychiatric Publishing.

Maat, S. D., Jonghe, F. D., Schoevers, R., & Dekker, J. (2009). The effectiveness of long-term psychoanalytic therapy: A systematic review of empirical studies. *Harvard Review of Psychiatry, 17*(1), 1–23.

Miller, S. (2012, May 13). Revolution in Swedish mental health practice: The cognitive behavioral therapy monopoly gives way [Blog post]. Retrieved from www.scottdmiller.com/feedback-informed-treatment-fit/revolution-in-swedish-mental-health-practice-the-cognitive-behavioral-therapy-monopoly-gives-way/

Pannucci, C. J., & Wilkins, E. G. (2010). Identifying and avoiding bias in research. *Plastic and Reconstructive Surgery, 126*(2), 619–625.

Pigott, H. E. (2015). The STAR*D trial: It is time to reexamine the clinical beliefs that guide the treatment of major depression. *Canadian Journal of Psychiatry/ Revue Canadienne de Psychiatrie, 60*(1), 9–13.

Pratt, L. A., Brody, D. J., & Gu, Q. (2011). *Antidepressant use in persons aged 12 and over: United States, 2005–2008*. NCHS data brief No. 76. Hyattsville, MD: National Center for Health Statistics.

Preskorn, S. H., Macaluso, M., & Trivedi, M. (2015). How commonly used inclusion and exclusion criteria in antidepressant registration trials affect study enrollment. *Journal of Psychiatric Practice, 21*(4), 267–274.

Rush, A. (2006). Acute and longer-term outcomes in depressed outpatients requiring one or several treatment steps: A STAR*D report. *American Journal of Psychiatry, 163*(11), 1905.

Shedler, J. (2012). The efficacy of psychodynamic psychotherapy. In R. A. Levy, J. S. Ablon, & H. Kächele (Eds.), *Psychoanalytic psychotherapy research: Evidence-based practice and practice-based evidence* (pp. 9–25). New York, NY: Springer.

Shedler, J. (2015). Where is the evidence for "evidence-based" therapy? *Journal of Psychological Therapies in Primary Care, 4*, 47–59.

Skårderud, F., & Fonagy, P. (2012). Eating disorders. In A. Bateman & P. Fonagy (Eds.), *Handbook of mentalizing in mental health practice* (pp. 347–384). Arlington, VA: American Psychiatric Publishing.

Stone, M., et al. (2009). Risk of suicidality in clinical trials of antidepressants in adults: analysis of proprietary data submitted to US Food and Drug Administration. *British Medical Journal, 339*, b2880.

Targum, S. D. (2014). Identification and treatment of antidepressant tachyphylaxis. *Innovations in Clinical Neuroscience, 11*(3–4), 24–28.

Thase, M. (2007). Cognitive therapy versus medication in augmentation and switch strategies as second-step treatments: A STAR*D report. *American Journal of Psychiatry, 164*(5), 739–752.

Turner, E. H., Matthews, A. M., Linardatos, E., Tell, R. A., & Rosenthal, R. (2008). Selective publication of antidepressant trials and its influence on apparent efficacy. *New England Journal of Medicine, 358*(3), 252–260.

Vitiello, B., et al. (2010). Long-term outcome of adolescent depression initially resistant to selective serotonin reuptake inhibitor treatment. *Journal of Clinical Psychiatry, 72*(3), 388–396.

Walker, E., Hernandez, A. V., & Kattan, M. W. (2008). Meta-analysis: Its strengths and limitations. *Cleveland Clinic Journal of Medicine, 75*(6), 431–439.

Westen, D., Novotny, C. M., & Thompson-Brenner, H. (2004). The empirical status of empirically supported psychotherapies: Assumptions, findings, and reporting in controlled clinical trials. *Psychological Bulletin, 130*(4), 631–663.

Chapter 3

The Relational Tradition
Landscape and Canon

Adrienne Harris

In this chapter, I describe the history and evolution of the Relational perspective, its theoretical underpinnings and ancestry, and its emergence as a powerful critique and alternative to the more classical movements in psychoanalysis.

But first, a word about comparative psychoanalysis. As I think now in 2017 of the distinct movements within the field, it strikes me that one of the important dimensions is the dynamic and interdependent aspect of analytic theory and analytic work. None of the traditions—object relations, self-psychology, modern Freudian, Kleinian, or relational—are, any more, exactly discrete entities. What were historically major differences appear now as more subtle distinctions. There are many points of influence among the dominant perspectives: some acknowledged, some disavowed, some ignored. Developments in the use of terms like enactment, countertransference, thirdness, intersubjectivity, to name just a few, cross back and forth among and between different schools of thought. Across many different points of view, for example, there is a strong conviction of the power of countertransference, its utility, and presence in much mutative action in treatments, even as this understanding is translated into many different modes of work and clinical process.

In thinking about how relational theory manifests something of its cultural and historical origins, Stephen Mitchell and I in 2004 launched a discussion with our colleagues and each other and asked, "What's American about American psychoanalysis?" and we were sometimes surprised by the answers.

Most centrally, we felt American (and certainly relational) thought emerged from the important background theories of pragmatics and semiotics, evolving from the mid-19th-century work of William James and C. S. Pierce. I draw on our essay here:

There are a number of aspects of William James's (1890, 1910, 1978) far-reaching thought that we might highlight in the light of the evolution of American psychoanalysis. James distrusted but did not repudiate abstraction. He was determined to ground any understanding in subjective experience, the immediacy and ongoing stream of conscious life. James sought to widen the scope of psychology from problems of knowing to include problems of believing or ethics. Passions are as crucial for ways of knowing as is mind. There are some familiar themes here: an instinctive pull for indeterminacy, for multiple ways of knowing. In James, this democratic, or perhaps more accurately egalitarian, impulse is grounded in philosophy, not ideology.

James (1978), writing on pragmatism, on the experience of the self, on his theory of radical empiricism, produced an important and influential network of ideas that feels quite familiar to relational analysts. His focus was on experience. His interest always lay in the particular instance, not the general concept. His focus on experience—not simply of things, but of things and relations—and his attention to a kind of hermeneutical circular relation between belief, desire, and action must strike an American (and particularly, an interpersonal psychoanalytic) reader as deeply familiar. This approach in philosophy and critical theory was, quite simply yet grandly, to understand the multiple intersections (James' term) between the individual's knowing of objects, the public shared nature of that knowing, and the problem of how one mind knows another. These ideas are strong anchors for contemporary American psychoanalysis where the intrapsychic and the interpersonal co-construct, where mind is simultaneously social, individual, public and private.

Certainly, one can read James in the light of Sullivan and interpersonal psychoanalysis, finding themes and preoccupations that cannot simply default to behaviorism. Because psychoanalysis, across its spectrum, insists on the centrality of meaning making, C. S. Peirce's (1955) theory of meaning could be seen as a background influence on perspectivalism and the contemporary preoccupations with intersubjectivity. Peirce built a complex triadic structure distinguishing the word, its meaning for the speaker, and its distinct but overlapping quasi-shared meaning for the listener. This complex model of meaning as intersubjective has had powerful influences in the academy.

(Mitchell & Harris, 2004, pp. 169–170)

In the history of psychoanalysis, the disruption and erasure of conversations about technique, or metapsychology, or theory has been costly. I think here of Freud's and the Freudians' split with Ferenczi (Heynal, 2002; Aron & Harris, 1994)—a split that kept the concept of trauma much too isolated, distinct, and polarized in relation to the concept of unconscious fantasy. Ferenczi is an important figure for the relational world, really a crucial ancestor, perhaps the ur-mother. To draw on Loewald's evocative image, the re-integration of Ferenczi into psychoanalytic cultures, a strong early project of relationalists, was an attempt to turn a ghost back into ancestor. The (re)turn to Ferenczi was also a hope for the emergence of healthy debate about technique as well as about trauma and its long sequalae in psychic life.

The question of influence and multiple perspectives is particularly critical in thinking about the relational tradition. Those of us in what might be termed the first generation at Psychoanalytic Dialogues (Aron, Altman, Bass, Benjamin, Bromberg, Davies, Dimen, Ghent, and Harris) were all, inevitably, some kind of immigrant, arriving at a relational address from a wide variety of background analytic cultures. There is an interesting distinction between "small r" and "capital R" relational perspectives, relationalists who like hybridity (mixed models), and ones who want to deepen and particularize a Relational tradition. My own inclinations are hybridic, but I think the dialogue within the relational world around these matters is very healthy.

Relational Ideas in Formation

The earliest papers Mitchell published in the late 1970s were criticisms of the canonical psychoanalytic work on homosexuality, which he charged as being insufficiently psychoanalytic and overly moralistic (Mitchell, 1981a, 1981b). One can see his determination to establish an alterity, a space of difference, and a critical engagement with drive theory. His early recognition of the destructive effects of moral judgments and pathologizing in the understanding and treatment of homosexuality were striking both in the trust he had in his own voice and vision, and in the attention to the social and regulatory (not a word he used) impulses in psychoanalytic theory.

In *Object Relations in Psychoanalytic Theory* (1983), Greenberg and Mitchell launched a consideration of a wide range of theories, marking what they termed a "radical alternative" to one person drive theory in the widely different work of Klein, Winnicott, Kernberg, and Kohut. Mitchell and Greenberg saw all these theorists, despite their difference, as joined in a fundamental commitment to the primacy of object ties and what, even then, was being termed "relational" experience. In this first book, the Jamesian perspective peeks out. Summarizing their work, they speak for theoretical and clinical approaches, to be judged on their utility (p. 380).

After 1983, in a series of books authored alone, Mitchell developed the relational perspective, considering metapsychological matters, clinical process, models of mind, and a richly textured sense of the dyadic flow of analytic work (Mitchell, 1988, 1993, 1997, 2000). His work was both constitutive of relational theory and dynamic, moving and open to transformation from inside and outside relational culture.

In his book *Hope and Dread* (Mitchell, 1993), he outlined the relational revolution, small r. It was to be a revolution in what the analyst knew (echoes of Lacan here) and a revolution in what the patient wanted (echoes of Ferenczi). By the end of his life, Mitchell had reconnected to an earlier and important figure, Hans Loewald, and his lens on early development.

Two-Person Psychologies

Two-person psychologies are perhaps the most dramatic concept that inaugurated the relational turn. Through the work and influence of Emmanuel Ghent, Winnicott's dyadic view of transitional space and transitional objects and his ideas of the power of interactions (in particular the constitutive effects of the infant's attempts to destroy and aggress against the other) produced a set of papers expanding our understanding of the use of relatedness as a crucial aspect to the formation of internal representations and to the establishment of distinctions between reality and fantasy (Ghent, 1990, 2002). Sadism and masochism, he argued, have at heart relational projects. For sadism, it was object finding and for masochism, it was a retreat from contact, or to use Ghent's preferred term, surrender.

For developmentalists like myself, this determination to see the social as constitutive of the individual spoke of the social and cognitive theories of Vygotsky (1978, 1986). In 2005, I wrote:

> We acquire language and language acquires us. We are inserted into and get some command over the experience of speech. But there is no

seamless fit between speech and self, text and subjectivity. The relation of speaking and being, including being a particular gender, is one of excess and gaps.

Vygotsky's interest in the intersect of speech and thinking focused on what we would call metacognition, a form of knowing he called co-knowing, and a form of consciousness and self-consciousness he thought as a multiple configured system (1978, 1986). Reflective functioning was a very particular capacity, derived out of the social experience of being known, spoken to, and thought about. The Vygotskian self is therefore private and public, social and personal, conscious and unconscious. A Vygotskian child emerges with an intentional or aspectual self, a formation born out of social relations and what psychoanalysts would now term intersubjectivity.

(Harris, 2005, p. 38)

For analyst/researchers like Beebe (Beebe and Lachman, 2005; Beebe, Knoblauch, Rustin, & Sorter, 2005; Seligman, 2003, 2005) and the Boston Change Group (1998), these ideas flowed from infant–parent observation. The potency and power of the early schemes of interaction created a template for subsequent forms of interaction. Beebe and Lachman (2005) established the concept of three forms of salience—ongoing regulation, rupture and repair, and heightened affective moments—as the ground of clinical and early relational life. Along with the work of the Boston Change Group (1998) on the power of "now" moments, and the range of attachment theorists, there was a focus on intense and abiding presence of nonverbal and preverbal forms of representation and interaction. Twoness was always an aspect of oneness.

For Hoffman (1998), in the context of his seminal work with Merton Gill, two-person-ness came as an aspect of social constructionism. In thinking of the ubiquity of social construction as an aspect of mind and of cure, Hoffman focused on the elements of suggestion, power, and intimacy in all analytic dyadic life. Jessica Benjamin's (1988) work on complementarity is a core idea that undergirds much relational thinking about two-person-ness. In the process of both forming attachments and negotiating separation, Benjamin stressed there was the potential for the emergence of new forms of relatedness, of distinct kinds of Thirdness in the process of negotiating subjectivity and objectivity. The dyad was always more than two-ness. In fact, as she argued and as we now see in many clinical encounters, too symmetrical and jammed a form of two-ness leaves both partners in the dyad caught in a sado-masochistic dance.

In another slant on two-person-ness, Stern (2010) examined the element of witnessing in clinical process, arguing that experience and self consciousness arise in the context of being witnessed and enactments are moments when the functioning of witness has collapsed and must be restored. On a micro-level, Stern, and on a macro-level, Gerson (2009) are both struggling with the impact of recognition or its collapse on processes of growth and self coherence or intelligibility.

Social Constructionism and Social Regulation

In pursuing the question of social construction of unconscious and intrapsychic as well as interpersonal life, the relationalists centered on the dyad, but increasingly felt the need to go beyond it. There are influences of Fromm (1941, 1947), and Levenson, drawn from the interpersonalist tradition, which made cultural formation an important element in individual psyche. But, perhaps more importantly, there were strong influences upon relational thought arising from encountering Foucault (1965, 1980, 1988), from critical theory and ideology critique, and from political activism. For those of us particularly working in the areas of gender and sexuality, the particular insights of Foucault, and for a next generation, Althusser (1971), Zizek (1989), and Levinas (1998), have been crucial. One intriguing aspect of these theorists is their demand of analysts to deploy certain self-consciousness in regard to method. We cure with contaminated tools.

Dimen (2003) is an exemplary relational figure whose attention was consistently attuned to the psychological, the political, and the social, as these forces play out in conscious and unconscious ways. Her work on sexuality, drawn from psychoanalysis, anthropology and feminism, insisted on the public-ness and privateness of sexuality. Disgust, excitement, excess all intersect and combust with the grids of power and regulation that manage and produce sexuality.

Ken Corbett (1999, 2009) situates his work both in a relational tradition and in queer theory. The dialogues between psychoanalytic theory and various movements of liberation and social activism are multi-directional and complex. Going back to the 1970s, one might see that in regard to feminism, the encounter of psychoanalysis (Chodorow, 1976; Dinnerstein, 1976) was fortuitous for those social movements. It took a lot of input from what was broadly described as psychoanalytic feminism, a theoretical practice that is more than solely or simply relational (see Elise, 1997, 2002; Chodorow, 1992, 1994) from a more Freudian and object relational approach, as well as Dimen, Goldner, Harris, Corbett, to alter the basic understandings in that political perspective.

In those early years, an analysis of theory as social regulation opened up a crucial and painful history of pathologizing of gender and sexual variance. In the 1980s, a movement began in the other direction, from activism to theory via critical theory, cultural studies, and many elements of postmodernism and post-structuralism. Queer theory (and its perhaps central figure from philosophy, Judith Butler) began to remake the psychoanalytic theories of gender, and sexuality. Queering psychoanalysis might be one way to describe the current projects in regard to gender, race, and class. Very broadly, many of these figures draw on and utilize some or many elements of relational theory.

In Corbett's work on masculinity (2010) and in the work on heterosexual masculinities (Reis & Grossmark, 2009), finally masculinity is being deconstructed, seen in its many limiting and traumatic implications. The traumatic effects of the pressure on making early separation normative for boys are something finally more visible. The complexities of masculinities finally join up with the deconstructing of femininity, which certainly begins with Freud. But with the new attention to deconstructive masculinity, the canonical has become symptomatic.

No identity category was immune from interrogation and resignification, to use a term of Judith Butler's (2005). This backdrop is foundational, but I think it is no accident many of us were drawn to psychoanalysis to deepen and engage with the social and political categories that had become compelling. Social construction has meant many things to relationalists, but for those working on gender and sexuality, the social was both micro and macro, the crucible of the family shot through with the grids of power and meaning through which social forces at many levels functioned to define and shape individual and collective lives.

The question of a cultural context for psychoanalytic theory and practice is an exceedingly complex one. In the original symposium on *What Is American about American Psychoanalysis?* (2004), cultural theorist Shirmeister was of the view that the initially positive reception of psychoanalytic ideas was in part due to America in 1912 still being a culture in mourning. One might see other periods of strain as well. The postwar period, deemed in one characterization as the Age of Certainty, is also a period of great trauma and difficulty, from the European refugee analysts bringing mid-century psychoanalysis to America (Jacoby, 1983) to the generation of American analysts working in the shadow of the postwar experience with veterans and the period of political repression and fear ushered in by McCarthyism, the black list, and the Cold War (Schrecker, 1986). The mourning attendant on the aftermath of the war, on the loss of progressive ideals and hopes in the Cold War era, as well as that suffered by the European community arriving in the United States in the 1930s and 1940s, all may have had a subtle but inexorable role in the structuring of psychoanalytic theory and practice in the postwar decades.

Multiple Self-States: Relational Metapsychology

Another key element in these transformations of questions of identity in relational thought is the long-standing relational preoccupation with multiple self-states and with a metapsychology in which shifting states of identity, powered by dissociative processes of differing intensities of magnitudes, account for many features of analytic dyadic work and the fluid ongoing nature of identity and identifications.

The work on shifting and multiple self-states inevitably led to a model of mind which featured vertical splits, the powerful presence of dissociation and dissociative processes in dyads and in individuals (Davies, 1994; Bromberg, 1998, 2006). Beginning with the powerful contributions of Davies and Frawley (1994) on the impact of sexual abuse on mental structure and psychic process, the relational work was perhaps first most known and most notorious for a strong use of analytic subjectivity and countertransference.

In this context, consider the evolution of the work of Philip Bromberg, an analyst both steeped in the interpersonal tradition and transformed in his encounter with Mitchell, Ghent, and Bollas who centers his interests in dissociative process that are used, among other things, to manage relational space. Paradoxically, dissociation is used in the service of certain kinds of false continuities and coherences. Intolerable and very shame-based self-states must be kept split off in order for the individual to avoid fragmentation.

Again, in a paradoxical circumstance, dissociation may be the glue (if that's the term) for attachment.

Development, Motivation, and Emergent Function

Ghent, early trained in object relations, in his seminal paper "Masochism, to submission, surrender," extends our view on development, motivation and emergent function. The object, he says:

> is needed "not because of the baby's impulse to destroy, but because of the object's liability not to survive" (an idea from Winnicott). The varieties of non-survival include retaliation, withdrawal, defensiveness in any of its forms, as overall change in attitude in the direction of suspiciousness or diminished receptivity, and finally, a kind of crumbling, in the sense of its losing one's capacity to function adequately as mother, or in the analytic setting, as analyst. This conception of development involving the difficult passage from object relating to object use implies a radical departure from the usual analytic notion that aggression is reactive to the encounter with external reality (the reality principle). Here it is destructiveness that creates the very quality of externality. But the main reason for this discussion of the development of the capacity for object usage is to explore its relation to surrender, masochism, and now, sadism. The essence of both transitional experiencing and the transition into object usage is the heady and wonderful world of creative experiencing wherein self and other have the opportunity to become real. A principal cause of failure in transitional experiencing is what has already been referred to as impingement by the caretaker. We have seen how this intrusiveness interferes with true experiencing or "coming into being" with the distressing result that for the infant to "exist," continuing impingement is required. Here we saw the beginnings of masochism. I have suggested also that in many people there is an impulse to surrender, perhaps in order to reengage that area of transitional experiencing, the miscarriage of which impulse or longing appears as masochism or submission.
>
> (Ghent, 1990, p. 125)

At the end of Mitchell's all too brief life, he had reconnected with an early affinity for Hans Loewald and was deeply interested in the emergence of self in the context of self and other. In *Relationality*, Mitchell (2000) noted the degree to which relational terms and ideas were visible throughout the psychoanalytic worlds. What he was not noticing so explicitly was the shifts in relational theory, in response to growth within the perspective and in response to critical demands to clarify the role and function of the unconscious in psychic life, as well as the fate and status of primitive states. In Mitchell's hands, Loewald emerges as a powerful visionary for the notion of human subjectivity as emergent within a relational matrix, one characterized from the earliest moments as a site of primal density from which object states and subjectivity emerge. Words catch fire in relational context, in dyadic affective life. The key for Loewald was balance, the constant vitalizing force of affect states and linguistic representations. For me, this positions Loewald and the relational ideas of early states and development more in parallel with Laplanche (1989), a theorist for whom the instability of inside/outside, self and other, excess and vitalization are key in the constituting of identity and sexuality.

The relationalist who has put Laplanche to most use is Ruth Stein, and here one might note the hybridity of her formation, Freudian and relational. In her prizewinning paper on sexuality as excess, Stein (2008) integrates classical ideas about excitement, Laplanchian accounts of the simultaneous and co-terminal constituting of sexuality and the unconscious, in an encounter with the other (surely a two-person account of sexuality) along with insights about shame and transgression from contemporary queer theory.

The central figures in this evolution of relational thinking are all people who bridge disciplines. From infant mental health, family systems, infant observation, developmental psychology and developmental psychopathology, a picture of developmental process and its impact on clinical experience emerges. Seligman's (2003) essay on this matter begins with a description of infant capacity, a description that then sets the stage for understanding the implications for the infant psyche of such capacious processing capacities.

Beebe and Lachman, most signally, and the Boston Change Group stress the potency and permanence of early dyadic life, the print of early transactions and nonverbal, affectively constituted experience as a template, both capable of transformation and also in certain ways immutable. The tension, between a theory of growth and a theory of the power of the past is a hot point in relational thinking, a place of debate and dialogue centering on how clinical experience is viewed (Beebe et al., 2005).

In the past decade, significant developments in neuroscience offer interesting points of conversation and integration (see Damasio, 1999 on the essential enmeshing of emotion and cognition; Gallese, 2009 on mirror neurons, and Beebe et al., 2005 on infant research). All these researchers are creating engaged fields of inquiry to think about what develops, what is interpersonal, and how relational matrices become intrapsychic. There are many strong arguments for the need for caution, for non-reductionist ways of thinking about interdisciplinary translations, but the utility—as metaphor, as theory building, as clinical listening—seem to me undeniable.

Clinical Process

While there are debates within the relational group about whether or even how to codify relational technique, it is in the area of technique or clinical process that the profound change relational psychoanalysis intended to effect in the field was first initiated.

It is in the realm of clinical process that the most pointed controversies and conflicts with the more classical world of psychoanalysis arose. Some of this debate was captured in an essay by Charles Spezzano (1998) ironically, but also exasperatedly, titled "How relational analysts kill time between disclosures and enactments." Relational theory is an example of a radical field theory, a theory where the social field and the individual are powerfully interdependent. Other examples of this kind of theorizing would include the post-Bionian work of Ferro (2015) and Lombardi (2009).

The implications for clinical work flowed for Mitchell and for others particularly interested in clinical process, from the ubiquity of counter-transference and the implications of a two-person psychology. Key figures in the evolution of clinical process ideas would be Bromberg, Aron, Hoffman, Davies, Bass, Pizer, Spezzano, Slochower, and more recently Ringstrom, Knoblauch, and from the related interpersonal side, Stern and Ehrenberg. How was the analyst to make use of his/her subjectivity? Was personal visibility or disclosure dangerous, or narcissistic, making the analyst more important than the patient, perverting and abusing treatment, gratifying either partner, avoiding having the patient work in more quiet, less interactive ways? Might such active and interactive treatments circumvent or occlude unconscious process? All these questions appeared in various forms in early reactions to relational ideas. But all these questions also arose from younger candidates and students interested in learning about relational theory and not finding it easy to know what to do.

Our understanding about countertransference and the analyst's subjectivity inevitably altered the power dynamics in the clinical setting. If you think that your presence (in ways knowable and unknowable) makes a difference in how and whether the analysand can think, speak, or feel, then that will lead to basic shifts in how you imagine the analytic setting. Everyone thinks that the patient can affect how the analyst is able to think, feel, or function. This has been true since Bion and Rosenfeld established the idea of projective identifications and projections as forms of communication. The question is, do you imagine that the process of disrupting the psychic function works in the other direction, from analyst to analysand? The related question is, how ubiquitous you find this dialectical movement and what do you do about such matters?

How you think of the frame, how it is established, what you think motivates the analyst or the analysand, and what information is relevant when you decide what to do or say or not say: all these questions compel relational analysts in thinking about clinical process. Relational clinical theory operates as a kind of radical system theory in which it is not possible to conceive of analysis as a more or less static scene with someone producing material to be understood (by speech or action) and someone else who knows. Relationalists are convinced that many elements in our work make us visible, and so function as disclosures. Aron (1991, 1992, 1996, 2001, 2006), and B. Pizer (2005) therefore look at explicit and implicit disclosures. Silence is no guarantee of opacity or even psychic space available for the analysand to work in.

Many analysts before Stephen Mitchell (Ferenczi, McLaughlin, Nacht, Jacobs, Little, Heimann, the Barangers, Racker, Ogden, and Renik) operated with some or many of these ideas that formed the ground for relational theory, even as they are put into practice in very different ways.

One early preoccupation had to do with power. Was analysis now a democracy, or anarchy? Aron, in particular, argues for a mix of mutuality alongside the maintenance of asymmetry, Hoffman for spontaneity and rules, the exercise of freedom, playfulness and interaction and for authenticity and responsibility. Davies' work is guided by her sense of the shifting self-states and the relational patterns played out between her and her patient who require active engagement. She writes that one of the most challenging demands on an analyst is the necessity of living as the patient's bad object, of seeing and saying when and how you might be imagined to be the perpetrator of abuse, and/or the potentially violent or collapsing significant other. These processes, projection, and projective identifications bring inevitable uncertainty to the relational clinical process, and we ask: "Whose life is this?" "Whose mind?" "Whose action?" "Whose meaning?"

What I find useful and necessary to add to considerations of intersubjectivity in clinical process is the idea of negotiation and paradox, most associated with Tony Bass, (2003, 2007), S. Pizer (1998), and Slochower (1996). If the analytic experience is one of ongoing negotiation around meaning, the clinical work has built in irreducible and often quite substantial uncertainty. In this regard, Bass, who has written about the frame and about the process of negotiations of both concrete and abstract matters in treatments, stands in the legacy of Ferenczi's ideas about mutual analysis. Bass (2003) works with the assumption that he is part of the process and the analysand's insights into his subjectivity need to be taken up. To work this way, Bass suggests, gives great freedom and creates tremendous demands on both partners for precision, and reflection.

Pizer, Aron, and Benjamin have focused on the experience of impasse, or the freezing of treatments, as a way to speak of the role of the analyst's subjectivity in transformation. S. Pizer (1998) looks at impasse as a sign of the collapse of negotiability, a deadening of creative vitality in both partners, perhaps a lapse in containment, inevitably, as Aron and others argue, a blind spot, a lapse in the analyst, whatever else has happened. Aron would see a variety of technical moves: interpretation, enactments (intentional and unintentional), and disclosures as kinds of ventilation, maintaining movement and psychic reflection in both participants.

An interesting variation on this question of analytic subjectivity is provided by Slochower (1996), who takes the more conventional idea in Winnicott and Bion of holding and containing, and sees its particular potency in treatments with very disturbed patients, for whom mutuality seems impossible. She sees holding as a kind of holding for the patient where the analyst contains the patient's ruthlessness, narcissism, and self-blame until the patient can begin to absorb these as self-states. Holding, then, is a kind of titrating of analytic failure. This model has both mutuality and asymmetry, and at least in some stages of the work, withholds analytic subjectivity while making intense use of it.

Countertransference is pursued in yet another way by Cooper (2000, 2010), who is interested in how the analyst holds theory, how our mental dialogues (what Stern might call witnessing) shape how we work, and often how we have to change how we work. Cooper's attention is to analytic reverie, what he terms its melancholic properties. In his hands, the analytic instrument is a highly complex, vivid set of processes, impeding and enabling progress in the work. There is a link, I would say, between Cooper's project in treatments to engage the patient in becoming curious about his/her body/mind and Cooper's model of the analyst's engagement with the field, broadly and deeply conceived. All these writers are crafting a model of clinical process in which dynamism is its permanent condition and impasse is a collapse in negotiation and the capacity for reflection and creativity.

My own interest in these questions of work in and on the counter-transference has centered on analytic vulnerability (Harris & Sinsheimer, 2008; Harris, 2009). To work in this way entails ruthless self-examination, but also protection against too ruthless a use of the self. Our ideals of analytic care often veer to the masochistic. We demand a great deal in our demands for self-scrutiny, and our understanding of the deep interdependencies of self and other, body and mind. This will require, in my view, both individual and collective managements: more disclosure to colleagues, more candor in situations where the analyst is in difficulty, more dialogue. Work by Gabbard (1994), Celenza and Gabbard (2003), and Dimen (2011) speaks to the field-wide dilemmas that boundary violations pose and the commitment to open dialogue as necessary correlative to the deeply private and often lonely conditions of our work.

A theme that goes back to Ferenczi, and is picked up in various ways by different analysts in different contexts (Racker, Nacht, Searles, McLaughlin), is an element in the relational canon in regard to work with countertransference. That is, change in the patient attends on, is ushered in, or impeded by, changes (or closures) in the analyst (Slavin, Harris, Ehrenberg). These questions of impasse and barriers to change centered in the analyst are often raised in the context of thinking about enactments and their place in mutative action. These questions are explored in regard to termination (Salberg, 2010) and in Rozmarin's (2007) Levinas-inflected analysis of how the analyst can recognize the patient without colonizing him/her.

New Directions

Social/Historical

Because of the presence in the earliest relational generation of strong interests in feminism, progressive thought and later in queer theory, categories like gender and sexuality were always under examination. More recently, class and race are held under a relational psychoanalytic lens. Relationalists working in these areas are also indebted to the work of Leary (1997, 2000) and Apprey (2006), writers more identified with a classical tradition. Altman has been at work on deconstructing the intersect of poverty and psychodynamic treatment—concerns that require confrontations in regard to internalized racism in analytic theory and analysts—and to the blindness in theories and institutions to the exigencies of class, culture, and race as they play into transference/countertransference processes more conventionally understood. His work, and that of Suchet (2007), Straker (2004), and White (2007) on race in the cultural context of apartheid, and of Hartman (2007) and Gentile (2007) on class and materiality as an aspect of embodiment and psyche, depends on the relational project of examination of countertransference and of seeing the deep imbrications of the social in the intrapsychic and thus in the clinical dyad.

Suchet (2007) and Hill (2008) track the ways race enters and splits early family relational life and thus the earliest attachments carry anguish, mourning, and creative links that often remain secrets even to the child who bears them. These ideas are quite relevant to many current social debates about the out-sourcing of child care, the divisions of class and race and ethnicity that are aspects of the changing nature of work (in First World and Third World women).

Political and social consciousness took a new turn in Aron and Starr's (2014) recent work about the way distinctions between psychotherapy and psychoanalysis were theorized. They explored how psychoanalysis, in an era when it had great cultural power, prestige, and status, and was overwhelmingly dominated by male physicians, defined itself by splitting off all that was vulnerable and precarious within the therapist. Nurturance and relatedness were split off into psychotherapy, leaving pure psychoanalysis as the champion of autonomy and individuality. From this angle, "relational psychoanalysis" was an oxymoron. Psychoanalysis was civilized, masculine, and promoted ego autonomy; psychotherapy was primitive, feminine, and relied on support and dependency.

There is a strong and old tradition in psychoanalysis predating relational work that seeks to use theory to do political critique and political work alongside the usual clinical practices. What was called the Freudian left was strongly influential in Europe in the interwar period, including the Frankfurt School, Reich, and many Berlin analysts (for an account of the transformations of a politically sophisticated psychoanalytic culture in the process of emigration and refugee flight, see Jacoby 1983). Relationalists, many of them formed in the intense crucible of the 1960s during the civil rights and anti-war and eventually feminist and gay liberation movements, have been working on this intersect of the social/political and the psychic/clinical. While the transformative aspects of drawing on categories of social identities are very exciting, this work is often borne out of the examination of painful aspects of the analyst/theorist's subjectivity and circumstances.

Trauma and Its Intergenerational Transmission

Trauma is, of course, an early preoccupation of relational thinkers. The long-term effects of early and cumulative trauma in the form of abuse, neglect, and various forms of psychic invasion or abandonment continue to dominate many clinical writings and projects. But there is also an interest in adult onset trauma on psychic and interpersonal life (Boulanger, 2002). One crucial aspect of these ideas is the transgenerational element. This concept has roots, I believe, in a number of sources, but particularly in the work of Abraham and Torok and their notion of encrypted identities, secrets passed in unconscious communications that remain secret to transmitter and receiver. Unconscious communication was of interest to Ferenczi and reflected his sense of the powerful forms of transmission—in speech, in bodily life, in ways of relating. These interests have been consuming for many relationalists, and are the focus of work on the body, considered in this next section.

Embodiment and Attachment

Within relational psychoanalysis, the body has become a central focus, clinically and theoretically. This might reflect one of the ways relational theorists have taken on critique. Had the turning of attention from one person to two-person-ness rendered the notion of the individual and the unconscious too shallow or too superficial? Had the intersubjective trumped the intrapsychic? In developing answers to these questions, relationalists were led towards other disciplines, philosophers of the body both general (Merlau-Ponty, Lakoff, & Johnson) and feminist/postmodern (Grosz & Butler). Thus embodiment is now a centerpiece to much developmental theory such that many forms of representation—for example, preverbal and nonverbal—are seen as the necessary ground to early memory, early attachment, and later relational strategies. We might see here the long legacy of Loewaldian ideas about the intermixing of primary and secondary process, a necessary balance to mature psyches.

Virginia Goldner (2014) demonstrates how couples work can be understood psychodynamically as the application of understanding of relational trauma in trapped and crisis-ridden couples. Drawing on work on early nonverbal attachment processes, Goldner applies a relational psycho-analytic lens to the analysis of couple processes in circumstances where, as she says, "the person who is one's safe haven and secure base, the one who heals/regulates and cares for you, is also the one who can hurt and frighten you" (p. 406). There is also a new and ethically demanding interest in the phenomena of transgender, where one can see the way topics that start on the outer edge of clinical experience, first read simply as pathology, migrate into the center. Looking at transgender phenomena means revising many ideas we have about the trauma of social regulatory anxiety for many gender experiences, the nature of the body and sexual difference, and the need to consider race, class, psychosis, as well as trauma and object relational history in our studies on gender identity (Corbett, 2009).

Conclusion

Relational psychoanalysis entails an understanding, sometimes reluctant, sometimes anxious, and sometimes jubilant and confident, that analytic work proceeds with an irreducible degree of uncertainty. We don't work knowing nothing, but our awareness, our clarity of purpose, our inten-tions, and our decisions—spontaneous or crafted—all have aspects of unconscious forces that render us incomplete masters in our own house. This is our challenge and our burden. If you believe, or have conviction, that mind is two-personish, that body and mind are interrelated and co-created, and that subjectivity arises first in the primal density that is social and interpersonal and elaborated in the networks of relational life, you are thus committed to a number of other key ideas that will guide how you work, how you see what is happening in a consulting room, and how you understand the mutative action of psychoanalysis and that for an individual to change a system will change, and vice versa.

Writing an essay on a theoretical/clinical movement in psychoanalysis is perhaps, inevitably, an act of imperialism, a form of colonization, planting flags in certain domains or fields of ideas. I began with the hope that we might see the powerful interrelations that theories have, even in periods of potent disagreement. I am aware that the previous paragraph might be subscribed to by many analysts not terming themselves relational. This seems hopeful to me. It is also my hope that here I have opened up an account of work whose producers think of themselves as relationalists, of one kind or another. Good ideas thrive from being shared.

References

Althusser, L. (1971). Ideology and ideological state apparatuses. In L. Althusser (Ed.), *Lenin and Philosophy and other essays*. New York, NY: Monthly Review Press.

Apprey, M. (2006). Difference and the awakening of wounds in intercultural psychoanalysis. *Psychoanalytic Quarterly, 75*, 73–93.

Aron, L. (1991). The patient's experience of the analyst's subjectivity. *Psychoanalytic Dialogues, 1*, 29–51.

Aron, L. (1992). Interpretation as expression of the analyst's subjectivity. *Psychoanalytic Dialogues, 2*, 475–507.

Aron, L. (1996). *A meeting of minds: Mutuality in psychoanalysis*. Hillsdale, NJ: Analytic Press.

Aron, L. (2001). Intersubjectivity in the analytic situation. In J. C. Muran (Ed.), *Self-relations in the psychotherapy process* (pp. 137–164). Washington, DC: American Psychological Association.

Aron, L. (2006). Analytic impasse and the third: Clinical implications of intersubjectivity. *International Journal of Psycho-Analysis, 87*, 349–368.

Aron, L., & Harris, A. (1994). *The legacy of Sándor Ferenczi*. Hillsdale, NJ: Analytic Press.

Aron, L., & Starr, K. (2014). *Defining psychoanalysis: The surprising relevance of racism, anti-Semitism, misogyny and homophobia*. New York, NY: Routledge.

Bass, A. (2003). Enactments in psychoanalysis: Another medium, another message. *Psychoanalytic Dialogues, 13*, 657–676.

Bass, A. (2007). When the frame doesn't fit the Picture. *Psychoanalytic Dialogues, 17*, 1–27.

Beebe, B., Knoblauch S., Rustin, J., & Sorter, D. (2005). *Forms of intersubjectivity in infant research and adult treatment*. New York, NY: Other Press.

Beebe, B., & Lachmann, F. M. (2005). *Infant research and adult treatment*. New York, NY: Routledge.

Benjamin, J. (1988). *The bonds of love*. New York, NY: Pantheon.

Boston Change Group (1998). Non-interpretive mechanisms in psychoanalytic therapy: The "something more" than interpretation. *International Journal of Psychoanalysis, 79*, 903–921.

Boulanger, G. (2002). Wounded by reality: The collapse of the self in adult onset trauma. *Contemporary Psychoanalysis, 38*, 45–76.

Bromberg, P.M. (1998). *Standing in the spaces: Essays in clinical process, trauma, and dissociation.* Hillsdale, NJ: Analytic Press.

Bromberg, P.M. (2006). *Awakening the dreamer: Clinical journeys.* Mahwah, NJ: Analytic Press.

Butler, J. (2005). *Giving an account of oneself.* New York, NY: Routledge.

Celenza, A., & Gabbard, G. O. (2003). Analysts who commit sexual boundary violations. *American Journal of Psychoanalysis, 51,* 617–636.

Chodorow, N. (1976). *The reproduction of mothering.* Berkeley, CA: University of California Press.

Chodorow, N. (1992). Heterosexuality as a compromise formation: Reflections on the psychoanalytic theory of sexual development. *Psychoanalytic Contemporary Thought, 15,* 267–304.

Chodorow, N. (1994). *Femininities, masculinities, sexualities: Freud and beyond.* Lexington, KY: University Press of Kentucky.

Cooper, S. (2000). Mutual containment in the analytic situation. *Psychoanalytic Dialogues, 10,* 169–194.

Cooper, S. (2010). *A disturbance in the field.* New York, NY: Routledge.

Corbett, K. (1999). Homosexual boyhood: Notes on girlyboys. In M. Rottnek (Ed.), *Sissies and tomboys: Gender nonconformity and homosexual childhood* (pp. 107–139). New York, NY: New York University Press.

Corbett, K. (2009). *Boyhoods.* New Haven, CT: Yale University Press.

Damasio, A. (1999). *The feeling of what happens: Body and emotion in the consciousness.* New York, NY: Harcourt Brace.

Davies, J. (1994). Love in the afternoon: A relational reconsideration of desire and dread in the countertransference. *Psychoanalytic Dialogues, 4,* 153–170.

Davies, J., & Frawley, M. G. (1994). *Treating the adult survivor of childhood sexual abuse: A psychoanalytic perspective.* New York, NY: Basic Books.

Dimen, M. (2003). *Sexuality, intimacy, power.* Hillsdale, NJ: Analytic Press.

Dimen, M. (2011). Lapsus linguae, or a slip of the tongue? A sexual violation in an analytic treatment and its personal and theoretical aftermath. *Contemporary Psychoanalysis, 47,* 35–79.

Dinnerstein, D. (1976). *The mermaid and the minotaur.* New York, NY: Harper & Row.

Ehrenberg, D. (1992). *The intimate edge: Extending the reach of psychoanalytic interaction.* New York, NY: Norton.

Elise, D. (1997). Primary femininity, bisexuality and the female ego ideal: A reexamination of female developmental theory. *Psychoanalytic Quarterly, 66,* 489–517.

Elise, D. (2002). The primary maternal oedipal situation and female homoerotic desire. *Psychoanalytic Quarterly, 22,* 209–228.

Ferro, A. (2015). *Reveries: An unfettered mind.* London, England: Karnac.

Foucault, M (1965). *Madness and civilization.* New York, NY: Vintage.

Foucault, M. (1980). *The history of sexuality.* New York, NY: Vintage.

Foucault, M. (1988). On power. In *Politics, philosophy, culture: Interviews and other writings 1977–1984.* New York, NY: Routledge.

Fromm, E. (1941). *Escape from freedom.* New York, NY: Avon.

Fromm, E. (1947). *Man for himself.* New York, NY: Fawcett.

Gabbard, G. O. (1994). Sexual excitement and countertransference love in the analyst. *Journal of the American Psychoanalytic Association, 42,* 1083–1106.

Gallese, V. (2009). Mirror neurons, embodied simulation, and the neural basis of social identification. *Psychoanalytic Dialogues, 19,* 519–536.

Gentile, J. (2007). Wrestling with matter: Origins of intersubjectivity. *Psychoanalytic Quarterly, 76,* 547–582.

Gerson, S. (2009). When the third is dead: Memory, mourning and witness in the aftermath of the Holocaust. *International Journal of Psychoanalysis, 90,* 1341–1358.

Ghent, E. (1990). Masochism, submission, surrender: Masochism as a perversion of surrender. *Contemporary Psychoanalysis, 26,* 108–136.

Ghent, E. (2002). Wish, need, drive: Motive in the light of dynamic systems theory and Edelman's selectionist theory. *Psychoanalytic Dialogues, 12,* 763–808.

Goldner, V. (2014). Romantic bonds, binds and ruptures: Couples on the brink. *Psychoanalytic Dialogues, 24,* 402–418.

Greenberg, J., & Mitchell, S. A. (1983). *Object relations in psychoanalytic theory.* Cambridge, MA: Harvard University Press.

Harris, A. (2005). *Gender as soft assembly.* Hillsdale, NJ: Analytic Press.

Harris, A. (2009). "You must remember this." *Psychoanalytic Dialogues, 19,* 2–21.

Harris, A., & Sinsheimer, K. (2008). *The analyst's vulnerability: Preserving and fine-tuning analytic bodies.* In F. Anderson (Ed.), *Bodies in treatment: The unknown dimension* (pp. 255–274). New York, NY: Taylor & Francis.

Hartman, S. (2007). Class unconscious: From dialectical materialism to relational material. In M. Suchet, A. Harris, & L. Aron (Eds.), *Relational psychoanalysis, Volume 3: New Voices* (pp. 209–226). Hilldale, NJ: Analytic Press.

Heynal, A. (2002). *Disappearing and reviving: Sándor Ferenczi and the history of psychoanalysis.* London, England: Karnac.

Hill, S. (2008). Language and intersubjectivity: Multiplicity in a bilingual treatment. *Psychoanalytic Dialogues, 18,* 437–455.

Hoffman, I. (1998). *Ritual and spontaneity in the psychoanalytic process: A dialectical-constructivist view.* Hillsdale, NJ: Analytic Press.

Jacoby, R. (1983). *The repression of psychoanalysis.* New York, NY: Basic Books.

James, W. (1890). *The Principles of Psychology.* New York, NY: Henry Holt.

James, W. (1910). *Psychology.* New York, NY: Henry Holt.

James, W. (1978). *Pragmatism.* Cambridge, MA: Harvard University Press.

Laplanche, J. (1989). *New foundations for psychoanalysis.* London, England: Blackwell.

Leary, K. (1997). Race, self-disclosure, and "forbidden talk": Race and ethnicity in contemporary clinical practice. *Psychoanalytic Quarterly, 66,* 163–189.

Leary, K. (2000). Racial enactments in dynamic treatment. *Psychoanalytic Dialogues, 10,* 639–653.

Levinas, E. (1998). *Otherwise than being.* Pittsburgh, PA: Duquesne University Press.

Lombardi, R. (2009). Symmetric frenzy and catastrophic change: A reconsideration of primitive mental states in the wake of Bion and Matte Blanco. *International Journal of Psychoanalysis, 90,* 529–549.

Mitchell, S. A. (1981a). The psychoanalytic treatment of homosexuality: Some technical considerations. *International Review of Psychoanalysis, 8,* 63–80.

Mitchell, S. A. (1981b). Psychodynamics, homosexuality, and the question of pathology. *Psychiatry: Journal of Interpersonal Process, 41,* 254–263.

Mitchell, S. A. (1988). *Relational concepts in psychoanalysis.* Cambridge, MA: Harvard University Press.

Mitchell, S. A. (1993). *Hope and dread in psychoanalysis.* New York, NY: Basic Books.

Mitchell, S. A. (1997). *Influence and autonomy in psychoanalysis.* Hillsdale, NJ: Analytic Press.

Mitchell, S. A. (2000). *Relationality: From attachment to intersubjectivity.* Hillsdale, NJ: Analytic Press.

Mitchell, S. A., & Harris, A. (2004). What's American about American psychoanalysis? *Psychoanalytic Dialogues, 2,* 165–192.

Peirce, C. S. (1955). *Philosophical Writings of Peirce* (J. Buchler, Ed.). New York, NY: Dover.

Pizer, B. (2005). Passion, responsibility, and "wild geese": Creating a context for absence of conscious intentions. *Psychoanalytic Dialogues, 15,* 57–84.

Pizer, S. (1998). *Building bridges: The negotiation of paradox in psychoanalysis.* Hillsdale, NJ: Analytic Press.

Reis, B., & Grossmark, R. (2009). *Heterosexual masculinities: Contemporary perspectives from psychoanalytic gender theory.* New York, NY: Taylor & Francis.

Rozmarin, E. (2007). An other in psychoanalysis: Emmanuel Levinas's critique of knowledge and analytic sense. *Contemporary Psychoanalysis, 43,* 327–360.

Salberg, J. (2010). *Good enough endings.* New York, NY: Taylor & Francis.

Schrecker, E. (1998). *Many are the crimes: McCarthyism in America.* Boston, MA: Little, Brown.

Seligman, S. (2003). The developmental perspective in relational psychoanalysis. *Contemporary Psychoanalysis, 39,* 477–508.

Seligman, S. (2005). Dynamic systems theories as a metaframework for psychoanalysis. *Psychoanalytic Dialogues, 15,* 285–319.

Slochower, J. (1996). *Holding and psychoanalysis: A relational perspective.* Hillsdale, NJ: Analytic Press.

Spezzano, C. (1998). How relational analysts kill time between disclosures and enactments: Commentary on papers by Bromberg and by Greenberg. *Psychoanalytic Dialogues, 2,* 237–247.

Stein, R. (2008). The otherness of sexuality: Excess. *Journal of the American Psychoanalytic Association, 56,* 43–71.

Stern, D. B. (2010). *Partners in thought: Working with unformulated experience, dissociation, and enactment.* New York, NY: Routledge.

Straker, G. (2004). Race for cover: Castrated whiteness, perverse consequences. *Psychoanalytic Dialogues, 14,* 405–422.

Suchet, M. (2007). Unravelling whiteness. *Psychoanalytic Dialogues, 17,* 867–886.

Vygotsky, L. (1978). *Mind in society.* Cambridge, MA: MIT Press.

Vygotsky, L. (1986). *Thought and language.* Cambridge, MA: MIT Press.

White, C. (2007). Fertile ground at the edge of difference: Self, other, and potential space. Commentary on paper by Gillian Straker. *Psychoanalytic Dialogues, 17,* 171–187.

Zizek, S. (1989). *The sublime object of ideology.* London, England: Verso.

Part II

Core Competencies

Chapter 4

Core Competency One: Therapeutic Intent

Steven Tublin

Introduction by Roy E. Barsness

The research revealed that an analytic treatment is first established by a clear understanding of the intent or purpose of the analytic endeavor. In the following chapter, Steve Tublin states:

> rendering his intent explicit compels the analyst to know, as much as that is possible, what he considers essential to a satisfying existence, what sort of mind he believes allows for the creation of such a life and what he is capable of doing, via the ritualized application of his craft to advance that aim.
>
> (p. 83)

Technique is thus first and foremost informed by intent. Ghent, in his seminal paper "Credo" (1989) states:

> ultimately a belief system that the analyst lives and works by . . . makes a very significant difference as to how one hears, what one hears, how one assembles what is heard, and how one conducts oneself in the analytic setting.
>
> (p. 170)

Participants in the research study held to a particular belief system and clearly oriented their work toward particular outcomes informed by their understanding of what constitutes change. Having a coherent understanding of the goal of treatment, made it easier to determine therapeutic action.

Properties of Therapeutic Intent

Core Competency One: Therapeutic Intent

1.1   An analytic treatment is first established by a clear understanding of the intent or purpose of the analytic endeavor.

    1.1.1   Increased capacity to experience and manage multiple affective states and to enjoy the full range of emotion

    1.1.2   Increased access to multiple aspects of the self without shame

    1.1.3   Ability to comfort and soothe oneself and to be self-reflective

    1.1.4   Ability to accept responsibility

    1.1.5   Ability to tolerate ambiguity and uncertainty

    1.1.6   Ability to be more truthful with oneself

    1.1.7   Ability to think more creatively and openly about one's past rather than to continue to repeat it

    1.1.8   Relief from internal constraints and rigidities that have become problematic

    1.1.9   A more imaginative and creative mind

    1.1.10 Increased capacity to love and to work; self-efficacy

    1.1.11 To engage in more meaningful and redemptive relationships

    1.1.12 Hope

Discipline and Freedom in Psychoanalytic Technique

In relational psychoanalysis, the issue of technique has often been viewed as, if not exactly a dirty topic, one that is a bit unseemly. The field's prominent theorists may concern themselves with grasping the nature of relatedness or the phenomenology of intersubjective experience, but technique, as Mitchell (1997) wryly noted, has become something for mere technicians, a lesser calling. When it has been addressed, relational technique has often been discussed in the negative. Theorists have dwelled primarily upon the technical constraints—anonymity, neutrality, and abstinence—limiting analysts' conduct in earlier paradigms. Relational theorists have successfully campaigned for the lifting of prohibitions on personal expression and self-disclosure (see Aron, 1996; Ehrenberg, 1992; Mitchell, 1997), leaving the relational analyst far freer than his classical predecessors to behave in a spontaneous, improvisational manner (Ringstrom, 2001, 2007)—one, many feel, that opens wide vistas for creativity in the analytic moment.

But the code or set of guidelines that lays out what the relational practitioner should actually do with this new freedom has remained insistently unarticulated. There are philosophical, practical, and political reasons for this lack of specification, and relational theorists have questioned whether it is preferable or even possible to articulate general technical "rules."

Thus, there is an inherent conflict in relational psychoanalysis between the freedom required to respond to contextually bound clinical moments and the discipline required to conduct a coherent, purposeful psychoanalytic treatment. In what follows, I discuss this tension between discipline and freedom as well as the efforts of several influential relational theorists to resolve it. My aim is to underscore the problems that follow when principles that guide clinical choices remain unarticulated, and the importance of clinical intent in shaping conscious technical choices

Freedom and the Burden of Choice

To begin with, contemporary relationalists embrace a radical eclecticism that denies them the comfort of a consensually accepted theory of mind upon which to build a set of technical principles. The relational clinician enjoys all the benefits of post-Kleinian, post-Winnicottian, post-Kohutian, neo-Sullivanian, postfeminist, queer theorist, Lacanian-inflected innovation. Whereas the mid-century Freudian faced strict limits in both the theoretical positions from which he might approach the clinical moment and tight restrictions on how he might then engage his patient, the contemporary relationalist has community sanction to borrow from a broad family of theoretical traditions and the techniques that correspond to them.

Moreover, in keeping with the postmodern sensibility that pervades relational theory, none of the many theories of mind and interaction, or techniques associated with them, can be considered "right" in an objective sense. The relational analyst is free to sample broadly and switch metaphorical frames in whatever direction seems clinically fruitful. Every moment of relational participation, therefore, presents a wide range of interactive possibilities with few, if any, strict criteria for distinguishing their utility (let alone "correctness"). A certain amount of both theoretical and technical heterogeneity now exists in all psychoanalytic schools, but the even-handed pluralism of relational theory has created a situation in which the analyst faces a broad menu of technical choices that can be exhilarating in its plenitude or panic-inducing in its boundlessness.

Let us consider the options in an instance where the analyst has the sense that he and his patient are stuck in an enactment with currents as yet undefined. For the relational analyst, the possibilities are just about endless:

he may venture an interpretation of the interpersonal mess (e.g., "I think I've fallen into treating you just like your father often did"), offer an affect-focused empathic comment (e.g., "You seem to be getting increasingly upset and I understand that's frightening for you"), or ask questions focusing on various aspects of the patient's experience: what he is thinking, what he is feeling, whether he was aware of anything about the analyst at that moment, or whether he too is confused.

Or the analyst can disclose aspects of his own experience. He can tell the patient about his emotional state (e.g., "Whenever we talk about your uncle, I get this vague feeling of dread"), or he can talk about his own life. He can say something like "I know the feeling; that happened to me once," or—why not?—"My wife gets very angry when I do that too." The befuddled analyst can simply confess, "I have no idea what is happening here." Or, grasping for a little inchoate inspiration, he can describe features of his own experience whose meaning eludes him, perhaps venturing something like, "I really don't know why, but I was just picturing X; does that resonate with something in your experience?" (Bollas, 1987). Beyond these, the contemporary relational clinician has community license to step out of the traditional analytic role entirely, as Hoffman (1994) demonstrated with his now iconic call to his panicking patient's internist.

Each of these technical interventions has elaborate, carefully considered theoretical justifications. Lost among this plenitude, however, is the sense that, while each type of intervention is justifiable, they derive from distinct and in some instances incompatible theories of therapeutic action. These stances can direct clinicians to different qualities of the patient or the interaction, and can require divergent clinical intents. For instance, a relationalist emphasizing a contemporary understanding of holding as essential in the treatment of certain patients (e.g., Slochower, 1996) may disagree with one who sees therapeutic impact primarily in the formulation of experience (Stern, 1983, 1997). A clinician following Ehrenberg's (1992) advocacy of work at the "intimate edge"—a position that emphasizes maximal contact with the patient and an accompanying affective intensity in the moment—will be trying to accomplish an altogether different thing than someone aiming to deconstruct the patient's too comfortably sealed life narrative (Levenson, 1988).

These clinicians will be operating from different conceptions of what makes a person who they are, what is causing their troubles, what the psychoanalytic encounter is about, and—most relevant for this discussion—

what they should do with their patient in order to most effectively promote psychoanalytic benefit. That is, their theories of therapeutic action, if rigorously embraced, will incline them to distinct families of interpersonal engagements, and therefore different techniques.

Relational psychoanalysis's focus on establishing plurality, openness, and creative flexibility in meeting the patient has provided a powerful antidote for clinicians who found established praxis confining and outdated. **But lost in this development has been the recognition that no amount of spontaneity, freedom, creativity, or play makes extended conversation psychoanalysis. It becomes psychoanalysis only when it is structured around a coherent theory of therapeutic action that defines the analyst's clinical intent—e.g., the working through of psychic conflict, the articulation of unformulated experience, and/or the provision of a new, generative relationship experience—that prescribes certain corresponding technical actions and discourages others.**

Freedom is, therefore, only part of the equation. The analyst must still choose. He must choose what to attend to, how to assign meaning, and what he must do to be of most use to his patient. On what basis, we might then ask, are those choices made? To which principles does the clinician adhere when engaging in the psychoanalytic process? How explicitly are these principles rendered, and how rigorously are they followed? The articulation of a theory of therapeutic action and an associated set of technical principles to which the analyst adheres constitutes a basis for the establishment of discipline.

Linking Theory and Technique

Crafting an analytic stance that balances the requirements of technical freedom and discipline is a new problem, for in the psychoanalytic paradigms that preceded the relational turn, technical principles were determined, in large part, by detailed conceptualizations of the dynamics of the patient's mind and symptoms. The near exclusive reliance on the interpretation of psychic conflict derived from a theory focused on impulse and defense and a profound faith in the mutative value of the analyst's properly delivered words.

So, if one subscribed to core premises of mid-century classical meta-psychology—specifically, that mental processes are beyond consciousness and structured by the id, ego, superego, drive, defense, and conflict, and that the correct interpretation is in itself mutative—then one had relatively few technical options available. While the community might debate the nature of defenses, the proper depth to which interpretations ought to be directed, or the ideal means of conveying this information, the analyst who accepted the defining premises of the classical psychoanalytic program was obligated to follow the principles of abstinence, neutrality, and anonymity. The logical structure of the theory required it.

As noted earlier, this is not the case within the relational world, where the various theories of mind and interaction do not obligate clinicians to specific technical actions. The reluctance to articulate a formal relational technique stems from a number of sources, most notably arguments derived from the postmodern and hermeneutic positions that call into question the analyst's authority, seeming omniscience, and claim to objectivity. As relational theory has evolved, it has increasingly emphasized multiplicity in the encounter: multiple interpretive frames that might be relevant, multiple self-states from which to speak and to address, and multiple meanings that might plausibly be assigned to the patient's and the dyad's experience. Taken together, these render the notion of a unitary, proper technique, as it has been traditionally understood, problematic.

A second premise advocated by relational theorists, the radical uniqueness of each psychoanalytic treatment (Fiscalini, 1994), further discourages formal discourse on technique. Recoiling from the seeming reductionism of orthodox Freudianism and retaining the Sullivanian celebration of detail in the development of the individual, relationalists have emphasized not only the uniqueness of the patient, but the uniqueness of the analyst, and, in keeping with the emphasis on two-person models, the uniqueness of the dyad (Levenson, 1972; Mitchell, 1993, 1997; Wolstein, 1994). This emphasis on the specifics of each analytic situation, in which the analyst seemingly carries nothing other than a store of clinical judgment into each new analysis, also defies any notion of general technique.

And last, the concept of enactment, while shared by much of the contemporary psychoanalytic world, has, in its embrace by the relational community, further complicated the notion of a prescribed technique. The presumed ubiquity of enactment implies that during any analytic exchange, the analyst, no matter how clear-thinking he might imagine himself to be, is also participating in an interpersonal drama driven by his own and/or his patient's relational schemas (Levenson, 1972, 1983). And, most crucially, this is thought to go on without awareness, the interaction residing in an unformulated state, the articulation of which lies at the core of psychoanalytic process

Thus, in the relational paradigm, the moment of engagement is shaped by both participants in ways they only partially understand (Bass, 2003; Renik, 1993). The analyst may know the general terrain of psychoanalysis, but makes no claim as to where the analysis needs to go. The psychoanalytic encounter can be characterized as the experiencing of a relationship interwoven by attempts to understand it as it evolves. As such, the patterning and themes that occupy the participants are emergent. That is, the meaningful features of dyadic interaction, the articulation of which will ostensibly lead to a richer and better life for the patient, cannot be predicted by qualities of either participant considered in isolation. The analysis is a joint product, the terrain of which becomes apparent only when it becomes apparent, and even then only provisionally, awaiting the next emergent feature and added interactive complexity.

The contemporary relational clinician is therefore accustomed to the idea that while he is interpreting, empathizing, judiciously disclosing, or just drifting off, he is also engaged in an interpersonal duet of uncertain emotional stakes, the meaning of which is often dissociatively unavailable to him and his patient (Stern, 2003, 2004). If one accepts that as one speaks, one acts (Greenberg, 1996; Searle, 1969), and that one can act with significant gaps in self-awareness, one is obliged to regard the notion of a consciously chosen therapeutic intent and supporting technical moves with a certain skepticism. The analyst now lives an insoluble riddle: he can no longer say with any certainty what he is actually doing, nor can he know why he is doing what he is trying to do. It seems misguided, in this framework, to prescribe, at least in any narrow, formulaic way, what the analyst should do.

Discipline amidst Freedom

Faced with these theoretical currents, relational theorists hoping to balance the pragmatic requirements of psychoanalysis with the relatively unregulated praxis of the postmodern era have found themselves in a bind. Many of those theorists were acutely aware of the risk implicit in advocating technical positions whose tenets might be interpreted too liberally. These theorists proposed various solutions to the dilemma of retaining a core of disciplines within a framework that grants broad interactive freedom.

These solutions, while sharing the relational emphasis on the analyst as a human, interacting presence, vary considerably in the degree to which they retain the traditional structure of analytic interaction. Some, as I argue below, begin with that structure, and advocate a targeted loosening of technical prescriptions they see as unnecessarily restrictive. Others privilege uniqueness and immediacy in the interaction, and offer a vision of psychoanalysis that more thoroughly dismantles traditional technique. The argument that follows is not an exhaustive review of relational opinion regarding technique, but a discussion of four influential theorists who demonstrate the tensions between the opposing needs—for freedom and for discipline—in relational psychoanalysis.

Four Theorists: Hoffman, Renik, Mitchell, and Stern

Irwin Hoffman, in a series of influential articles (Hoffman, 1983, 1991, 1994, 1996, 1998, 2006), elaborated a model of psychoanalytic technique oriented around the dialectical fluctuation between what he has termed "ritual and spontaneity."

For Hoffman (1998), it is ritual—the distinct setting, peculiar posture, asymmetric boundaries and roles, as well as the historic legacy of the analyst's position as healer—that gives the psychoanalytic conversation its strange, transformative power. Ritual lends the analyst a unique authority to influence central features of the analysand's mode of being in the world of others.

Hoffman's innovations have focused on his accounts of deviations from classical technique, but more recently, Hoffman (2006) has reemphasized the extent to which it is the oscillation between the two modes—spontaneity and ritual—that promotes analytic change. Although Hoffman has argued that the rigid adherence to prescribed technique deadens the psychoanalytic encounter, he has also maintained that without the cumulative work of traditional analytic inquiry, transference interpretation, and the insight gained thereby, these more natural, "nonanalytic" interactions would have little impact. Spontaneous engagement allows the analyst to be a living, creative human being with his patients, but it is the disciplined application of traditional analytic technique that confers new meaning upon his more casual interactions.

Hoffman's strategy, initially radical in its forceful rejection of the pillars of analytic restraint, appears, from a later vantage point, a conservative one. In it, much of traditional psychoanalytic method is preserved, though situated in a looser framework that allows for improvisation and personal presence. It is a strategy that retains an elaborate holding structure (i.e., discipline) that grounds the analyst's technical choices yet allows him to deviate in personally distinct and therapeutically compelling ways.

Owen Renik employs a similar strategy in which he retains a great deal of traditional technical structure while advocating the abandonment of prohibitions that have defined classical technique. Renik advocates openness with patients that has been anathema to much of the classical establishment (Renik, 2006). Arguing from the inevitability of the analyst's personal involvement in every aspect of the interaction, Renik (1993) has urged analysts to be more explicit about who they are, how they understand their patients' difficulties, and how they are emotionally involved in the proceedings.

Renik, like Hoffman, aims to liberate the analyst, but his short walks outside the boundaries of established technical orthodoxy are less an interspersing of "nonanalytic" moments than a more personally transparent mode of being a traditional analyst. Renik (1999) has urged analysts to "[play their] cards face up," arguing that analysts should "try to articulate and communicate everything that, in the analyst's view, will help the patient understand where the analyst thinks he or she is coming from and plans to go with the patient" (Renik, 1995, p. 485). He strives to make his personal involvement, his clinical understanding, and his immediate experience explicit and available to the patient.

Renik's innovative stance is driven by frank pragmatism. He finds that analysis simply works better when the patient is given access to the analyst's thinking. When Renik is open in discussing his understanding of the patient, the process, and aspects of himself that might influence his participation, he finds that patients are generally more open as well. They dwell less on the analyst's presence if it is demystified. Non-neutrality and personal presence, he argues, simply make for better analysis (Renik, 2006).

Renik's pragmatism provides him with a position from which he can establish a core of discipline. Self-disclosure is limited to experience related to the analytic process. Renik (1999, p. 533) therefore cautions that for "an analyst to play his cards face up does not mean that the analyst free-associates." His freedom operates in a context of disciplined adherence to both an established theory—Renik's conceptualizations and interpretations reveal a rigorous contemporary Freudian approach—and the received ritual that defines the psychoanalytic encounter.

So Renik, like Hoffman, resolves the need for discipline by retaining the bulk of the traditional framework from which he assertively deviates. Both theorists' innovations acquire meaning against the backdrop of an established metapsychology and elaborately ordered technical structure that relies on traditional inquiry and transference interpretation.

Influential relational writers arising from the Interpersonal School have taken a less structured approach to the issue of technique, one likely derived from the pluralism and flexibility inherent in the Interpersonal tradition (Fiscalini, 1994). In Stephen Mitchell's writing (e.g., 1997), the structure of inherited metapsychology and technique recedes farther than in Hoffman's and Renik's, forming more an implicit backdrop than a set of principles defining moment-to-moment clinical choices. For Mitchell, much of classical technique could be viewed as the performance of what he dismissively referred to as "procedures" (1997, p. x). Questions such as "What sort of frame should I maintain? Should I express my countertransferential experiences? Should I answer the analysand's inquiries?", Mitchell suggests, were formerly answered by consensually accepted rules (1997, p. x). But in his reconceptualization of the analytic encounter, where change involves the renegotiation of established dyadic patterns, each moment must be navigated without the benefit of principles that specify, beforehand, the right thing to do.

So, for Mitchell, the answer to the technical questions arising in each moment is "It depends." It depends on what has transpired between these two people before and on the meaning to this dyad of a particular course of action. It depends on the analyst's sense of whether an action might provide something new or repeat something old. It depends on whether the analyst and the patient can stand what might happen or live with what might not. The analyst can answer or not, disclose or not, or modify the frame. The issue is the meaning attributed to each choice in the unfolding of a given analysis.

This reconceptualization profoundly reframes the notion of discipline in psychoanalytic technique. Discipline, for Mitchell, does not pertain to the following of proper procedures—it is not what the analyst does—but to an elegantly nuanced habit of mind. The rigorous relational analyst, embedded in shifting, partially understood enactments with his patient, cultivates a stance of "self-reflective emotional involvement" (Mitchell, 1997, p. xi). Discipline requires the analyst's constant vigilance in considering, associating to, and emotionally resonating with his interactions with his patients.

Nevertheless, despite his insistence on broad technical freedom, Mitchell retains a connection to established psychoanalytic praxis. He likens studying psychoanalytic technique to the learning processes in sports or art. Learning how to play tennis, for instance, requires a rigorous immersion in basic technical skills. Personal style and creativity emerge only later from the bedrock of well-practiced competency. Mitchell seems to imply that self-reflection and interactive scrutiny underlying each clinical choice are best served by learning the techniques that form the basis of analytic restraint and then transcending them.

Mitchell's analyst is therefore constrained by tradition, but less directly than either Renik's or Hoffman's. Whereas the latter theorists remain rooted in traditional technique, but deviate in specific ways, Mitchell seems to have partially erased the lines that define the playing field. The status of traditional analytic technique has been downgraded from defining structure to historical legacy; discipline finds its origins not in proper technical steps, but in reflective participation and imagination. History provides not the procedures for managing that interaction, but the constructs the analyst employs to understand it.

In the work of Donnel Stern, another interpersonally oriented theorist, one encounters a deep respect for context (both cultural and immediate) and a philosophical commitment to freedom in the search for meaning—positions that dovetail smoothly with the postmodern spirit that infuses relational psychoanalysis.

Stern (2003, 2006, 2009), tries to resolve the paradox highlighted in this chapter: the need to place at the center of the analyst's actions a core of disciplined practice within a system that denies, on philosophical grounds, the validity of a priori technical principles. He does so by grounding psychoanalytic inquiry in principles derived from the hermeneutic philosopher Hans-George Gadamer (1975). For Gadamer, dialogue is the encounter of two culturally embedded persons, each possessed of their distinct biases or "prejudices." Prejudice, in this case, is to be understood not simply as distortion, but as the various culturally determined ways an individual encounters the world and renders it meaningful. Prejudice is thus both the source of meaning and its limitation. Through dialogue, one person encounters the biases of another and, in "genuine conversation" (Stern, 1997, p. 216), is led to reflect upon his own.

Stern (1997) emphasizes Gadamer's careful refusal to specify how one goes about achieving understanding. To advocate a method a priori is to risk embodying prejudice in the encounter itself. Method—or, for our purposes here, technique—should be subject to the same scrutiny and questioning as any other provisional understanding. Thus, Stern (1997, p. 216) argues, "one could even make the case on the basis of these ideas, that the concept of technique in psychoanalysis is specious."

Stern is careful, however, to back away from the seemingly anarchic state that Gadamer's position would imply for psychoanalysis. Because psychoanalysis requires something that distinguishes it from "ordinary conversation," Stern must retain some notion of technique, one that is explicitly socially constructed and provisional, but that still structures the dialogue. What, then, is Stern's disciplined Gadamerian analyst trying to do? What makes his interaction psychoanalytic rather than simply open-minded and concerned? For Stern, the analyst's actions aim to render dyadic experience meaningful, largely through the participation in and elaboration of enactment (Stern, 2003, 2004). It is the readiness to question multiple levels of prejudice and cultivate curiosity about what has been dissociatively excluded from linguistic articulation that forms the core of the analyst's discipline and technique. Thus, Stern (1990) has written of the analyst's need to "court surprise." Surprise is the mark of expectations defied, of prejudice revealed. Thus, Stern, like Mitchell, focuses less on what that analyst must do than on the cultivation of a state of mind that is the necessary precondition for any action.

Stern's clinical descriptions portray a disciplined mind in the acts of dyadic participation and internal surveillance and struggle. Yet Stern carries the reader only to the moment of realization, where the analyst, after much mental labor, intuits his internal limits, and in so doing reorganizes the dyadic context from which the interaction had derived its meaning. At that point, with the lights tentatively back on, when the analyst might raise his index finger, clear his throat, and choose how to use what he newly knows, Stern demurs. Like Gadamer, Stern refrains from explicit guidance on how, concretely, the analyst should capitalize on the hard-won interactive freedom.

To return to the now familiar categories: should the analyst at that moment offer a detailed interpretation of the enactment that until that moment had inhibited both participants? Well, sometimes, but why then and not other times? Should that interpretation include an account of the personal hurdles overcome? Or is shorter sweeter? And if one argues that a measure of personal disclosure is likely to enhance the interpretation's disruptive effect, what level of revelation is called for? Disclosure can mean the select transparency of Renik's playing our cards face up, but conceivably far more. If the interpretive moment is accompanied by a poignant memory, one that might amplify the impact of the statement, should the analyst consider laying it out, perhaps baring himself for the patient to experience as a real person with a history, with memories, and a mind that defends and regrets? Or should the analyst keep that domain of experience to himself? Stern, one must imagine, has his own answers to these questions. But in his privileging of freedom and the emergence of the unformulated, he does not offer principles for the general conduct of analyses.

This selective sampling of influential theorists demonstrates that the embrace of subjectivity and postmodern epistemology in relational theory has yielded widely diverse answers to the question of how to conceptualize discipline and technique. On the one hand, there are those that present a loosened version of traditional technique; on the other, there is a psychoanalysis that aspires to a disciplined application of craft while insisting on the absence, even the impossibility, of codified technique.

This wide variation, while quite real, is in some ways deceptive, for it would give the appearance that relational psychoanalysis, lacking a consensually agreed upon technical framework, can assume any form to which the patient and analyst agree. But this is obviously not the case. For all their commitment to uniqueness and freedom, relational clinicians are influenced by their relationship to a broader psychoanalytic community that sanctions certain theories and actions, and discourages others. It is to the often implicit role of the broader community in shaping relational technique that I now turn.

Technique and the Psychoanalytic Third

For each of the theorists discussed above, restraints on the analyst's conduct persist in varying degrees, derived from differing philosophical and clinical commitments. But beyond that, analysts' actions are powerfully influenced by their relationship to the containing forces imposed by the broader psychoanalytic community (Greenberg, 1999; Spezzano, 1998; Zeddies, 2001, 2002). Aron (1999) has used the term "psychoanalytic third" to refer to the presence of the community of practitioners as it affects the analytic dyad. Greenberg (1999) has argued that the broader psychoanalytic community both sanctions the analyst's authority and provides the boundaries that restrain the analyst's actions—a role that has grown with the receding of objectivist models and technical absolutes. Via journals, conferences, institutional training, and supervision, the community endorses certain theories of mind and interaction, certain "acceptable" modes of engaging patients, and discourages others. As a result, Hoffman's, Renik's, Mitchell's, and Stern's attempts to retain a rigorous core in a climate of technical freedom all occur within the boundaries established by the psychoanalytic third. So, while the analyst's momentary choices are many, they are not limitless. These constraints—which extend beyond sanctioned theory and technical steps to govern the analyst's demeanor toward the patient, and the leeway he allows himself in "spontaneous" deviations from doctrinal technique—live in the consulting room and influence the trajectory of treatment.

Conclusion

For the first generation of theorists and practitioners, relational psycho-analysis served as a counterpoint to the limitations of the dominant classical paradigm. It was, in its form and historical place, an opposition movement, and therefore defined by its dialectical relationship with the structure from which it deviated. That structure is retained in the work of Hoffman and Renik, who both preserve much of the traditional framework of classical theory and technique. Traditional structure is less visible in Mitchell's inter-personal variant, but persists in the form of a historical legacy that the con-temporary relationalist would absorb, and then transcend. And it recedes yet further for Stern, who retains analytic discipline as an ideal, but strongly privileges the illumination of prejudice over the codification of technique.

But clinicians and theorists encountering relational psychoanalysis, not as a vigorous alternative, but as an independent, freestanding orientation, enter a new, uncertain psychoanalytic world. For them, the technical prescriptions and their rationales, which were once the steel girders giving structure to the psychoanalytic enterprise, have become but faint lines on an architectural rendering. The new relational student learns many ways to comprehend his patient's experience, but he finds little that tells him what to say or how to be in order to most effectively promote change. The spontaneity, personal expression, and spirit of unique dyadic adventure that characterize relational psychoanalysis, when left to stand alone, turn out to have inadequate foundations upon which to define psychoanalytic praxis.

The four theorists reviewed above noted the risk that their words could be employed in the service of a psychoanalysis too rudderless to reliably traverse the choppy waters of emotional dyadic interaction. And their fears were justified, for as much as there has always been inspired clinical work, there has always been misguided, ineffective work as well. Whereas, among classical practitioners, this might have taken the form of an antiseptic technical correctness, in relational psychoanalysis there has been the risk of analyses devolving into mixed bags of technical moves, each one relational in the broadest sense, and each ostensibly justifiable, but theoretically incoherent when considered together. And, though it has not been the case that "anything goes," the embrace of spontaneity and personal expression has allowed clinicians so inclined to act in ways that simply felt right at the time.

Moreover, the reluctance among relationalists to prescribe technical principles has robbed the discourse of its capacity to meaningfully evaluate and constructively criticize analytic work. For a particular technical act to be judged better or worse, right or wrong, effective or ineffective, one must ask, "Relative to what?" These are judgments once made with respect either to accepted theories of mind and therapeutic action or to the broad technical principles explicitly derived from them. In the context of relational plurality and a philosophically enforced egalitarianism, with regard to analytic technique, the criteria against which such judgments might be made—or even the terms in which to craft critical debate—are absent.

So, although not everything goes, among relationalists there is neither consensus on what does "go" nor active discourse to address how one might even decide. In the wake of the relational rebellion, theorists must find a way of reinstilling rigor and discipline in psychoanalytic technique while retaining flexibility and basic humanness, and avoiding the artificial certainty of objectivism.

A preliminary answer, I propose, is to encourage relational theorists and clinicians to be more explicit about their preferred theories of mind and therapeutic action, and to take seriously the obligation that they act in accordance with those explicit beliefs. Relational analysts must choose among partially incompatible models, and both honor those choices and respect the implications of them. This will allow relational analysts to again entertain questions of what constitutes effective technique and what does not, what to do with certain kinds of patients or problems, and what actions to avoid. Clearly, these questions have never disappeared from classrooms and supervisory offices. But in an era marked by anti-authoritarianism and a deep respect for subjectivity, they have become the stuff of clinical wisdom, with attempts at more formal specification officially off-limits.

I am arguing, therefore, that discourse about relational technique be retrieved from the postmodern limbo to which it has been relegated while Psychoanalysis 1.0 rid itself of outdated objectivist principles. Toward that end, I propose a far looser definition of technique, one that is tied explicitly to varying and at times incompatible notions of analytic intent. It is intent, not the objectivist-tainted notion of correctness, that should guide the analyst's participation in the consulting room. **An intent-driven conceptualization of technique, while limiting the analyst's moment-to-moment actions, would force the analyst to be explicit about how his communicative acts—his interpretations, questions, empathic expressions, as well as the various jokes, reminiscences, and lexical gestures that establish his unique presence—are meant to drive a therapeutic process.**

For instance, whereas a commitment to the salutary effects of consistent attunement will incline the analyst one way, a belief in the role of mutual recognition and the requisite encounter with the Otherness of the analyst often leads, technically, in another direction (Ringstrom, 2010). So, too, does the privileging of affective intensity, the provision of a holding container, or the close attention to the flux of dissociated self–other configurations. These (and many other positions) are all relational, and widely endorsed by most in the field. But they are favored differently by different analysts, and the value attributed to partially conflicting positions like these may underlie various differences in technique found among practitioners. The relative salience given to these positions affects what the analyst attends to and then what he says, how he says it, and how he acts.

These matters—how minds work, what happens in intense interaction, how one harnesses the engine of human relatedness to alter the emotional functioning of another—constitute what one might term the means of psychoanalytic change. They are structured sets of ideas that provide a roadmap for how psychoanalysis works. The desired ends, however, are also subject to debate, and these too figure prominently in analysts' implicit clinical intents. What, in general terms, is the ideal psychoanalytic outcome? Where, after all that time and effort (and money), does the analyst hope the patient ends up? This introduces the complex issue of the analyst's personal values and the role these play in shaping his craft.

Most analysts would agree that it is improper to tell patients how to live their lives (e.g., how to raise children, whether to lose weight, what's the right amount of money). Nevertheless, analysts inevitably differ in their deepest philosophical commitments, and it is implausible to believe that these beliefs can be excluded from clinicians' conceptualizations of their craft. Stern (2009) argues that much of the theoretical heterogeneity one now encounters in psychoanalysis represents the elaboration of theories expressing disparate values. It is not an accident when a person chooses to be an analyst rather than a chef or sculptor (Tublin, 2002). But beyond that, Stern argues, the choice of what kind of analyst to be must likewise spring from deeply held beliefs—ethical, emotional, spiritual—about the fundamental meaning-giving themes of human existence.

Analysts working from disparate values, therefore, will aspire to different ends for their patients. And their values will incline them toward different intents that, in turn, will influence what they try to do each clinical hour.

These matters—the ends and means that underlie the approach to psychoanalysis—shape the thinking and actions of each analyst. Ghent's (1989) example, in which he challenged analysts to lay out their credo, to state, openly and clearly, "This is what I believe," has often been neglected, to the detriment of relational discourse. ⟵ *good point*

Rendering his intent explicit compels the analyst to know, as much as that is possible, what he considers essential to a satisfying human existence, what sort of mind he believes allows for the creation of such a life, and what he is capable of doing, via the ritualized application of his craft, to advance that aim. And, in a like manner, that explicit self-rendering forces that analyst to chart the areas where he disagrees with his colleagues and make claims regarding what he considers ineffective technique.

This exercise has obvious limitations. Foremost, it addresses only conscious intent. It does not address the unconscious wells from which the analyst's intent emerges. While a crucial component of training should be a questioning of the passions that make certain theories intuitively compelling and certain visions of life inspiring, experience tells us that this goal of self-knowledge is inevitably incomplete. Analysts can never know fully what motivates them in general, and even less what moves them in a particular treatment or clinical moment.

And, for this reason, relational technique, in this epistemologically modest era, will inevitably lack the bedrock certainty that guided clinicians working with modernist, objectivist premises. It is hard to imagine, given the way the psychoanalytic encounter is currently understood, a return to a sense that this or that interpretation, question, reassurance, or spontaneous expression would be the right thing to do in a given moment. But it is possible for analysts to state that certain kinds of things are right for them given their explicit theoretical commitments as they understand them thus far. Some actions follow from what one believes to be the nature of therapeutic action and the well-lived life, and others do not.

The relational turn has succeeded in casting off the limitations of orthodoxy. But relational freedom is bound by the pragmatics of the analytic task. As spontaneity acquires meaning and force only against the backdrop of ritual, so the freedom bequeathed the relational analyst becomes effective within the constraints imposed by therapeutic intent and the disciplined application of craft. What the analyst is free to be, and what he ought to do in the stumbling flux of each clinical hour, can now be the subject of rigorous debate, where the terms of psychoanalytic aspiration can be made explicit and subject to disagreement and evaluation.

References

Aron, L. (1996). *A meeting of minds: Mutuality in psychoanalysis*. Hillsdale, NJ: Analytic Press.

Aron, L. (1999). Clinical choices and the relational matrix. *Psychoanalytic Dialogues, 9*, 1–29.

Bass, A. (2003). "E" enactments in psychoanalysis: Another medium, another message. *Psychoanalytic Dialogues, 13*, 657–675.

Bollas, C. (1987). *The shadow of the object: Psychoanalysis of the unthought known*. New York, NY: Columbia University Press.

Ehrenberg, D. (1992). *The intimate edge: Extending the reach of psychoanalytic interaction*. New York, NY: Norton.

Fiscalini, J. (1994). The uniquely interpersonal and the interpersonally unique: On interpersonal psychoanalysis. *Contemporary Psychoanalysis, 30*, 114–134.

Gadamer, H.-G. (1975), *Truth and method*. G. Barden & J. Cumming (Ed. & Trans.). New York, NY: Seabury Press.

Ghent, E. (1989). Credo: The dialectics of one-person and two-person psychologies. *Contemporary Psychoanalysis, 25*, 169–211.

Greenberg, J. (1996). Psychoanalytic words and psychoanalytic acts: A brief history. *Contemporary Psychoanalysis, 32*, 195–213.

Greenberg, J. (1999). Analytic authority and analytic restraint. *Contemporary Psychoanalysis*, *35*, 25–42.

Hoffman, I. Z. (1983). The patient as interpreter of the analyst's experience. *Contemporary Psychoanalysis*, *19*, 389–422.

Hoffman, I. Z. (1991). Discussion: Toward a social-constructivist view of the psychoanalytic situation. *Psychoanalytic Dialogues*, *1*, 74–105.

Hoffman, I. Z. (1994). Dialectical thinking and therapeutic action in the psychoanalytic process. *Psychoanalytic Quarterly*, *63*, 187–218.

Hoffman, I. Z. (1996). The intimate and ironic authority of the psychoanalyst's presence. *Psychoanalytic Quarterly*, *65*, 102–136.

Hoffman, I. Z. (1998). *Ritual and spontaneity in the psychoanalytic process: A dialectical-constructivist view*. Hillsdale, NJ: Analytic Press.

Hoffman, I. Z. (2006). Forging difference out of similarity: The multiplicity of corrective experience. *Psychoanalytic Quarterly*, *75*, 715–751.

Levenson, E. (1972). *The fallacy of understanding*. New York, NY: Basic Books.

Levenson, E. (1983). *The ambiguity of change*. New York, NY: Basic Books.

Levenson, E. (1988). The pursuit of the particular: On the psychoanalytic inquiry. *Contemporary Psychoanalysis*, 24, 1–16.

Mitchell, S. (1993). *Hope and dread in psychoanalysis*. New York, NY: Basic Books.

Mitchell, S. (1997). *Influence and autonomy in psychoanalysis*. Hillsdale, NJ: Analytic Press.

Renik, O. (1993). Analytic interaction: Conceptualizing technique in light of the analyst's irreducible subjectivity. *Psychoanalytic Quarterly*, *62*, 553–571.

Renik, O. (1995). The ideal of the anonymous analyst and the problem of self-disclosure. *Psychoanalytic Quarterly*, *64*, 466–495.

Renik, O. (1999). Playing one's cards face up in analysis: An approach to the problem of self-disclosure. *Psychoanalytic Quarterly*, *68*, 521–539.

Renik, O. (2006). *Practical psychoanalysis for therapists and patients*. New York, NY: Other Press.

Ringstrom, P. (2001). Cultivating the improvisational in psychoanalytic treatment. *Psychoanalytic Dialogues*, *11*, 727–754.

Ringstrom, P. (2007). Scenes that write themselves: Improvisational moments in relational psychoanalysis. *Psychoanalytic Dialogues*, *17*, 69–100.

Ringstrom P. (2010). Meeting Mitchell's challenge: A comparison of relational psychoanalysis and intersubjective systems theory. *Psychoanalytic Dialogues*, *20*, 196–218.

Searle, J. (1969). *Speech acts: An essay in the philosophy of language*. Cambridge, England: Cambridge University Press.

Slochower, J. (1996). *Holding and psychoanalysis: A relational perspective*. Hillsdale, NJ: Analytic Press.

Spezzano, C. (1998). The triangle of clinical judgment. *Journal of the American Psychoanalytic Association*, *46*, 365–388.

Stern, D. B. (1983). Unformulated experience. *Contemporary Psychoanalysis, 19*, 71–99.

Stern, D. B. (1990). Courting surprise: Unbidden perceptions in clinical practice. *Contemporary Psychoanalysis, 26*, 425–478.

Stern, D. B. (1997). *Unformulated experience: From dissociation to imagination in psychoanalysis*. Hillsdale, NJ: Analytic Press.

Stern, D. B. (2003). The fusion of horizons: Dissociation, enactment, and understanding. *Psychoanalytic Dialogues, 13*, 843–873.

Stern, D. B. (2004). The eye sees itself: Dissociation, enactment, and the achievement of conflict. *Contemporary Psychoanalysis, 40*, 197–238.

Stern, D. B. (2006). Opening what has been closed, relaxing what has been clenched: Dissociation and enactment over time in committed relationship. *Psychoanalytic Dialogues, 16*, 747–761.

Stern, D. B. (2009). Shall the twain meet? Metaphor, dissociation, and coocurrence. *Psychoanalytic Inquiry, 29*, 79–90.

Tublin, S. (2002). But always behind in the count: A response to "Sluggers and Analysts." *Contemporary Psychoanalysis, 38*, 445–464.

Wolstein, B. (1994). The evolving newness of interpersonal psychoanalysis: From the vantage point of immediate experience. *Contemporary Psychoanalysis, 30*, 473–498.

Zeddies, T. (2001). On the wall or in the ointment: The psychoanalytic community as a third presence in the consulting room. *Contemporary Psychoanalysis, 37*, 133–147.

Zeddies, T. (2002). Sluggers and analysts: Batting for average with the psychoanalytic unconscious. *Contemporary Psychoanalysis, 38*, 423–444.

Chapter 5

Core Competency Two: Therapeutic Stance/Attitude

Nancy McWilliams

Introduction by Roy E. Barsness

Relational psychoanalysis was born out of radical critique of the authoritarian stance. The analyst does not view him/herself as the authority of the patient's internal/external world, but sees the relationship as a co-constructed event where authority resides in the understanding and working through of what transpires in the in-between of the analyst and the patient. This is clearly reflected in the participant's stance of collaboration, collaborative authority, a relentless curiosity of patient and the self of the therapist, and the interplay of the two, emotional risk-taking, exploration, and radical open-mindedness. In this chapter, Nancy McWilliams claims "authority about process but uncertainty about content," and elaborates on the findings in the research that supports a collaborative stance of curiosity and awe, complexity, deep identification with our patients, and the privileging of affect, alliance, and faith.

Properties of Therapeutic Stance/Attitude

Core Competency Two: Therapeutic Stance/Attitude

2.1 Relational psychoanalysis was born out of radical critique of the authoritarian stance.

    2.1.1   Radical open-mindedness

    2.1.2   Collaborative authority

    2.1.3   Relentless curiosity of patient/self/interplay of the two

    2.1.4   Emotional risk-taking

    2.1.5   Exploration

Core Competency Two: Therapeutic Stance/Attitude	
2.1.6	What happened and what is happening
2.1.7	What happened and what is happening
2.1.8	Follow the patient's lead by attending to the patient's affects and thoughts

The Psychoanalytic Sensibility

Despite differences among analysts, there are core values and understandings to which most would likely subscribe. This chapter concerns those commonalities. I have, rather arbitrarily, organized the elements of what W. H. Auden, in a poem mourning Freud's death, called a "whole climate of opinion" under themes of curiosity and awe, complexity, identification and empathy, subjectivity, and attunement to affect, attachment, and faith. These aspects are overlapping and therefore hard to isolate, and although it is impossible to describe a gestalt by breaking it down into component parts, I consider each briefly.

Curiosity and Awe

Most fundamentally, psychoanalytic practitioners take seriously the evidence that the sources of most of our behaviors, feelings, and thoughts are not conscious. Given recent neuroscientific discoveries, this conviction is increasingly shared by cognitive scientists and non-psychoanalytic psychologists, suggesting the possibility of an eventual integration of approaches. Yet, to psychodynamic therapists, it is not merely that these phenomena are *non*conscious; there is a dynamic organization to how we unconsciously register experience, an organization that prompts analysts to refer to *the* unconscious, both generically and in each of us. In any individual, this schema is seen as the result of unfolding interactions between the growing child and significant people in that child's world. Features of, and relationships with, these early figures come to be internalized in stable ways.

For anyone who has done analytic therapy, it becomes fascinating how non-accidental are the choices people make. We rationalize what we do, but like hypnotic subjects inventing explanations for why they unknowingly acted on a posthypnotic suggestion, we seldom, if ever, know all the determinants of our behavior. In intense experiences such as falling in love, we can glimpse how remarkably lacking in control we are over the emotionally powerful situations in which we find ourselves. Children of affectively intense parents often seek intensity; children of negligent ones find partners who ignore them. Daughters of alcoholic fathers bemoan their attraction to partners with alcohol dependency; sons of depressed mothers may be drawn like moths to the flame of unhappy individuals.

People are often aware of having a love object whose attractiveness feels irresistible, yet they are seldom certain why such a person is their "type." We are always operating at many levels beyond the verbal, rational ones, sending elaborate signals to each other with facial expressions, tone of voice, tilt of head, tension of body, perhaps even odors of pheromones. Proximity and chance affect our choices, but therapists who regularly hear clients' histories and witness their struggles are repeatedly struck with their unconsciously determined, repetitive, persistent interpersonal scripts. One man I treated, who as a child would come downstairs each morning to see his depressed mother staring into space with a cigarette in one hand and a coffee cup in the other, fell inexplicably in love with a woman he first noticed in his college cafeteria, staring into space with a cigarette in one hand and a coffee cup in the other.

Some people take pains to find a partner who is the polar opposite of a problematic parent, yet find, as they start to build a life with the person who was supposed to be an antidote, that their earlier experiences are eerily evoked in the new relationship. A patient of mine whose father had been episodically violent fell in love with a committed pacifist, someone she saw as so dedicated to nonviolence that she would never again have to live in fear. After a few months of marriage and several heated fights, she began suspecting that her husband's ideological pacifism expressed a not-entirely-successful effort to counteract his violent tendencies. Once again, she was worrying that the man she lived with was dangerous. She marveled at having managed to find her father despite diligent conscious efforts to lose him.

Therapists who work with dreams are consistently awed by how much data can be condensed into a few images and a story line. There is so much condensation in dream symbols that one cannot conceive of the brain's having that degree of power consciously. As Grotstein (2000) elaborated, dreams show the activity of various cooperating "presences" in the mind—"the dreamer who dreams the dream," "the dreamer who understands the dream," the actors, and the "Background Presence"—all intercommunicating and symbolizing experience into a narrative that "will organize and unify the data presented to the senses" (p. 24).

It is not difficult to see the evidence for unconscious processes in other people; it is harder to grasp the reality that we ourselves are inhabited and moved by forces beyond our access or control. For many psychoanalytic therapists, it was an incident in our own life or personal therapy that crystallized our sense of awe, moving our appreciation of unconscious motivation from intellectual deduction to visceral conviction. We remember, in the flash-bulb way people can recall where they were when they heard about a plane hitting the World Trade Center, a moment when the sense of pure wonder overpowered the protest of their pride. For me, it was when I realized that a public figure with whom I was oddly mesmerized had the same nickname as my father. For a colleague, it was when she dreamed about a "Thomas Malthus" when dealing with the fact that in her family, love was part of an economy of scarcity. She had no conscious knowledge that Malthus was an economic theorist who emphasized the limited nature of resources, and she was stunned that unconsciously, she had obviously registered this information. For a friend, it was when he discovered his depression had begun 30 years to the day after his father's death, a date he had not thought he knew.

The curiosity about how any individual's unconscious thoughts, feelings, images, and urges work together is the engine of the therapist's commitment and the bulwark of the patient's courage to be increasingly self-examining and self-disclosing. The assumption that we *don't know* what we will learn about a patient is both realistic and healing. One analogy for the role of analytic therapist—a role that claims authority about process, but uncertainty about content—is that of trailblazer. If one is in an alien jungle, one needs to be with someone who knows how to traverse that terrain without encountering danger or going in circles. The guide does not need to know *where* the parties will emerge from the wilderness, but does have the knowledge to make the journey safe. Even though there are reams of literature about dynamics that typically accompany various symptoms or personality types, thoughtful psychodynamic practitioners listen to each patient with openness to having such constructions disconfirmed. What Freud called "evenly hovering attention," what Bion and Ogden called "reverie," what Casement calls "unfocused listening" is perhaps the *sine qua non* of the analytic attitude: receptivity to whatever presents itself, and curiosity about the multitude of meanings it may have.

Awe is usually associated with spiritual themes, the numinous realm. It is intrinsically connected with humility, the acknowledgment that human beings are, as Mark Twain observed, "the fly-speck of the universe," and that each of us is impelled by countless forces outside our own awareness and control. It involves feeling very small in the presence of the vast and unknowable. Awe is receptive, open to being moved. It bears witness. It contrasts fundamentally with the instrumental, utilitarian mindset of the technical problem-solver or the pragmatic, can-do optimism of those who believe themselves fully in charge of their lives. Though not antiscientific, it views science more broadly than the logical positivist who converts vast, complex issues into simpler ones so that concepts can be operationalized and variables controlled.

Complexity

Analytic thinkers regard intrapsychic conflict or multiplicity of attitude as inevitable. Most of us can find in ourselves wishes to be old and young, male and female, independent and dependent, and so forth. Our adaptations to limits are irreducibly ambivalent. Freud construed the human animal as insatiable, always yearning, never satisfied—partly because human beings often want mutually exclusive things simultaneously. Post-Freudian analysts, who focus less on drives and more on relationship, nevertheless talk about paradox, ambiguity, dialectic, multiple self-states, and the perils of reductionism (e.g., Hoffman, 1998). A comment like, "She's doing that just to get attention," would not be an observation in a psychoanalyst's repertoire—at least not with the "just."

Robert Waelder (1937) seminally elaborated on the related psychoanalytic principles of "overdetermination" and "multiple function." Overdetermination connotes that significant psychological phenomena have multiple causes. A symptom important enough to instigate a trip to the therapist has typically resulted from many different, interacting influences, including, among others, one's temperament, developmental history, social context, identifications, reinforcement contingencies, personal values, and current stresses. Multiple function posits that any significant psychological tendency fulfills more than one unconscious function (e.g., it reduces anxiety, restores self-esteem, expresses an attitude unwelcome in one's family, avoids temptation, and communicates something to others).

Thus, a woman's anorexia may derive from the interaction of: (1) a background of parental overinvestment in her eating, (2) a history of sexual abuse, (3) a disappointment or loss, (4) a frightening developmental challenge, (5) an unconscious association of weight gain with pregnancy, (6) a history of being shamed for needing emotional nourishment, (7) a sense of having been neglected, (8) an experience of being admired for losing weight, and (9) repeated exposure to highly valued but unrealistic images of women's bodies. Her anorexia may unconsciously aim: (1) to achieve a sense of internal control despite efforts of others to control her, (2) to reduce her attractiveness to possible molesters, (3) to express grief, (4) to maintain a sense of being prepubertal, nonmenstruating, nonadult, (5) to reassure herself she is not pregnant, (6) to avoid criticism for self-indulgence, (7) to get her family's attention (8) to garner compliments, and (9) to conform to cultural definitions of beauty. Most analysts would consider this a short list for something as complex as anorexia, which may reflect other influences and fulfill other functions as well; for example, in some subcultures (modeling, dance) eating disorders are normative and assiduously reinforced.

As an undergraduate, I studied with an erudite political scientist named George Lanyi. Student lore held that to get a good grade from him, one should avoid attributing international political events to any one factor. One should consider the countries involved and address their economic situations, ethnic and religious compositions, historic allegiances and rivalries, leaders' personalities, internal factions' domestic agendas, beliefs about threats to their stability, ideological heritages, levels of economic development, sense of national mission, weather patterns, and so on. A friend referred to eschewing single-factor explanations as "Lanyi's balloon," implicitly contrasting it with "Occam's razor," the effort to account for any phenomenon with the simplest possible explanation.

Most empirical researchers embrace the principle of parsimony. For research purposes, parsimony is a useful assumption. But it is not necessarily the truth (Wilson, 1995). Both Occam's razor and Lanyi's balloon are fictions, assertions of preference for either simplified or elaborated theories of causation. The tendency of analytic therapists to prefer complex, intricate explanations over simple ones may express both their clinical experience and the temperament that originally inclined them toward in-depth, emotionally complicated work. We may eventually learn that some psychological phenomena have single causes, but in the meantime, psychoanalytic prejudice is to assume complexity.

Identification and Empathy

Psychoanalysts tend to view disturbances in functioning as extreme or maladaptive versions of universal human tendencies. Sullivan's conviction that "we are all more simply human than otherwise" (1947, p. 16) suffuses psychodynamic thinking. Not that those of us who practice psychodynamically are not perfectly capable as individuals of feeling a defensive superiority to others, whom we may objectify with our diagnoses and implicitly devalue in our zeal to distance from their problematic dynamics; my point is that analytic theories consistently stress our common human developmental pathways, vulnerabilities, and strivings. One goal of the personal psychotherapy required for analysts is to increase our capacity to identify with patients' struggles by finding comparable issues in ourselves.

There is a bias among analysts against categorizing problems in living as categorical disorders unrelated to an understanding of the varied functions that such conditions fulfill. Psychodiagnosis as actually practiced by psychodynamic therapists is holistic, inferential, contextual, and dimensional. Seemingly discrete problems can rarely be understood in isolation from the person in whom they exist. An articulate expression of this attitude appears in Roughton's (2001) article on his evolving understanding, over decades, of sexual orientation as a dimension of functioning independent of mental health or illness. In discussing specific sexual acts, he notes that, as in all psychoanalytic evaluation, it is the underlying psychic structure, motivation, and meaning, not superficial similarities of behavior, that count (p. 1,206).

Analytic therapists from Freud on have appreciated genetic, chemical, and neurological dispositions toward the serious psychopathologies as well as historical and current stresses that cause such tendencies to erupt as problems. There is an implicit consensus that under the constitutional and situational conditions affecting the patient, the therapist would have become similarly symptomatic. By temperament and training, psychodynamic clinicians trying to understand the hallucinating schizophrenic, the determined self-mutilator, the starving anorectic—even the sadistic psychopath—look to the psychotic, borderline, body-obsessed, and sadistic parts of themselves. They also expect, when working with anyone dealing with difficult personality problems, that their own similar issues will be activated. This tendency to identify with clients, and to mine that identification for increasingly deep empathy, contrasts with the responsibility felt by biologically oriented psychiatrists and most academic psychologists to take a more detached position.

Freud set the tone here. Although sometimes disdainful of people he was not interested in knowing better, he extended empathy toward some groups that were highly improbable objects of identification for individuals of his era, class, and profession. When many other physicians were dismissing women with conversion and somatization disorders as frivolous malingerers, Freud took them seriously and tried to understand them. His famous 1935 letter to the mother of a gay man (Jones, 1957, p. 195), in which he insisted homosexuality "is nothing to be ashamed of, no vice, no degradation, it cannot be classified as an illness," was striking in its refusal to consign people in sexual minorities to some lesser category of humanity (even if he did also view homosexuality, unfortunately for posterity, as an "arrest of sexual development"). And although the contemporary ear finds Freud's references to "savages" disturbingly racist, his main message was that "civilized" people have more in common with preliterate folk than their conceit of superiority warrants.

In a highly influential work, Bollas (1987) commented, "in order to find the patient, we must look for him within ourselves" (p. 202). The centrality of identification and empathy goes beyond a conceptual preference to the question of effectiveness. The main instrument we have to understand those who come to us is our empathy; the main delivery system of that empathy is our person. Whatever the benefit of more intellectual aspects of our understanding (theories, research, clinical reports), our capacity to "get" patients (or more accurately, to *approach* understandings that will inevitably fall short of completeness), and to convey our understanding in useful ways, rests mainly on our intuitive and emotional abilities. A chronic source of both pleasure and fatigue in psychodynamic work is the repetitive moving back and forth, trying to go inside the patient's subjectivity and then trying to come out and reflect on that immersion. Clients who feel their therapists are right but not empathic take their therapeutic medicine with a choking dose of shame, an affect that evokes compliance, oppositionality, or paralysis rather than receptiveness and emotional maturation. Clients who feel their therapists are wrong *but trying to identify* will not be shamed, and will continue their engagement in the therapeutic process as they try to make themselves understood.

Subjectivity and Attunement to Affect

Closely related to identification and empathy is the assumption that subjectivity, far from being the enemy of the truth, can promote deeper understandings of psychological phenomena than objectivity alone. A theoretical physicist presumably does not empathize with particles, but psychotherapists can use a disciplined subjectivity to draw testable inferences about a person's psychology. Some writers (e.g., Stolorow, Atwood, & Brandschaft, 1987) have defined psychoanalysis as the science in which sustained empathic inquiry is the primary observational mode.

The perils of subjectivity are obvious: we can distort in the service of our personal needs; we are limited by our backgrounds and assumptions; we cannot construct a cumulative science without objectively derived reliability and validity. But objectivity has liabilities, too. Researchers striving for objectivity may ignore data that cannot be operationalized, manipulated, or studied by randomized clinical trials; they may fragment complex, interrelated issues to make them researchable; they may be methodologically rigorous, but substantively vacuous. The more we learn about infant–caregiver interaction, the more we discover preverbal communicative processes that are hard to observe, describe, and count. Rather, we feel them.

Between infant and parent in the first year, there is a dance of right-brain-to-right-brain communication essential to optimal neural development and the achievement of secure attachment, affect tolerance, and affect regulation (Schore, 2014). The scrutinized emotional experience of a disciplined clinician can reveal a lot about what a client is communicating via facial affect, body language, and tone of voice. Analytic therapists embrace their subjectivity and learn from their affective reactions a lot about what their clients are trying to say.

Some years ago, a distinguished judge came to the attention of neurologists because an injury had damaged his frontal lobes such that he felt no emotion. Physiologically, he could have been the prototype for the rational man so idealized by Enlightenment philosophers and many contemporary researchers. All his decision-making was dictated by reason and logic rather than affective processes like sympathy, emotion, and intuition. The striking thing about his decisions is that they were often bizarre or glaringly self-defeating. Without emotionality, he seemed unable to understand the full meaning of his choices. Rather than being gloriously free of primitive contaminants that corrupt judgment, he was crippled by the absence of sensibilities that make good judgments possible. After his injury, he resigned from the bench because he understood that to render justice, one must be able to feel sympathy for diverse human motives. His predicament calls to mind Plato's charioteer, who needs not only the white horse of the will, but also the dark horse of passion to move ahead (see Damasio, 1994; Sacks, 1995, pp. 244–296).

 Early in his therapeutic endeavors, Freud learned there is a difference between intellectual and emotional insight; we can know something cognitively and yet not *know* it at all. To change, we need to appreciate our condition in a way that feels visceral, not just cerebral. That discovery has been made repeatedly by psychodynamic, existential, and humanistic therapists. Westen (personal communication, May 10, 2002) is probably right that CBT practitioners may soon call themselves "cognitive-affective-behavioral" therapists because the same phenomenon eventually impresses itself on all clinicians.

There is something about affect that is prerequisite for meaningful understanding and genuine change. Experience suggests that most people do not separate, individuate, and come to a benign acceptance of the past without going through a period of anger and even hatred toward the person or family or community or ideology from whose influence they are emerging. All known societies expect a grief process before a bereaved person resumes normal functioning. Overwhelming events become less traumatic once one can express emotional reactions to them. Empirical studies of emotion (e.g., Pennebaker, 1997) confirm the observation of generations of clinicians that affect plays a determinative role in growth and change. Without the capacity to appreciate the emotional worlds of their patients, therapists would be missing a huge chunk of data, and their effectiveness would be severely compromised.

Practitioners, unlike those who consider mental health issues from a greater distance, have no choice but to deal with affect: a client's pain or hostility or excitement can flood the interpersonal space. Affects are contagious; they induce complex emotional reactions in others. For a long time, psychoanalysts tried to follow Freud's prescription to keep a cool head despite patients' emotional storms, regarding anything other than a "benign physically attitude" as evidence of unworked-out emotional kinks in the analyst. Especially as we have seen more "difficult" patients, however, we have abandoned this rationalistic ideal. Of course we need to ponder the implications of a patient's outburst and restrain the natural tendency to act on our feelings while doing so. Of course we remember it is the patient, not the therapist, who may give free rein feelings in the office. As several analysts have commented, we try to be our "best self" with our patients, not our whole self. Psychoanalytic practitioners have rarely endorsed a let-it-all-hang-out philosophy. But we do attend closely to our subjective responses to our clients' emotions, and value what that practice teaches us.

Emotions may prove more consequential for human behavior than the instinctual drives privileged by Freud. Numerous psychoanalytic writers (e.g., Fosha, 2000), citing research in brain physiology and chemistry, argue instead for the primacy of affect. As we await more data, the subjective immersion of therapists, voluntary and involuntary, in the expressed and unverbalized emotions of their patients remains a critical source of information about what is "the matter" with a person, how that individual experiences what is wrong, what may have happened to create the problem, and what emotional processes may be necessary to recover from it.

I suspect that part of the psychoanalytic temperament involves an attraction to, or pleasure in, or inability to minimize strong affect. There seem to be marked individual differences in whether a person seeks and welcomes the experience of intense emotion or prefers to resist or subdue more passionate parts of the self. I have noticed that my students who are most naturally taken with psychoanalytic ideas are also frequently immersed in the arts: poetry, music, theater, dance, and other repositories of powerful emotionality. One characterized herself as an "affect junky." There are also individual differences in how much control we feel over emotions. Those of us who have no choice but to be filled with emotion may be attracted to psychoanalytic ideas because they give voice to our affectively suffused experience and help make sense of our intense, insistent inner lives. During the era when psychoanalysis wore the halo of medical prestige, many analysts may have been overly intellectualized and relatively impermeable to powerful emotions, but in recent decades, this kind of practitioner is rare.

Attachment

Psychodynamic clinicians see individual psychologies and psycho-pathologies as determined by complex interactions between lived experience and a person's constitutional makeup and normal developmental challenges. They view treatment as the opportunity for a new person—the therapist—

to facilitate a benign maturational process that naturally unfolds in an atmosphere of safety and honesty. Working collaboratively, the two parties find ways to help that process along when the patient gets stuck because of dangers that haunt the patient's history. As the markedly oppositional client of a colleague commented, with considerable sarcasm, "I'm finally getting it. You think I need a new experience. And you think *you* are gonna be that new experience?!"

Although analytic therapists hope to be ultimately assimilated by their patients as "new objects"—that is, as internal voices that differ significantly from those of people by whom their clients have felt damaged—they appreciate the fact that, because of the stability and tenacity of unconscious assumptions, they will inevitably be experienced as old ones. They consequently expect to absorb strong negative affects associated with painful early experiences, and help the client understand such reactions in order to move past them and learn something new that penetrates to the level of unconscious schemas. Most people in the analytic community have been struck by the wisdom in Greenberg's (1986) observation that if the therapist is not taken in as a new, good love object, the treatment never really takes off, but if the therapist is not also experienced as the old, bad one, the treatment may never end.

Any therapist becomes impressed over time with how hard it is to find a way to talk with someone that avoids getting subsumed into that person's preexisting personal schemas. Psychoanalytic approaches to helping people share an orientation to treatment that assumes an intimate, highly personal, affectively rich relationship in which both parties slowly become aware of the nature of the patient's unconscious assumptions and work past them to new ways of seeing and acting in the world. Young-Breuhl and Bethelard (2000) write about how "cherishment"—the sense of being affectionately and personally cared for by a devoted other—fosters the possibility and the will for change. Many psychoanalysts, starting with Freud, have credited love with the major role in psychotherapeutic healing (Bergmann, 1982; Shaw, Chapter 11 in this volume), even if what we mean by love is more like the Greek *agape* or the Japanese *amae* (Doi, 1989) than the romantic love more commonly celebrated in Western cultures.

The psychoanalysts John Bowlby, who pioneered the study of attachment, and Margaret Mahler, who studied the separation-individuation process in young children, have significantly influenced therapeutic practice. Their efforts to study human connections via infant–parent observation have

Never forget that Larisa knows everything

inspired far-reaching empirical and theoretical efforts, rich with implications for psychotherapy (Fonagy, Gergely, Jurist, & Target, 2002). Bowlby's hypothesis that attachment functions as a regulator of affect and a safety zone from which to explore has helped us appreciate the value of the therapeutic relationship over any interpretations issued by the therapist. Despite their relative indifference to many other areas of empirical study, psychodynamic practitioners have been avid consumers of attachment research findings, doubtless because relationship is the medium within which they work every day, and adapting oneself to each patient's attachment style is a continuing challenge.

As we learn more about attachment, we have new ways of understanding why the intimate emotional connection between therapist and patient is so critical to healing. **That we are inherently social creatures who mature in a relational matrix and require relationship in order to change is suggested by the well-established empirical finding that the alliance between patient and therapist has more effect on the outcome of therapy than any other aspect of treatment that has been investigated so far (Safran & Muran, 2000).** It is odd that so many people see psychoanalytic therapy as an endless, intellectual rehashing of childhood experiences when, in fact, one of its core assumptions concerns the raw emotional power of the here-and-now therapeutic relationship.

Faith

I have been ambivalent about writing about the role of faith in psychoanalytic therapy, for fear of offending readers who are uncomfortable with a term so rooted in religious and theological discourse. Moreover, because only a few analytic thinkers have written about faith, I have fewer scholarly underpinnings for an argument about the place of psychotherapeutic faith than for other topics. I considered substituting "belief," but that word is too cognitive and active (as opposed to visceral and receptive) to capture the phenomenon I want to convey. And "hope," another obvious candidate, and one with perhaps a more established place in psychoanalytic writing (e.g., Mitchell, 1993), connotes both less conviction and more expectation of something specifiable than I think the psychoanalytic sensibility contains.

Ultimately, notwithstanding the fact that many analytic clinicians who exemplify therapeutic faith are not theistic, "faith" seemed the best term for what I am trying to distill (Fowler, 1981). Religious language does capture certain dimensions of experience that secular language does not. It is not accidental that Freud, a rationalistic atheist, chose the word *psyche*, which translates as "soul," when theorizing about psychology, rather than writing about the mind or brain. So I am using the term advisedly, asking even readers with no affinity for the spiritual to consider that there is a leap of faith we invite our patients to make, and a keeping of the faith that we demonstrate to them.

What I mean by faith is a gut-level confidence in a process, despite inevitable moments of skepticism, confusion, doubt, and even despair. Analytic therapy has a kind of self-righting mechanism that iterates toward authenticity. Analysts have faith in the therapeutic project because they have experienced it themselves. They approach clinical material with an attitude akin to the "expectant waiting" of Quakers. They are loath to make predictions about just where the professional journey with any individual will go, but they trust it to take therapist and patient into areas that will ultimately strengthen the client's sense of honesty, agency, mastery, self-cohesion, self-esteem, affect tolerance, and capacity for fulfilling relationships. In that process, therapists have learned that the specific problems for which a person sought treatment (e.g., anxiety or depression or an eating disorder) will fade. Often, target symptoms remit quickly, while the client decides to continue in treatment to pursue related, more ambitious goals (including emotional inoculation against future problems) that take on increasing value as the process unfolds.

Very often, the kind of change the client originally envisioned is not the kind that occurs, only because what does occur is something the client could not have initially imagined. To move into areas that are emotionally new, we must proceed on a kind of borrowed faith. If the practitioner proceeds with integrity, the client will eventually feel trust in the therapist as a person; the therapist, meanwhile, exemplifies faith in the client, the partnership, and the process. A woman coming to treatment may want to learn how to relieve a depression, and instead learns to express previously unformulated feelings, negotiate for herself in relationships, identify situations that trigger depression, understand the connections between those situations and her unique history, blame herself less for things outside her control, take control over things that previously seemed impervious to her influence, and comfort herself when upset. As the therapeutic process evolves, she gradually loses the vegetative, affective, and cognitive symptoms of depressive illness. But more important, even though before the therapy she could conceive of feeling better, she could not have imagined the depth of authentic feeling that is now a reliable feature of her emotional landscape.

Sometimes people come for help getting out of a relationship, and instead find that they can make that relationship much more fulfilling than they had imagined. And sometimes the reverse happens: people enter therapy hoping to save or improve a relationship, only to decide eventually that the cost is too great, and separation is their only tolerable option. The faith of the therapist is not attached to a particular outcome, but to the conviction that if two people conscientiously put a certain effort in motion, a natural process of growth that has been arrested by the accidents of the patient's life thus far will resume and follow its own self-healing logic. This faith assumes that the effort to pursue the truth of one's experience has intrinsic healing value.

Postmodern theorists have cast unflattering light on scientific claims to "objectivity," "rationality," and efforts to discover "the truth" as an Enlightenment-era scholar like Freud hoped to do. But whether or not we can find *the* truth about any matter, we can try to speak truthfully about it. As Levenson (1978, p. 16) noted, "it may not be the truth arrived at as much as the manner of arriving at the truth which is the essence of therapy." The attempt to be emotionally honest is the wellspring of everything else that comes from analytic psychotherapy, and the cultivation of a relationship that fosters progressive approximations of emotional honesty remains the central task of the therapist. We may talk about this in ego psychological metaphors such as the analysis of defense, or via self-psychological appeals for accurate empathy, or in terms of relational notions about exploring subjectivity. We may hold as our image of a successful therapy Freud's notion of conquering repression, or Jung's individuation, or Bion's ideal of living in O, or Winnicott's true self, or Weiss and Sampson's abandoning pathogenic beliefs, or Lacan's idealization of the postsymbolic. Different psychoanalytic ideologies locate the activity of forthright acknowledgment differently, but all share a commitment to the mutual search for what feels true. It is this effort in which the psychoanalytic community has invested its faith.

Concluding Comments

I hope I have conveyed a sense of not just the figure, but also the ground of psychoanalytic thinking and practice. I have tried to talk about the central values, assumptions, convictions, temperamental inclinations, explanatory biases, and emotional tendencies that characterize psychodynamic treatments. Psychoanalytic therapy is not a set of technical interventions, but a body of knowledge, accumulated over years of practitioners' immersion in listening to their patients, understood in accordance with the mindset I have sketched out.

It is my deep conviction that the attitudes I have discussed—curiosity and awe, respect for complexity, the disposition to identify empathically, the valuing of subjectivity and affect, an appreciation of attachment, and a capacity for faith—are worth cherishing not only as components of a therapeutic sensibility, but also as correctives to some of the more estranging and deadening aspects of contemporary life. Their opposites—intellectual passivity, opinionated reductionism, emotional distancing, objectification and apathy, personal isolation and social anomie, and existential dread—have often been lamented by scholars and social critics as the price we pay for our industrialized, consumer-oriented, technologically sophisticated cultures. The cultivation of the more vital attitudes (Sass, 1992) that undergird the psychoanalytic sensibility just might be good for the postmodern soul whatever one's orientation to psychotherapy.

References

Bergmann, M. S. (1982). Platonic love, transference love, and love in real life. *Journal of the American Psychoanalytic Association, 30*, 87–111.

Bollas, C. (1987). *The shadow of the object*. New York, NY: Columbia University Press.

Damasio, A. R. (1994). *Descartes' error: Emotion, reason, and the human brain*. New York, NY: Grosset/Putnam.

Doi, T. (1989). The concept of *amae* and its psychoanalytic implications. *International Review of Psycho-Analysis, 16*, 349–354.

Fonagy, P., Gergeley, G., Jurist, E. L., & Target, M. (2002). *Affect regulation, mentalization, and the development of the self*. New York, NY: Other Press.

Fosha, D. (2000). *The transforming power of affect: A model for accelerated change*. New York, NY: Behavioral Sciences Research Press.

Fowler, J. W. (1981). *Stages of faith: The psychology of human development and the quest for meaning*. New York, NY: HarperCollins.

Greenberg, J. R. (1986). Theoretical models and the analyst's neutrality. *Contemporary Psychoanalysis, 22*, 87–106.

Grotstein, J. S. (2000). *Who is the dreamer who dreams the dream? A study of psychic processes*. Hillsdale, NJ: Analytic Press.

Hoffman, I. Z. (1998). *Ritual and spontaneity in the psychoanalytic process: A dialectical constructivist view*. Hillsdale, NJ: Analytic Press.

Jones, E. (1957). *The life and work of Sigmund Freud, Volume 3: The last phase, 1919–1939*. New York, NY: Basic Books.

Levenson, E. A. (1978). Two essays in psychoanalytic psychology—I. Psychoanalysis: Cure or persuasion. *Contemporary Psychoanalysis, 14*, 1–17.

Mitchell, S. A. (1993). *Hope and dread in psychoanalysis*. New York, NY: Basic Books.

Pennebaker, J. W. (1997). *Opening up: The healing power of expressing emotions* (rev. ed.). New York, NY: Guilford Press.

Roughton, R. E. (2001). Four men in treatment: An evolving perspective on homosexuality and bisexuality, 1965 to 2000. *Journal of the American Psychoanalytic Association, 49*, 1187–1217.

Sacks, O. (1995). *An anthropologist on Mars*. New York, NY: Knopf.

Safran, J. D., & Muran, J. C. (2000). *Negotiating the therapeutic alliance: A relational treatment guide*. New York, NY: Guilford Press.

Schore, A. N. (2014). The right brain is dominant in psychotherapy, *Psychotherapy, 3*, 388–397.

Stolorow, R. D., Atwood, G. E., & Brandschaft, B. (1987). *Psychoanalytic treatment: An intersubjective approach*. Hillsdale, NJ: Analytic Press.

Sullivan, H. S. (1947). *Conceptions of modern psychiatry*. New York, NY: Norton.

Waelder, R. (1937). The problem of the genesis of psychical conflicts in earliest infancy. *International Journal of Psycho-Analysis, 18*, 406–473.

Wilson, A. (1995). Mapping the mind in relational psychoanalysis: Some critiques, questions, and conjectures. *Psychoanalytic Psychology, 12*, 9–30.

Young-Breuhl, E., & Bethelard, F. (2000). Cherishment: A psychology of the heart. New York, NY: Free Press.

Chapter 6

Core Competency Three: Deep Listening/Affective Attunement

Stuart Pizer

Introduction by Roy E. Barsness

Listening is the sine qua non of most therapeutic approaches. What distinguishes the listening skills of the relational analyst is what Reik called listening with the third ear; Singer called the viscera and Ogden reverie. My own understanding of listening is a listening to the "conversation that is at hand," which attends to the affects, the body, the dissonances, the clumsiness, those things that are beyond the content of the words, seeking to find voice.

This level of deep listening was evident in the study where the participants used statements describing their own listening skills as: "I look deep within myself to find my patient." "I ask myself, what is my body saying?" "I wonder what is going on with us." "What are they repeating here with me?" The relational analyst listens for what the patient can no longer hear, deafened by his/her intellectual defenses that have built up walls around his/her emotional experiences. Therefore, the relational analyst seeks to be highly attuned and self-reflective, paying a great deal of attention to what is happening within their own mind and their own affective state, recognizing that what is being stirred within them is in part a transmission of the patient's internal and external world, yet unknown or unspoken. Attending to affect, one is better able to enter into the unconscious and disassociated aspects of the patient. The relational analyst prioritizes affect, recognizing that resonance at the emotional level is what leads to change. Stuart Pizer refers to this deep listening as generous involvement, and in this chapter speaks to how affective involvement is central in our work, while acknowledging the tensions inherent in the analyst's efforts of deep listening and attunement within the analytic dyad.

Properties of Deep Listening/Affective Attunement

Core Competency Three: Deep Listening/Attunement

3.1   The relational analyst seeks to be highly attuned and self-reflective.
    3.1.1   Deep attention to affect states
    3.1.2   Looks within him/herself to discover what is happening within the patient
    3.1.3   Attends to the effect of his/her own personality
    3.1.4   Attends to countertransference experiences as a means for understanding the patient

3.2   The relational analyst follows affective experiences both within him/herself, his/her patient, and in the relationship between the patient and him/herself.
    3.2.1   What is the patient triggering in the analyst—who, how, what, and why?
    3.2.2   Where is the affect?
    3.2.3   What is the patient trying to protect or avoid?

3.3   Intuition.
    3.3.1   Attends to "inklings" or having a "sense" of something
    3.3.2   Encourages his/her own mind to free-associate, wondering what his/her thoughts and affects have to do with the patient
    3.3.3   Attends to the uncanny with a curiosity as to what this may be saying about the unconscious

3.4   The analyst listens beyond content and pays close attention to the words, the affects, and the bodies of his/her patients.
    3.4.1   Where is this happening in their/my body?
    3.4.2   What is happening in the "us"?

3.5   The analyst is interested in all emotion, with particular attention to those emotions the patient (and the therapist) seek to avoid.
    3.5.1   Cannot ignore hate
    3.5.2   Cannot ignore love

The Analyst's Generous Involvement: Recognition and the "Tension of Tenderness"

As analysts or therapists, we possess a capacity for generous involvement simply by virtue of our being human, with our existence embedded in a relational context. Hence, generosity belongs to the composition of our therapeutic instrument—that is, the person we are as we engage with our patients. Thus, if generous involvement goes missing, we would do well technically to read it as a signal to ask ourselves when, why, and how we have disconnected from a caring relatedness with our patient.

My grandfather, who ran a newsstand in New York City, taught me, through embodiment and action, the essentials of an analytic process.

Educated to the sixth grade, Grandpa had a way of being that opened my heart to the essential meaning of the spirit of generosity.

Three unforgettable and transforming incidents have become for me, a metaphor for basic elements of analytic process. The first occurred during a rare visit to our apartment by my maternal aunt and uncle, who brought my grandparents for tea. The conversation quickly curdled into the recurrent fight between my mother and her sister, escalating to a scenario in which my mother yelled at everyone present. Pained by this familiar emotional violence, I quietly left the living room and took refuge in the kitchen, and closed the door to muffle the shrieking. A few minutes later, my grandfather opened the kitchen door, entered, closed the door behind him, and silently sat down with me at the table. No words. No commentary on the scene in the living room. The lesson I derived from this experience, as described in my earlier paper (Pizer, 2008), was the power of affective sharing, or communion. Essentially, Grandpa entered in as witness to my lonely sadness, wordlessly communicating through his embodied presence, "I'm with you." This moment captures for me the essential function of the analyst offering the patient in pain an affectively resonant witnessing presence.

The second incident occurred during the summer I stayed with my grandparents prior to my going off to college. One evening, my grandfather noticed my reading a *Playboy* magazine I had borrowed from his newsstand, and he recognized immediately that instead of gazing at the naked foldout, I was looking at tweed jackets in the "Fall Fashion Forecast for Men on Campus." I learned from my grandmother the next morning that my grandfather had joined her in their bedroom and said, "Stuart is afraid that he will go off to Harvard without the right clothes and feel ashamed. I won't let that happen to him." Following Grandpa's instructions, my grandmother took me to a shop on Fifth Avenue and had me fully outfitted with suit, tweed jacket, shirts, and ties. This experience shocked me into awareness that it is actually possible for a person to recognize what is going on inside another person, and to respond with "appropriate action" (Sullivan, 1953), and thereby provide for a recognized need. The profound impact of this experience taught me the second lesson that I now apply to understanding the essentials of analytic process: just as Grandpa's witnessing and recognition were not matters of indifference to him (he figuratively and also literally gave me all he had!), I believe that the analyst's recognition of the patient's need carries with it an internal tug toward offering some relevant provision.

The third incident happened when I was a graduate student on vacation in the Florida Keys with my aunt and uncle and grandparents. Grandma secretly conscripted me into driving my grandfather somewhere, anywhere, to get him away from my aunt's relentless shaming of him for his lack of education or "cultivated" interests. I drove north to take Grandpa to see the Everglades, all the way silently, and sullenly, resenting that I was once again coerced into accommodating my family's primitive emotional functioning. I tried to hide the rage I was barely containing by limiting conversation to a minimum. But I remained locked into feeling sorry for myself. As we approached the Everglades, Grandpa asked me to pull over at a farm stand. Returning with a paper bag, he reached it across to me so I could see the nectarines inside, and said, "Want one?" No lesson could be more powerful than that, or more relevant to analytic process. Grandpa's simple, direct, unspoken embodied gesture told me that he well understood the nuanced layers of my private experiencing, that he accepted me as I was, even as he saw me as I was, inclusive of my dark side, and yet in the face of my alienating mood, he could still offer me both a gift and a clear challenge that held us both in respect and declared our relationship. Natural, affectively compelling, and state shifting—and I received Grandpa's gift of a nectarine as the offering of a transformational intersubjective interpretation, one that adjusted our relational state in that moment (see Aron, 1992).

Grandpa's spontaneous and unselfconscious lessons informed my understanding of what the analyst's presence may offer in the face of the nonnegotiable: containment, acceptance, and recognition. I propose that all of us, as analysts, would do well to carry something like Grandpa's spirit into our therapeutic relationships, infusing our clinical subjectivity with a more preconscious, automatic, spontaneously enacted, and indeed, elementally motivated relational feature of our human involvement with the Other. When the baby in the high chair reaches out his spoon for Mama to have a taste, his gesture reflects something fundamental and intrinsic to human connection.

I suggest that generosity is an "innate property," "elemental" and "instinctual," yet I also assume that, as with the expression of most genetic potentials, generosity is contextually shaped—certainly by past developmental influence, and likely by conditions of the immediate moment. We are wired for attachment behavior, both care seeking and caregiving, yet relational factors will prejudice toward the development of secure, insecure, or disorganized functional patterns. We vary in our expression of universal instincts. And, to add further complexity, just as the capacity to recognize and reproduce rhythms and melodies seems to be a human universal, underwriting our potential for speech communication, we recognize variations in individual musicality. Generosity is a basic endowment, a reflection of shaping experiences, and, as Grandpa embodied, an individual gift.

Harry Stack Sullivan (1953) provided a compelling metaphor for the affective tug of analytic recognition in his concept of the "tension of tenderness." In Sullivan's interpersonal theory, in which the Self is constituted through the responses of others, we each come to recognize our own specific needs through what he called "appropriate action in the service of the need." I am reminded of the analytic patient Emanuel Ghent described, who had not recognized that she was shivering with cold until he got up from his chair and brought her a blanket. Sullivan begins with the basic needs, like oxygen and nourishment. Sullivan writes: "The alternation of need and satisfaction gives rise to experience or, if you will, *is* experience—needless to say, in the prototaxic mode." Sullivan defines the "prototaxic" mode as "the rough basis of memory . . . the crudest—shall I say—the simplest, the earliest, and possibly the most abundant mode of experience" (p. 29). Perhaps the prototaxic mode comes close to what Loewald referred to as a "primal density," a oneness of the joined infant–mother matrix prior to differentiation. This leads Sullivan to state a theorem: "The observed activity of the infant arising from the tension of needs induces tension in the mothering one, which tension is experienced as tenderness and as an impulsion to activities toward the relief of the infant's needs" (p. 39). Sullivan is specific in emphasizing that tenderness is very different from "love." And he proceeds with a very significant elaboration:

> The manifest activity by the mothering one toward the relief of the infant's needs will presently be experienced by the infant as the undergoing of tender behavior; and these needs, the relaxation of which require cooperation of another, thereon take on the character of a general need for tenderness.
>
> (p. 40)

And, although this generic need for tenderness is, for Sullivan, a derivative of "disequilibrium arising in the physicochemical universe inside and outside the infant," these generic needs "nonetheless . . . all require cooperation from another," leading Sullivan to assert, "thus, the need for tenderness is ingrained from the very beginning of things as an interpersonal need." And, in this primal density, via the empathic linkage between infant and mother, "the complementary need of the mothering one is a need to manifest appropriate activity, which may be called a general need to give tenderness, or to behave tenderly" (1953, p. 41).

Is this not Sullivan's particular language for what we know as the evolutionary necessity of attachment behavior linked to a caregiving system developed and activated in unison (see Bowlby, 1969)? Or Winnicott's declaration, "There is no such thing as a baby," and his notion of a mother's postnatal "temporary illness" or "primary maternal preoccupation"? In a 1992 paper, echoing Winnicott, I posited a state later in life, and relocated to a clinical context, that I called "primary analytic preoccupation" (Pizer, 1992)

An instinctual tug toward tenderness, or a spirit of generosity, in response to a recognized state of need in the Other is an inherent feature of our functioning attachment system. Or, as Trevarthan (2009) conjectures, perhaps we come into the world wired to seek community, relational embeddedness, or "we-ness." Perhaps Loewald's notion of a primal density, while metaphoric, points to the facts of our inborn nature.

Empathy and the Roots of Generosity: Attachment and "We-Ness"

The internal tug of the "tension of tenderness" as described by Sullivan, even the empathic linkage to the other's "tension of need" or "need for tenderness," the embodied pull toward an analyst's involvement and generous provision, may in part be grounded in our irreducible primordial oneness with the other at this earliest, deepest level. To borrow from Pogo, "We have met the other, and they is *us!*" Or, as Mitchell puts it, "For Loewald [1971], we are our objects, and our objects are us. The distinction between drives and objects is a developmentally later, secondary process superimposition upon the primal density in which self and other are not yet sorted out" (Mitchell, 2000, p. 40).

Why does the analyst's generous involvement with the "other" matter? Coltart (1992), describing the analytic attitude in an essay using as trope the good old English concept of "Manners Makyth the Man," wrote:

> The people whose manners we genuinely admire and enjoy are those who, without it being obvious, skillfully enhance our sense of significance and worth. All contact, whether conversational or silent,

is accompanied by an atmosphere of warmth and generosity; this promotes trust and openness.

(p. 137)

Adam Phillips and Barbara Taylor (2009), in a tract *On Kindness*, point out: "Even Charles Darwin, that darling of modern individualists, strongly rejected the view of mankind as primarily selfish, arguing for the existence of other-regarding instincts as powerful as self-regarding ones" (p. 97). In this short treatise, they offer some assertions about kindness that strike me as pertaining to generous involvement in an analytic context. They write, "It is kind to be able to bear conflict, in oneself and others; it is kind, to oneself and others, to forgo magic and sentimentality for reality. It is kind to see individuals as they are, rather than how we might want them to be; it is kind to care for people just as we find them" (p. 93).

If kindness is inherent to our human nature, and essential to our communal and evolutionary survival, Phillips and Taylor also remind us of some of what kindness is *not*: "Not a temptation to sacrifice ourselves, but to include ourselves with others. Not a temptation to renounce or ignore the aggressive aspects of ourselves, but to see kindness as being in solidarity with human need, and with the very paradoxical sense of powerlessness and power that human need induces" (2009, p. 114). These qualifiers, and more, as we shall see, are relevant to the framework of the analyst's generous involvement, the manifesting of the "tension of tenderness" while struggling with the rigors and conflicts of the analytic relationship and process.

The Analyst's Generous Involvement

What more, specifically, can be said about what the analyst's generous involvement is, and is not? Corpt (2011) asserts:

> By clinical generosity, I do not mean lax attention to the frame or sloppy guidelines of practice, but rather, a serious, and, at times, even unsettling re-evaluation and openness to amending any and all aspects of analytic practice in light of the patient's forward edge strivings.
>
> (p. 5)

She saw this as "holding open a horizon of possibility" that still holds in mind both self and other. Corpt also ventures a list of features of what she calls "clinical generosity."

Corpt's list resonates with what I have written about "containment, acceptance, and recognition" (see Pizer, 1998, 2008) as dimensions of generous analytic involvement, as I will briefly elaborate here. By containment, I mean a welcoming of the patient's multiplicity of states and feelings held in an abiding negotiated relationship. By acceptance, I mean the analyst's disciplined and willing receptiveness to the patient's feelings as well as the feelings evoked in the analyst while with the patient. The analyst sustains a tenacious struggle within himself to bear the patient's rage, hopelessness, dread, or anguish, thus conveying a fundamental human respect, a willingness to feel pain, confusion, self-doubt, and so on, in the service of an emergent process of negotiation. And certainly, the analyst's generous involvement may take the form of venturing a difficult confrontation of the patient that is likely to evoke painful consequences and the strain of a mutually challenging and stressful working through, which the analyst may feel inclined to spare him/herself. Indeed, generous involvement may well entail the analyst's surmounting feelings of frustration, anger, even antipathy, evoked in relating to a patient who pushes his/her buttons.

And, finally, the fundamental quality of therapeutic recognition is that the analyst is registering the imprint of a patient's state even while striving to preserve personal integrity and equilibrium. In these three primal modes—containment, acceptance, and recognition—the analyst faces a patient's nonnegotiable position and implicitly says, "I am with you."

As important as a functional delineation of what the analyst's generous involvement may include is recognition of what "generous involvement" is *not*. Here is a partial and not exhaustive list.

The analyst's generous involvement with the "other" is *not*:

- compassion, which is a *feeling with*; generous involvement entails a *moving toward the feeling*, being a witness who is not a bystander;
- furor sanandi—Freud's term for a "rage to cure," which became the criticism of Ferenczi's ventures into more active techniques (note: Ferenczi is, within psychoanalysis, an original voice of generosity toward his patients, yet his spirit of generosity, so worthy of note, seems so alloyed with projection of his own yearnings and idealizations, masochistic susceptibility, and reaction formation that I have not used his work as a conceptual model of generous analytic involvement);
- masochistic self-idealization;
- tolerance of being abused;

- boundary, or frame, crossings with a narcissistic "largesse";
- impulsive or compulsive bestowal of "gifts," whether they be material, or seductive idealizations, or disclosures out of the analyst's own urgency;
- grandiose presumption that "my love is healing";
- calculated "corrective emotional experience";
- guilty reparation;
- a denial of the analyst's moments of angry feelings toward the patient or an avoidance of feeling conflict;
- *noblesse oblige*, a condescending exercise of power or charity, or self-congratulatory "philanthropy";
- an act of "extractive introjection" (Bollas, 1987) that declares, "All goodness and love comes from me";
- disrespect for the patient's autonomy and agency;
- the analyst's passively obliging the patient—a "false self" act of compliance or pathological accommodation; or the analyst's passive acceptance or complicity in a "false self" act of compliance by the patient;
- finally, it is not an unreflective, defensive appropriation of the position of "good person," leaving the patient no alternative to a totalistic position of shame at being both an indebted beneficiary and the only "bad person" in the room (see Davies, 2004).

Perhaps we need to remind ourselves that all these traps and corruptions of "generosity" await us in process, and part of our analytic skill is to notice ourselves thus slipping. We need to remain alert to these dynamics that masquerade as generous caring but accompany our defensive avoidance of feeling our own personal suffering.

A Relational Conversation with Levinas' Suffering "Other"

At this point, I will introduce the radical ideas of Emmanuel Levinas to propose a relational counterpoint from within our psychoanalytic discourse field, while respecting the differences in Levinas' context of philosophical (ontological and ethical) discourse. I locate in generous analytic involvement some resonance with his assumption of our obligatory subjugation of self to the needs of the other. "To recognize the Other is to recognize a hunger. To recognize the Other is to give" (Levinas, 1969,

p. 75; see also Goodman, 2012). But Levinas' notion of obligation is and is not my idea of generosity. A French prisoner of war during World War II who lost many relatives to the Holocaust, a philosopher and Talmudic scholar, Levinas turned kindness, caring, and generosity on their head. For Levinas, kindness is not a privilege, not even a choice, and certainly is not extended from above. Radical in his positions, Levinas offers a challenge to our presumptions regarding autonomy, intentionality, choice, ownership of our separate subjectivity, and generosity. His message is humbling, however we subscribe to its specifics and complexities.

Levinas' (1969) ethical message begins with our encounter with the "other," a "stranger," who is not an abstraction, but the specificity of a face, in our face. This unfathomable "face," strange and transcendent, is infinitely beyond our categories, representations, and ideas. Startled awake by this face, we confront Infinity beyond our ken: "The way in which other presents himself, exceeding *the idea of the other in me*, we here call face" (Levinas, 1969, p. 50, original emphasis). As Orange (2011) writes: "The other (Autrui, the human other) presents me with an infinite demand for protection and care. The face says, 'You shall not kill . . . . You shall not allow me to die alone'" (p. 46). Or, for that matter, to suffer alone. And, as Orange further comments, "the response must be 'Me voici' (me here)" (p. 47). For Levinas (1985), paradoxically, "here I am" is an obligatory answer of a call from the Infinite Other, inherently the Divine, that is also our coming into being through responsiveness. And, as Orange comments, "I am indeed my brother's keeper, and there is no escape" (2011, p. 47). Levinas contends that the "face" of the other preexists us, looms above us, obliterating all question of our making, or having, a choice. No escape, no choice, except a protective recourse to familiar self-isolating defensiveness, complacent totalizing constructs, schizoid disconnection, a perpetuated experiential slumber. Indeed, for Levinas, our very subjectivity comes awake and into focus through our subjection, perhaps even subjugation, to meeting the face of the other with inexhaustible responsibility. Hospitality (both small and large, beginning with opening a door for a stranger) and provision are incumbent upon us. There is no charity (ego) and no "quid pro quo." We expect nothing in return. Asked whether the other, the stranger, bears the reciprocal innate responsibility toward us, our face, Levinas (1985) replied, "That is his affair" (p. 98).

Levinas does not extol a masochistic submission to misuse by the other. Although the suffering other faces us with an infinite demand—indeed, a demand that honors our own useful suffering—Levinas (1998) does not advocate our useless or passive suffering or tolerance of abuse or senseless brutalization, declaring all useless suffering to be "meaningless," "for nothing," and "precisely an evil" (p. 92). But he certainly puts a different spin on recognition and an inherent tug to respond to need.

How might we absorb the radical position of Levinas within a concept of the analyst's generous involvement with the "other" in clinical process, and the "tension of tenderness" within us that accompanies our recognition of the patient's need, affect, or state? Certainly we hold in common that to recognize is to give.

I turn to the moment when my grandfather reached the bag of nectarines toward me, saying, "Want one?" I do believe this was an act of hospitality in the Levinasian sense. But here is where I would like to introduce a counterpoint. I also think Grandpa was embodying another aspect of "recognition" in the best analytic sense, a gesture with his own particular tonality of "me here" in service to *your* suffering. I think Grandpa was effectively saying to me, "I see you," even "I see what's going on"—but not "I've got you pegged," or "I've got your number," and certainly not "I'll be slave to your mood." This message seems to me to introduce an aspect of recognition that can include something like challenge—but not confrontation, or collision, and certainly not denigration. It is like a gentler challenge that extends an opening for shifting my state, perhaps even grasping another perspective on myself at that moment with him—an invitation to join his reaching with a bag of nectarines with a reaching of my own, toward a self-reflective state shift that permits "being *with*."

Grandpa was asking nothing of me, no quid pro quo as in, "Now maybe you'll be less crabby company." But perhaps Grandpa was master of a different form of hospitality, not incompatible with Levinas (consistent with "That is his affair!"), offering the other, without presumptions of reciprocity, a particularly relational form of responsiveness that may not only serve the suffering other (as in "This is me here for you"), but also may serve usefully the suffering "we"! Perhaps we can locate here a dimension of the non-masochistic "one-for-the-other" when the self (of the analyst) and the other, at moments, might *both* be served by "one-for-the-we," holding in mind that the analytic "we" is in the service of a mission to attend usefully to the suffering of the Other. And generous involvement, on the part of a grandfather or an analyst, may represent the "tension of tenderness" expressed in recognition of the state, or need, of the *relationship*. Neither a self-involvement nor exclusively an involvement with the "other," this response tends to the relatedness of self and other—a step toward meeting the needs of both, without compromise. **And it seems to me, from a relational perspective, that therapeutic action is grounded in the analytic relationship, in its mutual affective involvement, its struggles, and its negotiations and adjustments and individual healing, of patient and analyst alike, moves forward with the healing relationship.** The analytic credo is remarkably Levinasian in its ethics. As Poland (2000), writes: "The capacity to appreciate the self and the capacity to appreciate the other do not simply go hand in hand: they are the same unitary phenomenon of growth seen from different angles" (pp. 29–30). And, invoking Levinas, Poland succinctly writes: "In the analyst's regard [witnessing the face of the Other]; looking and caring and separateness [interpretation] are one" (p. 32). Regarding Grandpa's gesture of hospitality toward our ongoing relationship, with a bag of nectarines, as analogous to an interpretation, I recall Aron (1992) stating: "Interpretation is the principal process by which analysts position and reposition themselves interpersonally in relation to their patients" (p. 504).

The Challenges of Generous Involvement: Nathan

Nathan was a world-class economist, the kind of teacher, theorist, researcher, and contributor who spends half his time on a plane traveling to conferences where he is usually a plenary speaker, if not the keynote. He has been awarded major recognition prizes in Economics. But, for all his significance in his field, he has repeatedly fallen short of full and complete application of himself in the refinement or completion of his projects.

What competed for his time and attention were a set of compulsive repetitions that could occupy a considerable portion of his day. Engaging daily in a regime of intense exercise, plus medication, in the effort to control his serious lipid disorder, he would nevertheless search town for the most bargain lunch at one of the fast food franchises, and consider it a triumph to save 23 cents while eating foods on his forbidden list. He "shopped" at bargain basements, painstakingly switching the price labels on sales items so that whatever item he brought to the register bore the deepest sale cut in price. Another secret triumph. On his travels by plane to and from conferences, he would steal the head sets. And, over the years, he had engaged in many affairs.

I first met him, many years ago, after his wife had found out about some of his affairs, and they consulted me together with the question of whether she could ever forgive him or trust him enough to remain in their marriage of 35 years. And what could Nathan change that might offer his wife something to go on for healing? She agreed to give him some time, under the condition that he commit himself to individual therapy with me. That being said, Nathan had, in his 62 years, been through several therapies, and analyses, and he and his wife shared doubt and skepticism that any therapy now would manage to crack the impenetrable nut of his destructive entitlement. His wife did not know about the other array of compulsions in Nathan's secret life, but she knew that she could not live with fearing more affairs.

Nathan began to see me twice weekly. A tall man, physically fit from years of endurance exercise, his thick black hair just yielding to a distinguished gray, he cut a commanding figure. His facial expression often looked like Robert De Niro in a perpetual state of annoyance. Nathan was a daunting elder for me to face in therapy. I knew the stakes, and committed myself to offering all I could as a therapist.

Nathan seemed to have no difficulty talking in therapy, but he was not quite talking to me. At least, I found it difficult in the first weeks to find my way into engaging any dialogue with him. I felt imposed on by him to sit still and receive his verbal barrage without interruption. I ventured telling him that he seemed to need to upload a lot of information into me before he might feel that I could think along with him about his life. Maybe in the fourth session, Nathan told me he loved to drive alone to New York, because he was free to stop on the highway at McDonald's and order whatever he wanted. "And no one sees me," he declared. Immediately I found myself saying, "Including you." He shot me a quick look, and then he proceeded with his narrative, leaving me with the sense that he would just barely let that one pass. I silently wondered, "Where is his superego?"

One session, about a month into our meeting together, stands out significantly. He began by telling me that walking to my office through Harvard Square, some "young Turk" had jaywalked, crossing his path. He had felt the impulse to yell, "Get out of my way," and to punctuate it with a shove. He managed to refrain. On that theme, he began to tell me what a tough kid he had been. He said he had long since learned that this resulted from his family situation. An only child, he was the focus of his mother's boundariless encroachments along with her histrionic shrieking fits. His father, meanwhile, would sit quietly in his chair, reading, leaving Nathan with the feeling that his father was abandoning him to handle this woman himself.

So, said Nathan, he had become a ruffian. He had killed squirrels. He had thrown a rock at the back of a girl's head as she sat on a park bench. He told me of these things with what struck me as a combination of matter-of-fact information and bragging. He declared that he felt entitled to his outlets, then and now, by virtue of the abusive maternal relationship. He emphasized one incident: at about age nine, he had been standing around with a few guys and began to dare them to pull a fire alarm. They all shrank back. He pulled the alarm, and they all fled. He just stood there, frozen. And, indeed, fire trucks soon arrived. A fireman, in full regalia, stepped down from the truck and loomed over him. Nathan reports that the fireman and he stood still for an endless moment, during which Nathan, transfixed, dreaded that the fireman would deliver him into the hands of his mother. Then the fireman said, "You shouldn't be doing things like that," and got back on the truck. Nathan just stood there on the sidewalk as they drove away.

Nathan then recounted for me another episode in his childhood that he considered important. He had contracted some childhood illness and needed hospitalization, for a week, in a children's unit at the time that, according to him, did not permit parental visits. I didn't know what to make of this, but listened. He said he had felt abandoned and scared. He said he was neglected there. As an illustration, he told me that over his bed dangled an empty light bulb fixture. No nurse or staff had attended to this for days. Curious, he had reached up and stuck his finger in the socket, and been singed.

The session now nearly over, Nathan turned to gather his coat and papers, and began to rise from his chair. "Oh yes," he said, "I'll be away next week at a conference. And I intend to have an affair with a colleague I've been with before."

What now?! Could I let him leave the room without a comment? (Levinas would say that I am responsible even for *his* responsibility.[1] Indeed, I felt that!) Would I be like a noninvolved bystander father? Would I be negligent staff, ignoring his exposure to scorching danger? (How might Nathan experience that "I am with him"?) I felt a sickening shudder of dread. My immediate "unthought known" was that an affair now would be a disaster. He would lose his marriage, and I doubted that he could survive this loss. Or, as bad, he would keep his secret from his wife, live with her in bad faith, and subvert their relationship, his therapy, his life. (How does my internal tug that cries, "I won't let that happen to him!" serve this moment?) Do I take a stand, tell him *not to*? He had barely allowed me to comment on his not watching his own sneak eating at highway stops. I felt sure that a directive from me would make me another "Young Turk" standing offensively in his way. And he would push past me and leave. I knew he was hurling a challenge at me—"OK, what will you do with me now!" In the mere seconds I had before Nathan walked out the door, I struggled with which mistake I should make. Silent abandonment? Antagonizing and alienating interference? I knew that I did not yet, if I ever would, have the authority with him to speak as a voice of conscience. I recognized this moment of his dire need, and his compact and contradictory state of surly isolation and wounded aloneness. We were both in conflict. I was enraged at him and worried for him at the same time. I felt intensely involved, and checkmated. (And I could not bear to leave him to walk out the door without my finding somehow, for that moment, a "bag of nectarines" to offer.)

And then I heard myself saying, "I wish we had that fireman in here right now."

Nathan remained in his seat. "Why?" he retorted, although now a puzzled look began to enter his face.

"Because I wonder what it would be like for you to spend some time with him now." Nathan gave me a more puzzled look, and left.

When he returned from his trip, Nathan began the next session by saying, "I didn't have the affair. And I didn't take the head set from the plane. I figured I'd have to come and tell you." Relieved, I tried to receive this with a quiet face. Our work was now engaged. As we then moved along, Nathan at times would wryly call me "Jiminy Cricket." I accepted this diminutive epithet with good humor because Nathan already was struggling with much shame to stay in the work with me, and this seemed to ease his bearing it. Besides, a young cricket may be allowed more freedom to sound off than a "young Turk."

After about a year of meeting, Nathan said to me, "You have been exquisitely tolerant of me, and forbearing, and gentle. If you hadn't been, I would have left long ago. But now, if I'm going to learn anything further, you will have to begin to tell me things about myself." And, following his expression of advice, need, and permission, I did.

Feeling tugged inside by the tension of tenderness in our deep affective involvement with what we recognize in the Other, both devoted and conflicted, we are moved to offer what we can of ourselves as therapists and analysts. As I have been defining the analyst's generous involvement,

it is not only an empathic witnessing, a "being with." It entails a "going forth" from within ourselves *toward* the patient's need.

I'll end with this quote from Shakespeare's *Measure for Measure*, Act 1, Scene 1:

> Thyself and thy belongings
> Are not thine own so proper, as to waste
> Thyself upon thy virtues, they on thee.
> Heaven doth with us as we with torches do,
> Not light them for themselves; for if our virtues
> Did not go forth of us, 'twere all alike
> As if we had them not.

Note

1   I thank David Goodman, PhD for this idea (see Levinas, 1985, p. 99), as well as for his generous conversations about Levinas (personal communication, June 2012).

References

Aron, L. (1992). Interpretation as expression of the analyst's subjectivity. *Psychoanalytic Dialogues*, *2*, 475–507.

Bollas, C. (1987). *The shadow of the object*. New York, NY: Columbia University Press.

Bowlby, J. (1969). *Attachment and loss, Volume 1: Attachment*. New York, NY: Basic Books.

Coltart, N. (1992). *Slouching towards Bethlehem*. New York, NY: Guilford Press.

Corpt, E. (2011). *Clinical generosity: An attitude deeply embedded in the contemporary self-psychology*. Presentation at the Annual Conference, International Association for Psychoanalytic Self Psychology, Los Angeles, CA.

Darwin, C. (1871). *The descent of man*. New York, NY: Penguin Classics, 2004.

Davies, J. M. (2004). Whose bad objects are we anyway? Repetition and our elusive love affair with evil. *Psychoanalytic Dialogues*, *14*, 711–732.

Ghent, E. (1995). Interaction in the psychoanalytic situation. *Psychoanalytic Dialogues*, *5*, 479–491.

Goodman, D. (2012). *The demanded self: Levinasian ethics and identity in psychology*. Pittsburgh, PA: Duquesne University Press.

Levinas, E. (1969). *Totality and infinity: An essay on exteriority* (A. Lingis, Trans.). Pittsburgh, PA: Duquesne University Press, 1961.

Levinas, E. (1985). *Ethics and infinity*. Pittsburgh, PA: Duquesne University Press.

Levinas, E. (1998). *Entre nous: Thinking-of-the-other*. New York, NY: Columbia University Press.

Loewald, H. (1971). On motivation and instinct theory. In *Papers on Psychoanalysis* (pp. 277–301). New Haven, CT: Yale University Press, 1980.

Mitchell, S. A. (2000). *Relationality: From attachment to intersubjectivity*. Hillsdale, NJ: Analytic Press.

Orange, D. M. (2011). *The suffering stranger*. New York, NY: Routledge.

Phillips, A. & Taylor, B. (2009). *On kindness*. New York, NY: Picador.

Pizer, S. A. (1992). The negotiation of paradox in the analytic process. *Psychoanalytic Dialogues, 2*, 215–240.

Pizer, S. A. (1998). *Building bridges: The negotiation of paradox in psychoanalysis*. Hillsdale, NJ: Analytic Press.

Pizer, S. A. (2008). The shock of recognition: What my grandfather taught me about psychoanalytic process. *International Journal of Psychoanalytic Self Psychology, 3*, 287–303.

Poland, W. (2000). The analyst's witnessing and otherness. *Journal of the American Psychoanalytic Association, 48*, 17–34.

Sullivan, H. S. (1953). *The interpersonal theory of psychiatry*. New York, NY: W. W. Norton.

Trevarthan, C. (2009). The intersubjective psychobiology of human meaning: Learning of culture depends on interest for co-operative practical work—and affection for the joyful art of good company. *Psychoanalytic Dialogues, 19*, 507–518.

Chapter 7

Core Competency Four: Relational Dynamic

The There and Then and the Here and Now

Lewis Aron

Introduction by Roy E. Barsness

Psychoanalysis has always recognized that past events, especially early developmental experiences, repeat themselves in the present. Therefore, relational analysts continue to attend to early attachment, developmental history, defensive structures, projections, transference and countertransference, asking themselves: "How has this person been shaped?" "What happened?" "What have they done with what happened?" Relational analysts, however, have expanded the emphasis on early parent–child relations, in particular the mother, to include other significant interpersonal relations as well as the influence of one's own culture and traumas that have shaped and formed a person's view of self.

Perhaps an even greater shift in relational theory is the attention to the "here and now" co-created between the patient and the analyst. In attending to this progression in analytic theory, analysts now consider such questions as: "What is being stirred in me?" "Why am I reacting in this way?" "How am I impacting this patient?" "Am I allowing myself to be fully immersed, with all my thoughts, all my feelings?" "What am I contributing within this relational milieu?" From this perspective, the relational analyst has modified the rationalistic interpretations of the Freudian era:

> from enlightening the patient about his life to helping him capture the nature of his emotional life in intimate detail . . . [furthermore] the emphasis [has] moved from understanding and

explaining of connections to concern with the present and an interest in immediate awareness of emotions.

(Singer, 1994, p. 195)

The analyst's current view is that working in the here and now not only offers insight to there and then, but is also an opportunity for a new relational experience. Thus the analyst engages the patient in direct relationship with him/herself, believing effective change comes from working through that which is co-created within the analytic dyad.

Historically, we have referred to the relational dynamic of there and then and here and now as transference and countertransference. In this chapter, Lewis Aron takes the reader beyond the binaries of transference/countertransference, introduces intersubjective theory, and offers the concept of the analytic third. Working within the intersubjective field shifts the emphasis of the treatment away from interpretation as the primary means for change to "working through" the inevitable impasses, enactments, and divides inherent in a co-constructed therapeutic relationship. To account for this, Aron (with reference to his colleague Jessica Benjamin) introduces the idea of the third as a means to conceptualize reflection and symbolization. The third, Aron notes, is:

an effort to create a psychic space within which to think together about ways in which patient and analyst are similar and different, merged and separate, identified and differentiated . . . a place where they are able to achieve a third position, beyond a transference–countertransference interlock [and] beyond binary thinking into transitional, symbolic space of thirdness and intersubjectivity.

(p. 137)

Properties of Relational Dynamic: The There and Then and the Here and Now

**Core Competency Four: Relational Dynamic:
The There and Then and the Here and Now**

4.1   Attend to past experiences, the "there and then," played out in the present.
    4.1.1   Early attachment
    4.1.2   Developmental history
    4.1.3   Defensive structures in both patient and analyst

4.1.4   Projection in both patient and therapist
4.1.5   Replication
4.1.6   Relational style
4.1.7   Transference/Countertransference
4.1.8   Culture
4.1.9   Trauma

4.2 Attend to the relational dynamic in the "here and now."
4.2.1   Engage the patient in direct relationship with the analyst, believing that the most powerful work is what emerges between the analytic dyad.
4.2.2   Attend to what happened in the past is happening in the therapeutic dyad
4.2.3   Pursues the question of what is going on in the in-between
4.2.4   Attends to how the analytic dyad is impacting and influencing one another
4.2.5   encourages the patient to be curious about the analyst
4.2.6   Attempts to avoid the temptation to "solve"

Clinical Implications of Intersubjectivity Theory

A bright, talented, and experienced supervisee presented a male patient who, following the calamity of 9/11, confided that he was not upset about the event, and in fact, found the whole thing exciting and energizing. In the aftermath of the attack, he was glued to CNN, enjoying the prospect of war. My supervisee told me she was privately horrified by his callousness. She had long known of his narcissistic tendencies, but given the horrific event, it disturbed her to think such raw aggression and pitilessness could so dominate her patient's mind. However, she was determined to make every effort to sustain an empathic stance, but doubted she could maintain an attitude in any way that felt genuine.

As her supervisor, I had the distinct advantage of not being caught up in the immediacy of the transference–countertransference enactment. I was able to help her see that there were many ways of understanding her patient's reactions on the basis of what we already knew about him. For one, her patient had a chaotic inner life, filled with images of violence, unconscious fantasies of bodily damage, and themes of sado-masochism. It seemed understandable her patient felt relief in the midst of the city's catastrophe, because, at least momentarily, the violence, chaos, and destructiveness were externalized, concretely taking place, for once, not in his own mind, but externally in the world of others.

Together we explored to what degree my supervisee had become fixed in her identification with the victims and the rescuers, thus locking her patient into his reciprocal identifications with the powerful and frightening terrorists. But, from the reverse perspective, how much was the patient being locked into one set of identifications pushing the therapist into identifying with the complementary roles? As Davies (2003) has written:

> Such cases of apparently inescapable therapeutic impasse always pose for me the dilemma that patient and analyst become prisoners of the coercive projective power of each other's vision; each becomes hopelessly defined by the other and incapable of escaping the force of the interactive pull to act in creative and fully agentic ways.
>
> (pp. 15–16)

What Davies refers to as the coercive projective power of each other's vision, and of being defined by the position of the other, is closely related to what Benjamin (1999) has called *complementarity*.

Complementarity

Identifications

My supervisee was caught between two contradictory organizations of her experience. She could be outraged at her patient's indifference and heartlessness, but then she felt unempathic and unresponsive to his therapeutic needs. She might get herself to identify with the patient's sadistic pleasures in the violence and destruction exploding around them, but this felt like a betrayal of herself and of her own experience and values. In her compensatory and exaggerated efforts to be empathic, she felt obliterated, while in her fantasized expression of authenticity, she risked annihilating her patient. The ostensibly contradictory options amounted to the same thing: dominate or be dominated, terrorize or be terrorized, kill or be killed; in each instance, someone is obliterated. She was trapped in this "complementarity" where each option, empathy or authenticity, was the simple inverse of the other. I was able to give her a nudge towards her relational compass, freeing her to take up more varied, more complex identifications and relational positions, which in turn, since the analytic dyad is a complex system, I suggested might encourage the patient to assume new roles. Davies and Frawley (1994) say it is essential that the analyst remain open to take up all of the patient's multiple unconscious identifications: victims and terrorists, rescuers and witnesses. My nudging the compass needle, which had become stuck between opposing binary poles, freed the treatment up to swing to alternative positions, creating space for multiple positions where previously there had been only a simple line between two fixed points.

Once in touch with the patient's chronic fear and internal battle, with the relief provided by the external concretization of his anguish, the supervisee no longer had to choose between victim and victimizer, between a sadistic and masochistic response, between doing or being done to, between empathy and authenticity. A third option reconfigured her experiential organization. Until then, patient and analyst had been caught in an extreme moment of negation where the acceptance of one person's subjectivity meant an obliteration of the other's. In Benjamin's words, they had become "thrown onto the axis of reversible complementarity, the seesaw in which our stances mirror each other" (1999, p. 203). There must be a move beyond this power struggle to a level of metacommunication that allows the dyad to return from complementarity to mutuality and recognition, and restore a process of identification with the patient's position without losing her own perspective, to move beyond submission and negation, reopening intersubjective space.

Identifications and the Primal Scene

I also found the psychoanalytic understanding of the conflicts of identification posed by the primal scene to be helpful in understanding the reactions of this patient and analyst. This is not in any way to reduce the horrors of 9/11 to infantile fantasy, but rather to gain an understanding of the conflicting reactions which require management when bearing witness to trauma. It is as if the patient had gone from containing a chaotic, violent primal scene being fought out within his own mind to becoming a witness to such a primal scene, but now as an observer struggling to maintain an identification with only one party to the scene. His therapist, in turn, had become caught up in observing the same external scene, and may similarly have struggled to contain her own terror by identifying rigidly with the other actor in the scene. One aspect of experiencing unconscious resonances of the primal scene is the intense conflict concerning with whom to identify, and we often manage such conflict by rigidly identifying with one actor and disidentifying with the other. This is perhaps the central conflict with which people struggle in witnessing the primal scene.

I have previously (Aron, 1995, 1996) elaborated on Britton's (1989) suggestion that the child's management of the primal scene facilitates the creation of a "triangular space," which allows for the possibility of being a participant in a relationship and observed by a third person, and of being an observer of a relationship between two other people. The child oscillates between moments of observation in which he or she is left out of some dyadic activity, and other moments of active participation as part of a dyad, where someone else is excluded. Here is the way Britton (1989) described it:

> The closure of the oedipal triangle by the recognition of the link joining the parents provides a limiting boundary for the internal world. It creates what I call a "triangular space"—i.e., a space bounded by the three persons of the oedipal situation and all their potential relationships. It includes, therefore, the possibility of being a participant in a relationship and observed by a third person as well as being an observer of a relationship between two people.
>
> (p. 86)

The Oedipus complex entails not just the child's viewing the parental relationship from the perspective of an excluded outsider; it entails the myriad fantasies of the child in which the entire system of family relations is experimented with and internalized. The little boy or girl is at one moment the small, excluded child barred from the gratifications of adult sexuality; at another moment the same child is the fantasized rival of the father for mother's love, and at the next is seeking a separate, private, and exclusive relationship with the father. Thus, it is in the oedipal stage that the child first alternates between observation and participation within what is now conceived by the child as a triangle. This fact is clinically important, because this oscillating function is the basis from which a person can participate in an analysis. Through this route, we learn to alternate among a variety of perspectives or vertexes. Benjamin and I argued that important varieties of triangulation also take place pre-oedipally and thirdness already exists within the mother–infant dyadic unit (Aron & Benjamin, 1999). Nevertheless, I believe, along with Britton, that significant transformations take place at the oedipal level, contributing to our capacities for reflexive self-awareness and lead to qualitative advances in intersubjectivity. While there is a pre-oedipal history of oscillation and participation, it occurs and is experienced as a series of dyads, rather than integrated into a triangular system.

o Oedpial dy namic
Maybe existrly in Polyamory

A Recap

To recapitulate: **dyads, couples, and systems tend to get stuck in complementary relations. This complementarity is characterized by a variety of splitting in which one side takes a position complementary to—the polar opposite of—the other side. If one is experienced as the doer, then the other becomes the done to (Benjamin, 2004a); if one is the sadist, then the other becomes the masochist; if one is the victim, then the other becomes the victimizer; if one is male, then the other becomes female; if one is active, then the other becomes passive. Polarities are split between the two members, and the more each one locks into a singular position, the more rigidly the other is locked into the opposing, complementary position, thus heightening the splitting and tightening the polarization.** At any time, the split may be reversed without significantly changing the structure of the complementarity. The active member may suddenly become passive while the passive member becomes active, thus their surface roles are switched, but the dyadic structure remains split between activity and passivity.

In the clinical example that we are discussing, the analyst experienced the patient as aggressively identified with the terrorists, now terrorizing her and hijacking the analysis. She did not want to submit to this terrorization, but felt done to, locked into a victimized position rationalized by her sense that she was "supposed to" empathize with her patient. She was locked into a structure she could not escape, and was tempted to attack her patient in return. She could confront him or intervene in a manner that would challenge his sadism, but in the very act of doing this, she might become the active, sadistic terrorist pushing him into the role of the passive, masochistic victim, hence achieving only a simple reversal.

Thirdness

Let's examine the structure of complementarity and the related conceptualization of thirdness. Drawing on Britton (1989) and Benjamin (2004a), I would like to use very simple mathematical ideas to explain the structure of this complementarity. These simple geometric terms are useful clinically in that they provide a clear, model of therapeutic impasses and how to transform them.

The structure of complementarity is best thought of as a straight line (remember the image of the compass needle stuck between two fixed points). A straight line has two end points opposite to each other. The line has no space; it exists in two dimensions only. You can move only forward or backward along the line; you cannot step outside of that line. Or think of two people on a seesaw, where one is on top and one is below. As long as they want to stay on the seesaw, the choices are either moving toward each other or further back toward the edge of the seesaw, thus slightly adjusting their relative power on the fulcrum. They can maintain their positions, or they can switch, creating a simple reversal. But the underlying structure is maintained; they are still on a straight line in which one's position on the seesaw determines the others. It is possible that each could be in a middle position, sitting evenly or level on the seesaw. But while this seems like an improvement—a more egalitarian, level relationship—it maintains the same structure of rigidity. They cannot both be up or down together, and one's push downward continues to pressure the other to swing upward. This is the model Benjamin (2004a) developed of complementary, doer–done to, push me–pull you relations, and it elegantly depicts what happens in therapeutic impasses and stalemates.

So how does one move from the structure of complementary relations to a more flexible arrangement? The two participants must find a way to go from being positioned along a line toward opening up space. I am referring, of course, to psychic space, transitional space, space to think, space to breathe, to live, to move spontaneously in relation to each other interpersonally. The conceptualization of the third models this state in demonstrating that a line has no space, whereas a triangle does. Britton (1989) spoke about being able to free himself to think to himself while with a patient, to take a step to the side within his own mind so as to create mental space. Picture this in terms of geometric space. While on a seesaw, one cannot take a step to the side; moving sideways is not an option. As soon as one steps to the side, a line has been transformed into a triangular space with room to think and to relate, enabling flexibility and freedom of movement. One's position within triangular space does not completely determine the position of the other, as it does on a seesaw.

One significant consequence of being stuck on a straight line in complementary twoness is that the line represents an unconscious symmetry.

Both partners on the seesaw mirror each other inversely; they are flip sides of each other; they inhabit reversible perspectives. This structural arrangement captures the mutual experience of their deep, generally unconscious, identification with each other. We know that the sadist identifies with the masochist, and vice versa, even if these identifications are repudiated in consciousness. Thus, when patient and analyst get stuck in complementarity, even while each feels "you are doing this to me, you are forcing me into this position," there remains a deep connection between them because they unconsciously recognize that they are locked together in this binary relation, however polarized. — *they need 'eachother' in order to stay in that postn*

Returning to my supervisee and her patient, when she could begin to think about her situation, she could see that he was not all sadistic terrorist, but also terrified hostage. When she could think about herself and realize she was locked into identification with the victims, she could begin to imagine other parts of herself and other identifications. Once she could take a step to the side, outside of the "push me–pull you" tug of war with her patient, other relational positions became immediately available to her. Thinking and feeling within the newly created triangular space allowed her to shift from the limiting structure of a polarizing flat line to a space with possibility and depth. A new configuration emerges that presents both patient and analyst with additional options for how they position themselves in relation to each other. Now they are enabled to renegotiate (Pizer, 1998). Rather than following the rigid and predictable back and forth movement of a seesaw, transference can begin to serve as a "strange attractor," allowing the emergence of surprisingly new configurations and unpredictable interpersonal adjustments.

The One-in-the-Third and the Third-in-the-One

The third is a concept popular across a variety of schools of psychoanalysis, but it is often defined ambiguously and inconsistently. For some, the third refers to something beyond the dyad, a context within which we emerge; for others, the third is an emergent property of dyadic interaction, and yet for others, the third is a dyadic achievement that creates the psychic space necessary for reflexive awareness and mentalization.

Benjamin (1988, 1990, 1995, 1998, 1999, 2002, 2004a, 2004b, 2005) addresses these issues by differentiating between what she calls the one-in-the-third and the third-in-the-one. When speaking about the one-in-the-third (which she has also called the nascent third or the energetic third), she is referring to that rhythmic or harmonic element of oneness that is essential to the experience of thirdness, or what I would suggest referring to as *mutual accommodation*. Benjamin clearly describes this in terms of two people sharing a pattern, a dance, a rhythm with each other. Think of the rhythms established by the mother–infant dyad in eye gaze, reciprocal speech, gestures, movements, and mutual mirroring. In discussing Sander's work, Benjamin (2002) has usefully described this as resembling musical improvisation, in which both partners follow a pattern that both of them simultaneously create and surrender to: a co-created third. With the phrase "the-one-in-the-third," Benjamin captures the experience of oneness, the mother–infant oneness or the oneness of a jazz band improvising in synch. Each member is not only accommodating to the other, but is also accommodating to the co-created rhythm that the couple has already established. The principle of mutual accommodation thus expands what we know to be ongoing mutual influence to include not only the ways two people influence each other, but also the ways in which they are continually influenced by the very patterns and rhythms they have previously established with each other.

It is critical to note that this form of thirdness may well be pre-oedipal, in that it emerges out of the mother and infant's accommodation to each other, as well as to their own prior accommodations. This form of thirdness does not require an oedipal father to sever the child's connection to mother. In arguing that thirdness emerges within the pre-oedipal, mother–infant dyad, Benjamin differentiates her ideas from those of Lacan, who saw the father as having to symbolize the third. For Lacan and many European analysts, as well as for others, including Ogden (1987), the mother–infant dyad is always triadic in the sense that the mother herself is engaged in the symbolic world, and it is the mother who contains the third element intrapsychically. In Benjamin's rhythmic third, however, the thirdness is a new creation emerging within the space of the dyad, rather than in the mind of one or the other participants alone.

Having spoken about the one-in-third, let us now take up Benjamin's third-in-the-one, which she also calls the symbolic or the moral third, to highlight a space for differentiation in what is ordinarily called oneness. Benjamin (2004a) illustrates this principle by referring to the term "marking" or "marked response." The idea of markedness was originally developed by Gyorgy Gergely, and is described by Fonagy et al. (Fonagy, Gergely, Jurist, &

Target, 2002), who elaborate a social biofeedback theory of affect-mirroring. Recent conceptualizations of "mirroring" emphasize that, no matter how well attuned a parent is to the infant's state, her mirroring facial and vocal behaviors never perfectly match the infant's behavioral expressions. The mother "marks" her mirroring response to her child to signal, so to speak, that it is *her* version of *his or her* response. It is markedness that indicates that it is not mother's affect display, but her reflection (her understanding, her version) of the infant's affect. The exaggerated quality provides a personal stamp or signature, signifying that it is neither a perfect reflection of the other, nor a completely natural response of the self. The infant recognizes and uses this marked quality to "decouple" or to differentiate the perceived emotion from its referent (the parent) and to "anchor" or "own" the marked mirroring stimulus as expressing his or her own self-state. To illustrate, when a mother sees her young child fall and bruise his or her knee, she exclaims "Ohhh" in such a way as to signify her empathy with the child's pain and fear. Nevertheless, the mother is not (or should not be) responding with the same degree of disorganization as her child. She both identifies with the frightened child and also marks her response (usually by some exaggerated feature) by signifying that she is not reacting exactly as the child is, and that she is separate. In the infant's experience, the parent's mirroring behaviors convey a sense of "nearly like, but clearly not identical to me." Nor are they viewed as real emotional expressions of the parent. They are neither realistic authentic responses of the self nor perfectly matched reflections of the other. Emotional attunement, mirroring, and empathy dialectically contain elements of authenticity and do not wipe out the features of either self or other. It is neither a sadistic destruction of the other nor a masochistic betrayal of the self. Therefore, mirroring, with its marked component, is a dyadic phenomenon, functioning as a differentiating third point emerging between the infant and the attuned parent. Think of the third here, once again quite literally, as constituted by three points: the child's immediate response, the mother's response identifying with her child's fear, and then that more adult, differentiated component of the mother's response in which she knows that the child is not dying and will get over it.

Thirdness thus emerges from within the dyad without needing a literal third object to intervene and separate mother from child. The marked response is thus an excellent example of the third-in-the-one or intentional third, in that it facilitates the differentiation of the self and other within their very connectedness. It should be clear that this understanding of mirroring is quite different from the classic Lacanian understanding, in that in this view of mirroring, the mother is not at all a united image providing false imaginary unification, but rather is split between two subjective positions, one aligned with the child and one distinct and marked. This will have clinical implications for the analyst, as we will soon see as we turn to examine how analysts' mirroring responses provide patients with access to their analysts' own inner conflicts and double-mindedness.

The one-in-the-third and the third-in-the-one are interconnected. Rhythmicity and markedness go together, with the former emphasizing connectedness, and the latter emphasizing difference; each is necessary to the other.

Clinical Implications of Intersubjective Theory and the Notion of the Third

One way to understand why contemporary psychoanalysis has become interested in the third is that thirdness is one way to conceptualize reflection and symbolization. It is a theory of thinking that transcends the mind in isolation, a relational theory of symbolization. I want to make the case that certain forms of the analyst's self-disclosure are best understood as legitimate and at times necessary attempts to create thirdness. By disclosing aspects of their inner processes, particularly their own inner conflict or self-disagreement, analysts conduct a dialogue with themselves in the presence of their patients, thus introducing a third element into the dyad. At times, these self-disclosures operate as strange attractors, breaking up the single-lined stuckness of the seesaw and introducing a third dimension, creating psychic space for reflexive awareness and mentalization.

Contemporary Kleinians view the third as an oedipal construct, conceiving the third as an aspect of the analyst's mind rather than a shared co-created experience. From this perspective, Britton (1989) understands his patient as attacking the third in the analyst's mind because it represents an oedipal rival third that cannot be tolerated. However, by placing exclusive emphasis on the oedipal situation, Britton, like most analysts who have written in this area, bypasses the important forerunner of triangular space that emerges from within the mother–infant dyad.

By way of example, Britton (1989) presents the case of Miss A's inability to tolerate knowledge of parental intercourse because accepting this triangular relation would entail a threat to an all too tenuous internal and external relationship to her mother. Any attempt on Britton's part to engage in a perspective outside Miss A's own was experienced as intensely threatening to her, and for a long time resulted in her becoming violent. Gradually, Britton learned to allow an evolution within himself of his own experience while articulating to Miss A his understanding of her point of view—something like what we call "mirroring." This progressively allowed Miss A to begin to think. Britton retains the oedipal metaphor and utilizes this imagery creatively, stating that parental intercourse could take place only if the knowledge of it did not force itself in some intrusive way into the child's mind.

Benjamin and I, however, argue that Britton's superb clinical sensitivity is better formulated in the following way (Aron & Benjamin, 1999). Britton constructed a relationship with Miss A in which he reflected back her own point of view as it was inevitably filtered through his own thought processes and emotional responsiveness. He successively elaborated his thinking about her point of view in such a modulated manner that she could gradually begin to identify herself with an image of him thinking about her, creating a sense of mutual identification or attunement, allowing her to gradually feel that he understood her experience sufficiently well. His thought became available as an object for her use, facilitating reflection wherein he did not intrude as a third element into their dyadic relationship. His response is consistent with the Kleinian view that conceives the third as an aspect of the analyst's mind rather than a shared co-created experience. Britton began to think *about* her point of view, but inevitably *from* his point of view.

Britton concludes that, since the patient cannot tolerate the analyst's thinking, all the analyst can do is to allow the evolution within him/herself of his/her own experience, and to articulate this to him/herself, while communicating to the patient only the analyst's understanding of the patient's point of view. Britton therefore calls for triangular space to be opened up only in the analyst's mind.

But it seems to me that this account really does not explain how this internal thinking in the analyst eventually leads to any shift in the patient. Does Britton mean to suggest that articulating understanding completely from the patient's point of view will eventually allow the patient to tolerate a third perspective? Perhaps. But I would argue that Britton, and all analysts, try as they might to stick with the patient's perspective, to articulate the world as it is experienced by the patient, inevitably introduce some difference, some marking of their reactions as different from the patient's.

Let us again think in very simple concrete terms about what it is that the analyst is doing. If the analyst is thinking silently about the patient in a differentiated way, without conveying any of that to the patient, then how does this create space between them? Sooner or later, at least in some small measure, doesn't the analyst have to demonstrate to the patient that the analyst can think about his/her own reactions? Doesn't the analyst have to have some kind of dialogue with him/herself, something in the form of: "I am of two minds about this idea, I can hold to two ideas, two points of view, some conflict or disagreement with myself?" It is the analyst's reflexive self-awareness that creates a third point within what was a simple dyad, a triangular space where there was only a line.

A superb account of this clinical process is "the dialectics of difference" described by Bollas (1989). Bollas encourages analysts to differ with themselves to express some conflict, for example about making a particular interpretation, or to explain to a patient something of the internal process that led to arriving at an interpretation. Bollas might disagree with himself, for example, saying to a patient that he feels his last interpretation was not quite right, and here is why. Bollas advocates this form of disclosure with the intention of helping patients gradually accept and articulate conflicts of their own.

Similarly, Hoffman (1998) advocates that analysts may at times reveal various conflicts about their analytic functioning, offering numerous examples where he would like to say X, but is worried about Y. He tells one patient he would like to offer her support about a particular activity, but worries that offering such support will encourage her dependency.

Bach (2003), like Bollas and Hoffman, also advocates analysts sharing with patients the inner workings of their minds, specifically emphasizing the importance of disclosing certain aspects of their own double-mindedness, ambivalence, or inner conflict.

I try, whenever possible, to explain the reasoning behind my comments and interpretations, and better yet, I allow the patient to witness my mind at work in the process of free-associating or making formulations, so that the interpretation becomes a mutual endeavor and is thereby much improved. It is especially useful for such patients to experience the analyst as he/she tries to deal with doubt and ambiguity, or as he/she tries to hold two ideas or two roles in mind at the same time, for it opens up the possibility of their doing the same. Most importantly, since I am implicitly asking my patients to trust me with their minds, I struggle to attain a position where I can trust them with my own mind and feel that I have nothing to hide from them (Bach, 2003, pp. 403–404).

Here is one further clinical illustration, from the work of McLaughlin (2005). McLaughlin, working with Mr. F, who was engaging in high-risk sexual encounters during the early years of the AIDS epidemic, tells the story of how closely he came to being pushed beyond his personal and analytic tolerance. In spite of his best efforts to remain neutral and non-intrusive and refrain from imposing moralistic or overly protective restraints in regard to Mr. F's anonymous homosexual encounters and cruising, McLaughlin could not conceal his own aversion and his wishes to restrain his patient, resulting in an impasse. Ultimately, for Mr. F the difficulty was not McLaughlin's concerns, but rather his dissembling and lack of directness about his feelings. Having arrived at this understanding, McLaughlin was able to directly disclose his own conflict and "to speak about the quandary of my wish to urge him to do the sensible thing, countered by my concern for his need for autonomy" (p. 220). It was this collaborative work and direct acknowledgment of the analyst's conflict that led to the resolution of the dangerous cruising behaviors and the associated analytic impasse.

The technical interventions described by Bollas, Hoffman, Bach, and McLaughlin begin to create analytic space by bringing in a third point of view. By disclosing their own difference with themselves or conflict or double-mindedness, what they are doing is saying, "I am of two minds about this intervention." They are saying, "OK, there are at least three of us here. There is you and then there is the I who wants to support you, and the I who is afraid of encouraging your dependency." Or they are saying, "There is the you who heard my last interpretation and felt whatever you felt, then there is the I who said it, and the I who now disagrees and feels somewhat differently." Benjamin (2004a) argues that, in an impasse structured along the lines of complementary twoness of doer–done to relations, analysts often may have to go first, revealing their own vulnerability before expecting this of the patient. It is not simply a matter of going first in the sense of sequence; rather, it is a matter of the analyst taking responsibility for participating in the push–pull by having said or done something that contributed to it. This relates to the all-important recognition that enactment and co-participation are essential and facilitative aspects of the analytic process. This does not mean that just any self-disclosure is clinically productive or that the analyst should just speak his/her mind or that anything goes—obviously not. The analyst's response must be marked. It must in some small way differentiate itself from the patient's response (the differentiating or intentional third or markedness), yet it also must reflect the analyst's accommodation to the needs and perspective of the patient and the various accommodations, rhythms, previously established between them (the rhythmic third as mutual accommodation and negotiation).

Returning to the initial clinical example, suppose the analyst could say something to the patient about her understanding of how his excitement about the attacks was understandable because it felt exhilarating to see the violence out there in the world, outside of himself, to identify with the excitement of having that much impact and control of the whole world. This could be said while genuinely identifying with the power and excitement of the power, without the analyst losing his/her own sense of the horror of the destructiveness. I think, however, that to say this would not simply be a mirroring of the patient's affective state, but would demonstrate markedness and the difference between the patient's reaction and what is captured by the analyst's interpretation. This point of difference leaves open an invitation to correct the analyst, to dialogue with him/her about the difference between his/her lived experience and what is captured by his/her remark, as well as negotiate the meaning of these experiences between them. Clearly, neither empathy nor negotiation is a steady process; rather, intersubjectivity is constructed and lost, ruptured and repaired (Beebe and Lachmann, 1994). This very process of rupture and repair may be well understood as drawing on the power of the third, the dialectic, or put another way, the negotiation of difference.

But consider another intervention. I could also see the analyst saying to the patient something along these lines: "Oh I see, I was missing something, I was so appalled by the violence and so saddened by the loss of life that I didn't want to let myself see that I also felt some excitement by the very power involved in the horror." Would it really be so surprising if, following an intervention like this, the patient could begin to notice that he also had more than one set of feelings about the disaster? Might not the patient react with something like: "Oh, you mean you can actually find the aggression exciting too?" "Can you at times really feel pleasure at innocent people's death the way I can?" The answer to the question, whether articulated to the patient or not, would be: "Yes, I can feel such excitement, and it is so appalling to me, so frightening to let myself feel such sadism, that I'd rather be repulsed by it in you than recognize and acknowledge it in myself." The analyst here is taking a step to the side; he/she is beside him/herself, dialoguing with him/herself, thinking out loud. Where until now there has been a simple line with patient and therapist at opposite ends, there is now triangular space with some increased room to move. As Benjamin (2004b) has written in commenting on the work of Davies:

 in order to speak about the coercive, hateful, or destructive aspects of the relationship, there must be a shift from destructive, table-turning tit for tat into the mode of feeling free to tell it like it is, to own up to feelings.

(p. 744)

As this illustration makes clear, I do not think of the third as describing a kind of analytic space that exists free of enactment. As Davies (2004) usefully clarifies, the third does not re-establish a form of objectivity free of distortion and co-participation. Rather, it is one step in an always shifting dynamic process, an effort to create a psychic space within which to think together about ways in which patient and analyst are similar and different, merged and separate, identified and differentiated. We should not expect the third to be a stable or static achievement. The nature of thirdness is that it is an ever-shifting, dynamic process. Intersubjectivity consists of a dialectic process of mutual recognition and breakdown into complementarity.

Transference–Countertransference as an Intersubjective Dyadic System

The conceptualization of thirdness presented here clearly rests upon the assumption that transference and countertransference constitute an intersubjective dyadic system continually influencing each other, and must be resolved in relation to each other. Exploring the nature of therapeutic impasses as long ago as 1959, Wolstein defined what he referred to as "transference–countertransference interlocks" (pp. 133–134). Wolstein, whose writing was dense and abstract, was a leading clinician and theoretician within the interpersonal tradition, and his work is hardly known among analysts of other schools, or for that matter outside New York, where he taught and practiced. Wolstein's early portrayal of analytic impasses is remarkably similar to what Benjamin and I have described in our work on the third. Wolstein argued that, in situations of interlock, transference and countertransference automatically emerge in correlation to each other's development. In situations of interlock, that area or dimension where the two co-participants are stuck, "neither participant is capable of free and independent movement" (1959, p. 135). Indeed, Wolstein used the same figures of speech that Benjamin and I have been using, speaking of the "reactive kind of push-and-pull cooperation" (Aron & Benjamin, 1999, p. 137) and of transference and countertransference as "interpenetrating" (p. 141). Wolstein points out that the end result of these interlocks is that either the patient finds a way to leave, or the analyst gives up, by coming to the conclusion that the patient is either too disturbed or unanalyzable. The alternatives to this bleak ending involve the analyst getting supervisory help, or preferably, turning to the person in the best position to make observations about the countertransference—namely, the patient.

In opening him/herself to exploring the countertransference by attending to the observations of the patient, the analyst transcends the dualism that structures the interlock. While not literally utilizing the language of the third, Wolstein anticipated and influenced much of the contemporary relational focus on the interplay of transference and countertransference, mutual enactments, mutual influence, and the intersubjective third. Just as Benjamin and I have placed special importance on the need for analysts to acknowledge their role in creating the impasse, so too Wolstein wrote:

> Once an interlocking of transference and countertransference sets in, the analyst may be said to need his patient's recovery because, in a sense, his own is actually involved. It is not simply a matter of invested time and energy; instead, a real opportunity for personal growth is at stake. This is the crucial dynamism in the experiential field that works toward a therapeutic outcome: both the analyst and his patient have now to find a way to a level of relatedness and integration that will be richer and more meaningful than the one they are capable of at this point.
>
> (1959, p. 169)

Consider the following everyday clinical illustration. A patient arrives minutes late, explaining that the New York City subways were once again running late. She had given herself plenty of time had only the trains been reasonably on time. The patient, however, may go on to blame herself. Of course it was her fault. She should have anticipated the delayed train schedule and left even earlier; it must have been her own resistance. She's not motivated enough, not a good enough patient. Now, of course, the analyst too can become caught up in one of, or alternate between, these two positions, blaming or excusing the patient. The analyst may alternate between wanting to interpret the patient's resistances to the treatment and wanting to interpret the patient's omnipotence in thinking that she can be and should be in such total control of all contingencies. Too often these polarities are enacted between patient and analyst on the seesaw of the transference–countertransference, where one party embodies the accuser and the other the defender, one championing omnipotence and one surrendering to forces beyond one's control. Or in traditional terms, one interprets and one expresses resistance. This back and forth, mutual projection of accusation and defense, interpretation and resistance, resembles the rigid attractor of the fixed seesaw. Here, patient and analyst can so easily become locked into a stalemate or impasse.

But consider what happens when the patient and analyst can play with the fantasy that the patient could control the timing of the trains, or joke about how she wanted to come late and that she wished the trains were delayed, or that she had calculated arriving just after the last train left the station. The patient needs to be able to do this lightly, not sarcastically or cynically or masochistically, moving beyond surrender to the objective facts or omnipotent control of reality, to play in transitional symbolic space (Gentile, 2001). Only with this third possibility, when the patient can entertain the fantasy that she purposefully made the trains late without getting caught up in exonerating herself by pointing to the concrete unavoidable realities and without becoming trapped in omnipotent, masochistic self-blame, guilt and shame—only then can she utilize her free-associative skills that permit the growth of mentalization and symbolization. This is the structure of analytic symbolization.

Let me elaborate several extensions of this illustration. Instead of a late train, consider a patient's playing with getting a cold that keeps him from attending a session, or a young single woman exploring why she never meets eligible men, or a man wondering why he repeatedly ends up working for demanding and authoritarian bosses, or another patient wondering why he always seems to find therapists who get bored and sleepy with him. In each of these instances, both the patient and the analyst can easily fall into the following three positions: (a) they hold the patient responsible, highlighting the patient's agency, but reinforcing omnipotence and masochism; (b) they exonerate the patient of all responsibility, emphasizing material reality and the patient's acceptance of what is beyond his/her control; or (c) the patient and analyst alternate between these two polarities in a series of simple reversals. Only when they are able to achieve a third position, transcending the first two, have they moved beyond sadomasochism, beyond a transference–countertransference interlock, beyond binary thinking, into transitional, symbolic space of thirdness and intersubjectivity.

Psychoanalysis has been plagued by its preoccupation with binaries, polarized between theorists and schools that emphasize drive or culture, self or object, attachment or separation, autonomy or relations, the individual or the social, the intrapsychic or the interpersonal. Within our own dialogue, we as psychoanalysts become stuck in impasses and stalemates, locked in heated battles of these polarized positions. Each theorist or school stares across the divide into its mirror image, locked in complementarity. Conceptualizing the third is one attempt to move beyond such oppositions and to create triangular space within which psychoanalysis too can think more freely, open dialogue, grow, and develop.

References

Aron, L. (1995). The internalized primal scene. *Psychoanalytic Dialogues*, *5*, 195–237.

Aron, L. (1996). *A meeting of minds: Mutuality in psychoanalysis*. Hillsdale, NJ: Analytic Press.

Aron, L., & Benjamin, J. (1999, March). *The development of intersubjectivity and the struggle to think.* Paper presented at the Spring Meeting, Division of Psychoanalysis (39), American Psychological Association, New York, NY.

Bach, S. (2003). A mind of one's own: Some observations on disorders of thinking. In R. Lasky (Ed.), *Symbolization and desymbolization: Essays in honor of Norbert Freedman* (pp. 387–406). New York, NY: Other Press.

Beebe, B., & Lachmann, F. M. (1994). Representation and internalization in infancy: Three principles of salience. *Psychoanalytic Psychology*, *11*, 127–65.

Benjamin, J. (1988). *The bonds of love: Psychoanalysis, feminism and the problem of domination*. New York, NY: Pantheon.

Benjamin, J. (1990). An outline of intersubjectivity: The development of recognition. *Psychoanalytic Psychology*, *7*, 33–46.

Benjamin, J. (1995). *Like subjects, love objects: Recognition and sexual difference*. New Haven, CT: Yale University Press.

Core Competency Four 141

Benjamin, J. (1998). *Shadow of the other: Intersubjectivity and gender in psychoanalysis*. New York, NY: Routledge.

Benjamin, J. (1999). Afterword. In S. Mitchell & L. Aron (Eds.), *relational psychoanalysis: The emergence of a tradition* (pp. 201–210). Hillsdale, NJ: Analytic Press.

Benjamin, J. (2002). The rhythm of recognition: Comments on the work of Louis Sander. *Psychoanalytic Dialogues, 12*, 43–53.

Benjamin, J. (2004a). Beyond doer and done to: An intersubjective view of thirdness. *Psychoanalytic Quarterly, 73*, 5–46.

Benjamin, J. (2004b). Escape from the hall of mirrors: Commentary on paper by Jody Messler Davies. *Psychoanalytic Dialogues, 14*, 743–753.

Benjamin, J. (2005, March). *Our appointment in Thebes: The fear of doing harm, and the need for mutual acknowledgement.* Paper presented at the annual meeting of the Division of Psychoanalysis (39), American Psychological Association, New York, NY.

Bollas, C. (1989). *Forces of destiny: Psychoanalysis and human idiom*. London: Free Association Books.

Britton, R. (1989). The missing link: Parental sexuality in the Oedipus complex. In J. Steiner (Ed.), *The Oedipus complex today: Clinical implications* (pp. 83–102). London, England: Karnac.

Davies, J. M. (2003). Falling in love with love: Oedipal and postoedipal manifestations of idealization, mourning and erotic masochism. *Psychoanalytic Dialogues, 13*, 1–27.

Davies, J. M. (2004). Reply to commentary. *Psychoanalytic Dialogues, 14*, 349–371.

Davies, J. M., & Frawley, M. G. (1994). *Treating the adult survivor of childhood sexual abuse: A psychoanalytic perspective*. New York, NY: Basic Books.

Fonagy, P., Gergely, G., Jurist, E. L., & Target, M. (2004). *Affect regulation, mentalization, and the development of the self*. New York, NY: Other Press.

Gentile, J. (2001, November). *Beyond privacy: Transitional intersubjectivity and the transitional subject.* Paper presented at the 24th Annual International Conference on the Psychology of the Self, San Francisco, CA,

Hoffman, I. Z. (1998). *Ritual and spontaneity in the psychoanalytic process: A dialectical–constructivist view*. Hillsdale, NJ: Analytic Press.

McLaughlin, J. T. (2005). *The healer's bent: Solitude and dialogue in the clinical encounter*. Hillsdale, NJ: Analytic Press.

Ogden, T. H. (1987). The transitional oedipal relationship in female development. *International Journal of Psychoanalysis, 68*, 485–498.

Pizer, S. A. (1998). *Building bridges: The negotiation of paradox in psychoanalysis*. Hillsdale, NJ: Analytic Press.

Singer, E. (1994). *Key Concepts in Psychotherapy* (2nd ed.). Lanham, MD: Jason Aronson.

Wolstein, B. (1959). *Countertransference*. New York, NY: Grune & Stratton.

Chapter 8

Core Competency Five: Patterning and Linking

Steven Knoblauch

Introduction by Roy E. Barsness

The analyst not only considers recurring themes and patterns and how they may be linked to the past and repeated in the here and the now, the analyst attunes to the patterns that emerge *within* the analytic relationship itself. Participants spoke of this as concentrating on patterns of synchronicity and asynchronicity, trying to get a "sense" of the shifts and patterns that happen between the analyst and the patient as they wonder what these shifts might mean. The linking of patterns within the analytic pair are often felt before they are known, appearing, as one participant remarks, "in very primitive ways . . . not from the frontal lobe and the left brain, but from the part of the brain that is registering it at the feeling level." Attending to this intersubjective patterning is evidenced in this study by comments such as "I attend to the artistry of how I am with the patient in the moment." "Everything within the hour has some organizing principle." "The patterning is organic and artistic." "Both [patient and therapist] occupy roles; the question is how is it being played out?" "What is the relationship doing, what can I be doing with my patient, and what is the patient doing to me?" "What are the patterns that we are establishing?" "How are these patterns impacting us right now?"

In this chapter, Steven Knoblauch, psychoanalyst and musician, refers to this process as a "polyrhythmic weave," likening psychoanalysis to the music of the samba, "highlighting in the subtle micromoments of a clinical interaction . . . the emergent affective meanings that are being constituted within the rhythmic dialogue."

Properties of Patterning and Linking

Competency Five: Patterning and Linking	
5.1	Listen for recurring themes and patterns and *within* the analytic dyad.
5.1.1	Shifts and patterns
5.1.2	Roles that are being assigned and played out
5.1.3	Matches and mismatches
5.1.4	Thoughts and affects
5.1.5	Bodily experiences

Patterning and Linking: The Structures and Fluidity of Emotions as a Field of Rhythmic Tensions

In this chapter, we address patterning and linking as a particular segment of a psychoanalytic treatment. Patterning and linking emerge out of the rhythmic underpinnings of affective experiences. This level of experience/communication is nonverbal, even though words also have an embodied dimension expressed through rhythm. You can sense this if you simply repeat a phrase or word and change the accent. For example, say the word "really" with a sharp staccato accent with the "real" spoken louder than the rest of the word, as if the speaker (you) is questioning the authority of what is being offered as real. Then say the word again, this time stretching the "rreeeeaaallly," in a way that slows the pace of your pronunciation and then trails off in volume with a decrescendo that communicates a sense of uncertainty. Now you are attending to the rhythmic (as well as tonal) dimension of communicative interaction which often emerges without reflection. You can feel this dimension as embodied and constituting what we can speak of as intuition. So, sometimes the meaning being communicated might seem quite clear and structured. At other times, such rhythms leave open a range of possibilities as meaning may still be fluid and in formation.

Much like jazz performance, patterning and linking is improvised, as the "musician" (analyst, or sometimes also patient) varies the original tune, inspired by changing affective states, bodily sensations, and nuance. These dimensions have been referred to as the *sub-symbolic* (Bucci, 1997). It is often on sub-symbolic dimensions of interaction that we experience powerful encounters of unconscious processes and deep attunements and intimacy within the therapeutic encounter. Attention to registrations within these dimensions can catalyze meaning-making (the symbolic), where the analytic couple locates metrics, insights, categories, images, and words that give meaning to sub-symbolic experience. But also, and of critical importance for understanding interactive processes, what is sub-symbolic can have affective impact without ever becoming symbolized.

The unique focus of the clinical narrative to follow allows us to think about the patterning and linking between two critical registers of inter-actional experience occurring in real time: (1) that which is expressed as structure with verbal categories for emotional experience such as the feel-ings of joy, sadness, excitement, disgust (the symbolic), and (2) that which is expressed as subtle and fluid (as opposed to structured) registrations of emotional experience (the sub-symbolic). Rather than viewing these as structured categories, they can be detected as crescendos, decrescendos, pauses, accents, rhythmic patterning of both matching and mismatching. We think of these musical thresholds as visceral responses reflected in voice, gesture, posture, face, muscle, and gaze. They occur as sighs, moans, shifting gaze up/down or side to side, with an emphasis on pressure or softness of words in addition to the semantic meaning being communi-cated. These fluid dimensions have also been called "vitality affects" by Daniel Stern (1985, pp. 157–161). With attention to the interaction between these two registers of emotional experience, we sense patterning and link-ing within the analytic encounter in micromoment exchanges shedding light on the past, present, and anticipated experience.

Clinical Illustration[1]

As Denise flopped herself into the chair in front of me, her chest rose, filling with air, as much as she could take in. Then, when fully engorged, she suddenly and swiftly released the gas, with a deep grunt . . . no, growl, much like the trumpeter Rex Stewart would punctuate the plaintive soundscape of an Ellington Depression-era dirge.

It was a cold, damp January morning, dark and lonely, with cloud cover obscuring the few hours of sunlight and relative warmth we are sometimes allowed during these short days of deep winter. Often, and particularly recently, Denise had begun sessions with a similar intake and outflow of air, but the quality of her body resonance, the complex interaction of her abdominal muscles, her throat constriction, and facial display had usually constructed a moan of despair. I was startled and moved in a way I had been when Ornette Coleman's alto saxophone would moan in his free-form jazz solos of the 1960s. Listening to Coleman, I would experience a visceral resonance in the back of my head, gut, and spine, a kind of internal downward spiral toward bottomlessness. Interestingly, I had never attended to Denise's moans with analytic curiosity until this morning. But now I was impacted noticeably by this shift to a grunt. Denise was clearly different, and her gesture cut a definite opening, a shift in my attention to her body and mine and the meanings that were being constructed kinesthetically.

My body? Well, before I could even begin to recognize the difference between now and then, or maybe, as the register in which recognition was first taking shape this morning (the symbolic), I found my gut swept with an indescribable sense that I can only call a soft sadness, a movement in muscles and hormones toward tears (the sub-symbolic). But I did not begin to cry. Rather, I too took in a deep gutful of air. I sensed how it seemed to regulate my sadness, slowing down the muscular constrictions and increasing skin temperature that accompanies the onset of tears. When I had filled to capacity, I released the breath, but with a different resonance, a deep, quiet sound that came from the chest area and was somewhere between a moan and a sigh. Our sound shapes briefly created an area of affective space, a space made possible (at this point, out of our awareness) for something new to begin to emerge. We had co-constructed a pause in time, a possibility of making meaning and some sense of things. But wait, not yet. Suddenly, we seemed to plummet in space as a parachutist out of a plane.

Our eyes met. We exchanged brief, nervous smiles. The tension in the muscles of our faces clearly suggested this was not fun. I could feel it in my response and see it in hers. Now the space was closing, as the time shifted. The rhythms of our "eye dialogue" here were quick and nervous, starting and stopping like the twists and turns that Bartok would command in his compositions, or Cecil Taylor would explode in his piano improvisations. These syncopations, combined with our earlier sound shapes, registered as feelings of uncertainty and hypervigilance.

What we knew from previous patterns and linking of the sub-symbolic to the symbolic is that Denise would feel depleted and hopeless in these states of uncertainty and hypervigilance. She would speak of her sense of failure and inability to measure up to anything of worth in her professional growth and personal life. She could find no satisfaction, no vitality in anything, not in her relations with her colleagues, not in her accomplishments, not in her intimate life. Nothing mattered. And yet she could see how others would tell her that she was performing effectively in her job, or that sex was satisfying and she and her lover were getting along well and fighting with more fairness as compared to earlier in their relationship. But no, nothing was good enough.

But now, something was shifting, a new pattern was emerging. The tug and pull now present between us was seeking new meaning. I noted that Denise seemed hopeless as before, but now rather than depleted, as we began to speak, her tone was strengthening and her rhythmic flow felt full with anger, a different affective texture for our context. Was hopelessness shifting to hope on some unformulated level of experience (Stern, 1997)? I couldn't tell at this point. I began to wonder about her satisfaction with me and the treatment, her inability to find anything good enough in what we were doing and in how responsive or not I had been or was being to her. I noted the parallel meanings to her life descriptions of our work and our relationship. She replied, slightly shifting to sadness, but then regaining the forward movement of her anger. Yes, she said, she was unhappy with what we were doing, or maybe not doing. Then, ambivalently, she once again began to shift, and stated that we had been making some progress. There were those sessions, she said, where she felt we seemed to get very close and deep. And in those brief moments, she did feel as though I was getting her, that she was feeling gotten. We then explored these moments as they occurred earlier, and found them to be shot through with erotic and destructive feelings constructing a kind of mutual devouring and engorging emotional experience of each other. As part of this experience, Denise noted that our week of sessions seemed to have a rhythm marked by a dissociated, devitalizing start and then climaxing in the last session of the week with feelings fraught with complex somatic and semantic encounters that were stimulating, if not overstimulating. But they were never enough. In fact, these encounters would then be drained of all feeling and meaning into some dissociated space by the beginning of the next week.

I had wondered with her in the past about how much she was experiencing me transferentially as devitalizing and as some version of her father. Denise had been very close to her father, and his death had exponentially potentiated her eating disorder and self-mutilating behavior, requiring a series of hospitalizations. I had suggested that maybe, in our weekly rhythms, the death of my affective responsiveness was a re-enacting of the loss of her father. I speculated that the unfolding affective patterning re-created in our work consisted not only of my lack of affect, but also the unbearable sense of her inability to continue to vitalize him or me, for which she either punished herself, as she had previously re-created in her starving and bleeding, or she had dissociated.

Her previous treatments had been a path back to relative satisfaction and relatedness that enabled her to pursue a somewhat successful athletic career as well as higher education for the current professional activity in which she was clearly excelling and developing status and recognition. Still, nothing had ever been enough. She could never hold onto—in fact, even ever feel—a sense of fulfillment or of having enough. We both sat in the silence of the long pause of despair that this emptiness, this absence of presence, had created between and within us. Again, we were constructing, though with significant pain, a space-expanding time warp, an opening for some new melody or syncopation to come forth and begin to constitute a new meaning between us.

I believe that by attending to our rhythms, this "never enough" pattern alerted me to a recognition that I had never asked about (or I had dissociated) of the time in her development when her eating disorder and self-mutilation had begun. We had always focused on the difficulty she had accepting the death of her father. We had never attempted to wonder about the fact that her difficulties had begun much earlier in life, as I now began to remember. My question of when her difficulties began was tentative, but clear. Denise responded to my query with a shift in body, rhythm, and tone. Her face and posture, relaxed. Her tone shifted from the punishing whine of adolescent anger to a lower register of sophisticated curiosity and collaboration. She began to recall how close she had been with her Dad as a child. In fact, she had almost been his little boy. They had done so much together athletically—biking, swimming, mountain climbing and running—she was her father's number one companion in these activities, which they filled themselves with as much as possible.

But now she remembered. It was when she began to grow breasts and her body shifted from that hermaphroditic phase that can be achieved in pre-puberty, but rarely sustained with the onset of menses, that she began to despair and self-destruct. I began to wonder whether her enacted symptoms were a crying out into the world by the "boy" companion she had been to her father and longed to be forever. I wondered of that young "boy's" sense of annihilation and that this version of herself was disappearing and if she felt it would be extinguished by her awful body which refused to obey her desire. The only thing to do was to punish her body, and so she did.

Her eyes widened and her voice shifted to a rhythmic vitality which I could recognize from the past, but never really see and hear as I was hearing now: the voice of that young boy, that subjective experience of being father's special companion that had been sequestered to the ghost realms by the curse of genetic physiology and against which Denise had battled with alcohol, drugs, food and blade, to no avail. Denise spoke more of her relationship with her father, of how wonderful those days were, and of how her father withdrew from her after puberty. It was as if their relationship had died.

Often in our work, in moments like this, our emotional closeness catalyzed powerful feelings of erotic desire or strange dystonic feelings of aggressiveness or fear. But I was now filled with a different set of sensations. I was then reminded of an early childhood experience she had had with boys in which they would play a game of holding someone's head under water until that person was close to drowning, and then at the last minute letting him up for air. There were times I felt as if she were pushing my head under water, forcing me into confusion and self-doubt as to whether or how I could ever be good enough for her as an analyst. As we talked about this, she noted that she had similar feelings as a patient, and as you would expect, this was in line with her self-doubt and denigrating feelings, with which she was constantly haunted. We had observed how much analysis could feel at times to both of us as if we are masochistically holding our heads under water for too long. Now, as I write this narrative, I can see how we constructed a sado-masochistic pattern. We did so by repeatedly enacting the dynamics of her internal struggle with her sequestered "boy" self whom she unconsciously rarely allowed up for air, but whose presence kept popping up in the rhythms and tones between us until now, when I finally could recognize and name him, and begin to sense what it might have felt like to be him.

This shift into vital lively rhythm and tone was suddenly perturbated again. Yes, the aggression seemed present as it had in our earlier patterns, and yes, I wondered if Denise was about to hold my head under once again. But then her verbal stream decelerated. The boyish enthusiasm had left her face and voice, and there was something touchingly girlish and sad in her expression. Her voice came from throat constrictions that construct higher frequencies, from the tonal realm of childhood discourse, a different version of herself. She looked directly into my eyes, her eyes wide with wonder and questioning. She noted that when she thinks of her father in her reveries, it is not the lively companion of her "boyhood." Rather, she sees the dying father gasping for his last breath on his hospital bed. As she spoke, my body filled with feelings that were not erotic, aggressive, or fearful. Rather, I found myself, now unable to use breath to regulate my sadness. A deep and initially indecipherable grief flowed up from within. Then, I experienced a brief internal memory fragment of my father lying in his death as I viewed him before his funeral. My eyes began to fill with tears. Sensing this palpable shift in me, Denise queried, "What's the matter?" There was a tender tone of motherly comfort in the delivery and flow of her utterance, suggesting still another self-state. I wondered if her inability to hold onto feelings of satisfaction with and relatedness to her achievements, colleagues, partner, and me were not colored by the unconscious and, until this moment, dissociated internal tie with her dead father. Stunned, she dropped her gaze to the floor and attempted to self-regulate. She looked up to say she never had considered this, but it felt true. This time, her voice shifted from a soft maternality to a deeper, firmer strength—should I risk saying, paternality? But, no, this was a different sense of authority or agency. This voice seemed to combine the resonance of the rich sounds of multiple self-states—a child's wonder, a mother's capacity to hold and absorb, and a father's capacity for delineation. In fact, these generational and gender stereotypic distinctions fail to discretely capture what more accurately seemed to wash and blur in the unparsed continuous sense of her hermaphroditic voice and body as I sat in my chair still trying to regulate my own flow of teary awe at the depth of connection and companionship that was momentarily filling our space together. Maybe for a moment we were both vulnerable little boys. Or maybe we were just both vulnerable in a heightened momentary flowing sense of self and other and loss, unfettered by discrete categorical distinctions of gender or age.

I close this description still wondering about how this unfolding patterning of tone and rhythm on kinesthetic and affective edges of shifting self-states had affected my own countertransferentially dissociated potential for multiplicity. I wonder how much I was experiencing of my mournful little boy crying with the little boy/girl whose loving father had also died and who couldn't be a little boy anymore. While at the same time I was holding a soft, safe place in time and space, recognizing, reflecting, and delineating in words the significance of the internal presences of an annihilated little boy/girl and dead father which had become black holes of emptiness in Denise's self-experience.

Discussion

As we reflect on the patterning and linking illustrated in this narrative, note that I have and will continue to use musical metaphors to re-present the fluid dimensions of emotional experience. Music carries emotional meanings without giving them a structured, distinct definition. Thus, musical thresholds of experience always carry complex and often difficult to tease out waves of feeling, not always able to be described, except maybe with poetic use of language.

I think of this level of registration as a polyrhythmic weave, a continuous and shifting patterning of accents and pauses built into the prosodic flow of sounds and symbols (worded categories), ebbing and flowing in its significance for attention. This vision provides a way to narrate in a language of process what cannot be narrated in traditional language of discrete categories. But also note how these different registers are mingled at times to create a sense of meaning emerging from what otherwise might be too complex and uncertain to formulate. So let's begin with patterns.

Patterns

One of the most basic elements of human interactional experience to which Freud and Breuer (Breuer and Freud, 1893, p. 15) first gave attention was patterning. In particular, they were interested in the ways humans stored and retrieved patterns of interaction as a process of remembering, compared with enacting or repeating patterns of human interaction without remembering the patterns through reflection. They believed that patterns that were either too intense or too weak to bear emotionally were not registered as categories for memory. This intensity or weakness triggers a process of self-protection from emotional collapse into unbearable guilt, shame, or humiliation. They called this process *repression*. When repressed, such patterns are not able to be linked to present patterned experiences in the imagination/experience of a person who, in fact, experienced such patterning previously.

However, Freud and Breuer also recognized that patterns of enactment were also a way of remembering, of linking the past with the present, and not just with words or visual symbols. Relational psychoanalysis has expanded Freud and Breuer's concept of enactment by emphasizing that when the emotional conditions associated with such patterns are evoked, we enact the patterns without first remembering them. This is a critical point for a relational approach to therapeutic treatment, and evidenced in the clinical narrative with Denise, where patterns emerged as both a product of our capacity for thinking and representing—the symbolic— and in our forms of relating—the sub-symbolic. For example, the narration opens with a description of the process by which Denise and I are communicating emotional experience cross-modally through tone and rhythm of vocalization as well as patterning of gaze. **Taking brief time and space for reflection, I was able to communicate a categorical expression (words) linking the patterning in the moment to a pattern of emotional hopelessness that has been threading through the treatment and which echoes earlier experience.** This illustration helps us to think more about emotional experience (emerging sub-symbolically) as we categorically represent it as feeling (symbolically).

Feelings

What is significant about giving attention to the fluid process dimensions of experience as narrated above is how such attention allows the therapist to move beyond the interpersonal—that is, what is going on, or said another way, what is the patient doing to herself and the therapist, and what is the therapist doing to him/herself and the patient? With attention to the sub-symbolic flow of vitality without giving it categorical meaning, space is created for the emergence of meanings related to the emotional registrations associated with what is going on, but not yet given categorical recognition.

Initially, this level of experience is not consciously detectable. Our attention is expanded beyond interpersonal patterning to what we call intersubjective patterning, where we feel, experience, and begin to create meanings out of what is emerging in our interaction. This kind of attention can help link what is going on between (the intersubjective) to what is going on within (the subjective). In the clinical illustration above, the initial experience of moaning, grunting, shifting in gaze (fluid process cues concerning the polyrhythmic weave), and attending to what is going on between, forms into a patterning that might be given categorical representation as hopelessness. This hopelessness within the patient impacts the therapist so he/she can recognize the significance of the emotional field (intersubjectivity) the two have created. It is the patterning in our vocal exchange and in the rhythms of exchange in our gazes which shape what is going on between. But the rhythms of this patterning also form scaffolding for emotional registrations about ourselves and each other, and what is going on within. For Daniel Stern (1997), attention to these vitality contours offers a window into inner emotional experience that is still too complex and uncertain to be given a formulation. Attention to the fluidity of these registrations as they occur in the present interaction can subsequently catalyze the emergence of categorization through the linking of these registrations to the clinical interaction and then to past experience.

Linking

The process of linking is very central to therapeutic change. Freud saw the analyst's work as making links between what is happening in the session to what happened in the past in order to dissolve the barrier of repressed memories. Building on Freud's ideas, Wilfred Bion (1959) addressed the ways patients attack links, often without conscious awareness that they are doing so. Our understanding is that patients attack links between present patterns of emotional experience and past patterns because the pain of remembering is too emotionally unbearable. Relational analysts have come to understand this kind of attack as a process of dissociation, a numbing or blotting out of emotional registration, a kind of emotional anesthetization.

In relational thinking, we sense the conflict patients experience over wanting to communicate the nature of their pain coupled with their fear of re-experiencing this pain as either too much for them or for us. This conflict often results in the pain being communicated to the therapist within an affective and unconscious patterning that re-enacts the emotional conditions that originally were too painful. The emotional pain associated with the pattern is dissociated and cannot be consciously named, yet emerges in the relational encounter or, as in the clinical illustration, "pops up" in the rhythms being constituted in the interaction.

To demonstrate, let's return to the metaphor of Denise pushing my head under water. In this pattern or rhythm, the patient re-experiences herself as either the aggressor (the doer) or the victim (the done to). And the complement is that the analyst is experienced as the opposite (Benjamin, 2004). In this interaction, Denise is the doer and I am the done to. Her initial response is to dissociate the feelings associated with her shame. But when I do not retaliate (i.e. become the doer to her) and am able to think about the idea of being pushed "below the surface," and to wonder with words about our patterning, I violate her expectations for me to become the doer. My violating her expectations for me to become the doer changes the expected patterning from the past and initiates a new patterning such that her dissociation begins to dissolve. This new patterning, these new rhythms reduce the unbearability of guilt, shame, or humiliation. This is made possible by attending to my inner emotional experience, my emotional vulnerability, intuitions, nuances, and embodied cues signaling me about the unbearability of staying above water for both of us. This shift in rhythm and its emotional significance is catalytic to making meaning from our patterns and rhythms. Dissociation for Denise begins to dissolve, and she begins to emotionally experience her grief over her father's death and what that might mean to her sense of self. This process, not an easy one, involved a struggle to sustain connection to unbearable affective experiences central to psychoanalytic work. Freud formulated it as conflict. However, struggle is not about resolution. Rather, it is about sustaining vitality as opposed to collapsing into states of deadness and emotional anesthetization.

Struggle to Sustain Connection versus Curing Conflict

Early classical psychoanalytic practice was based on the belief that when unconscious conflicts could be made conscious through interpretive work (the use of words to give meaning to what is unconsciously enacted), the patient's suffering would be alleviated and the patient's symptoms could be removed. The analyst would have to be able to recognize and provide words (categories) for what is going on emotionally. This at times could be a challenge, and often too difficult when the analyst's emotional state was overwhelmingly destabilized, as was noted in my struggle with Denise. Furthermore, contemporary relational thinking is no longer built on a goal of cure through interpretation and the lifting of symptoms (an artifact of a medical model of treatment), but on the goal of helping the patient expand his/her sense of self-expression (an expansion of possibility), and his/her capacity to recognize another through the intersubjective experience with the analyst. Recognition involves attention to sameness and difference between self and other. As noted in the case of Denise, attending to the tension of difference through the varying patterns that emerged, though initially emotionally destabilizing, these tensions brought about a reworking of meanings associated with past historical traumas. So, rather than cure, Denise and I—through sustained emotional engagement—were able to create a space of affective bearability which increased her ability to attend to multiple dimensions of self-expression. This process of emotional engagement facilitated an increased capacity for recognition of another, and an enhanced sense of mutuality and agency between self and others.

Complexity Theory suggests that recognition is an elusive process because, as we interact with others, we are continuously changing, sometimes dramatically, but often in subtle ways. Recognition, therefore, is not a goal, but a struggle to sustain an emotionally meaningful contact with one's own experience, and always in the context of the emotional experiences of others. This was the struggle evidenced in my work with Denise, where we sought to sustain connection in the midst of shifting affective states. Therefore, it is important to note that recognition often seems to lag behind the emotional meanings we and others struggle to experience and understand.

If we accept that recognition is a process of bringing into conscious reflection something that was previously unconscious, then we can see that recognition is pivotal to the process of therapeutic work with unconscious experience and the transferences and the countertransferences. Furthermore, we can see how attention to the subtle patterning of embodied registrations in self and other help us in this process of recognition.

The challenge in achieving moments of recognition is related in part to what the patient is able to bring to us that has been for him/her emotionally unbearable. Here, I wish to make a distinction between the idea of containment and navigation. Rather than try to contain that which has not attained a level of form or structure and is therefore quite fluid, we use our awareness of the complexity of emotional rhythms to navigate and contain.

Navigation versus Containment

In contemporary psychoanalytic writing, an idea first introduced by Wilfred Bion (1970) is used quite frequently to describe a process whereby emotions which are either too powerful or too weak to be reflected upon (given categorical representation) are transformed into something that can be useful for self-reflection and interpersonal relating. This is the concept of *containment*. When we contain an emotion, we are giving it articulation so that it can be experienced without flooding or shutting down our emotional responsiveness to ourselves or others (dissociation). This is a process whereby emotionally difficult experiences (i.e., unbearable guilt, shame, humiliation, etc.) can become "cooled off" or made bearable. This was demonstrated in the clinical illustration when I did not fulfill Denise's expected patterning associated with her emotional suffering. Though containment is a helpful and important technique, I would argue it is too limiting, and often forecloses important movements within the therapeutic relationship. Too often the technical guideline for containment involves some kind of interpretive strategy—that is, the use of words. While this strategy can be effective and the literature is full of examples, what are less frequently described are instances when words fail to contain. Often a failure in containment occurs because verbalization of the patient's experience by the analyst is experienced by the patient as a negative judgment, or even attack. When faced with such a dilemma, the analyst can become speechless, not as a strategy for giving the patient space to connect to his/her emotional/imaginative processes, but speechless out of fear, vulnerability, and/or hopelessness. This occurred in the moment when I came in touch with the grieving for my own father that resonated with Denise's loss. This is an important distinction, and one that therapists often have difficulty making. This difficulty arises because it is in just such moments of fear, vulnerability, and/or hopelessness that an analyst might be best served by shifting his/her attention from the question "What is going on?" to the question "What am I feeling, and how might this be related to what the patient is feeling?" **It is important to note that the question "What am I feeling, and how is this related to the patient?" is not to be answered with a cognitive formulation, but rather to be used to help the therapist connect to his/her inner emotional registrations, embodied as somatic or emerging as fantasies concerning desire or danger.** The moment when I began to tear up with Denise and the recognition and response that it catalyzed for her is an effective illustration of this process.

Therefore, to account for attention to the emotional fluidity of embodied registrations, I prefer to use the term *navigating* rather than containing. In a process of navigating, the therapist is holding affective patterns lightly, as softly assembled. The therapist is cautious about creating "too much" or "too little" emotional responsiveness that could constrict or foreclose.

Our intent is to meet the patient in a space that is not so much a place of matching, but a space for creating a pattern of connection that emerges as a midrange of emotional exchange. The rhythms in such a space have points of matching and mismatching. What is most useful and easier to attend to is not so much those points, but the larger patterning of syncopation or its failure. Syncopation, or weaving together of both points of match and mismatch and other dimensions of the exchange, can create a sense of connection or failure to connect. This polyrhythmic weave of the patient's and our gaze, posture, rhythms, and tonality, all on display in our bodies, catalyzes and destabilizes, fluidly forming and informing. These cues provide complex (and yes, often uncertain) washes of experience which can either slowly or quickly form into some sense of emotional meaning. This process of navigating seems to catalyze experiences of containment and formulation because the struggle to attend to the subtle, below-the-surface emotional cues creates a sense of shared struggle, shared commitment, a we-ness (see examples in the work of Spezzano, 1993, p. 47, and Nebbiosi, 2016, pp. 6–7). I have found this process that Daniel Stern (1997) calls communion a powerful form of human collaboration in the face of difficult and complex emotional stretches in psychoanalytic treatment.

Summary

With an extended illustration of a brief stretch of clinical encounter, we have examined how patterning and linking can occur with a different kind of attention than was initially thought to be catalytic in therapeutic treatment. Originally, attempts to cure emotional suffering psychotherapeutically were constituted with carefully thought through verbal interpretations of patterning that were assumed to lift repression and create links between present and past emotional experiences. But often, verbal interpretations can be experienced as attacks or intellectually distanced critical judgments that only contribute to an ongoing difficulty in recognizing and expressing emotional experience. In this chapter, we have expanded the linking process with a focus on the way that embodied registrations in both clinician and patient form into patterns. When these patterns are recognized, they help link emotional experiences to the past, each other, and to affects previously too intense to bear that have become dissociated and are not linked to recognizable emotional meanings occurring in real time. This process of attention and communication on these subtle registrations of embodied rhythms (the polyrhythmic weave) opens up previously closed or ignored possibilities for interactive experience and the emergence of emotional meaning. These meanings form into categories which we call feelings that help us to navigate the emotional dimensions of our interactions with others. In this way, we and our patients contribute to a process of recognition, expanding our sense of self and its impact on others, as well as their emotional impact on us.

Note

1   The clinical narrative is excerpted from a previously published paper (Knoblauch, 2005).

References

Benjamin, J. (2004). Beyond doer and done to: An intersubjective view of thirdness. *Psychoanalytic Quarterly*, *73*, 5–46.

Bion, W. R. (1959). Attacks on linking. *International Journal of Psychoanalysis*, *40*, 308–315.

Bion, W. R. (1970). *Attention and interpretation.* London, England: Tavistock Publications.

Breuer, J., & Freud, S. (1893). On the psychical mechanism of hysterical phenomena: A preliminary communication. In J. Strachey (Ed. & Trans.), *The standard edition of the complete psychological works of Sigmund Freud* (Vol. 2). London, England: Hogarth Press.

Bucci, W. (1997). *Psychoanalysis and cognitive science: A multiple code theory.* New York, NY: Guilford Press.

Knoblauch, S. H. (2005). Body rhythms and the unconscious: Toward an expanding of clinical attention. *Psychoanalytic Dialogues*, *15*, 807–827.

Nebbiosi, G. (2016). The smell of paper: On the usefulness of musical thought in psychoanalytic practice. *Psychoanalytic Dialogues*, *26*, 1–9.

Spezzano, C. (1993). *Affect in psychoanalysis: A clinical synthesis.* Hillsdale, NJ: Analytic Press.

Stern, D. B. (1997). *Unformulated experience: From dissociation to imagination in psychoanalysis.* Hillsdale, NJ: Analytic Press.

Stern, D. N. (1985). *The interpersonal world of the infant: A view from psychoanalysis and developmental psychology.* New York, NY: Basic Books.

Chapter 9

Core Competency Six: Repetition and Working Through

Karen J. Maroda

Introduction by Roy E. Barsness

The role of conflict has always been a central theme in psychoanalysis. The relational analyst expands traditional psychoanalytic theory on conflict, holding to the view that understanding intrapsychic conflict in and of itself is insufficient. Believing that deep change occurs at the emotional level, the relational analyst attends to the inevitable conflicts and impasses that emerge *within* the therapeutic relationship by the working through of differences, ruptures, entanglements, and enactments: "Although such ruptures of the alliance are the most stressful moments of the treatment, these 'collisions' of the therapist's and the patient's subjectivities also represent an intersubjective context of potential 'collaboration' between their subjectivities, and thereby a context of interactive repair—a fundamental mental mechanism of therapeutic change" (see Schore, Chapter 13 in this volume, p. 252).

In the chapter that follows, Karen Maroda speaks to inevitability of enactment and to its therapeutic potential, with an emphasis on:

> how ubiquitous it is and on how equally inevitable is the evocation of the analyst's past in terms of re-creating an emotional scenario. I want to emphasize that although it necessarily involves action, enactment is essentially an affective event. The action carries the purpose of fully expressing the intense emotion at the heart of the transference–countertransference exchange.
>
> (Maroda, 1998, p. 534)

Though enactments have generally been thought of as an unconscious event, Dr. Maroda extends our understanding of enactment as not only occurring unconsciously, but also at the conscious level. She contends that strong emotional experiences in the countertransference, especially negative ones, are rarely out of awareness. She then acknowledges that though therapists tend to be conflict-avoidant, therapeutic change occurs by facing and facilitating conflict within the therapeutic relationship.

Properties of Repetition and Working Through

Repetition and Working Through

6.1 As deep change occurs at the emotional level, the analyst attends to the inevitable conflicts that emerge in the relational dyad.
    6.1.1 Works through enactments
    6.1.2 Holds to the view of the necessity of destruction, survival and recognition
    6.1.3 Rupture and repair is inherent in any authentic relationship, and leads to change

Enactment and Beyond: Facilitating Constructive Conflict in the Therapeutic Relationship

Enactment has become the latest popular idea in psychoanalysis as we struggle to resolve the sticky problem of conflict between analyst and patient. As co-participants in the therapeutic relationship, we have been reluctant to initiate conflict through confrontation because of our perceived role as "good enough" caregivers who create a holding environment. Our job has been viewed as one where conflict is inevitable, but something we prefer not to be in charge of (hence the appeal of enactment as an unconscious to unconscious uncontrolled event).

Actually facilitating conflict has about as much appeal as dropping a baby on its head. Yet if we look closely at our relationships with our patients, we can tease out the threads of ongoing, often unspoken conflict. By definition, these conflicts are rooted in differences. These differences emerge due to the asymmetry and power relations between analyst and patient; in sexual tension; in differing values based on culture, sexual orientation, socioeconomic status, age and gender; in intergenerational competition, or in some perceived slight or insensitivity.

The relationship is not stagnant. Rather, it is an organic, ever-shifting one where different conflicts can dominate at different times. The challenge is knowing how to facilitate manageable levels of conflict, rather than avoiding them. This chapter focuses both on the theoretical issues of enactment, the analyst's fiduciary responsibility to facilitate conflict rather than waiting for it to happen, and on often unspoken conflicts that may go unrecognized for a variety of reasons, particularly the analyst's defense against being the "bad enough mother" (Mendelsohn, 2002).

If we closely examine the place of conflict in the analytic relationship, it becomes evident that we intellectually accept the desirability, if not necessity, of some degree of conflict inherent in the process. Transference–countertransference has never been described as an ongoing, harmonious event, yet as human beings, analysts naturally struggle with the reality of their patients noting their faults and/or being aggressive toward them. We cannot escape our hard-wired inclinations to defend ourselves and to either escape or resolve conflict as quickly as possible. Indeed, the issue of how much conflict, and for how long, is also a controversial topic. What constitutes negative therapeutic action (the eroding of the therapeutic alliance) versus the emergence of essential negative emotions and attributions (formally called the emerging transference neurosis)?

Safran and Muran's (2002) instructive book focuses on quickly repairing ruptures and restoring the therapeutic alliance, which is all well and good if the rupture is a potentially relationship-breaking one. But in the age of a psychoanalysis informed deeply by Winnicott's (1986) concept of "good enough" caretaking, and the extensive literature on attachment and affective attunement (Stern, 1985), might we be rushing to pick up the proverbial crying infant too soon? And in the age of diversity, might we be afraid of stirring any conflict with patients who are racially, sexually, religiously, ethnically, or otherwise different from ourselves, for fear of acting out of either conscious or unconscious bias?

For example, a first-generation Hmong patient, who I will call Pao, was newly graduated from business school, and presented with anxiety and depression. Incredibly symbiotic with his family of origin, he talked about them extensively, including his difficult childhood in a house overcrowded with extended family, situated in a poor neighborhood. Thirty years old, good-looking, sensitive, and intelligent, it seemed odd he had never had a long-term romantic relationship. He was a bit of a womanizer, flitting from one brief affair or one-night stand to another, but never committing. He spent his weekends returning to another city where his family lived, because he was very close to an aunt who had essentially raised and nurtured him while his mother worked and watched over their large extended family.

He had few friends. His peer friendships were mostly relatives and friends from childhood, who also lived in his home town. He took great pride in giving money to his family as soon as he began earning a good salary. He worried about their financial security, and dreamed of rescuing them financially. They were a genuinely loving and supportive family who immigrated to the US shortly before Pao was born. For me, the many healthy aspects of their family life made it more difficult to tease out the degree to which he was overly involved with them versus fulfilling his culturally expected role. He let me know that some people thought it was odd that he went home so often, but this was what was done in the Hmong community.

Initially, Pao said very little about his social life, other than noting that his goal of finding a loving woman and getting married seemed at odds with spending almost all of his free time with his family. He agreed, yet continued with this behavior. When he tried to stay put for the weekend, he became anxious and depressed, sometimes resulting in his going out and drinking too much. When I inquired about possible sources of his anxiety and depression, he would simply state that he felt lonely, or that he was overtired and sleep-deprived (which he often was), and when he "crashed" on the weekend, he experienced these emotions.

However, the longer I knew Pao, the clearer it was to me that he suffered from intense separation anxiety and dependency. He was completely lost whenever he had free time and couldn't be with his family. And although there was certainly a cultural component to his closeness with his family that might not apply to other ethnic groups in the US, his inability to separate enough from his family of origin to establish close relationships was indeed a therapeutic issue.

I was admittedly reluctant to pursue this issue with Pao, in part because he seemed to take offense when I first suggested that perhaps he could spend more time out socially rather than going home every weekend. I said he appeared to have not really ever left home. My comments were made within the first six months of treatment, and Pao was not ready to hear them. He let me know that I did not fully understand Hmong culture and what was normative within it. Having known other Hmong people, I knew this was not entirely true. What was true was that Pao was not ready to face this issue, and feared that I would not understand him because of our cultural differences.

After about a year of treatment, he asked me one day what I thought his real problem was. He accurately noted that although he was doing better at work (now up for a promotion, when he had been having some problems before), happy to be making more money, and also no longer clinically depressed, he still knew we had not defined his core issues. I decided that our relationship was now strong enough that I told him point blank that he suffered from severe separation anxiety. I couched this within the context of acknowledging the deep loving attachment he had with his family, noting that he didn't need to give that up. He just needed to find out who he was as a separate person and be able to tolerate this individuated state.

But that would never happen unless he took steps to practice being away from them—and he would have to tolerate bouts of anxiety and learn to manage them in order to achieve this. This was not welcome news to Pao, but this time, instead of seeing me as the unempathic "other," he understood that my confrontation was in his best interest. He said he knew I was right—that he couldn't possibly meet anyone as long as he was always with his family. He was also embarrassed by how dependent he was. He said he wanted to try and change.

The following months were marked by new optimism and enthusiasm on Pao's part, punctuated with loneliness and anxiety as he titrated his weekends, one with family, and one without. Sometimes he didn't make it all the way through on his own, getting in his car on Sunday and going to see his family. Eventually, he began to make attachments in the city and establish social routines, including dating. And there were times when he would slip into getting overly involved with family situations, increasing his family's dependence on him for money and advice. I confronted him gently on these issues, interpreting that the interdependency was both familiar and made him feel good when even his elders came to him to make decisions. The price of independence meant giving that up in exchange for other gratifications.

Given Pao's ambivalence about being separate from his family, it was not easy to continuously confront him with his behavior. The fact that he had earlier questioned my cultural sensitivity naturally made me more cautious. I could have escaped the discomfort that initially followed my confrontations of Pao by simply accepting what he said about his cultural norms. And I knew I risked losing him as a patient because of his intense loyalty to his family and, early in the treatment, his difficulty in finding any fault with them.

As you might expect, his view of me and responses to me echoed his relationship with his family. He was initially idealizing and deferent, which I found vaguely disquieting. Over time, when I noticed a slight frown or him physically turning away from me, I asked him what he was feeling. It took quite some time, but he eventually began to criticize me, and discovered that I was not the "perfect" analyst he thought I was. He was particularly irritated after a session where I gave him unsolicited advice (something I believe is rarely helpful, but ended up doing anyway). He responded with the deep resentment that he has harbored for years against his parents, who constantly infantilized him by worrying excessively about him and giving him advice he did not need or want.

Working effectively with Pao meant being willing to engage in a steady, low-level conflict that did not interfere with our basic strong therapeutic alliance, even when I had to challenge his behaviors that were to some degree culture-based or reinforced. The next natural progression was for me to help tease out his negative feelings toward me and realize that our relationship would not be destroyed by his finding me to be less than perfect. I believe my willingness to confront him on a regular basis minimized the need for enactment, which I see as occurring too frequently due to suppressed conflicts between analyst and patient.

Therapist Avoidance of Conflict

I believe, and have stated elsewhere (Maroda, 2010), that therapists are a particularly conflict-avoidant group due to our roles as soothers and peace-keepers in our families of origin. We deny some of our basic motivations for becoming analysts in the first place, which were to soothe and rescue family members in pain—particularly our mothers (Sussman, 2007; Jacobs, 1986). We deny our identification with our patients, primarily our own intense, ambivalent relations to our own mothers, and our desire to save them, along with our desire to be saved ourselves. This identification contributes to the avoidance of conflict that is rampant in therapeutic circles.

We also shun conflict to avoid separation and loss. If the patient leaves, have we failed as the "good enough caregiver"? To some extent, our mothers failed us, and we tried to rescue them, both out of love and a desire to restore them to good enough mother status. Ultimately, we did not have the power to heal them, only to momentarily soothe or entertain. So isn't each new treatment an attempt at both rescuing the mother anew and also a wish to be rescued ourselves, as Searles (1979) asserted?

As therapists, we are in a position to both observe and confront our patients with their maladaptive behaviors and misconceptions, and confirm their impact on others around them. But how many of us are comfortable doing this, or even see this as part of our responsibility toward our patients? Trying to find literature on the therapist's avoidance of conflict is indeed an act of frustration. Klein, Bernard, and Schermer (2010) provide one of the few brief references to therapist conflict avoidance, saying that **we tend to "confuse being nice with being useful."** Psychotherapy research (Farber, Berano, & Capobianco, 2004) has shown not only that therapists' assessments of outcome are much more positive than clients', but also that clients wish their therapists had pursued their "secrets" more aggressively and been more confrontational.

Most patients do not want to be confronted with their negative behaviors at the onset of treatment. They are understandably in pain and looking precisely for the soothing, empathic stance that we favor. But I firmly believe that a passive, accepting stance is not in the patient's best interest over time. And I agree with Hirsch (2008), who advises "a statute of limitations" (p. 186) on providing a holding environment. In supervising even experienced therapists, it is common that they avoid simple confrontations that are essential for keeping the boundaries, such as failure to pay the bill, and wanting to text after hours and on weekends. The typical rationalization centers on believing that the patient will come around when he/she is ready and will voluntarily cease the negative behavior. But from my experience, this rarely works out, particularly if we are talking about boundary issues. Rather, the therapist builds up resentment and discomfort, leading to some type of acting out or "enactment." Langs (1973) says therapists tend to be passive aggressive. Arriving late, cancelling or frequently rescheduling sessions, treating the patient with a noticeable patronizing air of superiority all point to a therapist who cannot bear his/her own negative feelings toward patients.

Bird's (1972) classic article on transference neurosis, which is basically a treatise on transference–countertransference conflict, has been oft-cited and admired, yet the lack of implementation of his ideas stands as a testament to our reluctance to be in conflict with our patients. Bird notes that Freud did say the resolution of a transference neurosis was required for a successful analysis, but he also notes Freud's mention of the difficulties involved. Bird says:

> Is he [Freud] saying, as I think likely, how very hard it is *on the analyst* to work effectively with the transference neurosis? We forget

sometimes that a neurosis is based upon conflict and that what is specific about a transference neurosis is the active involvement of the analyst in the central crunch of this conflict. The wear and tear of this abrasive experience can be considerable and must surely be one of the major reasons some analysts pull away from the transference neurosis and away from analysis itself.

(p. 278, original emphasis)

The profound difficulty in being in conflict with our patients (what Bird describes as allowing the transference neurosis to emerge) can be seen in the aforementioned trajectory of terms like "projection" and "projective identification." Projections involved the patient accusing the analyst of behavior or attitudes that were actually his/her own. Projective identification became the name for when the analyst or therapist began to unconsciously absorb intense, usually negative, feelings the patient was experiencing but could not directly express. Feelings of anger, despair, and/or hopelessness were cited in the literature as being "dumped" onto the unsuspecting analyst by the patient.

Over time, it became contradictory within the two-person, intersubjective perspective to "blame" the patient. The new emphasis was on how affect was mutually communicated within the therapeutic dyad, both consciously and unconsciously. Frequent references to projection and projective identification were gradually replaced with references to enactment, where patient and analyst join together, unconsciously, to mutually generate past conflicts that have become uniquely alive in the present.

The Classical analytic view, of course, revolved around a fairly standard set of thoughts, feelings, and behaviors that the patient established early in life in relation to his/her caregivers, and then re-created in any deep relationship. Within this view, the analyst merely inquires, makes interpretations, perhaps empathizes, remains neutral and steady; then one day the patient feels safe and sufficiently attached to take a critical stand against the analyst. From a classical perspective, this was totally impersonal. Analysts were seen as virtually interchangeable, and had no real *personal role* in stimulating the transference–countertransference conflict. Upon receipt of the patient's primitive hostile and sexual feelings, the analyst interpreted what he/she saw, usually referencing how the patient's feelings belonged more properly in relation to his/her early caretakers.

Within this context, the analyst did not contribute to the conflict, and was therefore not responsible and was found "not guilty" of any wrongdoing or bad intentions. It is obvious to anyone who reads this that this perspective could not be reasonably sustained, and it was, indeed, overturned more than 30 years ago by the British Independents (Balint, 1968; Bollas, 1986; Casement, 1985; Winnicott, 1953), who placed object-seeking as the primary human motivation rather than the gratification of drives; the interpersonalists (Horney, 1939; Fromm-Reichman, 1953; Levenson, 1987; Sullivan, 1953; Thompson, 1940), who also repudiated drive theory in favor of focusing on the patient's interpersonal relationships, both past and present; and the relational analysts (Aron, 1991; Bromberg, 1993; Davies & Frawley, 1992; Ghent, 1990; Greenberg and Mitchell, 1983; Hoffman, 1983; Mitchell, 1988; Maroda, 1998), who not only built upon the aforementioned emphasis on relationships over drives as the chief motivational force in human behavior, but also introduced the notion of the analyst's ongoing personal contributions to the current relationship with the patient and the need to address these in treatment.

The two-person movement redefined projective identification, not as an attempt on the patient's part to dump negative affect on the analyst and attempt to ruin the treatment, but rather a more innocent attempt at unconscious to unconscious communication of unbearable feelings (Aron, 1991; Hoffman 1983; Maroda, 1998; Renik, 1993, and many others). **We began to view the patient not as someone intent on ruining the treatment, but rather as co-creator of the relationship, trying desperately to communicate his reality in any way he could.** Concurrently, the very notion of a neutral observer was justifiably thrown out as unviable, and everyone from the British Independents to the Interpersonalists to the relational theorists began to redefine virtually every aspect of the analytic relationship within the parameters of a jointly created event.

Furthermore, in the last two decades, Allan Schore (2011) has made an invaluable contribution to examining the critical role of emotion in every relationship, from our earliest attachment to what transpires in the therapeutic dyad. His neuroscience findings have confirmed that psychoanalysts contribute to the ongoing dynamic relational dyad in a deeply emotional way that is both conscious and unconscious.

The relational analyst was also now on the hook for being a real human being, with real contributions to what happened moment-to-moment in the treatment, for better or worse. When conflicts arose within the treatment, marked by some untoward and unexpected behavior, from protracted silence to a mutual burst of anger, the term "enactment" gradually replaced references to projection and projective identification, because they placed all the responsibility for what was happening on the patient. Even "mutual projective identification" was abandoned because, as noted by Hirsch (1996), it fails to meet the standard inherent in enactment of some action taking place, which goes beyond the stimulation of emotion. New terminology was required to accurately describe analysis as a mutual, albeit asymmetrical, relationship where strong emotions are stirred up and acted out.

The New Emphasis on Enactment

The burgeoning of the two-person literature occurred in the 1980s, and the term "enactment" was coined by analyst Theodore Jacobs in 1986. Interestingly, he identified the analysts' early experience as the family peacemaker (referenced earlier in this chapter as a source of conflict avoidance) as something that was a potential source of unconscious distortion and acting out by the analyst.

For many colleagues, the experiences in childhood and adolescence of being an empathic listener to parents or other family members have played a role of importance in their choice of vocation. It is not a rare occurrence for the memories of these experiences to be evoked in the analytic situation. When these experiences are outside of awareness, the analyst's usually valuable empathic responses may contain enactments of those memories— enactments which, subtly, can alter and distort his perceptions and understanding (Jacobs, 1986, p. 296).

Chused (1997), McLaughlin (1991), Renik (1997), Hirsch (1996), and Levenson (1996) joined in the conversation about just what constituted enactment and whether or not it was something to be avoided or welcomed. Gradually, enactment has come to be broadly accepted as a mutually created unconscious to unconscious communication that results is some unplanned behavior. In my own work on enactment (Maroda, 1998), I defined it as follows:

> Enactment is an affectively driven repetition of converging emotional scenarios from the patient's and the analyst's lives. It is not merely an affectively driven set of behaviors; it is necessarily a repetition of past events that have been buried in the unconscious due to associated unmanageable or unwanted emotion.
>
> (p. 519)

The goals I had in writing that paper were to delineate enactment at a deeper level, promote understanding of its inevitability, and to emphasize that it was possible to minimize enactments through greater self-awareness and selective disclosure of ongoing countertransference feelings that typically precede an enactment.

At the same time, I understand and appreciate that enactment can signal a dynamic and transformational shift in therapeutic relationships, particularly if analysts are open to constructively expressing their disavowed feelings that are suddenly acted out. As I stated in 1998:

> Believing that giving the patient an emotionally honest response, in the moment, is essentially therapeutic—provided that the analyst expresses him/herself clearly and responsibly the majority of the time—is at the heart of accepting enactment as inevitable and potentially useful. Accepting that patient and analyst are fated to move each other in mysterious and unplanned ways leaves room for accepting being both the recipient and the stimulator of intense, unexpected emotion. And this acceptance leaves further room for exploring the most therapeutic ways in which to work through the re-created scenes from the past.
>
> (Maroda, 1998, p. 533)

Are Strong Emotions Conscious?

Levenson (1996), Renik (1997), and the Boston Change Process Study Group (2010) still contend that countertransference emotions cannot be experienced consciously, but rather come into awareness only after an enactment has taken place. The Boston Change Process Study Group has probably contributed the most to what I call the "enactment as moving train" position, due to their questionable application of neuroscience literature as a basis for elevating enactment to what could be labeled as the sine qua non of the therapeutic action of analysis.

Declaring that since most human communication is a right brain to right brain, unconscious experience, it stands to reason that knowledge of both the analyst's and patient's true inner emotions can only result from an unplanned behavioral event (see Modell, 2008) for a critique about this application of neuroscience. Thus, the role of the analyst is to provide a safe holding environment that promotes enactment. The analyst's skills come into play both in his/her ability to establish a genuine positive alliance and in the post-enactment processing. Ideally, the post-enactment processing leads to greater self-awareness, integration, and self-acceptance. As popular as this positioning of enactment has become in recent years, there are still those, in addition to myself, who question what Richards, Bachant, and Lynch (1997) have called "the valorization of enactment." For example, Chused defined enactment as "a *jointly created interaction*, fueled by unconscious psychic forces in both patient and analyst" (1997, p. 264, original emphasis). However, she goes on to make two very salient points:

> A patient's understanding of an enactment within the analytic relationship will be determined by the patient's psychic reality, by how he perceives and understands the analyst's behavior, not by the analyst's understanding of the enactment.
>
> (p. 267)

> An enactment can inform us, but it can also misinform us. The very issues that led to the enactment, the unconscious conflicts in the analyst that have been stimulated, are active at the time of the enactment and will call forth defenses in the analyst, including that of inaccurate self-understanding.
>
> (p. 268)

I agree with Chused that the notion that enactments are fairly benign and amenable to resolution and understanding denies the complexities of these events. Given that enactment is born of two sets of internal unconscious conflicts colliding simultaneously, the outcome seems as likely to go awry as to go well. I accept enactment as inevitable, but also remain skeptical about accepting it as the new "royal road to the unconscious." What do I propose instead?

First, I want to challenge the idea that strong countertransference emotions are almost always out of awareness and can only be known after they have been enacted. The research on affect has shown that strong affective responses, especially negative ones (which are more likely to be suppressed), are rarely out of awareness. It is hypothetically part of our hard-wired defensive system not to ignore threats of any kind.

I find that not only am I usually aware of my strong countertransference feelings, so are other clinicians I talk to and supervise. It is the exception, rather than the norm, that strong countertransference feelings are completely out of awareness over time. I think there is a marked tendency for most clinicians to minimize feelings that could potentially undermine the treatment, such as falling in love with a patient, being strongly sexually attracted to a patient, or being murderously enraged at one. Perhaps we would benefit from focusing more on the awareness of countertransference feelings and the inevitability of their being acted out in some way if they are not managed either intrapsychically or through an interpersonal exchange with the patient.

Subtle feelings can easily be repressed, but the more intense feelings, particularly intense negative feelings, are less likely to be out of awareness. This level of awareness applies equally to therapist and patient. Panskepp (2000) notes, however, that milder affective states can also remain in awareness, and "only become unfelt in the presence of too much competing cognitive activity."(p. 46)—a reason for analysts to interrupt the patient's defensive verbosity, even when it is entertaining or contains some insight.

The aforementioned research clearly debunks the notion that unconscious affective experience remains unconscious until it is enacted. **The very foundation of psychoanalysis is that unconscious feelings and thoughts can be brought into awareness and expressed, creating the necessary conditions for working through.**

Facilitating Conflict

There are numerous obstacles to therapists becoming less conflict-avoidant and more skilled at actually facilitating both conscious conflicts that can be observed, and the aforementioned out-of-awareness enactments. First and foremost are analysts' fears of facing their own conflicts with their early caretakers, especially regarding any primitive rage that may be difficult to manage and put into perspective in the current work with a patient (recall Jacobs' earlier definition of enactment, where he emphasizes the analyst's participation as being rooted in both his/her own early experiences and his/her desire to be a peacekeeper). I think that both personal analysis and training programs need to place more emphasis on therapists being more aware of their internal need to overcompensate for early aggressive feelings and accompanying guilt and shame, and should focus on actively debunking the myth of the therapist as an all-accepting, loving surrogate parent. I say this with full understanding that being a genuinely caring and empathic person is highly desirable in our profession. I am only interested in removing the exaggerated need for perfection, and the denial of primitive feelings that lie within all of us.

The second obstacle to therapists being more active and facilitating inevitable conflicts rather than extinguishing them as quickly as possible is the simple fact that there is little or no training provided in this area. We are trained to listen, trained to ask relevant questions, trained to respond empathically, trained to interpret. For the most part, we were not trained to actively engage in the process of being in conflict. The old model, which is still used extensively, is to listen to the patient's negative feelings toward us, acknowledge them, and move on.

The idea of expressing our own feelings in a well-thought out, in-control, manner that also retains emotion, thus engaging in an affective-driven exchange, remains somewhat alien, and even frightening. Volunteering observations of the patient may be equally uncomfortable. Particularly for neophyte therapists, I am sympathetic to the idea that it is better to play safe and do little if you don't really know what to do.

Yet I feel confident we can do a better job of stimulating both the patient's internal conflicts and the conflicts that are occurring in the therapeutic dyad. My experience with supervision has taught me that most therapists tire of their passive role, but are afraid of doing harm if they become more active without sufficient understanding of the therapeutic benefits of doing so. Getting this feedback from both new and seasoned therapists prompted me to provide guidelines for both using active interventions and assessing their effectiveness (see Maroda, 2010).

The Case of Jane—Intentions

Jane is a middle-aged, accomplished professor of literature who is accustomed to having admiring students taking her every word as Gospel and who debates her intellectual points with speed and dexterity. Presented with some disparity between her actions and her beliefs, or between her facial expressions and expressed feelings, she will quickly spin a narrative that serves her defenses at the moment. If I note a negative behavior or feeling of hers, or of someone close to her, she will often question my motives for doing so.

Panskepp (2000) speaks eloquently about the different styles and potentialities of the left and right brain, and the dance they do together, noting we commonly speak out one side of our mouth, with the left brain expressing the linguistic skills. Jane is a perfect example of this, as she literally pulls up one side of her mouth at the end of a defensive sentence. Panskepp says:

> The left hemisphere, in its appointed role of projecting an image of positive social desirability into the world, is not only an "interpreter" (Gazzaniga, 1998), but also a skilled confabulator, especially when it comes to trying to deal with emotional experiences, which are felt more intensely by its more passive and silent partner.
>
> (p. 243)

Jane has been feeling angry lately due to her husband's decision to make a job change requiring them to move an hour away and give up the home she has lovingly restored for the past ten years, including creating beautiful gardens she planted herself. Unable to express her anger at him for causing the move and for insufficiently discussing this decision with her, she has found herself getting unduly angry with a variety of service people and strangers.

The other day, she began her session by describing how she was walking back to her car in a store parking lot when a man yelled out to her, "Lady, can you get the hell out of the road?" She said that this incident really got under her skin, and she decided to watch and see where he parked and go over to him. Jane waited until he got out of his car, sized him up as normal enough-looking, and decided he was not a threat to her. She then walked up to him and said, "I'm so sorry if I was in your way." She said he didn't know what to say, stammered a bit, and then began apologizing to her. Jane felt the conversation went very well and they ended on a positive note, each wishing the other a good day.

Then she stopped talking and looked hard at me, which is her indication of "Tell me your thoughts." I said, "Well, my first question to you is, 'What were you feeling after he yelled at you and when you approached him?'" She laughed nervously, and said emphatically, "I was angry. And I felt embarrassed that he had yelled at me in public. But mostly I was angry." I followed with, "So you weren't really sorry that you were in his way. You went over to gain some power in the situation and get him to apologize to you. It was an opening gambit." She laughed again, and turned bright red. Jane then did what is characteristic of her—she began re-writing the scenario in a way that validated both her verbal expressions and her intentions.

She said, "Well, it's possible I was walking a little too far into the parking aisle, but it is a two-way lane, so there isn't much room for people walking to their cars. Still, perhaps I could have been over more."

"So you're saying that your approach to this man was really sincere?"

Jane responded with, "Well, yes, in a way." I reminded her that she had turned red when I verbalized my impression of her intentions.

Characteristically undaunted, Jane laughed, and proceeded with her rationalization. She said, "Even if I didn't express my feelings honestly at the moment, the outcome was undeniably good." (I was wondering to myself if the man involved would agree, since at some level he knew what she was doing. But then again, perhaps her gentle confrontation relieved his guilt and they both genuinely did feel better.) I responded to Jane by saying that I had no doubt that her way of dealing with difficult situations was often effective or adaptive in the moment. She said she felt that superficial social situations like this one didn't necessarily require emotional honesty, and it might even get in the way of a good resolution.

I agreed this was possible, but wasn't this emotional dishonesty characteristic of her exchanges with everyone, even loved ones? She admitted this was true, but still wondered if it doesn't serve her better than telling the truth. She also let me know she was not happy about being characterized as emotionally dishonest.

Over the years, I have become truly fascinated by Jane's instinctive, immediate, and largely unconscious ability to reframe either her own narrative or our joint dialogue whenever anything negative about her feelings or behavior emerges. Because she is so intelligent, this process is lightning quick, and it took me some time to recognize it as such during her treatment. Jane was raised to be the "perfect child" in a family that valued social standing and approval to excess. Negative attributes are simply unacceptable. Jane was taught to believe that she could, and should, transcend the baser instincts and self-interested behavior that characterize human nature.

Jane came to her next session and said she had been thinking about our exchange on and off since she left my office. She wanted to defend herself against my accusations of her having "sinister motives." I said, "Really? I don't recall the term 'sinister' being used in any way. I think this is why you need to defend against wanting to influence this man in a certain way and that you are labeling your minor manipulation of him as 'sinister.'"

Jane then began talking about having problems with her new computer. She called the customer service number and worked with a young man who she described and nice and helpful. But after a while she found herself getting increasingly irritated by him. He was having trouble solving her problem, and kept apologizing. She said, "You would think I would have liked it that he kept apologizing, but I didn't. The more he did it, the angrier I got, until I finally said to him, 'Please stop apologizing. What exactly are you apologizing for? I need you to stop and just talk to me about how we can solve this problem.'"

I responded by saying I found it intriguing that first she brought up her last session, where we had examined her honesty in an exchange with a stranger, then she free-associated to her conversation with the customer service representative. I said, "So let me see if I have this right. You became so annoyed with the customer service guy because his apologies were disingenuous. He was really just placating you as a technique for 'handling you' on the phone? He wasn't being emotionally honest."

She replied, "Yes, exactly." I noted how she minimized the effects when she was the one who was dishonest in an exchange with a stranger, but was very annoyed when the roles were reversed. She freely admitted she was reluctant to think of herself as emotionally dishonest because she loathed that quality in others. She naturally wanted to rationalize her behavior in the parking lot, but found no excuse for the annoying, patronizing behavior from the customer service representative on the phone. Then we both sat quietly for a minute or two. And she gave me that "What else can you add to this?' look. (I could clearly see that Jane was unusually open, was not continuing to defend her behavior, and seemed receptive to a genuine encounter with me. She was signaling that it was okay for me to go further.)

We talked a bit about her behaviors, and I asked if she could process more feedback. She said "Yes." I said that I noticed that when she gets really angry, she raises her voice, fake cries, and says, "I'm really hurt and upset about what you are saying to me." I told her that at those times, her facial expression, vocal tone, and body language (leaning forward and up) telegraph anger to me, not hurt.

She looked absolutely stunned, paused for a minute, then said, "That's exactly what my mother does. That's why I never confront her about anything. She gets really upset and says how terribly hurt she is. I just learned to back off." I said, "So her message to you is, 'You are hurting me and I want you to stop,' which was pretty effective when you were young and explains why you think you're a bad person if you express anger at people you love."

I always suspected her mother had done this to her, because it seemed so performative and Jane seemed so out of touch when she enacted it. But I knew the genetic interpretation would only tap into her guilt over her anger toward her mother and would result in her defending her mother rather than producing any insight.

So certainly this "lived moment" between Jane and me was therapeutic in a deep way that no interpretation alone could be. Her unconscious motivations and the resulting patterns of behavior reached the level of awareness only through this intense emotional encounter between us. I want to emphasize that this encounter relied heavily on my being willing to confront Jane with the contradiction that existed between her intentions and her actual behavior. And I also credit her for being willing to struggle mightily with her ego-dystonic internalization of her mother's manipulative behavior.

My relationship with Jane over the years has not been without enactments (she was prone to excessive gift-giving early in the treatment, which I did not respond well to). She is a very astute observer, and is often dead-on when she observes me. But she can also be quite intrusive. I think my relationship with her embodies the current discussion around enactment (Aron, 2003; Bass, 2003) that talks about the transference–countertransference dynamics that exist and are in play from day one. As stated previously, an enactment occurs when intense, usually negative, feelings are mutually stimulated and acted on without awareness. But they are part and parcel of an ongoing dynamic relationship between analyst and patient.

Jane was certainly one of the most challenging patients I ever treated, and it would have been easy to remain passive for too long in response to her narcissistic defenses and denial. But she needed a very active participant even though she always resisted it as much or more than she welcomed it.

In my opinion, it is becoming increasingly socially unacceptable in our culture to give honest negative feedback to people, even when they are asking for it. They are pacified instead as conflict avoidance grips our society, resulting in all manner of acting out, and little meaningful negotiation of relationships. This makes the role of the analyst or therapist as one who is not afraid to both speak and hear the truth, and work through the subsequent feelings, more important than ever.

In summary, I believe psychoanalytic theory has embraced the concept of transference–countertransference conflict and the necessity of an affect-based working through as the bedrock of therapeutic action. The past thirty years of theoretical innovation and acceptance of research on affect and attachment have thoroughly established the analyst as a co-participant in the intense relationship that characterizes deep therapeutic work.

Yet our role as passive peacekeepers seems to have dominated the clinical landscape. **The current emphasis on enactment, accentuating the analyst's inability to know what either he/she or the patient are feeling before it is acted out can fuel the analyst's acceptance of waiting for conflicts to occur rather than working to bring them out in the open. As new young therapists seek guidance in implementing a relational analytic method, it seems timely for us to translate our intellectual knowledge into clinical practice and overcome our reluctance to be in constructive conflict with our patients.**

References

Aron, L. (1991). The patient's experience of the analyst's subjectivity. *Psychoanalytic Quarterly, 1*, 29–51.

Aron, L. (2003). The paradoxical place of enactment in psychoanalysis: Introduction. *Psychoanalytic Dialogues, 13*, 623–631.

Balint, M. (1968). *The basic fault.* London, England: Tavistock.

Bass, A. (2003). "E" Enactments in psychoanalysis: Another medium, another message. *Psychoanalytic Dialogues, 13*, 657–675.

Bird, B. (1972). Notes on transference: Universal phenomenon and hardest part of analysis. *Journal of the American Psychoanalytic Association, 20*, 267–301.

Bollas, C. (1986). The transformational object. In G. Kohon (Ed.), *The British school of psychoanalysis: The independent tradition* (pp. 83–100). London, England: Free Association Books.

Boston Change Process Study Group (2010). *Change in psychotherapy: A unifying paradigm.* New York, NY: Norton.

Bromberg, P. M. (1993). Shadow and substance: A relational perspective on clinical process. *Psychoanalytic Psychology, 10*, 147–168.

Casement, P. (1985). *On learning from the patient.* London, England: Tavistock.

Chused, J. (1997). Discussion of "Observing-participation, mutual enactment and the new classical models. *Contemporary Psychoanalysis, 33*, 263–277.

Davies, J. M., & Frawley, M. G. (1992). *Treating the adult survivors of childhood sexual abuse: A psychoanalytic perspective.* New York, NY: Basic Books.

Farber, B. A., Berano, K. C., & Capobianco, J. A. (2004). Clients' perceptions of the process and consequences of self-disclosure in psychotherapy. *Journal of Counseling Psychology, 51*, 340–346.

Fromm-Reichmann, F. (1953). Personality of the psychotherapist and the doctor–patient relationship. *American Journal of Psychoanalysis, 13*, 13–17.

Gazzaniga, M. S. (1998). *The mind's past*. Berkeley, CA: University of California Press.

Ghent, E. (1990). Masochism, submission, surrender. *Contemporary Psychoanalysis, 26*, 108–136.

Greenberg, J., & Mitchell, S. A. (1983). *Object relations in psychoanalytic theory*. Cambridge, MA: Harvard University Press.

Hirsch, I. (1996). Observing-participation, mutual enactment and the new classical models. *Contemporary Psychoanalysis, 32*, 359–383.

Hirsch, I. (2008). *Coasting in the countertransference*. Hillsdale, NJ: Analytic Press.

Hoffman, I. (1983). The patient as interpreter of the analyst's experience. *Contemporary Psychoanalysis, 19*, 389–422.

Horney, K. (1939). *New ways in psychoanalysis*. New York, NY: Norton.

Jacobs, T. (1986). On countertransference enactments. *Journal of the American Psychoanalytic Association, 34*, 289–307.

Klein, R. H., Bernard, H. S., & Schermer, V. L. (2010). *On becoming a psychotherapist: The personal and professional journey*. New York, NY: Oxford University Press.

Langs, R. (1973). *The technique of psychoanalytic psychotherapy* (Vols. 1 & 2). New York, NY: Jason Aronson.

Levenson, E. (1987). An interpersonal perspective. *Psychoanalytic Inquiry, 7*, 207–214.

Levenson, E. A. (1996) Aspects of self-revelation and self-disclosure. *Contemporary Psychoanalysis, 32*, 237–248.

Maroda, K. (1998). Enactment: When the patient's and analyst's pasts converge. *Psychoanalytic Psychology, 15*, 517–535.

Maroda, K. (2010). *Psychodynamic techniques: Working with emotion in the therapeutic relationship*. New York, NY: Guilford Press.

McLaughlin, J. T. (1991). Clinical and theoretical aspects of enactment. *Journal of the American Psychoanalytic Association, 39*, 595–614.

Mitchell, S. (1988). *Relational concepts in psychoanalysis: An integration*. Cambridge, MA: Harvard University Press.

Mendelsohn, E. (2002). The analyst's bad-enough participation. *Psychoanalytic Dialogues, 12*, 331–358.

Modell, A. (2008). Implicit or unconscious? Commentary on paper by the Boston Change Process Study Group. *Psychoanalytic Dialogue, 18*, 162–167.

Panksepp, J. (2000). On preventing another century of misunderstanding: Toward a psychoethology of human experience and a psychoneurology of affect. Commentary by Jack Panksepp. *Neuro-psychoanalysis, 2*, 240–255.

Renik, O. (1993). Analytic interaction: Conceptualizing technique in light of the analyst's irreducible subjectivity. *Psychoanalytic Quarterly, 62*, 562–571.

Renik, O. (1997). Reaction to "Observing-participation, mutual enactment, and the new classical models" by Irwin Hirsch, Ph.D. *Contemporary Psychoanalysis, 33*, 279–284.

Richards, A., Bachant, J., & Lynch, A. (1997, July 25). *Interaction in the transference/countertransference continuum.* Paper presented at International Psychoanalytic Association Meeting, Barcelona, Spain.

Safran, J., & Muran, J. C. (2002). *Negotiating the therapeutic alliance.* New York, NY: Guilford Press.

Schore, A. N. (2011). The right-brain implicit self lies at the core of psychoanalysis. *Psychoanalytic Dialogues, 1*, 75–100.

Searles, H. (1979). *Countertransference and related subjects.* New York, NY: International Universities Press.

Stern, D. (1985). *The interpersonal world of the infant.* New York, NY: Basic Books.

Sullivan, H. S. (1953). *The interpersonal theory of psychiatry.* New York, NY: Norton.

Sussman, M. (2007). *A curious calling: Unconscious motivations for practicing psychotherapy* (2nd ed.). New York, NY: Aronson.

Thompson, C. (1940). Identification with the enemy and the loss of the sense of self. *Psychoanalytic Quarterly, 9*, 37–50.

Winnicott, D. W. (1953). Transitional objects and transitional phenomena: A study of the first not-me possession. *International Journal of Psycho-Analysis, 34*, 89–97.

Winnicott, D. W. (1986). The theory of the parent–infant relationship. In P. Buckley (Ed.), *Essential papers on object relations, Essential papers in psychoanalysis* (pp. 233–253). New York, NY: New York University Press.

Chapter 10

Core Competency Seven: Courageous Speech/ Disciplined Spontaneity

Roy E. Barsness & Brad Strawn

Introduction by Roy E. Barsness

The relational analyst holds to the notion that a patient needs to hear what is on the therapist's mind and how the therapist experiences the patient. Analysts take risks by stating what has come to their mind within the context of the therapeutic relationship. Risky though their speech may be, analysts offer their ideas from a non-authoritarian stance with tentativeness, curiosity and humility. Words are offered to the patient with a spirit of inquiry, exploration, and negotiation. Analysts consider their thoughts and affects and attempt to metabolize before they speak and while they are speaking. They are also willing to make a mistake in speaking, given their predisposition to follow the patient's response as the means for discovering understanding and meaning, rather than mere analytic interpretation. Interventions, thoughts, words come as conversations.

The research participants indicated that they do not operate from a script or from a formula. In fact, if they feel as though they are, they believe they may be missing or avoiding something. They live with the assumption that the encounter is unpredictable and unformulated, and because of that, they must follow the experience of their patient in direct relationship to the experience of the analyst.

One participant clearly captured the essence of courageous speech, and is quoted in full:

> [T]hough I am not sure-footed, I believe there is only one way to find out about his (speaking of a patient) coherence and his ability to link and that is by bringing my experience to him. I am reminded

of Ogden's chapter on the initial interview in his text, *The Primitive Edge of Experience*. He says, people say to be cautious what we say, because we don't know what the patient can tolerate. Ogden differs on this however, and believes that the question in the patient's mind is, "how much can you tolerate?" It seems important to go for the deepest level from the get go. What the patient is trying on or what is really going on in the patient's mind is "is there a place here for me?" Anna Freud said we have to calibrate how much of the patient's anxiety we expose. I would say if you have to do that, you are more likely calibrating how much anxiety you want to be exposed to. The participant goes on to say, I had another supervisor say, you can say anything you like as long as you know why you said it. This does not work however, because we don't know why things come to our mind, or why we say them. We don't know where these thoughts come from. We may have no idea. So we put it out there. The reason we put it out there is because we are trying to get a "scent" and "inkling"' of where this is coming from.

The above statement is further reflected by other comments that state: "Sometimes things just fly out of my mouth, which as long as I am there to explore this with the patient and it is connected to our experience, it is what is needed." "How do we know anything? By talking about what has happened." "I know that I can't have clarity unless I say something." "I recognize that because I am working with experience, the timing is always right because I am stating what it is that is happening." "I think that in some form the patient already knows what I am thinking anyway." "I do a lot of reflecting out loud. I suppose I am modeling the idea of looking inside while speaking outside." When to speak and what to say remains challenging, but it is evident that the relational analyst chooses to let the patient in on his/her thoughts believing that in doing so, the work is advanced.

What was striking about the practice of courageous speech was the humility that was evident in delivery. Participants made statements such as, "psychoanalysis is a discipline of restraining oneself with being courageous enough to speak to what is happening." It is about, "showing your emotions without being self-referential and maintaining the focus on the patient," and "speaking with curiosity, inquiry and exploration." "It is about "wondering why I might wish to say something and why I may wish to not say something, I need to always consider my motivations." The analysts stated that there is a caution to be "mindful of the compulsion to interpret when I want to feel clever," and to "see this work as a mutual endeavor," and to always "remain open to surprise."

In this chapter, my colleague Brad Strawn and I take a look at this particular competency—courageous speech/disciplined spontaneity—through the lens of acknowledging erotic arousal within the therapeutic relationship.

Properties of Courageous Speech/Disciplined Spontaneity

Courageous Speech/Disciplined Spontaneity

7.1 The analyst holds to the notion that the patient needs to hear what is on the therapist's mind and how the therapist experiences the patient.
- 7.1.1 Says out loud what he/she is thinking about and experiencing
- 7.1.2 Adheres to the ethic of honesty, both within the patient and within him/herself
- 7.1.3 Resists the urge for self-protection
- 7.1.4 The patient "knows" at some level the mind of the therapist, and thus it needs to be spoken
- 7.1.5 Clarity emerges from honest speech
- 7.1.6 Timing of speaking is adhered to by attending to what is happening in the moment
- 7.1.7 The general principle is to disclose, and then follow the patient's response
- 7.1.8 Must regulate his/her own shame, as it limits full involvement
- 7.1.9 Offers his/her ideas from a non-authoritarian stance, with tentativeness, curiosity and humility
- 7.1.10 Attends to how his/her interventions/words expand, clarify, and deepen the patient's experience
- 7.1.11 Needs to achieve an odd combination of restraint with being courageous
- 7.1.12 Shows emotions without being self-referential, and maintains the focus on the patient
- 7.1.13 Considers his/her own motivations for action and how this is relevant to the patient
- 7.1.14 Formulates thought and affect dialogically, and is open to the negotiation of ideas and affects
- 7.1.15 The goal in speaking boldly is to provide an authentic interaction
- 7.1.16 Is careful not to fill up space with his/her own needs or cleverness, but to keep the space open toward an understanding of the patient through the analyst's experience of the patient
- 7.1.17 Interpretation is only helpful to understand and consolidate what has happened experientially
- 7.1.18 Works the transference, rather than interpreting it

All Therapy Is Disclosure

From a relational psychoanalytic paradigm, all therapy is disclosure, and acknowledgment of what is actually presenting itself in the therapeutic encounter (most notably affective experiences and conflicts) requires considerable courage and discipline, but is a necessary factor for a successful therapy. Disclosure may appear in various forms, such as unconscious to unconscious uncanny experiences where both patient and analyst "know" something about the other and the use of words is not required. These unconscious moments of "gestalt" significantly shift the work into a deeper understanding of the other where the patient experiences a profound sense of the analyst's capacity to apprehend the patient's inner world (see Bollas, 2001; Bass, 2001). There are also times when the work calls for direct self-disclosure, where the analyst offers very clearly and consciously what he/she feels and experiences with his/her patient in direct relationship to the patient (see Davies, 2006; Maroda, 2004; Russ, 1999). But perhaps the most frequent "disclosing" of the analyst's self occurs in the daily routines of our work. We come to "know" one another through our words, our silences, movements, mistakes, impasses, and enactments. Here, in the back and forth of conscious and unconscious experiences, analysts strive to speak courageously by acknowledging deeply held feelings, conflicts, and thoughts bearing witness to the unfolding events occurring within the therapeutic relationship. In doing so, they try to find the words to speak courageously to the experience—even, and especially when, it is uncomfortable.

With this in mind, we speak of courageous speech as acknowledging and speaking to conscious and unconscious material that has emerged or is emerging into awareness within the therapeutic dyad. We do this by taking a look at the development of courageous speech through the history of disclosure within psychoanalysis.

As there is no such thing as a blank screen, everything we do is some form of disclosure, so it seems wise to talk about it rather than try and convince ourselves that we can hide it. As the therapist's experience is linked to the patient in both subjective and intersubjective ways, Bromberg (2006) believes that unconscious affects, thoughts, and fantasies are dissociated in both patient and therapist, so they must be processed in order to bring them into "cognitive symbolization through language" (p. 131). Transference–countertransference enactment is the process by which clients' dissociated self-states, or what Bromberg (2006) calls "trauma-derived emotion schemas" (p. 136), make themselves known. But because conscious and unconscious affects, thoughts, and fantasies are co-created in the analytic dyad and non-linear, therapists must put their own experiences into words in order to make sense of the enactment. As Bromberg states:

> the patient's pressure to force the analyst to give up his right to privacy is organized not simply by a need to know the analyst, but by a wish to know what the analyst knows about the patient but has dissociated.
>
> (Bromberg, 2006, p. 145)

This creates a situation that Owen Renik (2006) refers to as *flying blind*. Flying blind is admitting that all we really know is our experience of being with the patient, and subsequently we don't know with certainty what will provide a corrective experience. If patients' perceptions/feedback are ignored, interpreted away, or if patients are forced to explore without the therapist's authentic response, dialogue is effectively shut down and the dissociated will stay inaccessible (Bromberg, 2006). Furthermore, therapists must place their perceptions of themselves, their clients, and their interactions on the table, which may require the "analyst to say a good deal about him or herself—sometimes more than is comfortable" (Renik, 2006, pp. 54–55). When analysts play their cards "face up," it invites an opportunity for the analytic dyad to compare, contrast, and explore their perceptions. Karen Maroda (2004) suggests:

> The only tenable position for us to adopt is to focus on the nature of the interaction and the emotional states of the therapist and the patient at the moment to determine what approach is most genuine and humanly possible.
>
> (p. 21)

A Brief History of Countertransference Disclosure

The conceptualization of countertransference has a long and complex history. Freud first considered countertransference to be residual unanalyzed aspects of the therapist's past that threatened to interfere with the patient's transference and disrupt the therapy. Therefore, the analyst was to maintain analytic neutrality (i.e., not siding with the id, ego, or superego) and maintain a blank screen (i.e., not disclosing anything that might interfere with the patient's "pure" transference).

Contemporary psychoanalytic relational theories, such as multiple self theory and intersubjectivity, resist the conceptualization of an "independent mind" and see all interaction in therapy as transference–countertransference interaction. Thus countertransference is viewed as an intersubjective experience, and the use of countertransference as passage to a deeper understanding of the patient's internal and interpersonal world. With that in mind, Donna Orange (1995) wonders if we should drop the use of the word "countertransference" altogether, and instead refer to the therapist's and the patient's emotional reactions as co-transference. Gabbard (1996) has stated: "it is generally more clinically useful to consider transference and countertransference as a unit . . . a joint creation involving contributions from both patient and analyst" (p. 260). In agreement with these theorists, we contend that transference–countertransference theory should be repositioned from either/or and be replaced with concepts such as "trans-ferential experience" (Fosshage, 2000), "intersubjectivity" (Stolorow, Brandchaft, & Atwood, 1987), or the "interpersonal" (Mitchell, 1988). Transference–countertransference is then essentially perceived as an organism, as transactional, interactive, and perspectival—a relationship in which there is a "mutual, bi-directional, interactive influence" (Fosshage, 2000, p. 25). In this connection, past, present, and future collide, and require the analytic couple to make meaning of all aspects of a person's life as it now presents itself between the two, rather than the one. This complex human encounter gets at the matter of the self-in-relation, in an experiential, visceral way, and moves patients beyond an isolated, analyzed review of their past. The relational stance challenges a treatment where patients historically were:

> shadow companions, ostensibly invited on a mutually intimate journey, but traveling a course piloted by the analyst . . . [resulting] in an experience in aloneness, a tutorial in free association, replete with intellectual understanding of genetics and dynamics . . . sprinkled with interpretations that locate pathology within the patient.
>
> (Geist, 2009, p. 66)

The outcome of such an analysis was that the patient ended up with better explanations, but not a better life. What occurs in a relational analysis, however, is not just a good interpretation of the past, but a working through of the interactional conflict, staged and co-produced between both actors—therapist and patient—leading to a more meaningful interpersonal life. In this kind of analysis, we no longer hold to a benign neutrality or hold to the belief that we, as the therapist, are the authority, rather we are engaged in an intense intimate act of human relations.

It is important to note that this relativistic stance that privileges the co-created interaction between therapist and patient does not negate the individual and that individual's early object relations. The power of early attachment, developmental delays, and past traumas is not disputed. However, remembering and gaining insight from repressed memories is only one aspect of the work. The unconscious is made conscious not solely through interpretation of the past, but through direct encounter of an authentic relational response. Inquiry of the repressed is lived in the intricate, subtle, intersubjective, and inevitable conflictual interplay of the therapeutic relationship.

Patients' efforts to enlist us as co-designers of their past are most vulnerable to distortion and avoidance around issues of aggression and sexuality. We surmise that in heightened affective moments where these more primitive, socially constricted affective states appear, we tend toward sanitizing the therapeutic encounter, and capitulate to neutrality and interpretation, rather than attending to the intensity of the interaction between the analyst and the patient. It is our view that in the privatization of the therapist's thoughts and feelings, often distilled into precise interpretations, ignoring material or forbidding patients to talk about areas of their lives that make us uncomfortable, we forfeit authenticity: "Unable to maintain our usual emotional responsiveness in the face of losing control; we tend to act defensively to the patient's 'provocativeness'" (Geist, 2009, p. 176). However, as Geist has noted, it is "through heightened affective moments that the patient's self comes alive and feels real and more organized" (p. 175); it is therefore incumbent upon us to remain responsive and participative.

Conflict Regarding Erotic Disclosure in Contemporary Psychoanalysis

Even as relational theory has moved disclosure front and center, it is curious that some theorists give only marginal support to disclosure of erotic feelings. Perhaps it is this double standard around sexual arousal that caused one of Bollas' (1994) patients to comment on psychoanalysis as a "set-up, a seduction that refuses to assume responsibility for itself" (p. 576). His patient is correct, for despite the emphasis in relational psychoanalysis of lived intersubjective experiences, dyadic attachments, and affective attunement, the psychoanalytic literature, as discussed below, is replete with the dangers of the therapist acknowledging the erotic.

Although Bollas (1994) allows for a generative erotic transference that "implicitly recognizes the passion of a love relationship" (p. 589), he refers more commonly to the negative sexualized transference as the "blackness of hate" (p. 589), and implores the therapist to adhere to rigorous neutrality. Bollas' concern in breaking the analytic barrier of neutrality is that "something [is] now revealed of [the analyst's] true feelings or true self, from behind the screen of analytical neutrality . . . [and] the analysand [gains] what she wished namely, the desire to control her object" (p. 583). But we must ask, "Is change not made most possible when the screen of analytical neutrality is broken?" It seems that when the therapist's emotional veil is penetrated and an authentic response is offered, the patient is able to gain a greater sense of what his/her actions mean. Bollas contends, however, that by responding outside of neutrality, we arouse within patients their conviction that infantile sexuality will arouse the mother's "ire." Indeed, something is being aroused! But is it only ire? Is infantile sexuality only about aggression? Or does that "baby" also long for contact, touch, holding, affirmation of its body, and play? Rather than neutrality, it would seem important to enter into the quest of this infantile sexuality, to discover together what is hateful and what is love, and not defend against it.

Kumin (1985) also argued that erotic transference is a form of negative transference, and contended that both patient and therapist suffer from being objects of frustrated desire, and are therefore, expected to *behave* themselves—the patient by free-associating, and the therapist by maintaining a professional attitude. The rule of abstinence, he continued, "serves a protective purpose in the analytic situation, similar to that of the incest taboo in the family" (p. 16). Yes, the taboo of not having sex is a given, but unlike the taboo in the family, where not only having sex is taboo, but so is talking about it. Talking is *not* taboo within the analytic situation. *In fact, this is what we do. We talk about it!* Conversations that have been taboo can finally be released, uncensored, and spoken without constraint. Kumin's solution to this matter, however, is to abstain and to "produce the correct interpretation to reduce desire and resistance" (p. 16). It is not clear what he means by the "correct" interpretation, but he states that you know it is correct when "the analyst returns to the essential neutrality of feeling concerning the patient and the patient returns to productive free association" (p. 16). As to the *correct* interpretation, the best interpretation we have found is one that acknowledges what the patient and therapist have experienced and are experiencing, one that opens up a path toward an expansion of healthy and productive means of living with desire.

Masud Khan, who ironically upset his own career through sexual scandal, views the re-enactment of sexual arousal as a perverse collusion. He contends that the pervert wishes to "make known to himself and announce and press into another . . . his innermost nature as well as to discharge its instinctual tension" (cited in Kumin, 1985, p. 15). Rather than placing the patient in this locked position, we must ask, "What is the 'pervert,' if you will, pressing for?" The erotic is filled with aggressive action, and provokes vulnerability, rejection, retaliation, and shame, *but* it is important to recognize that that which is being pushed away is also what is most desired.

Gabbard (1998) contends that "direct disclosure of the analyst's sexual feelings toward the patient is an enterprise fraught with peril and must be carefully considered in terms of a risk–benefit equation" (p. 782). He goes on to say:

> disclosure of sexual feelings by the analyst is fundamentally different from disclosure of other countertransference affects. Acknowledgement of anger, for example, does not imply, either inside the consulting room or outside of it, in social situations, that violence will ensue.
>
> (p. 783)

This argument baffles, and if it is true, we wonder why we can talk about anger without violence, but we can't talk about sex without consummation. It appears as though, for Gabbard, acknowledgement of sex means sex between the participants will ensue. Although we understand Gabbard's (1998) reluctance to disclose because "our capacity for rationalization and self-deception in analytic work is remarkable" (p. 784), it is for this very reason we must be careful not to hold too much on our own. Rather, it seems incumbent upon therapists to bring to the patient what we experience, so that in some awkward way we are able to discover the veracity of what the arousal is seeking to communicate, rather than to consummate.

In contrast to these views of erotic as aggressive, perverted, and infantile, Ulanov (2009) reminds us that even for Freud, "the nucleus of love found in sexual love, includes our drive to make unities—within ourselves, in the world, and in our relation to the cosmos" (p. 92). Ulanov notes that

Fairbairn "saw libido as something that sought relation to another, not gratification" (p. 92). She agrees, and continues:

> Eros is the function of psychic relatedness that urges us to connect, get involved with, poke into, be in the midst of, reach out to, get inside of, value, not to abstract or theorize but get in touch with, invest energy, endow libido. Relatedness does not mean relationship . . . [rather] eros is like a huge spark that ignites our passion, and then confronts us with how we will live this fire in ordinary space and time. Eros brings us into the mysteries of desire to bond and believe in the other and ourselves as a unit, as a union that enhances both of us, and even gives something to the world, benefiting others, as if our living adds more to the sum of light available to everyone.
>
> (p. 93)

Ulanov's (2009) statement suggests that the erotic energy within a relationship exists as a spark towards unity, arousing us forward to a "sense of purpose, of going somewhere important, something that enlists body, soul, and spirit" (p. 90). Russ (1999) states: "if eros is a real vehicle for the profound effects of life, death, and the need for protection, merger, surrender, trust and bliss, the analyst should expect to be a full participant" (p. 613). Eros has a drive towards life and not death, therefore, "we must allow erotic responses, including attendant emotions, to become available for discourse with the patient" (Russ, 1999, p. 613).

Davies (1994) contends that the erotic urge drives us toward some purpose, and that:

> [the therapist's] unwillingness to regard her sexual responses, as a significant aspect of the countertransferential process, [creates] a perverse scenario, rather than an increasingly intimate one . . . [her fear is] that which masquerades as analytic neutrality may in many cases represent the reenactment in the transference of a countertransferentially induced gratification of the patient's eroticized masochism rather than an enhanced capacity for intimacy and erotic mutuality.
>
> (p. 7)

Davies contends that it is incumbent upon both patient and therapist to enter the risk. She states: "if aspects of the analyst's unconscious participation in the therapeutic drama remained unexpressed and therefore, unexplored, whole areas of the patient's unconscious experience may be kept out of full participation in the interpersonal arena of reconfigured meanings" (p. 11). We must confront the anxiety of participation as it "prevents analysts from addressing sex where it is and makes them see it where it isn't. The solution, according to Dimen (2003) is to talk about sex . . . seriously with humor and with pleasure" (p. 158).

By way of example, a female therapist reported to us her discomfort and anxiety due to frequent compliments about her clothing from a male patient, and asked him to stop. She continued: "He seemed somewhat confused, but was apologetic, and he did indeed stop." And in her mind, the treatment progressed. We, however, contend that the intervention may have negatively impacted the therapy and circumscribed other areas of exploration for her patient, which subsequently became inaccessible. Treatments that invoke abstinence by placing certain behaviors off limits run the risk of limiting thoughts and affects, compromising deeper exploration, restoration, and transformation.

From our experience, as will be demonstrated in the following vignettes, **interacting defensively with our patients diminishes our capacity to understand what is unfolding, circumscribes the complexity of a delicate interplay, and ultimately damages the relationship. We posit a reconsideration of the transference–countertransference relationship that affective states (sex and aggression) must be considered from a variety of vantage points: the patient's perspective, the perspective of the therapist, that which has been dissociated, and the interaction of the two.** Within a relational model and from a shared perspective of embodiment (Anderson, 1982; Brown & Strawn, 2013), the therapeutic relationship is viewed as co-constructed, and therapists are not only objects of a patient's projection, but must "recognize that the analysand and analyst variably co-create the transferential experience [and the] analyst [must be] alert to address, and acknowledge his contribution" (Fosshage, 2000, p. 34).

Case Vignette: Mary

Mary came from a highly abusive home where over the course of several years, her father had sexually abused her, ending at age 18 in a ménage à trois between her father and his girlfriend. During the course of Mary's childhood and adolescence, her mother married the same two men, Mary's father and stepfather, five different times. The patient was an attractive, articulate woman who held to a belief that her only means of getting attention was through sex. A highly charged erotic transference–countertransference reaction ensued. The tension between desire and aggression began to dominate our work. As the sparks of eroticism grew, rather than addressing the tension, the therapy languished under the protection of the therapist becoming neutral and emotionally unavailable, the banter and the play that had characterized the earlier work replaced with indifference and calculated interpretations.

In contrast, Davies (2006), speaking to this tension of desire and aggression, stresses the importance of creating "a psychic bridge" (p. 673) between aggression and sexuality, stating:

> Sensual pleasures, erotic tenderness, intimate murmurings . . . into whose arms we fall and melt and merge . . . is the object with whom we experience pleasure, cohesion, satiation and a sense of fullness and completeness . . . and yet its survival is precarious [for] it must be protected from the aggression also spilling in our relationship . . . the object who arouses . . . the object who teases, tortures and holds us captive, awaiting ultimate release . . . these are the fantasies that involve aggression, shame, domination and submission, the power dimensions of who loves more, who needs more . . . the fantasies that unite the self with a taunting, teasing, ever-alluring, bad exciting object.

(p. 674)

This dissociation, the unbearable of the wanting and the not getting, was the drama being played in our work. Part of what was driving our enactment was "the patient's deep conviction that [I, akin to her father] . . . didn't want to know her dissociated self-state crashing against the urgent need to let [me] know" (Benjamin, 2009, p. 444). My patient had learned early that her father's affections were sexualized and her only means for connection with him was through her body. Consequently, in her attempt to get my attention, she vowed that if I did not sleep with her, she would kill herself. Overwhelmed, I shut down. This long and painful impasse was broken when, in exasperation, the patient declared, "I swear to God you are asexual." Finally aroused, I spontaneously said, "In this room, in this moment, with you, I am. For your threat to kill yourself if I do not go to bed with you scares me, and I have shut down." This unadulterated response acknowledging the tension *between* us helped us make meaning of the reprise of the abusive nature with her father. And slowly, within this more spacious and honest space, she began to feel that her deepest longings could perhaps be expressed, but not exploited. Disclosure ushered us toward more imaginative play, effective regulation of fantasies, and an increased ability to work within the tension of desire and aggression. Davies (2006) captures this shift in our work in this way:

> The capacity to experience pleasurable anticipation must not be overwhelmed by frustration and rage, nor can its fantasized elaboration be inhibited and potentially shut down by an overly restrictive and primitively bifurcated notion of "goodness." A sense of playful adventure, mischievousness, naughtiness, the capacity to tease and not torture, to allure and not torment, to attract without holding captive . . . [to] no longer live entirely within either to the exclusion of the other.
>
> (p. 676)

Our work did take a new direction when we were able to remain in a state of playful adventure, instead of an overly restrictive and primitively bifurcated notion of goodness. We did better when we talked, acknowledging how her/our seductions evoked both feelings of love and of hate, as well as how her despair, her threat of killing herself, rendered me afraid and impotent. As we were able to explore the sexual arousal actively in pursuit of us, while holding to the tension that neither of us wanted it to end in a tryst, we learned that the sexiness of our relationship, though about sex, and arousal, was also about making contact, finding meaning, being valued, and about love. Had I not been so preoccupied by my own sexual guilt and fear that consummation followed arousal, we could have held that "bodily arousal, excitement and tension [does not hold any] guarantee of immediate satisfaction or release" (Davies, 2006, p. 272), and we would have been able to move toward a place of satisfaction and release that would be life-altering and may not have led to her suicidal dramas. I believe that had I had the courage to have stayed in the game earlier than I did, my patient would not have reached such points of despair within the enactment. The concern that I hold several years past this treatment is: did the enactment last too long, and become more of an acting out, because of my long refusal to acknowledge the erotic tensions between us, our mutual feelings of arousal, and in particular my defense against it? I believe so, and believe that as my work has matured, I have been more at the ready, less defensive, and more willing to acknowledge what exists between me and my patient, and the inevitable enactments have been less contaminated by my fears, and thus more fertile for the analysis.

Twenty-one years following the termination of our work, this patient and I had the opportunity to meet once again. Midway in our conversation, she brought up those two long years of our highly eroticized, sexually charged six-year relationship. She stated, "It must have been awful for you." I responded, "It was awful for both of us, and in fact, I felt responsible for a good deal of what was occurring at that time." I acknowledged that because of my inability to hold the tension of her desire and aggression, our work was placed in serious peril. She went on to say that she was not so sure I was the cause of her wish to act out, but was grateful I had never acted upon her sexually during that time. She said, "I wanted you so much." I responded, "And yet, in many ways, you didn't want me at all." She became thoughtful for a time, and then quietly said, "I have never thought of that before, but you are right, I didn't want you that way, but it was the only way I knew how to make contact with you."

This early professional experience confirmed the danger of not working with all of the tensions—the aggressive and the erotic and every emotion in between that emerges between the therapeutic couple. Benjamin (2009) offers some balm for our errors, noting that:

> our failure to link is inevitable, and to be unable to link feelings and parts is a natural part of our procedure, a liability intrinsic to our work, and not the failure that it feels like. Self-correction is our way of life.
>
> (p. 443)

Though I remain convinced that my actions or inaction were cause for some of our enactments, I am relieved and grateful that my patient and I had the opportunity for self-correction that was made possible through the act of acknowledging the fear of the arousal between us and my strong defense of talking about it.

The next vignette illustrates the use of acknowledging the erotic tension earlier—before it becomes expressed in troublesome enactments. It is also an example of *flying blind*, in which the therapist didn't premeditate an answer to the patient's question. He couldn't have planned a response, in part, because the question was asked in an oblique manner. Rather, by fully entering into the collaborative transference–countertransference dialogue and trusting the process, the therapist responded in a non-defensive, authentic, and immediate manner. In either case—erotic tension acknowledged after the fact or in the moment—the work is either salvaged or advanced.

Case Vignette: Julia

Julia was a 20-something woman socialized within the conservative Christian tradition to fear her sexuality and to dissociate it as bad/sinful. Her highly religious family, especially her father, never talked about sex, and if they did, it was in hushed and shameful tones. Not surprisingly, Julia came to therapy in part because of difficulty relating to men. She identified as heterosexual, but felt guilty about her sexual longings, which led to her feeling that she had no clue how act sexually with a man. With men from her own religious tradition, she found they either fled from sexual feelings, or damned the torpedoes of their values and engaged in all manner of sexual behavior, short of intercourse. With men who didn't share her religion, Julia could engage in sexual behavior, but only for the man's pleasure, and never her own.

As a sexual transference–countertransference developed, Julia began to have sexual dreams and entertain sexual fantasies, and became increasingly flirtatious. Julia was attractive, and at times I became uncomfortable (perhaps dissociative at points), as she would press me for reactions regarding my feelings about her. I began to hypothesize that she needed to know if I experienced her as a sexually attractive woman, capable of impacting me. Did she need to know that our experience was mutually pleasurable, that she had an impact on me, and did she need to repeat and experience the past in the present within the protection of the analytic frame?

There appeared to be two primary issues. First, Julia needed to know that her sexual feelings didn't have to be dissociated; she could be playful with sexuality without fear. I determined that there was a high degree of safety between us—Julia shared her fantasies in a way that indicated she was aware our talk wouldn't lead to consummation. However, this did not answer her question of how I felt toward her. Did I enjoy her flirting with me? Did I experience her as an attractive young woman, and could she experience pleasure knowing I did? I admit I felt anxious when I became convinced Julia was pressing me for this information and new experience.

I was certain this new experience was happening between us in unspoken ways, but was unclear whether I needed to verbalize it or consider what I would say if she eventually asked me outright. I did find her attractive, and found myself aroused by her dreams and flirting. I attempted to sit comfortably silent with my countertransference, hoping that an unconscious-to-unconscious communication would be enough to assist her with the developmental needs I perceived her to be working through. But I also worried what might happen, or be communicated to her, if we never moved this interaction into the realm of language. In my own conflicted state, I honestly hoped we could keep it in the area of the unspoken! What if owning my attraction would be too arousing for her and for me?

While all of this was occurring, I had a second experience; sex, attraction, and even affection were clearly in the air, but I had a distinct feeling I was not just being sexually aroused, but because of her father's inability to mirror her as a developing sexual young woman, I conceptualized, at least in part, that her sexual transference was paternal. My sense was that she needed a father figure who could acknowledge/admire her sexual maturing self without taking advantage of her.

In one session, she had been especially forthcoming about a sexual dream, and said, "You are probably tired of me sharing all my sexual fantasies about you." Understanding this comment as a question, and an opportunity for a new experience, I wondered what to say. I felt I could hide behind my understanding of her developmental need and make some kind of interpretation—suggesting she was needing an admiring father figure (which I think she did in fact need)—or I could take a risk of sharing my erotic countertransference, allowing her to know her impact on me, and provide a new kind of experience of herself as a sexual woman, capable of impacting a man without shame or demand, and allowing her that pleasure. In openly acknowledging my countertransference, I feared overwhelming her with my sexual subjectivity and possibly placing her, once again, in the position of needing to deny her own feelings/needs in service of a man in her life (e.g., guys she dated, her father, even her God). The question that quickly came to me was framed rhetorically: "You don't think I enjoy being admired by an attractive young woman?" She smiled, and sincerely responded, "Thank you for saying that," then paused and said, "Thank you for helping me with this."

Acknowledging what we both knew accomplished two things: first, it provided a new developmental experience for Julia, where she had a paternal figure admire and welcome her emerging sexuality without exploitation, and second, our acknowledgment allowed her to own dissociated aspects of herself, and to own that she was sexy and she could arouse a man, and experience pleasure without shame and fear. While my response seems measured and restrained, my subjective experience was far from it! As noted above, I was deeply concerned about the impact this kind of acknowledgement (my pleasure in her attraction and my attraction) would have on Julia. Yet I believe that what came out of my mouth was a combination of both my understanding of our interaction as pressing for a developmental new experience and a kind of playfully safe sexual flirting that had been in the room for some time. I believe that she experienced me as delighting in her womanliness, sexuality, and power, even admiring it, while not exploiting it for my own gain.

It is important to note that acknowledging the obvious did not increase Julia's sexual fantasies (i.e., seduce her or overstimulate her), nor did it decrease our ability to explore the multiple meanings of her sexual feelings (i.e., contaminate the transference). We continued to explore her sexual long-ings, and her conflicted feelings about giving and receiving pleasure. We processed defenses against sexual longings and how she used me as a "test case," to figure out what she wanted in a man. But I also believe that together, Julia and I practiced and experienced how to give and to receive love.

It would be nice to report that I had all these issues figured out before Julia pressed me into service, but I didn't. I was in fact "flying blind" and trusting my patient would teach me what she needed. For this reason, I "chose"—if one can really say that—to play my cards "face up" with her when the moment arrived.

As we bring our vignettes to a close, we wish to note that it is common in the literature to speak of the erotic only as transference phenomena, and in fact our vignettes imply this very thing. However, as Kuchuck (2012) posits:

> if we consider the intersubjective nature of our work . . . we cannot always know with whom these feelings begin. My hunch is that it is often the analyst who first experiences these feelings, whether cons-ciously or not . . . [but] regardless of where the feelings begin, the important point is that the analyst's erotic state often mirrors or creates space for a similar state in the patient.

(p. 554)

Is there danger in acknowledging erotic feelings? Yes, but often, in not doing so, impasses and enactments ensue. And if these erotic feelings, impasses, and enactments are not addressed, spoken of, and worked through, the work is stalled and the patient is not helped. So yes, there can be danger in speaking courageously to these intense moments in our work, but what we have argued for and demonstrated in our vignettes is that there may be more danger in not doing so.

Metabolization

In our effort to encourage courageous speech, we also emphasize that spontaneity is "disciplined" and not random nor thoughtless. As the clinical vignettes above have demonstrated, acknowledgments are hard fought, especially so when erotic and aggressive affective states are deeply stimulated. We also noted that acknowledgement is inevitable, and essential to advancing therapeutic work. **As we continue to advance the idea that the patient has the right to our minds and our affects, we also contend there are certain disciplines associated with speaking courageously that challenge recklessness and careless disclosures.**

First, it is helpful to remember that interaction includes inaction—that in-between place to ponder, catch one's breath, organize and metabolize. In fact, spontaneity without discipline may too quickly "solve the limits of knowing, or more precisely foreclose the necessity of unknowing that [is] vital to analytic exchange" (Corbett, Dimen, Goldner, & Harris, 2014, p. 311). Second, Corbett also reminds us of the importance of retaining other analytic practices within the realm of the spontaneous, such as:

> Containing, waiting, associating, soliciting the patient's associations, wandering into reverie, wandering back out, dreaming, debating, practicing what one might say, silently interpreting, consciously contemplating, bridging, linking, cataloging, pacing, being lost, tolerating being lost, sequencing, listening, listening through hovering attention, listening more acutely, listening with an ear of theory, inquiring, momentarily stepping out of the bond, taking a break, remaining silent, debating silence, debating theory, considering when and/or if to bring a feeling or a thought forward, and at what point in the hour, what point in the week.

(p. 640)

Attending to this these various modes requires pause and contemplation. For example, a rule of thumb we have adopted when we feel a strong urge to speak is that it is most likely not yet the time to do so. As an example, one of us recently found ourselves eager to blurt out what was believed to be a very well crafted interpretation, but then had a hunch that the eagerness to speak was motivated more by a need to impress the patient and show prowess than it was by helping the patient expand his/her self-awareness.

On the other hand, we must be cautious when we find ourselves reluctant to speak courageously. In these situations, we invite the patient to explore our resistance "out loud" in terms of why we might be reluctant to speak our thoughts and experiences. Usually in this cooperative effort, a place of safety and timing for the disclosure takes place. To further guide us, we turn to Steven Kuchuck (2009), who in some ways offers a "decision tree" in helping us regulate our disclosures. He does this by speaking to our narcissistic reasons for disclosing and narcissistic reasons for not disclosing. Believing that each of these is beneficial in developing discipline in speaking courageously we offer them in their totality.

Narcissistic self-regulatory reasons analysts do disclose:

- wish or need to brag or show off;
- wish or need to talk about ourselves rather than more passive listening;
- loneliness, isolation, fatigue;
- need for mirroring, approval, and/or love;
- parentified wish to please and gratify patients' stated wish to know about us;
- discomfort with transference distortions (idealizing or devaluing) and/or a general wish to control how we are perceived;
- maintenance of false-self presentation.

Narcissistic self-regulatory reasons analysts do not disclose:

- maintenance of false-self presentation;
- wish or need to be seen in a specific manner—usually involving the need to be idealized;
- wish or need to avoid feeling vulnerable;
- guilt due to feeling like one is breaking taboos by separating from mother/father (Freud), early analysts, supervisors, teachers, mentors;

- maintenance of ego-ideal of the neutral nondisclosing analysts;
- shame of exposure (Freud said we use the couch so as not to be stared at—perhaps also to hide and not be seen);
- power (Kuchuck, 2009, p. 1022).

Lastly, in regulating our speech, we contend that the psychoanalytic technique of expanding the question can often be used defensively by the therapist. Psychologists are well known for turning the question back on the patient. In using this "technique," we suggest that as long as our motivation to return the question is to create a more imaginative space, we are on good ground. If, however, we use it to deflect our own anxieties, we are being harmful. It is essential that we are able to determine the difference between holding a question promoting deeper reflection and withholding a question used to protect our vulnerability.

To speak courageously, the analyst must have a healthy respect for anxiety and tension without feeling threatened, hold direct requests for acknowledgment non-defensively and with curiosity, value his/her words as a means for exploration rather than as correctness, and finally, follow the patient's response. Following the flow of the analyst–patient relationship recognizes that what we *say* to our patients is second in command to how we *work* what is said and experienced into the interplay of the dyad. Essentially, we play, we wonder, and we ask: "Has collaborative inquiry increased and is our patient freer to engage more deeply with themselves and with others?"

We began this chapter with the statement that there is no such thing as a blank screen, and everything we do is some form of disclosure/acknowledgment. We end by encouraging readers to come to trust themselves:

> enough to act on impulse and mistrust ourselves enough to pause and reflect. Technique, has to do with *self-reflection, reflection in action, reflection before action and reflection after action*, balancing the hermeneutics of suspicion with the hermeneutics of faith with an emphasis on mutuality, mutual influence, mutual recognition, mutual accommodation, mutual negotiation and mutual change, which of course implies the uniqueness of each person and each dyad and our community of other selves and dyads.
> (Aron, 2008, pp. 119 and 135, emphasis added)

References

Anderson, R. S. (1982). *On being human: Essays in theological anthropology.* Pasadena, CA: Fuller Seminary Press.

Aron, L. (2008). The question of technique (Msg. 13). Message posted to http:// iarpp.net/archive/2008 Dec IC 13

Bass, T. (2001). It takes one to know one; or whose Unconscious is it anyway? *Psychoanalytic Dialogues, 11,* 683–702.

Benjamin, J. (2009). A relational psychoanalysis perspective on the necessity of acknowledging failure in order to restore the facilitating and containing features of the intersubjective relationship (the shared third). *International Journal of Psychoanalysis, 90,* 441–450.

Bollas, C. (1994). Aspects of the erotic transference. *Psychoanalytic Inquiry, 14,* 572–590.

Bollas, C. (2001). Freudian intersubjectivity: Commentary on paper by Julie Gerhardt and Annie Sweetnam. *Psychoanalytic Dialogues, 11,* 93–105.

Bromberg, P. M. (2006). *Awakening the dreamer: Clinical journeys.* Mahwah, NJ: Analytic Press.

Brown, W. S., & Strawn, B. D. (2013). *The physical nature of Christian life: Neuroscience, psychology and the church.* Cambridge, England: Cambridge University Press.

Corbett, K., Dimen, M., Goldner, V., & Harris, A. (2014). Talking sex, talking gender—a roundtable. *Studies in Gender and Sexuality, 15,* 295–317.

Davies, J. (1994). "Love in the afternoon": A relational consideration of desire and dread in the countertransference. *Psychoanalytic Dialogues, 4,* 153–170.

Davies, J. M. (2006). The times we sizzles, and the times we sigh: the multiple erotics of arousal, anticipation and release. *Psychoanalytic Dialogues, 16,* 665–686.

Dimen, M. (2003). *Sexuality, intimacy and power.* New York, NY: Analytic Press.

Fosshage, J. (2000). The meaning of touch in psychoanalysis: A time for reassessment. *Psychoanalytic Inquiry, 20,* 21–43.

Gabbard, G. O. (1998). Commentary on paper by Jody Messler Davies. *Psychoanalytic Dialogues, 8*(6), 781–789.

Geist, R. (2009). Empathy, connectedness, and the evolution of boundaries in self psychological treatment. *International Journal of Psychoanalytic Self-Psychology, 4,* 165–180.

Kuchuck, S. (2009). Do ask, do tell? Narcissistic need as a determinant of analyst self-disclosure. *Psychoanalytic Review, 96,* 1007–1025.

Kuchuck, S. (2012). Please don't want me: The therapeutic action of male sexual desire in the treatment. *Contemporary Psychoanalysis, 48,* 544–562.

Kumin, I. (1985). Erotic horror: Desire and resistance in the psychoanalytic situation. *International Journal of Psychotherapy, 11,* 3–20.

Maroda, K. (2004). *The power of counter-transference: Innovations in analytic technique.* Hillsdale, NJ: Analytic Press.

Mitchell, S. (1988). *Relational concepts in psychoanalysis.* Cambridge, MA: Harvard University Press.

Orange, D. M. (1995). *Emotional understanding: Studies in psychoanalytic epistemology.* New York, NY: Guilford Press.

Renik, O. (2006). *Practical psychoanalysis for therapists and patients.* New York, NY: Other Press.

Russ, H. (1999). Leaving chastity behind: The analyst's use of her sexual response. *Psychoanalytic Psychology, 16,* 605–616.

Stolorow, R. D., Brandchaft, B., & Atwood, G. E. (1987). *Psychoanalytic treatment: An intersubjective approach.* Hillsdale, NJ: Analytic Press.

Ulanov, A. (2009). Countertransference and the erotic. *Journal of Religion and Health, 48,* 90–96.

Chapter 11

Core Competency: Love

Daniel Shaw

Introduction by Roy E. Barsness

As was noted in Chapter 1, Grounded Theory Analysis allows the researcher to search for a central explanatory concept or core category which is intended to capture the essence of what has been studied. In this study, I could not escape an overwhelming concept that kept pushing to be named. I was reluctant to name it, because it is too human, and I was afraid it would sound too "soft" for research. But it refused to not be recognized. And it is this—what lies at the heart of a psychoanalytic treatment is love. It came up in three ways. First, interviewees stated it directly by simply saying, "I love my patients." Second, I found myself "loving" my interviewees as I was "caught up" in how they expressed themselves with so much joy, care, and compassion for their patients. I found myself "touched" by the intimacy that evolved in their work as they risked themselves emotionally and intellectually, wholeheartedly engaging the analytic process. Third, love came to be defined by the very kind of relationship analysts provide—a relationship that requires of themselves honesty and risk-taking, a deep immersion in the affective lives of the other, and a devotion to scrutinize non-defensively their own selves in an attempt to understand, feel, and grasp the internal and interpersonal world of another. The analyst is willing to resist the urge for self-protection, surrender certainty, and engage in the inevitable conflicts, misrecognitions, and ruptures, and to stay in the conflict until it is worked through. The analyst's relentless "ethic of honesty"—a Freudian technique that Freud believed an essential requirement in the patient—is now valued by these relational analysts as a requirement also in themselves. It is this honesty that births an unusual authenticity rarely found in human relations, and the primary factor that engenders change and transformation in our patients' lives.

As I vetted this study, I discovered that some analysts were uncomfortable with the word "love" and some even stated that they didn't love all of their patients, giving me pause to reconsider love as a core category. So how did it get included? First, it was in the data. Second, just as this research study was developed from a student pushing for clearer practices, it was also a student who encouraged me to include it. Students were aware of the research I was conducting, and many even participated in the literature review for the study. I told them about this thing called love, and that it was controversial. There was a student who had been in the class for two semesters and who had said little to nothing the entire time. I sensed his engagement, but was often curious about his silence. Now, at the end of the semester, having said our goodbyes, he approached me and quite intensely said: "Don't ever shy away from love . . . you have brought it, you have lived it, I have bought it, and I believe it . . . and now, as a new practitioner, I have seen it. Don't ever give up on love."

It should be made clear that we don't "decide" to love a patient, and in fact, if love is in the air, we know that negative affective states are not far behind (and perhaps vice versa). However, isn't the very tangle of the therapeutic relationship, where we experience the intensity of the full range of emotions, including love and hate, not some form of love? In this chapter, Daniel Shaw addresses this question as he speaks to love within the therapeutic relationship.

On the Therapeutic Action of Analytic Love

Ari was a patient who was not easy to love. Aged 40 when he began to see me, his marriage was falling apart and he was pervasively angry and anxious. His daily marijuana smoking for 20 years, along with cigarettes, was literally making him sick.

Ari is physically imposing, athletic, muscled like a bull, with a military and soccer background. He wears an expensive watch, a diamond earring, and a leather jacket. He shaves his head close, and rides a motorcycle around town and across country. At first meeting, he spoke gruffly, volubly, bitterly, loudly, and without pause. Even if I wished to speak, he would not allow me. I noticed how often I felt anxious about speaking to him, fearing I might misspeak and he would explode with rage—and possibly assault me. Ari spent most of a year splenetically venting, about his wife, son, partners, and employees. Feeling shut out, I shuttled between resentment, detachment, and intimidation. Eventually, I understood that I was with-drawing and withholding a necessary confrontation, in retaliation for the narcissistic injury I felt about my perceived lack of effect on him. This helped me to reorganize and mobilize the assertiveness I needed in order to reach Ari. One day, I finally raised my voice and said, quite loudly, "You know, I would like to say some things to you, but I'm afraid if you don't like what you hear, you will bite my head off, possibly literally."

Ari looked up at me with his sharp, penetrating eyes, and I was scared. I was then surprised to see Ari's eyes go moist. He said sadly, "I'm just like my father, this is what I do to everyone, my wife, my son, everyone, just like my father did."

I said, "It must be awfully lonely, with everyone afraid of you like that. He looked up at me, silently. I added, "You know that song 'Desperado?'"

"Yes, I know it," he said, still looking intently at me.

"You remind me of those lines, 'You better let somebody love you, before it's too late.'"

Ari looked down and began to weep. My very mixed feelings about Ari melted into unexpected warmth, respect, and tenderness, and I thought, "I really love this guy." I was then able to feel safer confronting his obsessional anger. I was in a position to address the tender, wounded part of him which he had wanted not only to hide, but also, with great trepidation, to show. This shift between us allowed Ari to reveal traumatic aspects of his history that he felt ashamed of and hurt by.

Ari is one of many analysands I have come to love. Each analytic dyad I have been a part of has had its own unique history of how love did or did not develop, and how it was or was not expressed. What is this thing called "analytic love"? What do we do with it? How does its presence or absence affect our work?

In psychoanalysis, analyst and analysand inevitably and necessarily become intimately involved with each other, intellectually and emotionally. At the heart of this endeavor is a search for love, for being lovable, for the remobilization of thwarted capacities to give love and to receive love. This may at first seem a more fitting description of the analysand than the analyst, but consider our choice of profession. Is it not likely that we chose our work, at least in part, because it affords us the means of realizing the aim of being especially important to—especially loved and valued by—our analysands?

We have long been free to discuss hating our analysands (Winnicott, 1947), and more recently, to discuss having sexual feelings for them, including disclosing such feelings (Davies, 1998). It is less often that we discuss our feelings of tenderness and affection with the kind of thoughtfulness and seriousness of our other discussions. Erotic or aggressive countertransferences are now widely conferred the status of therapeutic agents, and natural warmth, openness, and expressiveness are no longer considered antipsychoanalytic. Yet case presentations where feelings of tenderness, affection, and love are openly expressed are often greeted with the suspicion that the analyst has "acted out" his/her narcissistic need to cure, by posing as an impossibly perfect parent to a perennially infantilized patient (Freud accused Ferenczi of "furor sanandi"—passion for curing—on similar grounds).

This gap in our developmental and clinical theories was noted long ago by Ian Suttie (1935), who asked: "in our anxiety to avoid the intrusion of sentiment into our scientific formulations, have we not gone to the length of excluding it altogether from our field of observation?" (p. 1).

In this regard, for the last century many psychoanalysts have taken their lead from Freud, shunning the concept of "cure through love" as antitherapeutic. When Freud advises Eitington that "the secret of therapy is to cure through love" (quoted in Falzeder, 1994), he is referring to the therapeutic traction provided by the *patient's* transference love for the *doctor.* Freud had very little to say of the doctor's love for the patient, and was concerned with distancing himself from therapies that promoted sentimental, spiritual, and hypnotic types of cures.

Freud erred when he sought to inoculate psychoanalysis from the potentially dangerous effects of analytic love and the recruitment of the analysand into pathological accommodation to satisfy the analyst's need for power and control (Brandchaft, 1994). He did so by enjoining the analyst to suppress his/her love altogether. Of course, one might argue that seduction for the purpose of attaining control and domination over another might often happen in the name of love, but on the other hand, professional neutrality, abstinence, and deliberate withholding of gratification can be equally manipulative means of maintaining domination and control over others.

While analytic love is by no means exiled today, I think it is fair to say that it is not readily and universally embraced either. With the popularity of concepts such as Winnicottian holding and Kohutian empathy, this statement may seem surprising. But what I wish to focus on is the analyst's love in a broader sense, not just specific components of love, such as holding, empathy, or recognition.

I have had the experience, as we all have, of successfully treating patients who have been treated unsuccessfully by a colleague. And yet the former analyst had conducted the treatment correctly, and I have been led to ask myself: "What did I do more than he?" I have also had the experience of being unable to cure a patient, and ask myself what I did less for him than for others. For a long time, this problem worried me, until I reached the conclusion that in one case or the other, it was to my own deep underlying attitude towards the patient that I had to attribute the responsibility of success or failure. Nacht (1962) said: "no one can cure another if he has not a genuine desire to help him; and no one can have the desire to help unless he loves, in the deepest sense of the word" (p. 210).

Was Nacht ahead of his time? Or was he attuned to something deeply rooted in psychoanalytic theory of which his contemporaries, of the 1960s, had lost sight? The story of the acceptance or rejection of analytic love as a valid therapeutic agent begins early in the history of psychoanalysis, most notably with what Lothane referred to in his article "The feud between Freud and Ferenczi over love" (Lothane, 1998).

It was at the critical juncture concerning the nature of the analyst–analysand relationship that Freud and Ferenczi, Freud's closest disciple, encountered irreconcilable differences. Ferenczi eventually came to see the quality of love, specifically the mutual exchange of tenderness between parent and child, as crucial to development and central to the understanding of human motivation. He emphasized these themes in contradiction to Freud's emphasis on sexual and aggressive drives as the foundation of the structure of the human psyche. Ferenczi saw the ability to generate mutual tenderness between analyst and analysand, constituting mutative new relational experiences (Fosshage, 1992), as essential to cure. Ferenczi saw transference not primarily as an expression of infantile id pressures, which through analysis would be made conscious and renounced, but rather as a forum for the analysand to re-enact and work through traumatic developmental experiences within the parent–child matrix. Ferenczi believed this could be achieved optimally with an analyst who was authentic and emotionally alive, rather than with one who was neutral and abstinent. Ferenczi's analysand Clara Thompson (1943) summarized his views succinctly when she said that Ferenczi "believed that the patient is ill because he has not been loved" (p. 64). **"Ferenczi reasoned: if the analytic situation is a repetition through the transference of the childhood situation, the same things must be important in analysis—the patient must need to feel loved and accepted by the analyst" (Thompson, 1964, p. 77).**

While Ferenczi's attempts at mutual analysis are often perceived as the worst-case scenario of analytic masochism, Ferenczi clearly came to recognize both the power and the limits of analytic love. In his *Clinical Diary* (1932), he speaks of the futility of pretending more friendliness toward the patient than one really feels (pp. 35–36). Similarly, in his final paper, Ferenczi wrote that children:

> cannot do without tenderness, especially that which comes from the mother. *If more love or love of a different kind from that which they need*, is forced upon the children in the stage of tenderness, it may lead to pathological consequences in the same ways as the frustration or withdrawal of love.
>
> (1933, p. 164, italics in original)

The greatness of Ferenczi's contribution lies in his persistent effort to understand and make therapeutic use of his feelings about his analysands at a time in analytic history when countertransference feelings were considered a sign only of the analyst's insufficiently eradicated neurosis.

In accord with Ferenczi, Ian Suttie and Suttie's wife Jane, also an analyst and the English translator of many of Ferenczi's papers, believed that what children want first and foremost is to receive *and* give loving tenderness with their parents and other caregivers. Suttie's relational alternative to drive theory focused on the importance of the bond between mother and child. In deliberate contrast to the work of Melanie Klein (1932), Suttie saw the wish for mutually exchanged love, and not instinctual forces of envy and aggression, as the organizing force in development.

In perhaps his most cogent and enduringly relevant observation, Suttie (1935) found that "tenderness itself was tabooed in our culture and science—tabooed more intensely even than sex—and that even psychoanalytic investigation and treatment was sharply limited by this bias" (p. 5). Suttie sought to "put the conception of altruistic (non-appetitive) love on a scientific footing" (p. 3), and in so doing, to make a clear case for a fully interpersonal, as opposed to id-driven, model of development. Anticipating Fairbairn's claim that the infant is object-seeking, Suttie's alternative to drive theory was "the conception of an innate need-for-companionship which is the infant's only way of self-preservation" (p. 6). He wrote:

> In the beginning of life none of the transactions between mother and infant could be distinguished . . . as "giving" or "getting" in the sense of "losing" or "gaining." The mother gives the breast, certainly, but the infant gives the mouth, which is equally necessary to the transaction of sucking" [p. 38] . . . . I consider the child wakes up to life with the germ of parenthood, the impulse to "give" and to "respond" already in it. This impulse, with the need "to get" attention and recognition, etc., motivates the free "give and take" of fellowship.
>
> (p. 58)

Continuing with Suttie's (1935) theory, he, like Michael and Alice Balint after him, deplored the demand in Western culture that children, for the sake of impatient parents, prematurely relinquish their rights to be childish—that is, dependent and in need of secure attachment. In contrast to Freud, he saw pathology as rooted less in oedipal jealousy and fear of the father, but rather in the thwarted need for the mother, which "must produce the utmost extreme of terror and rage, since the loss of mother is, under natural conditions, but the precursor of death itself" (p. 16). Pathology arises for Suttie not just when the mother fails to give adequately, but especially when the infant feels its own gifts are rejected by the mother. He says: "The rejection of the child's 'gifts,' like any failure to make adequate response, leads to a sense of badness, unlovableness in the self, with melancholia as its culminating expression" (p. 50). Forecasting Fairbairn's (1943) idea of "moral defense," Suttie described how the child "exonerate[s] the mother by condemning the self" (1935, p. 45). And anticipating Winnicott's (1960) concept of the false self, Suttie took note of the infant's "impulse to earn love by becoming what is wanted" (1935, p. 45), similar to the defensive strategy of identification with the aggressor that Ferenczi spoke about in 1933. For Suttie, "the 'overcoming of resistances' might almost be paraphrased as the development of a trust in the analyst-parent which will be capable of surviving the reproaches arising from repressed anxiety and rage" (1935, p. 217). The analyst must survive the child's/analysand's hate and destruction, an assertion Winnicott (1969) would later elaborate as a cornerstone of his own theory.

As noted, Michael Balint's and Suttie's views are remarkably similar. Balint (1937) introduced his concept of primary love specifically to refute Freud's concept of primary narcissism, believing, like Ferenczi and Suttie, that human beings are relationally oriented from the beginning. In the stage of primary love, mother and child ideally live interdependently, with boundaries blurred, in "an harmonious interpenetrating mix-up" (Balint, 1968). He saw the origin of psychopathology in disruptions and failures of this primary love experience. Analysands would then seek to use their analysis for the purpose of making a "new beginning," to "free himself of complex, rigid, and oppressive forms of relationship to his objects of love and hate . . . and to start simpler, less oppressive forms" (p. 134). Balint states:

> the analyst . . . must allow his patients to relate to, or exist with, him as if he were one of the primary substances . . . . [H]e must be there, must always be there, and must be indestructible—as are water and earth.
>
> (p. 167)

Some may see Balint as suggesting here that the analyst be constantly capable of an intrinsically false, utopian kind of bottomless empathy. In this interpretation, Balint is seen as endorsing a clinical technique that promotes the analyst's masochistic self-effacement, leading undesirably to the infantilization of the analysand, and to the exaltation of the analyst as an impossibly perfect parent. I believe, rather, that Balint is poignantly describing a particular form of analytic love, evoked by analysands deeply in touch with traumatic developmental experience, in which the analyst attempts as much as possible to set his/her own needs and analytic agendas aside. The analyst provides the analysand a new beginning with his/her nonimpinging, abiding presence, offered in the service of the analysand's efforts at reparative self-delineation. The idea here is similar to Winnicott's (1958) concept of the development of the capacity to be alone, to feel alive and real, in the presence of the other.

Although Fairbairn says virtually nothing about the role of analytic love in therapeutic cure, he is explicit, more than any other theorist, about the role of love in development and pathology:

The greatest need of a child is to obtain conclusive assurance (a) that he is genuinely loved as a person by his parents, and (b) that his parents genuinely accept his love. It is only in so far as such assurance is forthcoming in a form sufficiently convincing to enable him to depend safely upon his real objects that he is able gradually to renounce infantile dependence without misgiving. . . . Frustration of his desire to be loved as a person and to have his love accepted is the greatest trauma that a child can experience.

(Fairbairn, 1941, pp. 39–40)

With love so central to Fairbairn's theory, it is puzzling that he did not seem to consider the role love might play in analytic treatment. Whatever his reasons for this omission, Fairbairn's emphasis on love leads to the idea that the analyst's love, and how that love is exchanged and regulated in the analytic dyad, will play a central role in the recovery of the analysand's capacity to love and be loved.

Although Loewald was a passionate Freudian, his early work with Sullivan and Fromm-Reichmann (Mitchell & Black, 1995, p. 186) may have been an important conceptual link to the Ferenczian relational concepts that emerge in his work. Although comparing the analyst's functions to those of parents is as old as psychoanalysis itself, Loewald's formulation of this analogy is particularly significant because of the linkage he makes between love and respect, where he speaks of the parents' *"love and respect* for the individual and for individual development" (Loewald, 1960, p. 229, italics added). In Loewald's formulation, the parent holds and mediates to the child a hopeful vision of the child's potential, a vision based in an empathic, loving, and respectful recognition of the child's emerging identity. Loewald (1979) wrote that "it is the bringing forth, nourishing, providing for, and protecting of the child by the parents that constitute their parenthood, authority (authorship), and render sacred the child's ties with the parents" (p. 387).

Thus, for Loewald, analytic work is optimally conducted as a medium in which the analyst's love and respect for individual development serves to revive the analysand's derailed developmental processes—caused by failures in the regulation of love and respect in the parent–child matrix.

Teicholz (1999) points out the resonance between the work of Kohut and Loewald. Kohut's concept of the archaic selfobject can be linked with Ferenczi's stage of tenderness between infant and mother and Balint's stage of primary love (p. 102). Teicholz notes that *"Kohut's selfobject concept expressed an insistence on a lifelong, mutual interpenetration of selves, rather than on autonomy"* (p. 34, italics in original). This prorelational view of health led Kohut to recommend that the analyst protect and accept the analysand's idealization, rather than attempt to interpret it away. Kohut believed that this would allow disrupted developmental processes, based on the unavailability of a sufficiently idealizable archaic selfobject, to have a second chance to resume and take on new, more mature forms with the analyst. Kohut's ideas about the acceptance of the analysand's idealization seem especially congruent as well with Fairbairn's position of child development regarding the crucial importance for the child to have a sense that his/her love is recognized, felt, and welcomed—that is, that his/her love is good.

Although originally concerned with empathy primarily as the optimal psychoanalytic tool with which to gather data (Kohut, 1959), Kohut (1984) eventually asserted that the analyst's empathy was in and of itself a therapeutic agent (p. 74). With his emphasis on the importance, in both development and the clinical situation, of the recognition of mirroring, idealizing, and twinship selfobject needs, and with the privileging of an empathic listening perspective (Fosshage, 1997), I believe Kohut identified crucial ways in which love is provided and experienced between parent and child and in the analytic dyad. Ironically, but not surprisingly, given the climate of his day, he did so without actually using the word "love."

Discussion

Regarding the goals of contemporary relational psychoanalysis, Mitchell (1993) poses a series of questions:

> How does life come to feel real? significant? valuable? What are the processes through which one develops a sense of self as vital and authentic? How are these processes derailed, resulting in a sense of self as depleted, false, shallow?
>
> (p. 24)

To facilitate the analytic exploration of these central questions, I maintain an ongoing focus on the analysand's experience of parental love, which I see as crucially determining the analysand's sense of vitality and sense of the purpose and meaning of life. In seeking to understand the person before me, I assume that experiences of loving and being loved are either figure or ground at any given point in the analytic process. I seek to learn how these experiences have shaped their central organizing principles. For many, I have found that framing their relevant issues in these terms promotes access to dissociated affect and experience.

So how do we define analytic love? Analytic love is often left undefined, perhaps because it may at times resemble parental love, fraternal love, charitable love, friendly love, or erotic love. But it isn't any of those things. It is a thing unto itself.

I offer two defining principles. The first is expressed by Loewald (1960) in his statement that for things to go well, analysts must have "*love and respect for the individual and for individual development*" (p. 229, italics mine). For Loewald, it is not just love, but the joining of love with respect that constitutes the crucial components of the parental role in human development. If parental love is present, but *respect* for the individual and individual development is not, as when the child is treated primarily as a narcissistic extension of the parent (Miller, 1981), and in cases of abuse, neglect, and exploitation by parents, then there will be illness. Loewald implies that faith and belief in human potential is a defining characteristic of analytic love. **The analyst's love and respect encourage analysands whose experiences of deprivation of love, or of love without sufficient respect, have been overwhelmingly discouraging.** Loewald's phrase "love and respect" implies a sense of awe and reverence for human potential, and not just the parent–child bond as sacred, but also the analytic bond.

The second principle of analytic love is the analyst's commitment to the analysand's safety. Loewald's (1960) reference to parental love and respect as a kind of positive neutrality refers to the abstinence involved when a parent makes the effort to refrain, as best as possible, from narcissistically exploiting the child. Similarly, analysts who love and respect the analysand's capacity for development, and see the analysand as inherently worthy of love and respect, will seek to keep their love free from narcissistic, sexual, and other forms of exploitation. This is one of the major ways the crucial asymmetry (Aron, 1996) of the analytic relationship is upheld.

How do we get to analytic love? It does not happen simply by our own efforts. No doubt, many parents fall instantly in love with their babies the moment they are born, but often a parent's love grows slowly, in tandem both with the infant's emerging sense of self and with the infant's increasingly noticeable recognition of the parent. As Suttie pointed out, children have much to give parents, and not just vice versa. The same must be said for the analytic relationship. By responding to our therapeutic efforts, analysands provide us with a sense of efficacy, pride, and purpose, all of which constitute vitalizing selfobject experience (Bacal & Thomson, 1998). We sustain our analytic purpose with even the most difficult of analysands because we hope they will get better and that what we provide will be healing. As an analysand becomes aware of the deepening of our loving feelings, the analysand is not only affirmed, but encouraged in evoking those feelings in us. Both analyst and analysand feel valued, and recognized, for what they have to give, inspiring the other to succeed in reaching the goals of treatment. Mutuality in this interplay is vitalizing for the analyst, and therapeutic for the analysand (Aron, 1996).

I believe that in many cases, stalemates occur when the analysand is not progressing enough to provide the analyst with sufficient evidence of the power and impact of the analyst's love. In this situation, the analysand's withdrawal stimulates the analyst's frustration and counter-withdrawal because the analyst's vulnerability to the problematic aspects of his/her own history of loving and being loved have been stimulated.

Bacal and Thomson (1998) address this issue in terms of the selfobject needs of the analyst; some are ubiquitous, while others are specific to each analytic dyad. In my own case, when I feel that my love, in the form of my best analytic effort, is rejected, I find myself tempted to focus on how the analysand "provoked" or "elicited" my aversion. This is usually a sign that I am narcissistically wounded and preoccupied. In that state, I am at a disadvantage in terms of considering all the possible meanings of the analysand's behavior.

I hope that in an analysis I conduct, my patient and I are able to experience a full range of feelings for each other (Aron, 1996). **Without having avoided taking on sex and aggression, in the end, I would hope that our predominant feelings would include respect, understanding, acceptance, empathy, admiration, caring, the sincere wish for the other's happiness and fulfillment, and love.**

Let me return now to Ari. After the turning point I described earlier, Ari ceased ranting and began to tell his story. I was able to learn how his father dominated everyone around him, especially Ari, his only son. A successful, self-made man bitterly estranged from seven brothers, Ari's father worked hard, went bankrupt, and rebuilt his business, ultimately dying in his fifties of a heart attack. Ari's mother worked full-time and devoted herself to trying to assuage her husband. She did not intervene when father frequently slapped Ari's face for a wide variety of infractions. Ari was able to remember these incidents, with full affect. One in particular stood out and was especially painful. When his father wanted him to smile for a picture, Ari would have difficulty because of a defective tear duct, making it painful to have the sun in his eyes. Because Ari would squint when he had to pose, his father would smack him, shouting, "Now smile, goddamn it!" Childhood pictures of Ari were generally taken following a painful and humiliating slap by his father.

Perhaps most shameful of all, and something of which Ari rarely spoke, were the few times he saw his father slap his mother.

I was particularly struck by Ari's history of problems with school, and his identity in his family as a wild screw-up, because in spite of his difficulty with anxiety and rage, he was exceptionally hardworking, intelligent, and articulate. Ari and his wife were already preparing their son for high school examinations, hoping to enroll him in one of the best schools in New York, which in fact he later attended. As we explored this, I was able to ask him why he hadn't been helped to learn in the ways he was helping his son to learn. Was he ever helped to do better in school, or were his experiences of being accused, reproached, and humiliated all he could remember? Were his potentials recognized and nurtured at all? What did his mother think about or do about his father's frequent violence?

Ari began to grieve and weep, openly, in session after session. He wept for his own mistreatment, and for his repetition of this mistreatment with his wife, son, and employees. He wept for the guilt he felt of betraying his parents by acknowledging the abusive and neglectful dimensions of their behavior. I was deeply moved by Ari's tears. I felt honored that he could let himself be this vulnerable, and my loving feelings for him deepened. Now more in touch with the way his father had used anger against him, I was able to interpret to Ari his identification with his father, and how he treated his wife, son, and employees much as his father had treated him. I could confront him in this way because I believe we both knew that we trusted each other. I told him that he was in a war to the death with his wife, and that if one of them didn't try to make peace, they would go on living over each other's dead bodies. I repeated this many times.

Eventually, Ari reported that he was changing his behavior, that he had made love to his wife for the first time in two years, and that he was changing his attitude at work, calming down and managing conflict more smoothly. Ari reconnected with his deep love for his wife, transcending his grievances against her. The next year and beyond, he focused on calming himself down, gaining more detachment, learning when to keep his mouth shut, when to apologize, how to communicate more effectively.

It was powerfully moving to hear the ways that Ari was opening up and sharing himself with his son, to see his pride in and respect for his son, and although he had never heard a word of encouragement from his father, was making sure that his son would hear it from him. I loved Ari for this, certainly in connection with my own resonant feelings about both my father and my son, feelings that were often powerfully called forth while listening to Ari. I loved the tender aspects of himself he let me see, and his honesty and courage in engaging the analytic process.

The essence of this new experience, in Ari's case and in general, is that love can be experienced by both analyst and analysand as having greater vitalizing power than hate and fear. The challenge the analyst faces is to find a place from which to help the analysand choose love over hate, again and again, in spite of the many dangers the analysand faces in so doing.

I am aware that the way I have presented my work with Ari will be perceived by some as endorsing, in the name of analytic love, provision, direction, reassurance, and exhortation, all shibboleths of "proper" psychoanalysis. In a drive model, where interpretation is the exclusively permissible intervention, such forms of responsiveness indeed will have no proper place. But in a relational model that acknowledges the centrality of love and the necessity and inevitability of the analyst's emotional participation, I believe that these kinds of responses cannot be condemned automatically. These analytic modes were appropriate and beneficial in our work, as were the many struggles and negotiations we managed that often mobilized a good deal of aggression and conflict. Authentic analytic engagement will necessarily include a fluid, oscillating, and often simultaneous use of the analyst's capacity for empathic attunement as well as skill in negotiating difference toward mutual recognition. There cannot be any truly intimate human relationship without both relational experiences.

Conclusion

Is it necessary for the analyst to love the analysand in order to create a new relational experience that is curative? I don't presume to offer a universal, definitive answer. When, how, and whether the analyst experiences this love—and if it is experienced, whether or not it is ever made explicit—is co-determined from within each unique analytic dyad. I do not wish to imply that analytic love is a technique that can be used in certain ways to guarantee certain results. Analytic love, like any other meaningful love, is not a demand to be loved in return, or an attempt to control, or a deal you make in which you give the analysand love and the analysand gives you health. The understanding and acceptance of analytic love as a therapeutic agent is also influenced by the values of the analytic community, and determined by the extent to which our theories do, or do not, include and accept love as central in development, pathology, and technique. While significant contributions have been made by the theorists I discussed earlier, the complicated and crucial place of love in their work has yet to be more fully articulated and integrated into our theory and practice.

Hoffman (1998), speaking of the ironic and ambiguous aspects of the analyst's influence and authority, concludes that it is nevertheless our responsibility to use the power vested in us "in a way that is as wise, as compassionate, and as empowering of the analysand as possible" (p. 10). In a similar vein, I am saying that analytic love is indeed complicated and dangerous, and like all loving, carries the potential for devastating disappointment. This knowledge, rather than leading us to ignore, omit, or cancel our love, seems instead a call to persist in loving, as authentically, deeply, respectfully, and responsibly as we can.

References

Aron, L. (1996). *A meeting of minds*. Hillsdale, NJ: Analytic Press.

Bacal, H., & Thomson, P. (1998). Optimal responsiveness and the therapist's reaction to the patient's unresponsiveness. In H. Bacal (Ed.), *Optimal responsiveness* (pp. 249–270). Northvale, NJ: Jason Aronson,

Balint, M. (1937). Early developmental states of the ego: Primary object-love. In M. Balint (Ed.), *Primary love and psycho-analytic technique* (pp. 90–108). New York, NY: Liveright.

Balint, M. (1968). *The basic fault*. New York, NY: Tavistock.

Brandchaft, B. (1994, March). *Structures of pathological accommodation and change in analysis*. Paper presented at the Association for Psychoanalytic Self Psychology, New York, NY.

Davies, J. M. (1998). Between the disclosure and foreclosure of erotic transference–counter-transference: Can psychoanalysis find a place for adult sexuality? *Psychoanalytic Dialogues, 8*, 747–766.

Fairbairn, W. R. D. (1941). A revised psychopathology of the psychoses and psychoneuroses. *International Journal of Psychoanalysis, 22,* 250–279.

Fairbairn, W. R. D. (1943). The repression and the return of bad objects (with special reference to the "war neuroses"). *British Journal of Medical Psychology, 29,* 327–341.

Falzeder, E. (1994). My grand patient, my chief tormentor: A hitherto unnoticed case of Freud's and the consequences. *Psychoanalytic Quarterly, 63,* 297–331.

Ferenczi, S. (1932). *The clinical diary of Sándor Ferenczi.* J. Dupont (Ed.) (M. Balint & N. Z. Jackson, Trans.). Cambridge, MA: Harvard University Press, 1988.

Ferenczi, S. (1933). Confusion of tongues between adults and the child. In M. Balint (Ed.), *Final contributions to the problems and methods of psycho-analysis* (E. Mosbacher, Trans.) (pp. 156–167) London, England: Karnac, 1980.

Fosshage, J. (1992). Self psychology: The self and its vicissitudes within a relational matrix. In N. Skolnick & S. Warshaw (Eds.), *relational perspectives in psychoanalysis* (pp. 21–42). Hillsdale, NJ: Analytic Press.

Fosshage, J. (1997). Listening/experiencing perspectives and the quest for a facilitative responsiveness. In A. Goldberg (Ed.), *Conversations in self psychology: Progressive self psychology* (pp. 33–55). Hillsdale, NJ: Analytic Press.

Hoffman, I. (1998). *Ritual and spontaneity in the psychoanalytic process.* Hillsdale, NJ: Analytic Press.

Klein, M. (1932). *The psycho-analysis of children.* London, England: Hogarth Press.

Kohut, H. (1959). Introspection, empathy, and psychoanalysis. *Journal of the American Psychoanalytic Association, 7,* 459–483.

Kohut, H. (1984). *How does analysis cure?* Chicago, IL: University of Chicago Press.

Loewald, H. (1960). On the therapeutic action of psychoanalysis. In *Papers on Psychoanalysis* (pp. 221–256). New Haven, CT: Yale University Press.

Loewald, H. (1979). The waning of the Oedipus complex. In *Papers on Psychoanalysis* (pp. 384–404). New Haven, CT: Yale University Press, 1980.

Lothane, Z. (1998). The feud between Freud and Ferenczi over love. *American Journal of Psychoanalysis, 58,* 21–39.

Miller, A. (1981). *The drama of the gifted child.* New York, NY: Basic Books.

Mitchell, S. (1993). *Hope and dread in psychoanalysis.* New York, NY: Basic Books.

Mitchell, S. (2000). *Relationality.* Hillsdale, NJ: Analytic Press.

Mitchell, S., & Black, M. (1995). *Freud and beyond.* New York, NY: Basic Books.

Nacht, S. (1962). The curative factors in psycho-analysis. *International Journal of Psychoanalysis, 43,* 206–211.

Suttie, I. (1935). *The origins of love and hate.* New York, NY: Julian Press.

Teicholz, J. (1999). *Kohut, Loewald, and the postmoderns.* Hillsdale, NJ: Analytic Press.

Thompson, C. (1943). The therapeutic technique of Sándor Ferenczi: A comment. *International Journal of Psychoanalysis, 24,* 64–66.

Thompson, C. (1964). *Interpersonal psychoanalysis.* M. Green (Ed.). New York, NY: Basic Books.

Winnicott, D. W. (1947). Hate in the countertransference. In *Through paediatrics to psycho-analysis: Collected papers* (pp. 194–203). New York, NY: Basic Books.

Winnicott, D. W. (1958). The capacity to be alone. In *The maturational processes and the facilitating environment* (pp. 29–36). New York, NY: International Universities Press.

Winnicott, D. W. (1960). Ego distortion in terms of true and false self. In *The Maturational processes and the facilitating environment* (pp. 140–152). New York, NY: International Universities Press.

Winnicott, D. W. (1969). The use of an object and relating through identifications. In *Playing and reality* (pp. 86–94). London, England: Tavistock.

Part III

New Frontiers

Chapter 12

Relational Psychoanalytic Ethics

Professional, Personal, Theoretical, and Communal

Roy E. Barsness & Brad Strawn

Ethics is considered a core requirement in all curriculums for mental health practitioners, and demonstration of ethical proficiency is a requirement for licensure. And although the Code of Ethics within the mental health professions speaks to the integrity, dignity, and respect of our patients, it tends to primarily concern itself with professional liabilities (e.g., protection, do no harm, etc.) procedural ethics (e.g., privacy and confidentiality; record keeping, etc.) and the overall reputation of the discipline. What we seek to develop in this chapter is an ethic that subsumes and exceeds liabilities and procedures, positioning our ethics and our actions deeply within the person of the therapist and the therapeutic relationship itself. Most people today associate ethics with little more than a set of rules by which to temper one's behavior. However, in the past 20 years or so, ethics and ethical decision-making in psychotherapy have extended further than a clinician's behavior, to include ethical issues embedded within the very theories and techniques of psychotherapy and psychoanalysis (Doherty, 1995; Browning & Cooper, 2004; Meissner, 2003; Nicholas, 1994; Richardson, Fowers & Guignon, 1999; Rubin, 2004).

Browning and Cooper (2004) posit that schools of psychotherapy contain implicit ethics such as what is normal/abnormal, good/bad, how one ought to live life in relationship to others and self, and a even a vision of the "good life." Therefore, schools of psychotherapy can be conceptualized as ethical systems. Yet while these theories contain implicit ethics about a "way to live," they are neither cognizant nor explicit about the underlying philosophical commitments that *may or may not* inform their ethics. Philosophical ethicist Alasdair MacIntyre (2007) contends that this is because the Enlightenment project, in its attempts to create objectivity and universals, decontextualized ethics from any particular tradition, philosophical or religious. This leaves ethical reasoning and the implicit ethical theories utilized by psychotherapists practicing from a *thin ethic* which Dueck and Reimer (2009) define as "acontextual explanations of behavior and [assumption of] universal laws that are relationally abstract" (p. 124). As opposed to a thin ethic, a *thick* ethic is "historically particular, symbolically complex, and ethically maximalist" (p. 123). It is an ethic that places morals, values and images of "the good life" within cultural, ethnic, racial, socioeconomic and spiritual contexts. When clinicians operate from a thin ethic, they unwittingly resort to "lowest common denominator ethics" (Dueck, 2016, personal communication) which are supplied by a professional association or licensing board.

In this chapter, we argue that changes brought about through postmodernity, growing cultural awareness, and changes in psychoanalytic theory itself require psychoanalysis to pursue the development and practice of a thick ethic. This is clearly echoed by Goodman and Severson in their recent text, *The Ethical Turn: Otherness and Subjectivity in Contemporary Psychoanalysis* (2016), which claims:

> The rise of attachment and mentalization research, neuroscientific emphasis on our "social" brains, and the "relational turn" in several dominant theoretical models have all contributed to an *emphasis on moral considerations in human identity, development, and relationships*. relationality has become the occasion for ethics to be considered anew.
>
> (p. 3, italics added)

This chapter seeks to develop a thick ethic around four strands of thought, to assist in the development of a responsible *and* relational ethic, the *professional* ethics offered by our various organizations in which we locate our work (psychiatrist, psychologist, social worker, mental health practitioner), the *theoretical* ethics offered by the guidelines implicit in our chosen theories of practice, *the personal* ethics born out of our personal narratives, and the *communal* ethic informed by the moral responsibility to love and care for the other that calls forth a deep responsibility for the care of our patients beyond the codes of our disciplines, our theories, and our personal narratives.

Four Strands of Thought in Developing a Relational Ethic

The First Strand: Professional Standard Codes of Ethical Practices

Standard Codes of Practice are outlined by a professional association and/or licensing board. They are typically concerned with boundary issues such as dual relationships, appropriate and inappropriate therapeutic behavior, and the protection of clients, therapists, and the profession. When ethical codes are functioning at their best, they are in place for the safety and protection of our clients, practitioners, and the profession as a whole. These are agreed upon codes, vetted by a professional organization, and often hard learned through mistakes and litigation. These Codes of Practice absolutely need to be internalized by all clinicians, and are usually taught early in clinical training. Professional ethical codes, as they should, err on the side of patient protection. Perhaps no one has done more to write about the damage that occurs when these codes are violated than Glen Gabbard (2016) and Gabbard and Celenza (2003). Their chilling work deserves close and serious attention by both new and seasoned therapists.

The Second Strand: Theoretical Orientations

The second strand of psychotherapeutic ethics refers to what a therapist/analyst should or shouldn't do, as informed by their therapeutic orientation. The original psychoanalytic ethic established by Freud was an ethic of certainty. Freud "knew" and based his theory on the "fact" that mental health was dependent upon bringing forth repressed memories by making the unconscious conscious. The "weight of psychoanalytic technique was on the side of the knowledge of causes" (Summers, 2005, p. 222). Therefore, Freud himself ascribed to an ethic that anything other than offering his knowledge (e.g., interpretation) was considered unethical. Cognitive Behavioral Treatment models, which originally were seen as the great challengers to psychoanalysis, ironically share an ethic similar to Freud's, in that CBT also tends toward the prescriptive and is dependent upon the certitude of the model. It is the certainty of these two models that directs the therapist's ethical actions. We contend, therefore, that all therapeutic models have implicit ethics based on their theory.

So what is the "ethic" behind the relational model?

Changes to psychoanalytic theory which include object relations, self-psychology, and relational theories have led theorists over time to emphasize the therapeutic role of the analytic relationship itself (in juxtaposition to a model), as they have become frustrated with the classical model of analyst authority and interpretation as the primary conduit towards change. Summers (2005), as well as Maroda (personal communication, 2016), provocatively doubt, however, that the field of relational psychoanalysis has fully come to terms with the implications of these relational changes, and would argue that determining an ethic within the relational model is difficult because of the varied opinions on what exactly constitutes a psychoanalytic treatment.

Rather than getting bogged down in arguments between various schools, Summers (2005) goes on to suggest that psychoanalytic ethics will best be guided by "what the analyst uses to steer herself through the patient's world . . . intimately linked to her model of therapeutic action" (p. 220). Summers, attending to his own understanding of theory and therapeutic action, proceeds to propose an ethic that we feel does capture, in general, a relational psychoanalytic ethic. He states:

> The psychoanalytic ethic is the willingness to suspend presumptive knowledge in order to meet the uniqueness of the patient's experience, understand its structure and workings, and then make it possible for the patient to create new ways of being . . . . It is the analytic *process*, the way of aiding the patient's becoming himself, that defines the uniqueness of psychoanalytic therapy . . . . The ethic is the willingness to make contact with all aspects of the patient, both known and unknown, and let this encounter work on the analyst, to be influenced, as much as to influence.
>
> (Summers, 2005, p. 236)

We elaborate on this statement by considering two operating principles—honesty (Summers' idea of letting the encounter work on the analyst to be influenced as much as to influence) and fluidity (his idea of suspending presumptive knowledge). We believe these two principles are synchronous with the relational model and address the implications in the transition from the original psychoanalytic ethic of certainty to an ethic of relationality.

Honesty

Foundational to the practice of psychoanalysis, Freud required the patient to adhere to the rule of complete honesty. Although this was Freud's "assignment" given to his patients, we as therapists would be wise to assign this rule to ourselves. Privileging authority over honesty, certainty over transparency, relationships often descend into secrets and manipulations, communication breaks down, and the risks of boundary violations are heightened.

We use an interesting story from our shared legacy to illustrate the cost of authority over honesty by recounting Jung's account of the demise of his and Freud's relationship. Jung says:

> Freud had a dream—I would not think it right to air the problem it involved. I interpreted it as best I could, but added that a great deal more could be said about it if he would supply me with some additional details about his private life. Freud's response to these words was a curious look—a look of the utmost suspicion. Then he said, "But I cannot risk my authority!" At that moment he lost it altogether. That sentence burned itself into my memory; and in it the end of our relationship was already foreshadowed. Freud was placing personal authority above truth.
>
> (cited in Beebe, 1999, p. 616)

By placing personal authority above truth and honesty, Freud lost a friend and demonstrated not only how difficult it is to give up authority, but how this approach can be relationally deadening as well.

In Chapter 10, we spoke of disclosure/acknowledgement, in the harrowing case of Mary, who threatened to kill herself if her therapist did not go to bed with her. Though technically no professional ethical boundaries were breached, we suggested that perhaps a more serious violation occurred. In the therapist's inability to reach into his own fears, his constrictions, deep affective states, and his default into relying only on the code of ethics of his association, the patient was objectified. When the therapist withdrew into "good" behavior, the patient whose personal history sought contact through seduction and sexual conquest was forced to continue to objectify the therapist in much the same manner she had "learned" from her past, which caused her to descend into the similar chaos encountered in the abusive relationship with her father. Essentially caught in an impasse in the clash of what Benjamin (2004) refers to as the doer (the aggressor) and the done to (victim), patient and therapist treated each other as objects, one seeking to exploit, the other feeling exploited, this objectification of doer and done to ricocheting back and forth, passing off and pissing off, as therapy limped along. This objectification left the dyad focused on their individual selves—on the patient's desire and the therapist's safety—without consideration of the other's experience. It was an unethical discord, as it refused, in its fear, to consider together the context, the intentions and the experience of the other.

When it became apparent that conducting the dizzying ethical dilemmas only from an external ethic (i.e., in not gratifying her wishes and choosing to hide and protect by relentlessly interpreting her behavior as transference) was not working, the therapist "turned" toward the patient and addressed the dynamic out loud by offering his own subjectivity, and the treatment shifted. As interpretations ceased and were replaced with questions such as "What are we going to do here?" "What is ethically correct here? "What will bring life to us?" "What is this seduction seeking?" "How can we better see and be seen?", the analytic encounter began to take on new shape. This stance of honesty released the patient to a broader imagining, and rather than acting out on the threat, the analytic couple was able to speak more boldly of desire, of the limits of desire, and of love.

What was discovered was that an externally imposed "applied" ethic alone was insufficient as it did not take into account the suffering with and for the other, and the analyst's ethical responsibility of "bearing" the traumatized other. The analyst could not provide what Stolorow calls a "'relational home' in which the traumatic experience, with all of its disorganizing consequences, can be welcomed and held" (cited in Orange, 2015, p. 3). What did work was a relationally negotiated ethic supplied via honesty and safety, where the therapist did not act as the distant third, but as part of the relational context. It was, as philosopher Martin Buber so poignantly stated, that change occurs when we eventually lay our hands:

[i]n the wound of the other and learn: this concerns you (the patient, not just me, my fears, my concerns that) . . . it may strike him (the psychologist) that the orientation . . . and the treatment of the therapist have changed unawares and that if he wishes to persist as a healer he must take upon himself a burden he had not expected to bear.

(cited in Agassi, 1999, p. 116)

Since that time, and in the therapist's frequent recollections of this difficult time in their work, he has reflected upon what would have happened when terrorized by Mary's threats had he just said, "Well we just can't do that!—an ethic informed out of ethical codes of his association, but also, as we will see later, out of a moral ethic that sought the dignity of the other. Perhaps the quest would have changed, and inquiries such as "So now what are we going to do?" "What have we done?" might have followed. Simply imagining these varied responses offers relief from the press to violate the frame, and a fresher mind open to discovery. It was the therapist's lack of honesty which compromised the integrity of the therapy. In the therapist's inability to acknowledge his/her own personal limitations and the limitations inherent in their work, the patient could not find *his/her* "no," and kept pressing to find the boundary. When the therapist was able "to in part lay his hand in the wound" rather than using his/her authority, fueled by fear, the honest response did not limit the patient; rather, it opened up new possibilities of expression and connection, as well as expanding both the patient's and the therapist's imaginations. We contend that it is therapeutic honesty that captures part one of Summers' (2005) psychoanalytic ethic, "which is our willingness to make contact with all aspects of the patient, both known and unknown, and let this encounter work on the analyst, to be influenced, as much as to influence" (p. 236).

Fluidity

Our understanding of the second operating principle within the strand of theoretical ethics—fluidity—is best understood through the lens of set theory. Sorenson (1996) states: "western thought is dominated by bounded set thinking, in which set membership is determined by essential characteristics, clear boundaries, uniformity of membership and static classifications" (p. 183).

If we appreciate the contemporary relational psychoanalytic model as one that endorses the centrality of relationality, dynamic non-linear boundaries, and that the power differential is negotiated by the therapist and the patient, thus radically changing the very concept of therapeutic authority, we need to reconsider our ethics beyond bounded sets. In contrast, centered sets are interested in what is at the center of the set and if action is moving toward that center:

What matters is what's at the center more than what's at the edge . . . .
Boundaries emerge out of relationship to the center. Boundaries are
penultimate concerns; the heart or the center of the set is of primary
importance. Objects within the set are variable rather than uniform,
and dynamic rather than static.

(Sorenson, 1996, p. 183)

In describing our ethic from within a relational psychoanalytic
orientation, the center of the set is a movement toward a particular relational
configuration that attends to the ever-emergent emotional landscape
developing between the analytic pair. Shane (2006) states that within such
an orientation:

nonlinear aspects of the boundary are neither preset nor based on
predictable cause-and-effect connections or on unvarying standards.
Rather, they are based on personal and interpersonal considerations,
as well as on any constraints arising individually and interpersonally
between patient and analyst.

(p. 45)

Just as the psychotherapeutic frame within a relational approach to psychotherapy needs to be fluid and mutually engaging, to remain theoretically
consistent throughout our practices, we must also locate our ethics fluidly by
attending specifically to each relational dyad. The psychoanalytic frame and
the setting of boundaries and technique are not concise, economical, nor
formulaic. Rather, they must bend to the variegated contours of the uniqueness of each interpersonal encounter while always determined by a center
that is willing, as Summers has stated, to "suspend presumptive knowledge
in order to meet the uniqueness of the patient's experience" (Summers, 2005,
p. 236).

Though a boundary ethic is ostensibly established to protect the patient,
it is often used for therapist self-protection from the uncomfortable affective states generated in the countertransference experience. The foundational bedrock of relational psychoanalysis, however, is that it is the depth
and quality of the relational interaction that yields meaning and change
in our patients' lives. This requires an awareness of how two people
effect one another, the need to speak candidly about the experience, and a
willingness to get lost for a while as together, patient and therapist sort out

messages seeking voice and resolve. From early on, psychoanalysis has believed that "what turns the scale is not intellectual insight, but the relationship to the doctor" (Freud, 1921, p. 90). This is not an "anything goes" ethic, but a contemporary relational theory ethic that espouses the operating principles of honesty and fluidity which lead to genuine connection and safety.

This second strand, theoretical ethics, if it is situated in a centered set—that is, a relational configuration that is not pre-set and attends to personal and interpersonal considerations—trends towards developing what we have referred to as a "thick" ethic. It does so because inherent in its stance, authority is co-determined and the analytic work is considered as a living and dynamic partnership. It is the therapeutic relationship that is the determinant of our ethics, not our certainty or knowledge. Within the relational model, we situate ourselves relationally as "subjects," not as "objects." We stand toward our patient as a Thou requiring us to "turn" toward the other (patient), listen with an ear to confirm the other, and address the other as a sacred subject. We do this by responding honestly and with fluidity, offering our authentic thoughts, affects, and experiences, respectfully, and with humility.

But is relationality enough?

The Third Strand: Personal Ethics

Philip Cushman (1995) and Richardson et al. (1999), in their hermeneutic critiques of psychology and psychotherapy, suggest that our theory of relationality is not enough. Rather, they would argue that our ethics come from somewhere, and are informed by something other than "choice" of model or what our associations may dictate. Browning and Cooper's (2004) critique of psychotherapeutic ethics is that our theoretical models and/or association standards do not take into account one's history, including one's unacknowledged culture, including, but not limited to, ethnicity, race, socioeconomic status, religion, and so on, and that these are not dead and buried, but are actual living, breathing influences which shape one's understandings in numerous and unconscious ways, literally impacting how one makes sense of one's present experiences in the world.

What this demands of psychoanalysis is that we cannot pretend that we as individuals or our theories and our practice are objective, neutral, or in any way disconnected from history, "pre-understanding," or context/

culture. Even more importantly, Cushman (1995) and Richardson et al. (1999) assert that even our psychotherapy theories are products of the social locations in which they are developed, because the theorists themselves were contextualized in time and place. These writers worry that when psychotherapies present themselves as objective and neutral practices, free from moral or ethical influences and concerns, they become "unwitting conspirators with and reinforcements of the dominant social and cultural ethos of our age, i.e., the rational-choice processes of the market and the individualistic and consumerist ethic that it encourages" (Browning and Cooper, 2004, p. 9). Cushman goes so far as to state that by being so contextualized in the culture from which it develops, psycho- therapy may unwittingly and unknowingly perpetuate the very problems it is attempting to repair. These problems may include, but are not limited to, consumerism (e.g., an empty self that must be filled) and individualism (e.g., an autonomous self that looks to itself as a source of truth and knowledge). The ethic that is unknowingly embedded within much of psychotherapy theory and emerges in treatment is what MacIntyre (2007) refers to as emotivism—where the self is the sole arbitrator for truth and ethical decision-making. Subsequently, ethics become a matter of personal preference. In similar ways, this critique has been used in the vast literature on cultural psychology, which psychoanalysis is just now attempting to incorporate, noting the Western bias of most psychotherapy theories and the violence that can accrue when these theories are forced on patients from diverse cultures (Dueck & Reimer, 2009).

Crucial to our point is that while psychotherapy and psychoanalysis have attempted to present themselves as moral neutral activities, divorced from any traditional moral or religious systems, Doherty (1995) and Browning and Cooper (2004) convincingly demonstrate that schools of psychotherapy are in fact "practical moral philosophies" (p. 7) or *cultures*, and are not neutral:

> By "culture" I mean a system of symbols and norms that guides a society or group by providing general images of the nature of the world, the purpose of life, and at least some of the basic principles by which life should be lived. It is often thought that the modern psychologies are basically scientific and to this extent do not provide answers to life's meaning. But it is my argument that most of the prominent modern psychologies [psychoanalysis included], in addition

to whatever scientific value that they may have, do indeed cross over into what must be recognized as types of positive cultures—cultures, indeed, that possess religio-ethical dimensions.

(p. 4)

So while psychoanalytic theories contain these implicit ethics or "cultures," they are thin ethics because they have become decontextualized from any *explicit* cultural and communal narratives often found within traditional religious, spiritual, and moral systems, leaving them in the realm of ethical emotivism. Theories, therefore, traffic in the realm of ethics—that is, how one should live one's life, theories of normal and abnormal, and so on, but in fact are bereft to answer these larger moral questions. Not having a clearly articulated thick ethic, most psychoanalytic theories degenerate to a treatment Fromm called "social adjustment," as opposed to "cure of the soul" (Fromm, 1950, p. 65). Subsequently:

> The end goals of contemporary psychoanalytic treatment are assumed according to their perspective theories, and the focus of the therapeutic process is solely upon technique and effectiveness in transforming human persons into well-adjusted individuals.
>
> (Wright, Jones & Strawn, 2014, p. 41)

Relational psychoanalysis has, either by intent or by accident, seemed to move the discussion of ethics located in the individual to ethics embedded in the other (e.g., the relational turn). The way that this has been addressed within the relational approach is to consider ethics in the "we" or the "us," thus thickening our ethic. However, unless relationality is grounded in something beyond itself, it may fall into the same trap as any other decontextualized theory. And given our propensity for denial and rationalization, we risk entering into destructive relations by calling certain relationships ethical when they may simply be meeting our own personal preferences and needs (i.e., having sex with patients, reckless disclosures, touch, gifts, withholding, increasing sessions for one's own needs only, etc.) or mirroring the implicit thin ethic of the larger cultural milieu (e.g., individualism and consumerism).

As we continue to consider the impact of "cultures" within our orientations and the various ways they are languaged and how they "orient" us, we must consider our own personal contexts and their impact when considering our ethical choices. We are exposed to and subsequently choose our ethics from the kitchen tables of our past, our institutions that trained us, the personal experiences that have shaped us, and the cultures that formed us. In developing a moral ethic (Strand Four) we seek the assistance of philosophers Emmanuel Levinas and Martin Buber, but we pause here as we note how Levinas and Buber's personal contexts (Strand Three) influenced their own moral ethics.

Buber's life was dominated by a deep love for the Torah, Hasidic stories, and mysticism. He was exiled from Nazi Germany, and lived in Jerusalem while holding a deep passion and concern for those suffering in Palestine. His mother, who abandoned him as a child, influenced his ideas of mismeeting and his subsequent "discovery" of I/Thou and genuine encounter. Levinas was a revered teacher of the Talmud, and a French philosopher influenced by Bergson, Husserl, and Heidegger. He was a traumatized survivor of the war, during which he was imprisoned for five years and everyone in his family was murdered. He later said that his entire life "was dominated by the presentiment and the memory of the Nazi horror" (Levinas, 1990, p. 291). His primary ethic—responsibility for the other—emerged from his response to this horror. For both of these philosophical giants, their ethics emerged from their personal narratives and their devout Judaism.

We also acknowledge that our ethics emerge from within our own context and narratives which are deeply embedded in the Judeo-Christian traditions and the doctrine of the Trinity, which taught us to love one's neighbor as oneself, to regard the other more highly than oneself, and to treat the other with reverence and as a holy other. What we are suggesting is that when we speak of personal ethics, each of us must consider their ethical stance from within their own particular context. Why? If we are not clear "what" influences us from within our own context/culture/tradition and its impact on what we do, we are left in danger of unknowingly and unwittingly repeating, acting out, and dominating the therapeutic theater from our own personal biases.

The Fourth Strand: Communal Ethics

Ultimately, responsibility implies not only fidelity to codes of professional ethics or attending to a particular therapeutic stance or a deep awareness of our cultural/context. We are moral beings who are wired to consider our lives and the lives of others from within a moral hermeneutic. Something is called forth from the very person of the therapist/analyst, and we are left to ask: "what constitutes our own moral center or hegimonikon, as the Ancient Greeks and Romans would have called it? Where do we hear the voice of the daimon [spiritual force] of conscience of responsibility?" (Orange, 2015, p. 32).

Here, the ethical question is: "Who am I, and what is my responsibility to you—my other?"

Given the cautions noted above about implicit ethics embedded in our theories which mirror culture, we argue that Strand Four—the Communal—must *explicitly* contextualize itself in thick ethical traditions (philosophically and spiritually) that embrace culture, and communal narratives that are particular, historical, resist reductionism, and embrace specificity, complexity, humility, and human dignity. For this reason, we ground our work in the philosophical, ethical/religious traditions of Emmanuel Levinas and Martin Buber. In doing so, we are not assuming that this is *the* tradition that all readers may be drawn to, but offer it as a position and a possibility, as well as an invitation, for readers to consider what determines their own moral ethic. Second, as will be noted, ethics within relational psychoanalysis recently has been deeply influenced in particular by Levinas, and we wish to expand the discussion. Third, we are not offering Levinas and Buber up as the patron saints of the Communal Ethic, disconnecting the reader from their own traditions. On the contrary, we contend that just as the ethics of these two philosophers emerged from their own traditions (Judaism), they exemplify for us the importance and the necessity of moral ethics formed out of and from one's own tradition. Consequently, this requires clinicians to reflect upon their own traditions and their influences on their ethical decision-making (Wright et al., 2014).

With this in mind, we have noted that in considering ethics from within the realm of moral ethics, relational psychoanalysis recently leans towards a Levinasian view (see Goodman and Severson, 2016; Orange, 2015). The Levinasian idea of the face of the other—and his concept of responsibility—parallel much of what we think of when we talk of asymmetry within relational psychoanalysis, and Levinas' radical self-for-the-other is an important contribution to our consideration of ethics. However, as relational psychoanalysis has shifted into intersubjectivity and co-construction, we must also attend to the self-within and between-the-other and the implications thereof. Here we find Buber's I/Thou and his Distance and Relation useful. The cross-fertilization of the two, however, seems essential, as both seek a way of being with the other that is profoundly dignified in fostering a deep and respectful ethic of the other. It is the response-ability to the other that grounds the two philosophies together.

For Levinas, defining an ethic is a radical asymmetrical relationship. The "other" must exceed oneself. One's own needs, wants, desires, must be forfeited for the sake of the other. He states: "I become a responsible or ethical 'I' to the extent that I agree to depose or dethrone myself—to abdicate my position of centrality—in favor of the vulnerable other" (Levinas, cited in Cohen, 1986, pp. 26–77). From this view, when we address our patients, we address them with no expectation in return. At the moment of our encounter, an obligation is placed upon us where the patient is considered "more than me, more than my equal" (Levinas, cited in Critchley, 2002, p. 14). Orange (2011) explains:

> the other (*Autrui*, the human other) presents me with an infinite demand for protection and care. The face says, "you shall not kill (*tu ne tueras point*). You shall not allow me to die alone . . . the response [toward the other] must be 'Me voici'" (me here).
>
> (pp. 46–47)

This is a profound and sobering command—a command that exceeds the ethics of our associations that say "do no harm," placing a deep responsibility upon us in Levinas' positioning of "me here" and "you shall not die alone."

As we take up this sobering command, we wish, however, to enlarge Levinas' ethic with a relational perspective in mind. We would suggest expanding Levinas' "*me here*" not only from "me here for me to take you in, and stand for you," but also "*me*" here for you (the patient) to also be able to see—to see the other, in order to find your own "*me*" here, with the understanding that well-being is not only to be seen but to also see. To have a "self," Mitchell (1993) reminds, "needs a protagonist, someone who does things and to whom things happen" (p. 145), or as Summers (2005) offers, "to be influenced, as much as to influence" (p. 236).

Therefore, we are not only the suffering servant therapist who contains all projections, survives all attacks. The patient also comes to see us as having a separate subjectivity. In fact, according to Benjamin, "mutual recognition is the capacity to see others as equal subjects . . . and the reciprocating experience of the other's acknowledgement of oneself" (cited in Hoffman, 2011, p. 12). In Chapter 6 in this volume, we see Stuart Pizer expanding Levinas' thinking in his suggestion that:

> Perhaps we can locate here a dimension of the non-masochistic "one-for-the-other" when the self (of the analyst) and the other, at moments, might *both* be served by "one-for-the-we," holding in mind that the analytic "we" is in the service of a mission to attend usefully to the suffering of the Other.
>
> (p. 114)

Buber also held to an asymmetrical idea of the therapeutic relationship, and was quite adamant about this in his conversations with Carl Rogers. Buber insisted that the therapeutic relationship was asymmetrical and an unequal dialogue bounded by tragedy. We believe, however, that he inadvertently gets to the idea of mutual recognition when he states: "the [therapeutic] relationship would be ended when the patient was able to experience the psychotherapist's side of the relationship" (Buber, 1970, p. 182). Relational psychoanalysis would agree, but adds that recognition is on a developmental trajectory, and that this "successful" ending that Buber speaks about that ends in mutual recognition was the result of many mutual moments occurring throughout the treatment.

Whereas Levinas' primary ethic is situated in his responsibility to the other, Buber, on the other hand, believed that the primary movement of human life and one's own existence is dependent upon the other. For Buber, relationships are twofold. There is the I–It world that objectifies, categorizes, and reduces the other to what the observer observes, and there is the I–Thou world that stands open for mutual reciprocity, where "when I address you as a 'Thou' I enter into direct relationship with you as a uniquely whole person, not merely as an identity" (Buber, 1970, p. 19).

What is important in this stance is Buber's concept of distance and relation. To meet the other, one must stand in contrast to the other, to stand with their whole being. This differs from Levinas, whose authentic expression of his own being never comes into consideration. For Buber, both persons need to be present in their difference as much as one can be. For health to occur, the patient seeks to be confirmed *and* to confirm. Buber says it this way:

> the basis of man's life with man is twofold, and it is one—the wish of every man to be confirmed as what he is, even as what he can become,

by men; and the innate capacity in man to confirm his fellow men in
this way.

(Buber, 1947, p. 12)

The basic words I/Thou can only be spoken with one's whole being. The
basic word I–It can never be spoken by one's whole being (p. 54). If
the goal of our work is for our patients to speak from their whole being,
then we too will be met in some way by them. They can only heal if they
feel they have also in some way had an impression of us, or have observed
a movement and change in us in which they have played a part. In the end,
Buber states: "I felt I have not the right to want to change another if I am
not open to be changed by him" (cited in Agassi, 1999, p. 249).

Ethics can quickly turn into conversations of "oughts." Apart from egre-
gious violations that sicken, as well as questionable analytic interpretations or engagements where we might raise our technical eyebrows, we
suggest that ethics not be based on an "ought," but rather, an embodied
thick ethic rooted in intersubjectivity, regard for the other, truthfulness,
advocacy, and mutual recognition. In considering what we "ought to do or
ought not to do," we borrow again from Martin Buber, whose "ought" is
grounded in his conception of authentic existence. From Buber's perspective, our ethical decisions extend beyond the "ought." This requires a
deeper responsibility to be faithful stewards reflective of our motivations
and our intentions, confirming what is good, truthful, and honoring, and
measuring our actions by our contribution to human flourishing. It is a
"lived" ethic where the ethical "responsibility is brought back from the
province of *specialized* ethics, of an 'ought' that swings free in the air, into
that of lived life. Genuine responsibility exists only where there is real
responding" (Buber, 1947, p. 16, italics added). "Real" responding is at the
core of relational psychoanalysis, embedded in theoretical concepts such as
intersubjectivity and mutual recognition, where ethics are not viewed as
static, or controlled by those in authority, but more poignantly, they are to
be lived in the lively dynamics of human connection and encounter.

In working with this chapter, we wondered about our draw, and the draw
for many in the analytic community, to the ethical considerations of
Levinas and Buber. We believe it is because both theorists resist discussing
rules, or dictums alone (Strand One), but rather, as one continues to
saturate oneself with their philosophies (the deeply embedded Strand
Three of their personal context), one begins to "feel" something, something

calling deep within the human condition of our mutual need for contact, our need to be honored, dignified, loved, and respected. We discover an ethic dependent upon the dignity of the other, the sacredness of the other, and we discover it in our guts and within our common humanity, not only in our texts, our theories, and our rules.

Conclusion

Before we review the four strands, it is important to note that in working out our ethics from within our associations, our psychoanalytic orientations, and our own personal cultural contexts, and in developing a communal/moral ethic, we would suggest a need for a kind of "distanciation" (Ricoeur), which Browning and Cooper (2004), describe as:

> the human capacity for reflectivity that makes it possible to both be conscious of one's historically conditioned beginning point but also partially distance or detach oneself from it, not in any absolute way but to some degree. Objectivity suggests absolute detachment; distanciation points to the simultaneous use of one's historical horizon and yet partial detachment from it to examine and test that very horizon.
>
> (p. 11)

This kind of distanciation, although always partial, can allow practitioners to critique the implicit ethics of their own theories and to acknowledge the particularity of their contextualization (e.g. ethnicity, race, socioeconomic status, religion, etc.) as well as their own cultural and moral traditions.

In developing our psychotherapeutic ethic, we have offered four interlocking strands we believe are critical to the foundation of an ethical professional life. In Strand Four—Communal Ethics—we make the claim that we must clearly embed our theory in a thick ethic. We have attempted to do this through an understanding of the value of the human person and the responsibility we bear to act towards the other with sacredness and dignity as understood within the ethical context of Emmanuel Levinas and Martin Buber, which resonates with our own Judeo-Christian context. In Strand Three—Personal Ethics—we have suggested that we must know ourselves within our own cultural context and the influences of our familial, religious-spiritual formations and how our personal "cultures" influence us in our ethical decision-making toward the other.

In Strand Two—Theoretical Orientations—we have suggested we must know the implicit ethics within our orientations. We have noted that in the relational model, we have moved from a model of certainty toward an ethic of relationality. Lastly, in Strand One—Professional Ethics—we have affirmed that the ethics of our professions guide and offer a certain level of safety for both the therapist and the patient. We ask, though, how safe is safe, if one's ethics are guided by a system not grounded within the analytic dyad, within our own personal narratives, within an ethic rooted in our own traditions, and within an ethic informed by our responsibility to the other?

Why have we gone down this path? Why the four strands? Why the emphasis upon a Communal Ethic? First, because we see it as good practice. Second, because the relational model has shifted ethics from the authority implicit within a model to an ethic situated within the therapeutic encounter. This requires of us to attend anew to our own convictions, traditions, and anthropologies. Third, we contend that a communal ethic— an ethic grounded in an anthropology of the nature of the person and the responsibility we bear in assisting one in the discovery of "becoming"— *thickens* our theoretical orientations and the ethics of our associations. These four strands—our professional, theoretical, personal, and communal ethics—overlap and interlock. Together, they strengthen each other, deepening our ethical awareness, and offer a greater accountability in our clinical work.

References

Agassi, J. (1999). *Martin Buber on psychology and psychotherapy: Essay, letters and dialogues*. New York, NY: Syracuse University Press.

Beebe, J. (1999). Integrity in the psychoanalytic relationship. *Psychoanalytic Review, 86*, 607–626.

Benjamin, J. (2004). Beyond doer and done to: An intersubjective view of thirdness. *Psychoanalytic Quarterly, 73*, 5–46.

Browning, D. S., & Cooper, T. D. (2004). *Religious thought and the modern psychologies*. Minneapolis, MN: Fortress Press.

Buber, M. (1947). *Between man and man*. London, England: Routledge.

Buber, M. (1970). *I and Thou* (W. Kaufman, Trans.). New York, NY: Touchstone, 1923.

Cohen, R. (1986). *Face to face with Levinas*. Albany, NY: State University of New York Press.

Critchley, S. (2002). *The Cambridge companion to Levinas*. London, England: Cambridge University Press.

Cushman, P. (1995). *Constructing the self, constructing America: A cultural history.* Reading, MA: Addison Wesley.

Doherty, W. (1995). *Soul searching: Why psychotherapy must promote moral responsibility.* New York, NY: Basic Books.

Dueck, A., & Reimer, K. (2009). *A peaceable psychology: Christian therapy in a world of many cultures.* Grand Rapids, MI: Brazos Press.

Freud, S. (1921). Group psychology and the analysis of the ego. In J. Strachey (Ed. & Trans.), *The standard edition of the complete psychological works of Sigmund Freud* (Vol. 18). London, England: Hogarth Press.

Fromm, E. (1950). *Psychoanalysis and religion.* New Haven, CT: Yale.

Gabbard. G. (2016). *Boundaries and boundary violations in psychoanalysis* (2nd ed.). Washington, DC: American Psychiatric Publishing.

Gabbard, G., & Celenza, A. (2003). Analysts who commit sexual boundary violations: A lost cause? *Journal of the American Psychoanalytic Association, 51*(2), 617–637.

Goodman, D., & Severson, E. (2016). *The ethical turn: Otherness and subjectivity in contemporary psychoanalysis.* New York, NY: Routledge.

Hoffman, M. (2011). *Toward mutual recognition.* New York, NY: Routledge.

Levinas, E. (1990). *Difficult freedom: Essays on Judaism.* Baltimore, MD: Johns Hopkins University Press.

MacIntyre, A. (2007). *After virtue: A study in moral theory* (3rd ed.). Notre Dame, IN: Notre Dame University Press.

Meissner, W. W. (2003). *The ethical dimension of psychoanalysis: A dialogue.* Albany, NY: State University of New York Press.

Mitchell, S. (1993). *Hope and dread in psychoanalysis.* New York, NY: HarperCollins.

Nicholas, M. (1994). *The mystery of goodness and the positive moral consequences of psychotherapy: Exploring altruism, responsibility, egalitarianism, justice and honesty.* New York, NY: Norton.

Orange, D. (2011). *The suffering stranger: Hermeneutics for everyday clinical practice.* New York, NY: Routledge.

Orange, D. (2015). *Nourishing the inner life of clinicians and humanitarians: The ethical turn in psychoanalysis.* New York, NY: Routledge.

Richardson, F. C., Fowers, B. J., & Guignon, C. B. (1999). *Re-envisioning psychology: Moral dimensions of theory and practice.* San Francisco, CA: Jossey-Bass.

Rubin, J. B. (2004). *The good life: Psychoanalytic reflections on love, ethics, creativity, and spirituality.* New York, NY: State University of New York Press.

Shane, E. (2006). Developmental systems of self-psychology. *International Journal of Psychoanalytic Self Psychology, 1*, 23–46.

Sorenson. R. L. (1996). "Where are the nine?" *Journal of psychology and theology,* 24(3), 170–196.

Summers, F. (2005). Therapeutic action, epistemology, and the ethic of psychoanalysis. *International Journal of Applied Psychoanalytic Studies, 2*, 220–236.

Wright, R. W., Jones, P., & Strawn, B. D. (2014). Tradition-based integration. In E. D. Bland & B. D. Strawn (Eds.), *Christianity and psychoanalysis: A new conversation* (pp. 37–54). Downers Grove, IL: Inter-Varsity Press.

Chapter 13

The Right Brain and Psychoanalysis

Allan Schore

In 2009, the American Psychological Association invited me to offer a plenary address, "The Paradigm Shift: The Right Brain and the relational Unconscious." In fact, that was the first time an APA plenary address was given by a member in private practice, and by a clinician who was also psychoanalytically informed. Citing 15 years of my interdisciplinary research, I argued that a paradigm shift was occurring not only within psychology, but also across disciplines, and that psychology now needed to enter into a more intense dialogue with its neighboring biological and medical sciences. I emphasized the relevance of developmental and affective neuroscience (more so than cognitive neuroscience) for clinical and abnormal psychology. And so I reported that both clinicians and researchers were now shifting focus from left brain conscious cognition to right brain unconscious emotional and relational functions (A. N. Schore, 2009), consistent with a statement only a few years before where the APA explicitly articulated its newfound emphasis on the relational foundations of psychotherapy. In 2006, the APA Presidential Task Force on Evidence-Based Practice boldly stated:

> Central to clinical expertise is interpersonal skill, which is manifested in forming a therapeutic relationship, encoding and decoding verbal and nonverbal responses, creating realistic but positive expectations, and responding empathically to the patient's explicit and implicit experiences and concerns.
>
> (p. 277)

This relational trend in psychotherapy had largely evolved from seminal contributions of psychodynamic clinicians, including Sullivan (1953), Kohut (1971), Mitchell (1988), and more recently, Bromberg (2011).

Over this same period, in parallel to psychological advances in psychotherapy, the paradigm shift to a relational "two-person psychology" had
also progressed within neuroscience, especially in the discipline of interpersonal neurobiology. In this chapter, I briefly summarize my work in
that field, utilizing the relational perspective of regulation theory (A. N.
Schore, 1994, 2003a, 2003b, 2012) to model the development, psychopatho-
genesis, and treatment of the implicit subjective self. This interdisciplinary
work integrates psychology and biology in order to more deeply understand precisely how relational experiences, for better or worse, impact the
early development of psychic structure and the emergent subjective self,
and how these structures are expressed at all later stages of the lifespan,
especially in psychotherapeutic contexts. My studies continue to describe
the fundamental role of the early developing right brain in relational processes. In the following, I briefly present interpersonal neurobiological
models of attachment in early development, in the therapeutic alliance, in
mutual therapeutic enactments, and in the therapeutic change processes.
This work highlights the fact that the current emphasis on nonconscious
relational processes is shared by, cross-fertilizing, and indeed transforming both psychology and neuroscience, with important consequences for
clinical psychological models of psychotherapeutic change. Regulation
theory strongly supports currently evolving psychodynamic models of
psychotherapy, especially in the treatment of early-forming attachment
trauma.

Interpersonal Neurobiology of Attachment: Interactive
Regulation and the Maturation of the Right Brain

A major contributor to the current relational trend derives from recent
advances in attachment theory, now the most influential theory of early
social-emotional development available to science. Following John
Bowlby's (1969) seminal contributions, over the last two decades I have
utilized an interdisciplinary relational perspective to describe and integrate
the developmental psychological and biological processes that underlie the
formation of an attachment bond of emotional communication between
the infant and primary caregiver (A. N. Schore, 1994, 2003a, 2003b, 2012).
Modern attachment-relational theory (J. R. Schore & A. N. Schore, 2008)
is essentially a theory of the development of affect regulation, and thus
emotional development. During attachment episodes of right-lateralized

visual-facial, auditory-prosodic, and tactile-gestural nonverbal communications, the primary caregiver regulates the infant's burgeoning positive and negative bodily based affective states, thereby shaping the development of the early maturing right brain (A. N. Schore, 1994, 2003a, 2003b, 2012).

At the most fundamental level, the right brain attachment mechanism is expressed as interactive regulation of affective-autonomic arousal, and thereby the interpersonal regulation of biological synchronicity between and within organisms. During dyadic attachment transactions, the sensitive primary caregiver implicitly attends to, perceives (recognizes), appraises, and regulates nonverbal expressions of the infant's more and more intense states of positive and negative affective arousal. Via these communications, the mother regulates the infant's postnatally developing central and autonomic nervous systems. In this co-created dialogue, the "good enough" mother and her infant co-construct multiple cycles of both "affect synchrony" that up-regulates positive affect (e.g., joy-elation, interest-excitement) and "rupture and repair" that down-regulates negative affect (e.g., fear-terror, sadness-depression, shame). Internal representations of attachment experiences are imprinted in right-lateralized implicit–procedural memory as an internal working model that encodes nonconscious strategies of affect regulation. Recall that Bowlby (1969) asserted that these internal representations of attachment operate at levels beneath conscious awareness.

In support of this model, Meaney and his colleagues offer neuroimaging research of neonates at the beginning of the first year, and conclude:

> In early life the right cerebral hemisphere could be better able to process . . . emotion ([A. N.] Schore, 2000; Wada and Davis, 1977). . . . These neural substrates function as hubs in the right hemisphere for emotion processes and mother and child interaction.
>
> (Ratnarajah et al., 2013, p. 193)

Tronick's research on infants in the middle of the first year demonstrates that under relational stress, six-month-old infants use left-sided gestures generated by the right hemisphere. They interpret these data as being "consistent with [A. N.] Schore's (2005) hypotheses of hemispheric right-sided activation of emotions and their regulation during infant–mother interactions" (Montirosso, Cozzi, Tronick, & Borgatti, 2012, p. 826). Using near-infrared spectroscopy, Minagawa-Kawai and colleagues' fMRI study of infant–mother attachment at the end of the first year observed: "Our results are in agreement with that of [A. N.] Schore (2000) who addressed the importance of the right hemisphere in the attachment system" (Minagawa-Kawai, Matsuoka, Dan, Naoi, Nakamura, & Kojima, 2009, p. 289).

Furthermore, my work in developmental neuropsychoanalysis models the early development of the unconscious (versus the later forming conscious) mind. These studies echo a basic premise of classical developmental psychoanalysis that the first relational contact is between the unconscious of the mother and the unconscious of the infant (Palombo, Bendicsen, & Koch, 2009; J. R. Schore, 2012). Throughout the lifespan, implicit psychobiological regulation, operating at nonconscious levels, supports the survival functions of the right brain, the biological substrate of the human unconscious (Joseph, 1992; A. N. Schore, 1994, 2003b, 2012). Consonant with this proposal, Tucker and Moller assert: "The right hemisphere's specialization for emotional communication through nonverbal channels seems to suggest a domain of the mind that is close to the motivationally charged psychoanalytic unconscious" (2007, p. 91). Indeed, a growing body of studies document that unconscious processing of emotional information is mainly subsumed by a right hemisphere subcortical route (Gainotti, 2012), that unconscious emotional memories are stored in the right hemisphere (Gainotti 2006b), and that this hemisphere is centrally involved in maintaining a coherent, continuous, and unified sense of self (Devinsky, 2000; McGilchrist, 2009). From infancy throughout all later stages of the lifespan, right-lateralized rapidly acting emotional processes are centrally involved in enabling the organism to cope with stresses and challenges, and thus in emotional resilience and well-being.

Right Brain Attachment Communications within the Therapeutic Alliance

Regulation theory dictates that early social-emotional experiences may be either predominantly regulated or dysregulated, imprinting secure or insecure attachments. In marked contrast to the optimal growth-facilitating attachment scenario described earlier, in a relational growth-inhibiting early environment of attachment trauma (abuse and/or neglect) the primary caregiver of an insecure disorganized-disoriented infant induces traumatic states of enduring negative affect in the child (A. N. Schore, 2001, 2003a).

This caregiver is too frequently emotionally inaccessible, and reacts to the infant's expressions of stressful affects inconsistently and inappropriately (massive intrusiveness or massive disengagement), and therefore shows minimal or unpredictable participation in the relational arousal regulating processes. Instead of modulating, she induces extreme levels of stressful stimulation and arousal, very high in abuse and/or very low in neglect. Because she provides little interactive repair, the infant's intense negative affective states are long-lasting.

A large body of research now highlights the central role of insecure attachments in the psychoneuropathogenesis of all psychiatric disorders (A. N. Schore, 1996, 2003a, 2012). During early critical periods, frequent dysregulated and unrepaired organized and disorganized-disoriented insecure attachment histories are "affectively burnt in" the infant's early developing right brain. Not only traumatic experiences, but also the defense against overwhelming trauma, dissociation, is stored in implicit-procedural memory. In this manner, attachment trauma ("relational trauma," A. N. Schore, 2001) is imprinted into right cortical-subcortical systems, encoding disorganized-disoriented insecure internal working models that are nonconsciously accessed at later points of interpersonal emotional stress. These insecure working models are a central focus of affectively focused psychotherapy of early forming self pathologies and personality disorders. There is now consensus that deficits in right brain relational processes and resulting affect dysregulation underlie all psychological and psychiatric disorders. All models of therapeutic intervention across a span of psychopathologies share a common goal of attempting to improve emotional self-regulatory processes. Neurobiologically informed relational infant, child, adolescent, and adult psychotherapy can thus potentially facilitate the intrinsic plasticity of the right brain.

Recall that Bowlby (1988), a psychoanalyst, asserted that the reassessment of *nonconscious* internal working models of attachment is a primary goal of any psychotherapy. These interactive representations of early attachment experiences encode strategies of affect regulation, and contain coping mechanisms for maintaining basic regulation and positive affect in the face of stressful environmental challenge. Regulation theory dictates that in "heightened affective moments" (A. N. Schore, 2003b), the patient's unconscious internal working model of attachment, whether secure or insecure, is reactivated in right-lateralized implicit-procedural memory and re-enacted in the psychotherapeutic relationship.

In light of the commonality of nonverbal, intersubjective, implicit right brain-to-right brain emotion transacting and regulating mechanisms in the caregiver–infant and the therapist–patient relationship, developmental attachment studies have direct relevance to the treatment process. From the first point of intersubjective contact, the psychobiologically attuned clinician tracks not just the verbal content, but the nonverbal moment-to-moment rhythmic structures of the patient's internal states, and is flexibly and fluidly modifying his/her own behavior to synchronize with that structure, thereby co-creating with the patient a growth-facilitating context for the organization of the therapeutic alliance. As the right hemisphere is dominant for subjective emotional experiences (Wittling & Roschmann, 1993), the communication of affective states between the right brains of the patient–therapist dyad is thus best described as "intersubjectivity."

In accord with a relational model of psychotherapy, right brain processes that are reciprocally activated on both sides of the therapeutic alliance lie at the core of the psychotherapeutic change process. These implicit clinical dialogues convey much more essential organismic information than left brain explicit, verbal information. Rather, right brain interactions "beneath the words" nonverbally communicate essential nonconscious bodily based affective relational information about the inner world of the patient (and therapist). Rapid communications between the right-lateralized "emotional brain" of each member of the therapeutic alliance allow for moment-to-moment "self-state sharing," a co-created, organized, dynamically changing dialogue of mutual influence. Bromberg (2011) notes: "Self-states are highly individualized modules of being, each configured by its own organization of cognitions, beliefs, dominant affect, and mood, access to memory, skills, behaviors, values, action, and regulatory physiology" (p. 73). In this relational matrix, both partners match the dynamic contours of different emotional-motivational self-states, and simultaneously adjust their social attention, stimulation, and accelerating/decelerating arousal in response to the partner's signals.

In the clinical literature, Scaer (2005) describes essential implicit communication patterns embedded within the therapist–client relationship:

> Many features of social interaction are nonverbal, consisting of subtle variations of facial expression that set the tone for the content of the interaction. Body postures and movement patterns of the therapist . . .

also may reflect emotions such as disapproval, support, humor, and fear. Tone and volume of voice, patterns and speed of verbal communication, and eye contact also contain elements of subliminal communication and contribute to the unconscious establishment of a safe, healing environment.

(pp. 167–168)

These implicit right brain/mind/body nonverbal communications are bidirectional and intersubjective, and thereby potentially valuable to the clinician. Meares (2005) observes:

Not only is the therapist being unconsciously influenced by a series of slight and, in some cases, subliminal signals, so also is the patient. Details of the therapist's posture, gaze, tone of voice, even respiration, are recorded and processed. A sophisticated therapist may use this processing in a beneficial way, potentiating a change in the patient's state without, or in addition to, the use of words.

(p. 124)

Neuroscience characterizes the role of the right brain in these nonverbal communications. At all stages of the lifespan, "The neural substrates of the perception of voices, faces, gestures, smells and pheromones, as evidenced by modern neuroimaging techniques, are characterized by a general pattern of right-hemispheric functional asymmetry" (Brancucci, Lucci, Mazzatenta, & Tommasi, 2009, p. 895). More so than conscious left brain verbalizations, right brain-to-right brain visual-facial, auditory-prosodic, and tactile-gestural subliminal communications reveal the deeper aspects of the personality of the patient, as well as the personality of the therapist.

In order to receive and monitor the patient's nonverbal bodily based attachment communications, the affectively attuned clinician must shift from constricted left-hemispheric attention that focuses on local detail to more widely expanded right-hemispheric attention that focuses on global detail—a characterization that fits with Freud's (1912) description of the importance of the clinician's "evenly suspended attention." In the session, the empathic therapist is consciously, explicitly attending to the patient's verbalizations in order to objectively diagnose and rationalize the patient's dysregulating symptomatology. However, he/she is also listening and interacting at another level, an experience-near subjective level, one that implicitly processes moment-to-moment attachment communications and self-states at levels beneath awareness. Bucci (2002) observes: "We recognize changes in emotional states of others based on perception of subtle shifts in their facial expression or posture, and recognize changes in our own states based on somatic or kinesthetic experience" (p. 194). These nonverbal communications are examples of "primary process communication." According to Dorpat (2001), "The primary process system analyzes, regulates, and communicates an individual's relations with the environment" (p. 449). He observes: "Affective and object-relational information is transmitted predominantly by primary process communication. Nonverbal communication includes body movements (kinesics), posture, gesture, facial expression, voice inflection, and the sequence, rhythm, and pitch of the spoken words" (p. 451). The right brain thus processes "the music behind the words."

The organizing principle of working with unconscious primary process communications dictates that just as the left brain communicates its states to other left brains via conscious linguistic behaviors, so the right nonverbally communicates its states to other right brains that are tuned to receive these communications. Bromberg (2011) concludes:

> Allan Schore writes about a right brain-to-right brain channel of affective communication—a channel that he sees as "an organized dialogue" comprised of "dynamically fluctuating moment-to-moment state sharing." I believe it to be this process of state sharing that . . . allows . . . a good psychoanalytic match.
>
> (p. 169)

Writing in the psychiatry literature, Meares (2012) describes "a form of therapeutic conversation that can be conceived . . . as a dynamic interplay between two right hemispheres."

On the matter of the verbal content—the words in psychotherapy—it has long been assumed in the psychotherapeutic literature that all forms of language reflect left-hemispheric functioning of the conscious mind. Current neuroscience now indicates this is incorrect. In an overarching review, Ross and Monnot (2008) conclude: "Thus, the traditional concept that language is a dominant and lateralized function of the left hemisphere is no longer tenable" (p. 51):

Over the last three decades, there has been growing realization that the right hemisphere is essential for language and communication competency and psychological well-being through its ability to modulate affective prosody and gestural behavior decode connotative (non-standard) word meanings, make thematic inferences, and process metaphor, complex linguistic relationships and non-literal (idiomatic) types of expressions.

(p. 51)

These data suggest that the early responding right brain, which is more "physiological" than the later responding left, is involved in rapid bodily based intersubjective communications within the therapeutic alliance.

Intersubjectivity is more than a communication or match of explicit verbal cognitions or overt behaviors. Regulated and dysregulated bodily based affects are communicated within an energy-transmitting intersubjective field co-constructed by two individuals that includes not just two minds, but two bodies (A. N. Schore, 2012). At the psychobiological core of the co-constructed intersubjective field is the attachment bond of emotional communication and interactive regulation. Implicit intersubjective communications express bodily based emotional self-states, not just conscious cognitive "mental" states. The essential biological function of attachment communications in all human interactions, including those embedded in the therapeutic alliance, is the regulation of right brain/mind/body states. Intersubjective, relational, affect-focused psychotherapy is not the "talking cure," but the "affect communicating cure."

Transference–Countertransference Communications within Mutual Enactments

Regulation theory's relational perspective allows for a deeper understanding of the critical intersubjective brain/mind/body mechanisms that operate at implicit levels of the therapeutic alliance, beneath the exchanges of language and explicit cognitions. One such essential mechanism is the bidirectional transference–countertransference relationship. There is now a growing consensus that despite the existence of a number of distinct theoretical perspectives in clinical work, Freud's concepts of transference and countertransference, have been expanded and (re-)incorporated into all forms of psychotherapy. Transference–countertransference affective transactions are currently seen as an essential relational element in the treatment of all patients, but especially the early forming severe psychopathologies.

In such cases, implicit right brain-to-right brain nonverbal communications (facial expressions, prosody-tone of voice, gesture) convey unconscious transference–countertransference affective transactions, which revive earlier attachment memories, especially of intensely dysregulated affective states. Gainotti (2006b) observes: "the right hemisphere may be crucially involved in those emotional memories which must be reactivated and reworked during the psychoanalytical treatment" (p. 167). In discussing the role of the right hemisphere as "the seat of implicit memory," Mancia (2006) notes: "The discovery of the implicit memory has extended the concept of the unconscious and supports the hypothesis that this is where the emotional and affective—sometimes traumatic—presymbolic and preverbal experiences of the primary mother-infant relations are stored" (p. 83). Transference has been described as an expression of the patient's implicit memories. These memories are expressed in "heightened affective moments" as transferential right brain-to-right brain nonverbal communications of fast-acting, automatic, dysregulated bodily based states of intensely stressful emotional arousal (e.g., fear-terror, aggression-rage, depression-hopeless despair, shame, disgust). Right-lateralized implicit-procedural emotional memory also encodes the dissociative defense against re-experiencing relational trauma, and thereby generates dissociated (unconscious) affects.

Recent psychodynamic models of transference now contend, "no appreciation of transference can do without emotion" (Pincus, Freeman, & Modell, 2007, p. 634). Clinical theoreticians describe transference as "an established pattern of relating and emotional responding that is cued by something in the present, but oftentimes calls up both an affective state and thoughts that may have more to do with past experience than present ones" (Maroda, 2005, p. 134). This conception is echoed in neuroscience, where Shuren and Grafman (2002) assert:

> The right hemisphere holds representations of the emotional states associated with events experienced by the individual. When that individual encounters a familiar scenario, representations of past emotional experiences are retrieved by the right hemisphere and are incorporated into the reasoning process.
>
> (p. 918)

Research now indicates that the right hemisphere is fundamentally involved in autobiographical memory (Markowitsch, Reinkemeier, Kessler, Koyuncu, & Heiss, 2000).

Transference–countertransference transactions are expressions of bi-directional nonconscious, nonverbal right brain-mind-body stressful communications between patient and therapist. These reciprocal psycho-neurobiological exchanges reflect activities of both the central and autonomic nervous systems. Behaviorally, the patient's transferential communications are expressed in nonverbal, visual, auditory, and gestural affective cues that are spontaneously and quickly expressed from the face, voice, and body of the patient. Countertransference is similarly defined in nonverbal implicit terms as the therapist's autonomic responses that are reactions on an unconscious level to nonverbal messages.

As the empathic clinician implicitly monitors the patient's nonverbal transferential communications, his/her psychobiologically attuned right brain tracks, at a preconscious level, the patterns of arousal rhythms and flows of the patient's affective states. Clinicians are now asserting that "transference is distinctive in that it depends on early patterns of emotional attachment with caregivers" (Pincus et al., 2007, p. 636), and describing the clinical importance of "making conscious the organizing patterns of affect" (Mohaupt, Holgersen, Binder, & Nielsen, 2006, p. 243). Converging evidence from neuroscience now indicates: "Simply stated, the left hemisphere specializes in analyzing sequences, while the right hemisphere gives evidence of superiority in processing patterns" (Van Lancker & Cummings, 1999, p. 95). Even more specifically: "Pattern recognition and comprehension of several types of stimuli, such as faces, chords, complex pitch, graphic images, and voices, has been described as superior in the normal right hemisphere" (Van Lancker Sidtis, 2006, p. 233).

But in addition, the therapist is implicitly tracking his/her own counter-transferential responses to the patient's transferential communications, patterns of his/her own somatic countertransferential, interoceptive, bod-ily based affective responses to the patient's right brain implicit facial, prosodic, and gestural communications. Via these right brain mechanisms, the intuitive psychobiologically attuned therapist, on a moment-to-moment basis, nonconsciously focuses his/her right brain countertransferential broad attentional processes upon patterns of rhythmic crescendos/decre-scendos of the patient's regulated and dysregulated states of affective auto-nomic arousal. Freud's dictum "It is a very remarkable thing that the *Ucs* of one human being can react upon that of another, without passing through the *Cs*" (1915, p. 194) is thus neuropsychoanalytically understood as a right brain-to-right brain communication from one relational unconscious to another. In this manner, "The right hemisphere, in fact, truly interprets the mental state not only of its own brain, but the brains (and minds) of others" (Keenan, Rubio, Racioppi, Johnson, & Barnacz, 2005, p. 702).

Right brain-to-right brain transferential–countertransferential unconscious communications between the patient's and therapist's "internal worlds" represent an essential relational matrix for the therapeutic expression of dissociated affects associated with early attachment trauma, and thereby "subjectively unconscious danger" (Carretie, Hinojosa, Mercado, & Tapia, 2005) and "unconscious emotion" (Sato & Aoki, 2006). These affective communications of traumatized self-states were neither intersubjectively shared nor interactively regulated by the original attachment object in the historical context, but now the patient has the possibility of a reparative relational experience. Right brain bodily based dialogues between the relational unconscious of the patient and the relational unconscious of the affectively sensitive empathic therapist are activated and enhanced in the "heightened affective moments" of re-enactments of early relational trauma. Enactments are now seen as powerful manifestations of the intersubjective process and expressions of complex, though largely unconscious self-states and relational patterns (for an extensive interpersonal neurobiological model of working in clinical enactments, see A. N. Schore, 2012).

The relational mechanism of mutual enactments represents an interaction between the patient's emotional vulnerability and the clinician's emotional availability (the ability to "take" the transference). It is most fully operational during (inevitable) ruptures of the therapeutic alliance, described by Aspland, Llewelyn, Hardy, Barkham, and Stiles (2008) as "points of emotional disconnections between client and therapist that create a negative shift in the quality of the alliance" (p. 699) that act as "episodes of covert or overt behavior that trap both participants in negative complementary interactions" (p. 700). Although such ruptures of the alliance are the most stressful moments of the treatment, these "collisions" of the therapist's and patient's subjectivities also represent an intersubjective context of potential "collaboration" between their subjectivities, and thereby a context of interactive repair—a fundamental mechanism of therapeutic change. This co-created emergent relational structure within the therapeutic alliance contains a more efficient feedback communication system of not only right brain communications, but also right brain interactive regulations of intensely dysregulated affective states associated with early relational trauma.

Indeed, the essential biological homeostatic functions of affective, bodily based, intersubjective attachment communications in all human interactions, including those embedded in the psychobiological core of the therapeutic alliance, are involved in the regulation of right brain/mind/body states. The importance of this right limbic-autonomic connection is stressed by Whitehead:

> Every time we make therapeutic contact with our patients we are engaging profound processes that tap into essential life forces in ourselves and in those we work with . . . . *Emotions are deepened in intensity and sustained in time when they are intersubjectively shared.* This occurs at moments of *deep contact.*
>
> (2006, p. 624, italics added)

In such moments, intersubjective psychobiological resonance between the patient's and clinician's relational unconscious generates an interactively regulated amplification of arousal and affect, and so unconscious affects are deepened in intensity and sustained in time. This increase of emotional intensity allows dissociated affects beneath levels of awareness to emerge into consciousness in both members of the therapeutic dyad.

"Heightened affective moments" of the treatment afford opportunities for right brain interactive affect regulation, the core of the attachment process. In a seminal article in the clinical psychology literature, Greenberg (2007) describes a "self-control" form of emotion regulation involving higher levels of cognitive executive function that allows individuals "to change the way they feel by consciously changing the way they think" (p. 415). He proposes that this explicit form of affect regulation is performed by the verbal left hemisphere, and unconscious bodily based emotion is usually not addressed. This regulatory mechanism is at the core of verbal-analytic understanding and controlled reasoning, and is heavily emphasized in models of cognitive behavioral therapy. In contrast to this conscious emotion regulation system, Greenberg describes a second, more fundamental implicit affect regulatory process performed by the right hemisphere that rapidly and automatically processes facial expression, vocal quality, and eye contact in a relational context. This type of therapy attempts not control, but the "acceptance or facilitation of particular emotions," including "previously avoided emotion," in order to allow the patient to tolerate and transform them into "adaptive emotions." Citing my work, Greenberg asserts: "it is the building of implicit or automatic emotion regulation capacities that is important for enduring change, especially for highly fragile personality-disordered clients" (2007, p. 416).

Right Brain Relational Mechanisms of Therapeutic Change

In cases of early attachment maturational failures, especially histories of relational trauma, deep emotional contact and implicit interactive affect regulation are central mechanisms of right brain psychotherapy change processes. Recall that the hallmark of trauma is damage to the relational life (Herman, 1992). The repair and resolution of relational trauma therefore must occur in a therapeutic relational context, the core of the change mechanism. The clinical work involved in traumatic re-enactments involves a profound commitment by both participants in the therapeutic dyad and a deep emotional involvement on the part of the therapist. These types of cases, difficult as they may be, represent valuable learning experiences for the therapist, and they call for expert skills (A. N. Schore, 2012). Ultimately, effective psychotherapeutic treatment of early evolving self pathologies (including personality disorders) can facilitate neuroplastic changes in the patient's right brain, which is dominant for attachment functions throughout the lifespan. This interpersonal neurobiological mechanism allows optimal longer-term treatment to potentially transform disorganized-disoriented attachments into "earned secure" attachments.

That said, the developing right brain system is relationally impacted in all attachment histories, including insecure organized and secure attachments. Regulation theory's transtheoretical clinical perspective that describes the basic psychoneurobiological processes of therapeutic action applies to all patients, insecure and secure, and to all forms of psychotherapy. Changes mediated by affectively focused, relationally oriented psychotherapy are imprinted into the right brain, which is dominant for the nonverbal, implicit, holistic processing of emotional information and social interactions (Decety & Lamm, 2007; Hecht, 2014; A. N. Schore, 2012; Semrud-Clikeman, Fine, & Zhu, 2011). The right brain is centrally involved in implicit (versus explicit) affectivity, defined as "individual differences in the automatic activation of cognitive representations of emotions that do not result from self-reflection" (Quirin, Kazen, Rohrmann, & Kuhl, 2009, p. 4012). It also predominates over the left for coping with and assimilating novel situations, but also for emotional resilience (see A. N. Schore, 2012). These adaptive functions are mobilized in the change processes of psychotherapy.

Long-term treatment allows for the evolution of more complex psychic structure, which in turn can process more complex right brain functions (e.g., intersubjectivity, empathy, affect tolerance, stress regulation, humor, mutual love, and intimacy). The growth-facilitating relational environment of a deeper therapeutic exploration of the unconscious mind can induce plasticity in both the cortical and subcortical systems of the patient's right brain. This increased connectivity in turn generates more complex development of the right-lateralized biological substrate of the human unconscious, including alterations of the patient's nonconscious internal working model that encodes more effective coping strategies of implicit affect regulation, and thereby adaptive, flexible switching of self-states in different relational contexts.

The intrinsically relational aspect of regulation theory also models the reciprocal changes in the clinician's right brain that result from working repeatedly with therapeutic processes (A. N. Schore, 2012). Recall the APA's characterization of clinical expertise as "interpersonal skill," expressed in "encoding and decoding verbal and nonverbal responses" and "responding empathically to the patient's explicit and implicit experiences." With clinical experience, psychotherapists of all schools can become expert in "implicit relational knowledge" and nonverbal intersubjective processes that enhance therapeutic effectiveness. The professional growth of the clinician reflects progressions in right brain relational processes that underlie clinical skills, including affective empathy, the ability to tolerate and interactively regulate a broader array of negative and positive affective self-states, implicit openness to experience, clinical intuition, and creativity (for references, see A. N. Schore, 2012). In a very recent comprehensive overview of laterality research, Hecht (2014) states:

> Mounting evidence suggests that the right hemisphere has a relative advantage over the left hemisphere in mediating social intelligence-identifying social stimuli, understanding the intentions of other

people, awareness of the dynamics in social relationships, and successful handling of social interactions.

(p. 1)

I would argue that clinical experience enhances the therapist's right brain "social intelligence."

Regulation theory proposes that the core clinical skills of any effective psychotherapy are right brain implicit capacities, including the ability to empathically receive and express bodily based nonverbal communications, the ability to sensitively register very slight changes in another's expression and emotion, an immediate awareness of one's own subjective and intersubjective experience, and the regulation of one's own and the patient's affect. Over the course of the treatment, in an array of emotionally charged clinical exchanges, the empathic therapist is flexibly accessing a storehouse of affective experiences gained over the course of his/her career. A relational perspective of professional development dictates that the continuously evolving psychotherapist frequently reflects upon the subjective experiences of *being with* patients, including not only *the patients'* unique personalities, but also *their own* conscious and especially unconscious intersubjective co-participation in the therapeutic process.

In order to be optimally effective in treating the regulatory and relational deficits of both psychiatric and personality disorders, the expert clinician learns how to fluidly access not only the patient's left-lateralized conscious mind and explicit self, but even more importantly, the patient's right-lateralized unconscious mind and implicit, bodily based self. This principle applies to clinical psychology's models of both assessment and treatment. Interestingly, as opposed to verbal questionnaires that measure explicit functions, projective tests, such as the Rorschach and Thematic Apperception Test, directly tap into right brain implicit functions (Hiraishi, Haida, Matsumoto, Hayakawa, Inomata, & Matsumoto, 2013). Indeed, Finn (2012) is now applying regulation theory to Rorschach assessments of right brain attachment failures (see also the use of the Adult Attachment Projective Picture System by Finn, 2011, and the Operant Motive Test by Quirin et al., 2013).

In addition, the *explicit knowledge* the psychologist acquires from studying the rapidly expanding amount of clinically relevant interdisciplinary research is essential to professional growth. My ongoing studies indicate that the current explosion of information on early social-emotional development, attachment, relational trauma, unconscious processes, and developing brain functions is directly relevant to clinical models of psycho-therapeutic change. The expanding knowledge of the biological and medical disciplines that border psychology needs to be incorporated into and thereby update our professional curriculum, training, and internship programs, where it can promote more effective relational and therapeutic skills.

The practice of psychotherapy is not just explicitly teaching the patient coping skills. Rather, it is fundamentally relational: the therapeutic alliance, the major vector of change is, in essence, a two-person system for self-exploration and relational healing. At all points in the lifespan, this emotional growth of the subjective self that supports emotional well-being is facilitated in relational contexts, as described above. The importance of "context" is currently highlighted by all scientific and clinical disciplines. For most of the last century, science equated context with the organism's physical surround; this has now shifted to the social, relational environment. All human interactions, including those between therapist and patient as well as researcher and experimental subject, occur within a relational context, in which essential nonverbal communications are transmitted at levels beneath conscious awareness, thereby activating/deactivating basic homeostatic processes in both members of an intersubjective dyad. The ubiquitous expression of the relational unconscious in the thera-peutic alliance strongly supports psychodynamic, interpersonal models of psychotherapy, as well as amplifying Sigmund Freud's call for paradigm-shifting scientific explorations of the unconscious in everyday life.

At the beginning of this chapter, I suggested that a paradigm shift is now occurring across a number of disciplines, from left brain conscious cognition to right brain unconscious, relational, emotional functions. Writing in the neuropsychoanalytic literature on "Emotions, unconscious processes, and the right hemisphere," Gainotti (2006a) concludes: "[T]he right hemisphere subserves the lower 'schematic' level (where emotions are automatically generated and experienced as 'true emotions') whereas the left hemisphere the higher 'conceptual' level (where emotions are consciously analyzed and submitted to intentional control)" (p. 71).

In his masterly review of brain laterality research, Iain McGilchrist (2009) asserts:

> If what one means by consciousness is the part of the mind that brings the world into focus, makes it explicit, allows it to be formulated in

language, and is aware of its own awareness, it is reasonable to link the conscious mind to activity almost all of which lies ultimately in the left hemisphere.

(p. 188)

On the other hand:

The right hemisphere, by contrast, yields a world of individual, changing, evolving, interconnected, implicit, incarnate, living beings within the context of the lived world, but in the nature of things never fully graspable, always imperfectly known—and to this world it exists in a relationship of care.

(p. 174)

Psychotherapy, "a relationship of care," can alter more than the left-lateralized conscious mind; it also can influence the growth and development of the unconscious "right mind." It is undoubtedly true that both brain hemispheres contribute to effective therapeutic treatment, but in light of the current relational trend that emphasizes "the primacy of affect," the right brain, the "social," "emotional" brain, is dominant in all forms of psychotherapy.

References

APA Presidential Task Force on Evidence-Based Practice. (2006). Evidence-based practice in psychology. *American Psychologist, 61*, 271–285.

Aspland, H., Llewelyn, S., Hardy, G. E., Barkham, M., & Stiles, W. (2008). Alliance rupture resolution in cognitive-behavior therapy: A preliminary task analysis. *Psychotherapy Research, 18*, 699–710.

Bowlby, J. (1969). *Attachment and loss, Volume 1: Attachment.* New York, NY: Basic Books.

Bowlby, J. (1988). *A secure base* (2nd ed.). New York, NY: Basic Books.

Brancucci, A., Lucci, G., Mazzatenta, A., & Tommasi, L. (2009). Asymmetries of the human social brain in the visual, auditory and chemical modalities. *Philosophical Transactions of the Royal Society of London B: Biological Sciences, 364*, 895–914

Bromberg, P. M. (2011). *The shadow of the tsunami and the growth of the relational mind.* New York, NY: Routledge.

Bucci, W. (2002). The referential process, consciousness, and the sense of self. *Psychoanalytic Inquiry, 5*, 766–793.

Carretie, L., Hinojosa, J. A., Mercado, F., & Tapia, M. (2005). Cortical response to subjectively unconscious danger. *NeuroImage, 24*, 615–623.

Decety, J., & Lamm, C. (2007). The role of the right temporoparietal junction in social interaction: How low-level computational processes contribute to metacognition. *The Neuroscientist, 13*, 580–593.

Devinsky, O. (2000). Right cerebral hemisphere dominance for a sense of corporeal and emotional self. *Epilepsy & Behavior, 1*, 60–73.

Dorpat, T. L. (2001). Primary process communication. *Psychoanalytic Inquiry, 3*, 448–463.

Finn, S. E. (2011). Use of the Adult Attachment Projective Picture System (AAP) in the middle of long-term psychotherapy. *Journal of Personality Assessment, 95*, 427–433.

Finn, S. E. (2012). 2011 Bruno Klopfer Distinguished Contribution Award: Implications of recent research in neurobiology for psychological assessment. *Journal of Personality Assessment, 5*, 440–449.

Freud, S. (1912). Recommendations to physicians practicing psycho-analysis. In J. Strachey (Ed. & Trans.), *The standard edition of the complete psychological works of Sigmund Freud* (Vol. 12). London, England: Hogarth Press, 1957.

Freud, S. (1915). The unconscious. In J. Strachey (Ed. & Trans.), *The standard edition of the complete psychological works of Sigmund Freud* (Vol. 14). London, England: Hogarth Press, 1957.

Gainotti, G. (2006a). Emotions, unconscious processes, and the right hemisphere. *Neuropsychoanalysis, 7*, 71–81.

Gainotti, G. (2006b). Unconscious emotional memories and the right hemisphere. In M. Mancia (Ed.), *Psychoanalysis and neuroscience* (pp. 151–173). Milan, Italy: Springer Milan.

Gainotti, G. (2012). Unconscious processing of emotions and the right hemisphere. *Neuropsychologia, 50*, 205–218.

Greenberg, L. S. (2007). Emotion coming of age. *Clinical Psychology Science and Practice, 14*, 414–421.

Hecht, D. (2014). Cerebral lateralization of pro- and anti-social tendencies. *Experimental Neurobiology, 23*, 1–27.

Herman, J. L. (1992). *Trauma and recovery*. New York, NY: Basic Books.

Hiraishi, H., Haida, M., Matsumoto, M., Hayakawa, N., Inomata, S., & Matsumoto, H. (2012). Differences of prefrontal cortex activity between picture-based personality tests: A near-infrared spectroscopy study. *Journal of Personality Assessment, 94*, 366–371.

Joseph, R. (1992). *The right brain and the unconscious*. New York, NY: Plenum Press.

Keenan, J. P., Rubio, J., Racioppi, C., Johnson, A., & Barnacz, A. (2005). The right hemisphere and the dark side of consciousness. *Cortex, 41*, 695–704.

Kohut, H. (1971). *The analysis of the self*. New York, NY: International Universities Press.

Mancia, M. (2006). Implicit memory and early unrepressed unconscious: Their role in the therapeutic process (how the neurosciences can contribute to psychoanalysis). *International Journal of Psychoanalysis, 87*, 83–103.

Markowitsch, H. J., Reinkemeier, A., Kessler, J., Koyuncu, A., & Heiss, W. D. (2000). Right amygdalar and temperofrontal activation during autobiographical, but not fictitious memory retrieval. *Behavioral Neurology, 12*, 181–190.

Maroda, K. J. (2005). Show some emotion: Completing the cycle of affective communication. In L. Aron & A. Harris (Eds.), *Revolutionary connections. Relational psychoanalysis, Volume II: Innovation and expansion* (pp. 121–142). Hillsdale, NJ: Analytic Press.

McGilchrist, I. (2009). *The master and his emissary*. New Haven CT: Yale University Press.

Meares, R. (2005). *The metaphor of play: Origin and breakdown of personal being* (3rd ed.). London, England: Routledge.

Meares, R. (2012). *A dissociation model of borderline personality disorder*. New York, NY: W. W. Norton.

Minagawa-Kawai, Y., Matsuoka, S., Dan, I., Naoi, N., Nakamura, K., & Kojima, S. (2009). Prefrontal activation associated with social attachment: Facial-emotion recognition in mothers and infants. *Cerebral Cortex, 19*, 284–292.

Mitchell, S. A. (1988). *Relational concepts in psychoanalysis*. Cambridge, MA: Harvard University Press.

Mohaupt, H., Holgersen, H., Binder, P.-E, & Nielsen, G. H. (2006). Affect consciousness or mentalization? A comparison of two concepts with regard to affect development and affect regulation. *Scandinavian Journal of Psychology, 47*, 237–244.

Montirosso, R., Cozzi, P., Tronick, E., & Borgatti, R. (2012). Differential distribution and lateralization of infant gestures and their relation to maternal gestures in the Face-to-Face Still-Face paradigm. *Infant Behavior & Development, 35*, 819–828.

Palombo, J., Bendicsen, H. K., & Koch, B. J. (2009). *Guide to psychoanalytic developmental theories*. New York, NY: Springer.

Pincus, D., Freeman, W., & Modell, A. (2007). A neurobiological model of perception: Considerations for transference. *Psychoanalytic Psychology, 24*, 623–640.

Quirin, M., Kazen, M., Rohrmann, S., & Kuhl, J. (2009). Implicit but not explicit affectivity predicts circadian and reactive cortisol: Using the implicit positive and negative affect test. *Journal of Personality, 77*, 401–425.

Quirin, M., et al. (2013). Neural correlates of social motivation: An fMRI study on power versus affiliation. *International Journal of Psychophysiology, 88*, 289–295. doi:10.1016/j.ijpsycho.2012.07.003

Ratnarajah, N., et al. (2013). Structural connectivity in the neonatal brain. *NeuroImage, 75*, 187–194.

Ross, E. D., & Monnot, M. (2008), Neurology of affective prosody and its functional-anatomic organization in right hemisphere. *Brain and Language, 104*, 51–74.

Sato, W., & Aoki, S. (2006), Right hemisphere dominance in processing unconscious emotion. *Brain and Cognition, 62*, 261–266.

Scaer, R. (2005). *The trauma spectrum: Hidden wounds and human resiliency.* New York, NY: W. W. Norton.

Schore, A. N. (1994). *Affect regulation and the origin of the self.* Mahweh, NJ: Lawrence Erlbaum.

Schore, A. N. (1996). The experience-dependent maturation of a regulatory system in the orbital prefrontal cortex and the origin of developmental psychopathology. *Development and Psychopathology, 8*, 59–87.

Schore, A. N. (2000). Attachment and the regulation of the right brain. *Attachment & Human Development, 2*, 23–47.

Schore, A. N. (2001). The effects of relational trauma on right brain development, affect regulation, and infant mental health. *Infant Mental Health Journal, 22*, 201–269.

Schore, A. N. (2003a). *Affect dysregulation and disorders of the self.* New York, NY: W. W. Norton.

Schore, A. N. (2003b). *Affect regulation and the repair of the self.* New York, NY: W. W. Norton.

Schore, A. N. (2005). Attachment, affect regulation, and the developing right brain: Linking developmental neuroscience to pediatrics. *Pediatrics in Review, 26*, 204–211.

Schore, A. N. (2009, August 8). *The paradigm shift: The right brain and the relational unconscious.* Invited plenary address to the American Psychological Association 2009 Convention, Toronto, Canada. Retrieved from www.allanschore.com/pdf/SchoreAPAPlenaryFinal09.pdf

Schore, A. N. (2012). *The science of the art of psychotherapy,* New York, NY: W. W. Norton.

Schore, J. R. (2012). Using concepts from interpersonal neurobiology in revisiting psychodynamic theory. *Smith College Studies in Social Work, 82*, 90–111.

Schore, J. R., & Schore, A. N. (2008). Modern attachment theory: The central role of affect regulation in development and treatment. *Clinical Social Work Journal, 36*, 9–20.

Semrud-Clikeman, M., Fine, J. G., & Zhu, D. C. (2011). The role of the right hemisphere for processing of social interactions in normal adults using functional magnetic resonance imaging. *Neuropsychobiology, 64*, 47–51.

Shuren, J. E., & Grafman, J. (2002). The neurology of reasoning. *Archives of Neurology, 59*, 916–919.

Sullivan, H. S. (1953). *The interpersonal theory of psychiatry.* New York, NY: W. W. Norton.

Tucker, D. M., & Moller, L. (2007). The metamorphosis. Individuation of the adolescent brain. In D. Romer & E. F. Walker (Eds.), *Adolescent psychopathology and the developing brain* (pp. 85–102). Oxford, England: Oxford University Press.

Van Lancker, D., & Cummings, J. L. (1999). Expletives: Neurolinguistic and neurobehavioral perspectives on swearing. *Brain Research Reviews, 31,* 83–104.

Van Lancker Sidtis, D. (2006). Where in the brain is nonliteral language? *Metaphor and Symbol, 21,* 213–244.

Wada, J. A., & Davis, A. E. (1977). Fundamental nature of human infant's brain asymmetry. *Canadian Journal of Neurological Science, 4,* 203–207.

Whitehead, C. C. (2006). Neo-psychoanalysis: A paradigm for the 21st century. *Journal of the Academy of Psychoanalysis and Dynamic Psychiatry, 34,* 603–627.

Wittling, W., & Roschmann, R. (1993). Emotion-related hemisphere asymmetry: Subjective emotional responses to laterally presented films. *Cortex, 29,* 431–448.

Chapter 14

Sex, Gender, and Desire

Karol Marshall & Roy E. Barsness

We, the authors, reside in a fairly liberal state that was one of the first states to legalize same-sex marriage, and within a liberal, sex-positive city where the streets are relatively safe and inclusive of diverse lifestyles. We are aware this is not necessarily true for the lives of many within our country who are stigmatized and continue to face sexual discrimination on a daily basis. We are also aware that the complexity of human sexuality continues to rapidly shift and change. For example, definitions of human sexuality have morphed over the years from people at one time simply being described in binaries such as gay/straight to a broader notation of GLBTQ to GLBTQIA2-S (T: Transgender or Transsexual; Q: Queer or Questioning; I: Intersex; A: Asexual or Ally; 2-S: Two Spirit, a Native American term for those who walk in two worlds—female and male). Other evidence of change is that during the writing of this chapter, the term "gender-fluid" was officially entered as a new term in the *Oxford Dictionary*. As Bob Dylan, author, poet, musician, once wrote: "the times they are a changin'."

In view of the shifting landscape of sexuality, it seemed to us that our own thinking about sexual desire and gender identity could benefit from a thorough updating of our understanding of diverse aspects of contemporary theory and the science of sex. Furthermore, though we both consider ourselves open and accepting— an openness that carries over into our clinical offices—we also recognize that our very own particular ideas lurk behind our apparent open-mindedness. Our ways of experiencing and reflecting on sex, gender, and desire, as well as our perceptions of those around us, are quite personal, nuanced, and individual.

Initial Questions

Despite all of our experience and training, we discovered we actually had many questions about sexuality, including:

- How should sexual phenomena best be categorized? How can we minimize traditional dualisms even as we realize that they are sometimes helpful?
- How is an individual's physical "sex" usually determined?
- How and when do people become "gendered"?
- When and how do people establish their preferred sexual objects?
- To what degree are these three—sex, gender identification, and sexual preference—related?
- To what extent are these facets of a person set by genes, or in the womb in other ways?
- What in sex, gender identification, and object preference changes through postnatal life experience?
- How does psychoanalytic understanding contribute to thinking about sex, gender identity, and desire?

Theory and Data outside Psychoanalysis

The study for this chapter began with Marshall's search for contemporary science and research on sexuality. This search led her to the latest scientific journals, for example *Archives of Sexual Behavior*, an online peer-reviewed journal, as well as contemporary textbooks such as *Neuroscience* (Purves et al., 2008) and *Human Sexuality* (LeVay & Baldwin, 2012). These sources are frequently updated and rich with explanations, charts, and images. She had in mind her early study of a body of research (Marshall, 1977) then widely cited in the psychological literature. Although those studies and conclusions had been accepted as established, when studied more closely, she found the entire body of work to be a house of cards. This experience taught her that "science" is less conclusive than it often appears, and she once again recognized the need to be thoroughgoing in her efforts to learn about work outside her own discipline. Little did she realize how drastically her ideas of what was "true" would be pushed from one direction to another in the process (see Marshall, 2009).

Questions about sexual desire and gender identity are so sensitive and politically controversial that new understandings have a difficult time making it into public awareness. Results of complex, multi-factorial studies are reported too early, publicized too widely, subjected to oversimplification and misunderstanding, and embroidered with unsustainable "conclusions." People are passionately concerned about sex; invested people and groups sometimes make it impossible for new findings to be published. Politicians mislead and inflame the public; advances are deliberately twisted to serve particular ends. The press is constrained and politicized; researchers are harassed, attacked, and threatened (cf. Dreger, 2008).

Disturbing work by Money (1955) illustrates the risks of theory-driven error. This prominent sexologist had decided that cultural factors were pivotal in sexual identity, so when he was consulted about a young child whose penis had been damaged in infancy, he decided the problem would be best dealt with through early surgical intervention to provide the 17-month old boy with female genitals. Money augmented the child's surgically created female genitals with female hormones, thinking cultural forces could then help the child develop a clearly feminine gender identity. He believed gender was culturally determined, and predicted the child would come to think of itself as female. It eventually emerged, however, that this individual, "John/Joan," rejected the surgically and culturally created female sex to return to a male sexual identity. Tragically, "John/Joan/John" ended his life by suicide at the age of 38.

Money's particular understanding, combined with an eagerness to help, led to assumptions about the social mutability of gender that led him to make a fatal error. As neuroscientist Purves put it: "A grievous mistake was made by failing to understand the influence on the brain of circulating androgens during early sexual development" (Purves 2008, p. 782). Fausto-Sterling (2000) pointed to Money's inadequate appreciation of how the process of forming a gender identity begins in the very first months of life and involves a lot more than genital structure and cultural influence. The chemistry of the brain and early socialization are also key components of this story.

We form ideas about ourselves and others that seem to make sense. Ramachandran, a prominent neuroscientist, demonstrated how this can lead to misconceptions (Ramachandran & Blakeslee, 1998). He devoted much of his attention to individuals with brain pathology, seeking to illustrate how sensory and sense-making processes function in normal mental life as well as in pathological situations. In his lectures, Ramachandran demonstrated touching a blindfolded person's nose in a rhythmic pattern while that person touched someone else's nose with the identical pattern.

He showed that after several seconds, the blindfolded subject was likely to develop the conviction his own nose had somehow moved several feet from his face. As he said, "This simple experiment not only shows how malleable your body image is," but also helps us recognize that self-perception is a process of extracting correlations from the world so as to produce a functioning model of the self, even if that model is unlikely to be realistic. He said, "Your body is a phantom, one your brain has constructed for convenience" (Ramachandran & Blakeslee, 1998, p. 58). If a subject in Ramachandran's clinic can become convinced his nose is several feet long, we can imagine that a person's or a scientist's beliefs about his/her science or his/her gender or his/her sexuality might be due to peculiarities in play when observations are being made, regardless of how these beliefs might strain credulity. What is important to recognize is that people create belief systems that seek to make sense out of complex phenomena even if these ideas are inherently unreasonable. Changing times and changing perspectives are likely to result in changing personal understandings.

One of the most cited scientists (Ioannidis, 2005) has cautioned that studies are less likely to be true when:

> the studies in the field in question are small, when effect sizes are small, when there are a number of tested relationships [and] when there is greater flexibility in designs, definitions, outcomes, and analytical modes, when there is greater financial and other interest and prejudice, and when more teams involved in a field are chasing statistical significance.
>
> (p. 1)

As Ioannidis concluded: "For many current scientific fields, claimed research findings may often be simply accurate measures of the prevailing bias" (p. 6). This is undoubtedly true for sex and gender studies, as most of the factors listed by Ioannidis are in play when studying sex differences in the brain.

Three Interactive Processes

It is helpful to think of all aspects of sexuality, as with all of psychology, as interacting lifelong developmental processes, rather than specified, easily labeled, dichotomous states. This interactive, developmental model may seem relatively straightforward; however, all too frequently even the most rigorous and respected theorists and scientists—that is, LeVay & Baldwin (2012) and Bailey, Vasey, Diamond, Breedlove, Vilain, and Epprecht (2016), who will be cited here—at times collapse or blur dimensions that may not be the focus of their immediate attention.

To begin to address this concern, Jordan-Young (2010) suggested being clear about three interactive processes:

1. *organic sex*—the form and functionality of "material body";
2. *gender*—the individual's identity or self presentation as either masculine or feminine;
3. *sexuality*—the individual's sexual desires and preferences.

Organic Sex—the Form and Functionality of Material Body

What part of the sexual equation is a person born with? Although scientists and the public tend to be concerned about the sex and gender of the neonate, it is difficult to study life at that juncture. Environmental factors immediately come into play, making isolating the effects of genes and prenatal hormones quite difficult. From time to time, promising observations are celebrated, such as: "This part of the brain is bigger or more active in this or that gender." However, these provocative leads tend to fade to a limited handful of relatively reliable differences that may or may not be the product of development rather than its cause. It is, however, clear to many scientists that the essential human physical and neurological structure of the self, including sex and gender, originates in the interaction of genes and prenatal hormonal condition, and is not simply genetic (LeVay & Baldwin, 2012; Bailey et al., 2016). Fluctuating factors present in the mother's uterus influence the presence and action of hormones (cf. Auyeung et al., 2009; Bailey et al., 2016), and these prenatal genetic and environmental conditions determine chromosomal sex, undifferentiated fetal sex, differentiated fetal gonadal sex, fetal hormonal sex, and genital sex (Fausto-Sterling, 2012). Furthermore, the sexual differentiation of the brain begins in the last half of pregnancy, where "early hormonal influences do produce some sex differences in brain structure, function and chemistry" (LeVay & Baldwin, 2012, p. 100). Differences in brain functioning have been correlated with biological sex. These are most clear when they concern reproductive and parenting behaviors, "but they also include aspects of general cognitive and emotional style: emotion, memory, vision, hearing, processing faces, pain perception, navigation, neurotransmitter levels, stress action on the brain and disease states" (Cahill, 2006, p. 477).

Studies of specific sex differences focusing on complex interactions discovered that males, for example, have faster fear conditioning than females. This pattern however, interacts with various factors such as chronicity of the stressful situation, presence of social stress, presence of physiological stressors, and whether the stress hormone cortisol is administered. Clearly, biological sex matters, but situational and hormonal factors matter as well (Andreano & Cahill, 2009).

Another series of studies differentiated people with two types of cognitive tendencies, "empathizers" and "systematizers." Cognitive neuroscientist Baron-Cohen (2003) demonstrated an "empathic" approach toward experience to be more common in women, while a "systematizing" approach is more commonly found in men. He made the case that these cognitive styles are a consequence of biological (genetic and hormonal) factors prior to birth (Baron-Cohen, 2003). Researchers in his lab showed a link between fetal testosterone and the development of sex-typical play in children. High levels of prenatal testosterone were related to increased male-typical play behavior in boys. Auyeung et al. (2009) concluded that some personal traits or preferences that we may think of as directly dependent on cultural context and familial experiences have biological underpinnings that contribute to the shape of sex and/or gender identity.

Jordan-Young (2010) challenged these conclusions, however, with a "Not so quick!" (p. 50). In her careful analysis of the research on brain sex differences, she disagreed with many of these generalizations, maintaining that studies of the gendered brain are "[a] hodgepodge rather than a solid structure." She concurs that a size difference in the volume of a small organ in the brain, INAH3, does seem to correlate with sex; however, amazingly, she found this to be the only solidly confirmed sexual difference in brain anatomy. She concluded, "Sex differences in the human brain are subtle and elusive" (p. 50), and that "the basic sense of male or female is not set in stone by androgens in the uterus, although androgens do seem to have some effect" (p. 108). So, though form and functionality of the material body is known to be biologically determined, Jordan-Young's analysis pushed her to a fuller recognition of how sexual differences in the brain are also largely formed through environmental shaping.

Gender Identity—the Individual's Identity or Self-Presentation

Since the last half of the 20th century, American scholars (notably Money, 1955) have explored how people may usefully be recognized to be not only biologically determined—that is, "sexed"—but also "gendered"—that is, situated as sexed beings within cultural settings. Substantial bodies of research have emerged attempting to clarify how these cultural factors operate in the formation of "gender identity" (Butler, 1990).

Fausto-Sterling (2012), for example, illustrated how the contemporary cultural preference for certain colored clothes for babies and children can be understood as a result of behavioral shaping of gender roles. Pink, popularly associated with girls, didn't become the color of choice in America until some time after 1930. This cultural preference became important for girls in this country via behavioral "rewards" and "punishments." Thus, if wearing pink elicits compliments that please the girl, she will feel happy wearing pink and will be likely to choose pink when she can. This simple example makes social shaping seem easy to understand. The mechanism becomes operational as soon as an individual is born into a social, relational context. Its power is sometimes blatant, while at other times it is less easy to decode. We see people doing and preferring things that to the observer seem aversive rather than rewarding. Although specific mechanics may be obscure (and call for more complex ways of understanding the roots of behavior), the behavioral process is easily understood.

This is also demonstrated by Jordan-Young (2012), who interviewed 20 influential brain organization researchers, and concluded: "What went under the umbrella terms masculine and feminine—wasn't stable" (pp. 130–131). Shifting assumptions by researchers went unrecognized, untheorized, and unstudied. To illustrate, studies on "femininity" done before 1980 measured different dimensions of "femininity" than studies done later in the century, after the arrival of birth control and freer sexual expression. Female sexual desire and behavior in the 20th century, was often loosely labeled "female sexual behavior," without details.

The power of the interaction between gender and culture was further illustrated by a meta-analysis study conducted by Lawrence (2009) on the prevalence of two different types of transsexual people in cultures that foster individualism or collectivism. She found that cultural individualism was correlated with the prevalence of male/female transsexuals who prefer male (androphilic) or female (gynephilic) sexual objects. Cultures that fostered collectivistic social patterns were correlated with more homosexual (attracted to men, androphilic) trans-people, and vice versa for trans-persons attracted to women. Cultures that fostered collectivistic social patterns were correlated with more homosexual (attracted to men, androphilic) trans-people, and vice versa for trans-persons attracted to women. Culture type accounted for 77% of the variance. Clearly, culture type has a powerful relationship with this aspect of gender dysphoria. It is important to note that if the two different types of trans-men (gynephilic and androphilic) are grouped together, these cultural correlations disappear. Lawrence's meta-analysis of the incidence of two clusters of male to female transsexuals revealed an important aspect of the male trans experience. Gender dysphoria is not simply a question of being born or made "that way." How you experience your gender and who you identify with are likely to differ in cultures with different values.

As mentioned earlier, gender is a contemporary construct, useful for conceptualizing social roles and "the entire collection of mental and behavioral traits that, to a greater or lesser degree, differ between males and females . . . aside from the primary and secondary sex traits" (LeVay & Baldwin, 2012, p. 103). Currently, the determination of gender in the United States varies from state to state. In some places, birth gender is determinative; a person is born either male or female. In others, a diagnosis and treatment of gender dysphoria is necessary. In others, the law simply accepts that a person's gender is what they state it to be, regardless of their current body anatomy or what might be written on their birth certificate. Jordan-Young (2010) has argued persuasively that for scientific purposes, feminine and masculine should not be thought of as two extremes on one dimension of gender. She espouses:

> thinking of these two clusters of characteristics as different from and perhaps orthogonal to each other. An individual might then be seen as clearly masculine and feminine, neither masculine or feminine, or characterized by one or the other gender role cluster.

(p. 159)

Sexuality—the Individual's Sexual Desires and Preferences

Neuroscientist LeVay summarized studies of sexual object choice, suggesting that sexual orientation could be viewed as an aspect of gender (LeVay & Valente, 2004). He proposed that the key attribute defining sexual orientation would be the gender to which a person is attracted. Rather than labeling people by the *sameness* or *difference* of the sex of their sexual object (homosexual or heterosexual), he recommended highlighting the *gender* of the object: androphilic (attraction to men) or gynephilic, (attraction to women). Most, although not all, men are gynephilic, and most, but not all, women are androphilic. Sexual orientation is a highly gendered trait, although not so highly gendered as gender identity. This proposed reframing of the study of sexual object and gender identification, shifting the focus from identity to object, was enormously distressing to many individuals who were not comfortable with such a radical rethinking of gender identity.

As Fausto-Sterling described the response to LeVay's work, "He became the center of a firestorm . . . the language of the public debate soon became polarized," with terms like "genetic, biological inborn, innate, and unchanging" being contrasted with "environmental, acquired, constructed, and choice" (Fausto-Sterling, 2000, p. 26). Established categories were pitched against each other in contentious opposition, rather than being open for ongoing nuanced scientific dialogue.

How do you determine a person's sexual orientation? In some studies, self-report is accepted, while in other studies, genital response to sexual stimuli is measured and used to define sexual orientation. When both sorts of data are collected, they often differ from each other. Such differences (which may be glossed over in reports) make for real ambiguity when interpreting results. Furthermore, many individuals have objects of desire that do not fit within this framework and whose desire focuses on a wide variety of stimuli that can be sexually arousing—spanking, cutting, bondage, fetish objects, animals, parts of bodies, deceased bodies, as well as parts of one's own body—rather than on gender-sorted categories of people. Recognizing this range of objects of desire makes room for our mental models to more accurately consider patterns present in sexual desire.

Many theories attempt to find explanations of sexual orientation. As we have said, there are a great variety of objects of sexual desire, some more fixed, some more fluid; nonetheless, many disciplines study desire from within a dichotomous structure, considering the dichotomy of same and opposite sexual desire. Biological theories tend to look for causality of desire by focusing on prenatal factors. Studies of identical twins raised apart suggest that genes do have a significant influence on sexual orientation. LeVay and Baldwin (2012) state that "Genetic factors account for as much as half of the overall diversity in men's sexual orientation. [In women the influence of genetics was] weaker but still measurable" (p. 377). Jordan-Young (2010), on the other hand, stated the problem was thinking of genes as "static, concrete building blocks" (p. 271). She emphasized: "Gene expression is a dynamic, contingent process that is responsive to both specific conditions during development and to random events" (p. 271). Other studies of sexual orientation point to the possibility that androgen hormones, or the baby's sensitivity to the hormones, may cause atypical sexual orientation.

Six scientists from diverse biological and sociological disciplines (Bailey et al., 2016) recently presented a comprehensive overview of what is currently considered known about the formation of sexual object desire. In their overview of data on differing causal hypotheses, including hormonal, genetic, social environmental, they stated there is:

> more evidence supporting nonsocial causes of sexual orientation than social causes . . . . This evidence includes the cross-culturally robust finding that adult homosexuality is strongly related to childhood gender nonconformity; moderate genetic influences demonstrated in well-sampled twin studies; the cross-culturally robust fraternal-birth-order effect on male sexual orientation; and the finding that when infant boys are surgically and socially "changed" into girls, their eventual sexual orientation is unchanged (i.e., they remain sexually attracted to females). In contrast, evidence for the most commonly hypothesized social causes of homosexuality—sexual recruitment by homosexual adults, patterns of disordered parenting, or the influence of homosexual parents—is generally weak in magnitude and distorted by numerous confounding factors.
>
> (Bailey et al., 2016, p. 46)

From a different perspective, Jordan-Young (2010) was skeptical: "The overall evidence that early hormones affect sexual orientation is murky, at best" (p. 146). In 2010, she stated flatly, "There is no evidence linking early hormone exposures with sexual orientation in genetic males with typical rearing" (p. 197).

Clearly, what "causes" same-sex desire is a subject of controversy rather than certainty. Jordan-Young proposed that when studying "orientation," it would be helpful to make clearer distinctions. We should distinguish between identity, behavior, and desire, which may or may not be correlated. As she states, "It makes a great deal of difference which [factors] are used as a gauge of orientation" (p. 196). Kuchuck (personal communication, 2016), asks:

> if we are to question what leads to same-sex desire without also asking why some people are heterosexual, bisexual or otherwise inclined in their sexual attractions and behaviors, we are implying that there is something unusual or otherwise deviant or "wrong" about same sex attraction and/or orientation. The fact is, we don't really know why people are attracted to the same or opposite sex. To suggest otherwise, especially when the question is only posed to non-heterosexuals, is to risk the assumption of pathology. Secondarily, to my mind, that question obfuscates the much more important inquiry into what prevents people and societies from embracing diversity of any kind. It seems to me that a more relevant and useful question would be why and how shame, fear, and other familial, religious, and cultural prohibitions persist and interfere with a person's ability to desire and love.

As we can see, just as in gender identity, sexual orientation is a complex matter influenced by a number of factors. Diamond (2009), in research on the concept of sexual fluidity in women, reported that over the course of two years, two-thirds of 100 young female subjects shifted their stated sexual identity—many shifting repeatedly. Diamond (2014) went on to study the phenomenon of fluidity in men. Her study, conducted on 159 adult women and 179 adult men who identified as gay/lesbian, bisexual, and heterosexual, allowed participants to choose more than one identity. This differs from most research that typically uses forced-choice/either/or methodology in determining sexual identity; 36% of lesbian women and 39% gay men selected at least one other identity.

Her findings were as follows:

- less than half of self-identified gay men and lesbians in this study said that they were only attracted to people of the same sex during the last year;

- 42% of lesbians said that they had masturbated to a male fantasy recently;
- 31% of gay men said they had masturbated to a female fantasy recently;
- 9% of self-identified lesbians and 12% of self-identified gay men reported actually having sex with someone of the other sex during the last year;
- 50% of heterosexual women and 25% of heterosexual men reported having at least some recent same-sex attraction;
- 35% of heterosexual women and 24% of heterosexual men reported masturbating to a same-sex fantasy in the last year;
- 2% of heterosexual women and 9% of heterosexual men reported actually having same-sex contact in the last year.

One other finding worth noting is that, among those who had previously "come out," 84% of women and 78% of men reported that they had changed their sexual identity label at least once.

Discussion

Returning to our initial questions, this limited exploration of cross-disciplinary studies makes it clear there are no solid answers. We repeatedly discover the importance of not being naïvely overtaken by what is attributed to other disciplines. Science works in a chain-like process, moving forward and back, venturing into new territory and then returning to revisit ideas previously accepted or rejected. All this means we need considerable mental flexibility when thinking about scientific research.

Despite the lack of clear answers, a number of important ideas can be carried back to our clinics. Rather than specific bits of knowledge, so very likely to change with time, these have to do with better ways of thinking about sex and gender:

- We would best think about biological sex, gender, and sexual desire as three intertwining aspects of the sexual being: organic—the material body; gender—how one identifies; sexuality—one's desire.
- "Nature" and "nurture" are co-occurring and always interactive.
- Development and change are continual and ongoing.

- Femininity and masculinity are helpfully thought about as fluid, co-occurring dimensions rather than a single continuum.
- Sexual orientation can be thought of as made up of three changeable factors: sexual behaviors, identity, and sexual desire.
- Aspects of specific situations affect the self-perception and presentation of sexuality.
- People form theories to try to understand their experience. These theories powerfully shape what they see and think.

Psychoanalysis/Science

What now? How can we psychoanalysts think about this collection of provocative and provisional information? We can well afford to add these important refinements to our thinking about human sexuality, augmenting the ways we work with our own psychoanalytic models.

Troublesomely, psychoanalysis has tended to be marginalized in many discussions of sexuality. Green (2002) says that "With the decline of psychoanalytic influence for explaining the development of sexual identity . . . and sexual orientation . . . researchers have sought 'biological' origins behind these bedrock features of humanhood" (p. 463). Bailey et al. (2016), recently put it this way:

In general, psychoanalytic theorists came to blame a dysfunctional relationship between children and their parents for children's homo-sexuality, which they saw as a pathological outcome. Culprits included emotionally distant fathers and overbearing mothers. These hypotheses had the empirical limitations of most psychoanalytic hypotheses . . .— namely, that they stemmed from therapists' observations filtered through the lens of highly speculative theory rather than from systematic scientific studies.

(p. 83)

Even though psychoanalytic thinking has completely disavowed the ideas cited here, the wider community of scientists continues to think that these ideas characterize our point of view. This historically based misunderstanding of psychoanalysis continues to operate as a barrier to interdisciplinary dialogue. So we are faced with the important question, "Can psychoanalysis establish relevance in the study of human sexuality?"

Relational Psychoanalysis

While other schools of psychoanalysis have developed useful studies and ways of understanding sex, we will focus on the substantial contributions of relational psychoanalysis. In part, this strength is a byproduct of the close ties between relational psychoanalysis and academia. Relational psychoanalysis has a long history within the New York University Postdoctoral Program, including ongoing dialogue with other disciplines such as anthropology, sociology, history, and feminist and queer studies (see Aron, 1996). Stephen Mitchell, one of the original founders of relational psychoanalysis, assimilated ideas from ancient Greece through 20th-century psychoanalysis, from Freud, through Klein and Winnicott. Mitchell built on this broad understanding of philosophy and psychoanalysis to develop innovative ways of understanding the human experience. Twenty-eight years ago, in an article entitled "Gender and sexual orientation in the age of postmodernism: The plight of the perplexed clinician," he stated: "the best position for the clinician in the land of postmodernism includes, in addition to claiming considerable knowledge about many things, not claiming to know things we don't know, and probably never will know" (Mitchell, 1997, p. 72).

Building on Mitchell's stance of humility and wisdom, relational psychoanalysis has tackled many aspects of the human experience, including groundbreaking understandings of sex. The numbers of relational theoretician/clinicians who have written and taught about sexual theory and practice are more than can be summarized in this overview. For a more extensive review, we refer you to "Talking sex, talking gender—a roundtable," where four of the most eminent thinkers in the field of gender and sexuality discuss the current trends (Corbett, Dimen, Goldner, & Harris, 2014). Also, in Chapter 3 of this volume, Adrienne Harris outlines explicitly the influence of feminism, queer theory, liberation theory, and culture on the development of relational theory, signaling that from its inception, human sexuality has played a significant role in relational psychoanalytic theory.

Fundamentally, and importantly, psychoanalysis insists that much of what motivates us is unconscious, and not adequately reduced to an experience-based model of learned behaviors. Our tradition also recognizes that we are subject to internal conflicts and inconsistencies that add yet more complexity and mystery to our emotions and behaviors. Our discipline also holds to a particular clinical relationship characterized by acceptance of diversity and ambiguity; a non-authoritarian, explorative stance; and openness to working within dissonant internal and interpersonal spaces. Furthermore, the relational model's shift toward vigilant reflection and use of counter-transference as a means toward understanding the patient's intrapsychic and interpersonal world requires the analyst to attend to his/her own personal sexuality as a path towards understanding the sexuality of others.

One of the most influential theorists in the arena of sex and psychoanalysis was Muriel Dimen, anthropologist, psychoanalyst, founding member of relational psychoanalysis, and long-time editor of the journal *Studies in Gender and Sexuality*. Her death in 2016 silenced her clear, bold thinking about sex. Her text *Sexuality, Intimacy, Power* (2003) wrestled with the problems of binaries and their implicit hierarchies; underlined the importance of unconscious processes in sexuality; pointed to the subversive action of concepts of difference; and called on us to "give up all determinism" in order to think about desire. Dimen worked to restore ambiguity and tension to the discussion of desire, advocating for paradox, difference, multiplicity, and uncertainty. Dimen regarded sexuality as a complicated aspect of being that begins unconsciously in the womb and remains an enigma throughout our lives.

Theoreticians such as Dimen who promote recognition of unconscious enigmatic motivators provide a particularly important contribution to the psychoanalytic understanding of sex as they theorize the unpragmatic, the irrational, and in fact the erotic aspect of sex. Most recently, Atlas (2016) has drawn further attention to the "enigmatic," addressing not only the sensible, practical, measurable aspects of experience, which she labels the pragmatic, but also the enigmatic aspects, characterized by opacity, riddles, and ambiguity. She suggests that the body, the mother, death, and desire are agents for accessing these unknown places of the psyche. Repeatedly, Atlas attends to the senses, the unspoken knowledge of the body, especially the female body, replete with discharges, secrets, pregnancies. Her clinical writing offers valuable examples of how psychoanalytic understanding, more fully considered, can help in thinking about and working with dimensions of sexuality that are difficult or impossible to explain with behavioral or "scientific" models.

Saketopoulou, also an innovative relational writer and thinker, concerns herself with such complex topics as perversion and transsexualism. She opens up the complexity of bodily sex, gender identity, and sexual desire to "the anguish felt in response to the body's primary and secondary sexual characteristics" (2014, p. 780). For her, gender isn't simply a performance, as Butler (1990) may seem to imply, but "something that people are" (Saketopoulou, 2014, p. 780). She contends that "The analytic task is to help the patient . . . disturb the fixed relationship between the materiality of the flesh and gendered experience . . . to allow language and symbolism to enter these knotted psychic spaces" (p. 782).

As a legacy from Jung, we have an understanding of the role of co-occurring male and female qualities. His concepts of anima and animus organize an appreciation of how, despite our gender identification, we carry conscious and unconscious psychological qualities of the opposite gender. Psychoanalysts Gabbard and Wilkinson (1996) discuss this further in their comments on gender fluidity when they say:

> The psychoanalytic situation presents both the analyst and the analysand with a fundamental dialectical tension between nominal gender and gender fluidity. On the one hand, each member of the dyad is nominally male or female. On the other hand, in the transference/ countertransference dimensions of the process, both are subject to wide-ranging identification (and counteridentifications) with both male and female figures that render each of them, in a psychological sense, relatively genderless . . . . In the patient's unconscious effort to transform the analyst into the transference object, the analyst will be perceived as at times male, at times female, at times homosexual, at times heterosexual and at still other times various blends of genders and sexual orientations.
>
> (p. 463)

Harris (2005) proposed we think of gender as softly rather than rigidly "assembled." In a more recent symposium, she stated:

> [I think of] gender as a necessary fiction. The crucial thing about these categories is to hold them very lightly. In the theoretical sense we need a model in which gender categories can be a matter of life or death for some, and fluid and variable and transformable for others. This is where for me chaos theory becomes important, especially the chaos theory idea of soft assembly.
>
> (Corbett et al., 2014, p. 296)

As we can see, the formation of identity is complex, varied, and dynamic. The self is not unitary, but is constituted by a multiplicity of mental representations, early object relations, varying interpersonal relations, and deep affective states that shift and shape understanding. Bromberg (1998) speaks of the "human personality functioning as a shifting configuration of multiple self-states (what Freud calls 'part-egos') . . . an ongoing dialectic between multiple realities of both people at the interface of language and selfhood" (p. 54). This indicates that the self is formed in-relation, in multiple ways, and in multiple settings and encounters. From Bromberg we learn to respect the role of dissociation and splitting—mechanisms that allow the self to think in sectors when the full range of self-awareness would be overwhelming. To remain coherent, the individual must navigate through discordant realms of cognitive and emotional experience. Filtering, sequestering, denying, splitting, and dissociating are used to keep from mental chaos.

Stern (2002) advances Bromberg's intersubjective stance with his understanding that the multiple self is not only determined intersubjectively—that is, the self constituted by "identifications with the other's response to the self" (p. 694)—but also intrapsychically. He contends that:

> adopting a horizontal dynamic systems model (identity formed in a person's relational experience) does not necessitate abandoning a more "vertical" structural model (the self in relation to itself); in fact, one achieves a fuller complexity of understanding by retaining and integrating both the horizontal and vertical dimensions of psychic structure.
>
> (p. 694)

Cooper-White (2011) summarizes this well when she says:

> These states are not monolithic but in themselves encompass whole worldviews, ranges of affect, systems of meaning making and tendencies to particular types of bodily activity. In this theory, we are not understood as a unitive, integral Self, but as a conglomerate of self states, affect states and entire personalities formed in identification with objects or part-objects we have internalized from our experiences of other persons since birth. These self-states and internal personalities, further, do not function as autonomous, structured "beings" but

continue to grow and change in unconscious dynamic interaction, both among themselves internally, and in connection other persons beyond the "self."

(p. 197)

What we see in discussing complex identity formation is that the self in general, and the sexual self in particular, is not fixed, rather it is in flux. This does not infer fragmentation—that is, a pathological uncohesive, unreliable self. Rather, multiplicity is the capacity to play and live within the tension of the diversity of the self in all of its various affects, desires, identifications "as a multiple organized, associationally linked network of parallel, coexistent, at times conflictual, systems of meaning attribution and understanding" (Davies, 1998, p. 195).

Summary

In this brief overview, we have been introduced to the complexity of nonpsychoanalytic models and understandings of the many aspects of sexual being. We have also quickly surveyed some of the contributions of contemporary relational psychoanalysis. We are challenged to continue to work with many differing models in order to best understand the domains of the body, gender, and sexual desire. We continue to ask: "Can we recognize that the body is something that is really there at the same time we recognize the powerful psychic roles of our attachments and our cultures? Can we handle fluidity and flexibility while acknowledging that there is something inherently enigmatic within us that influences our gender identities, our sexual desires, and our erotic behaviors? Can we try to think about this complexity without displacing some of the very models that have the most to offer thinking about sex and gender: the role of the unconscious, the enigmatic, and the multiple and diverse understandings of the sexual self?"

As we have discovered, the complexities of each individual, including sexuality, are myriad, including fundamental incoherence deeply rooted in original enigmas. When we meet in the consulting room, differing complexities come together. Relationships, and all of existence, physical, sexual, and psychological, are beyond easy contemplation. Sex, gender, and desire emerge, over time, individually as well as in relationships, through complex interactions of social, cultural, psychological, biological, psychodynamic, neurological, and genetic forces. We must think of each individual and his/her psychological world as coming to be in a multi-factored field, and what we should be speaking of is "paradoxes and spectrums, not contradictions and mutual exclusion" (Phillips, 1997, p. 158).

As we continue to search to find meaningful ways to assist our patients with the choices confronting them within the complexity of their own identity and sexuality, we conclude with timeless and resonant words from Mitchell (1997), who reminds us that "it is the task of the analyst to help the patient confront those choices not with vertigo, but with a sense of extraordinary opportunity" (p. 72). By enhancing our ability to think fluidly and flexibly, we open up a richer field upon which to build day-to-day clinical relationships.

References

Andreano, J. M. & Cahill, L. (2009). Sex influences on the neurobiology of learning and memory. *Learning Memory, 16*, 248–66.

Atlas, G. (2016). *The enigma of desire.* New York, NY: Routledge.

Aron, L. (1996). *A meeting of the minds.* New York, NY: Analytic Press.

Auyeung, B., et al. (2009). Fetal testosterone predicts sexually differentiated childhood behaviour in girls and in boys. *Psychological Science, 20*, 144–48.

Baron-Cohen. S. (2003). *The essential difference: The truth about the male and female brain.* New York, NY: Basic Books.

Bailey, J., Vasey, P., Diamond, L., Breedlove, S., Vilain, E., & Epprecht, M. (2016). Sexual orientation, controversy, and science. *Psychological Science in the Public Interest, 17*(2), 45–101.

Bromberg, P. (1998). *Standing in the spaces.* Hillsdale, NJ: Analytic Press.

Butler, J. (1990). *Gender trouble: Feminism and the subversion of identity.* New York, NY: Routledge.

Cahill, L. (2006). Why sex matters for neuroscience. *Nature Reviews: Neuroscience, 7*, 477–484. doi:10.1038/nrn1909

Cooper-White, P. (2011). *Braided selves.* Eugene, OR: Cascade Books.

Corbett, K., Dimen, M., Goldner, V., & Harris, A. (2014). Talking sex, talking gender—a roundtable. *Studies in Gender and Sexuality, 15*, 295–317.

Davies, J. M. (1998). Multiple perspectives on multiplicity. *Psychoanalytic Dialogues, 8*, 195–206.

Diamond, L. (2009). *Sexual fluidity: Understanding women's love and desire.* Cambridge, MA: Harvard University Press.

Diamond, L. M. (2014, February). *I was wrong! Men are pretty darn sexually fluid, too.* Invited keynote presented at the Society for Personality and Social Psychology Preconference on Sexuality, Austin, TX.

Dimen, M. (2003). *Sexuality, intimacy, power*. New York, NY: Analytic Press.

Dreger, A. D. (2008). The controversy surrounding the man who would be queen: A case history of the politics of science, identity, and sex in the internet age. *Archives of Sexual Behavior, 37*, 366–421.

Fausto-Sterling, A. (2000). *Sexing the body: Gender politics*. New York, NY: Basic Books.

Fausto-Sterling, A. (2012) *Sex/gender biology in a social world*. New York, NY: Routledge.

Gabbard, G. O., & Wilkinson, S. M. (1996). Nominal gender and gender fluidity in the psychoanalytic situation. *Gender and Psychoanalysis, 1*, 463–481.

Harris, A. (2005). *Gender as soft assembly*. New York, NY: Analytic Press.

Ioannidis, J. P. A. (2005). Why most published research findings are false. *PLoS Med, 2*(8), e124.

Jordan-Young, R. M. (2010) *Brainstorm: The flaws in the science of sex differences*. Cambridge, MA: Harvard University Press.

Lawrence, A. (2009). Societal individualism predicts prevalence of nonhomosexual orientation in male-to-female transsexualism. *Archives of Sexual Behavior, 39*(2), 573–583. doi:10.1007/s10508-008.9420-3

LeVay, S., & Valente, S. M. (2004). *Human sexuality*. Sunderland, MA: Sinauer Associates.

LeVay, S., & Baldwin, J. (2012). *Human sexuality*. Sunderland MA: Sinauer Associates.

Marshall, K. (1977). Empathy, genuineness, and regard: Determinants of successful therapy with schizophrenics? A critical review. *Psychotherapy: Theory, Research & Practice, 14*, 57–64.

Marshall, K. (2009). The embodied self. *Journal of Analytical Psychology, 54*, 677–696.

Mitchell, S. (1997). Gender and sexual orientation in the age of postmodernism: The plight of the perplexed clinician. *Gender and Psychoanalysis, 1*, 45–74.

Money, J. (1955). Hermaphroditism, gender and precocity in hyperadrenocorticism: Psychologic findings. *Bulletin of the Johns Hopkins Hospital, 96*, 253–264.

Phillips, A. (1997). *Keeping it moving*. In *The Psychic Life of Power*. Palo Alto, CA: Stanford University Press.

Purves, D., et al (2008). *Neuroscience*. Sunderland, MA: Sinauer Associates.

Ramachandran, V. S., & Blakeslee, S. (1998). *Phantoms in the brain*. New York, NY: Harper Press.

Saketopoulou, A. (2014). Mourning the body as bedrock: Developmental considerations in treating transsexual patients analytically. *Journal of American Psychoanalysis, 62*, 773–806.

Stern, S. (2002). The self as a relational structure: A dialogue with Multiple Self-Theory. *Psychoanalytic Dialogues, 12*(5), 693–715.

Chapter 15

Considering Culture from a Psychoanalytic Perspective

Pratyusha Tummala-Narra

Psychoanalytic theory has been criticized for neglecting issues of social context and identity and for privileging internal life over external realities of clients in psychotherapy (Brown, 2010; Wachtel, 2009). However, many psychoanalytic scholars over the past two decades have examined various aspects of social context as it relates to intrapsychic and interpersonal processes (Akhtar, 2011; Altman, 2010; Leary, 2006). The present chapter aims to extend psychoanalytic contributions to the understanding of culture and diversity as an essential component of psychoanalytic psychotherapy. In the following sections, I discuss how cultural competence has been defined in professional psychology, a critique of psychoanalytic approaches to social context, recent psychoanalytic scholarship that addresses issues of social identity, and the ways in which psychoanalytic theory can both be transformed by and transform existing understandings of cultural competence in professional psychology.

Cultural Competence in Professional Psychology

Multiculturalism, identified as the "fourth force" in psychology (Pedersen, 1991), aims to "encourage inclusion and enhances our ability to recognize ourselves in others" (Comas-Díaz, 2011). The multicultural counseling movement in mental health paralleled the Civil Rights movement of the 1950s and 1960s (Arredondo & Perez, 2003; Hurley & Gerstein, 2013). Psychologists began to challenge the universal applications of psychotherapy approaches rooted in Euro-American cultural values and norms. Further, the multicultural movement in psychology, along with feminist psychology, has challenged traditional approaches to psychotherapy for rarely addressing issues of power, privilege, and more broadly, social context. From this view, Western-based psychotherapies, such as psycho-analytic, cognitive behavioral, and humanistic therapies, have historically decontextualized, ahistoricized, and depoliticized individual development. Multicultural psychology involved a turn toward new models that would explain minority and majority group identities as rooted in the context of particular social (gendered and racialized) interactions. The new frame-works that emerged recognized that existing approaches to psychotherapy may actually contribute to internalized oppression and a compromised sense of agency (Atkinson, Morton, & Sue, 1998; Comas-Díaz, 2011; Helms, Nicolas, & Green, 2010). In 2003, the American Psychological Association developed guidelines for providers of services to ethnic, lin-guistic, and culturally diverse clients which support the place of context in a client's life and call for culturally competent practices. Stanley Sue (1998) suggested that the essence of cultural competence involves scien-tific mindedness, which encourages therapists to resist premature conclu-sions about clients who are from a different sociocultural context than themselves, dynamic sizing, which involves the therapist's ability to appropriately generalize and individualize client's experiences such that stereotyping is minimized, and culture-specific expertise, which involves the therapist's specific knowledge about his/her own sociocultural context and that of the clients with whom he/she works. Derald Wing Sue (2001) further elaborated on the need to address universal, group, and individual levels of personal identity, emphasizing that therapists tend not to attend to the influence of individuals' connection with groups, such as ethnic or religious groups, on their psychological well-being.

Culturally competent therapists aim to engage with several tasks: (a) develop (the therapist's) self-awareness; (b) develop general knowledge about multicultural issues and the impact of various cultural group mem-bership; (c) develop a sense of multicultural self-efficacy, or the therapist's sense of confidence in delivering culturally competent care; (d) understand unique cultural factors; (e) develop an effective counseling working alli-ance in which mutuality and collaboration are emphasized; and (f) develop intervention skills in working with culturally diverse clients (Constantine & Ladany, 2001; D. W. Sue, 2001). The term "cultural competence" often evokes feelings of anger, helplessness, and frustration among academics and clinicians, and can even be experienced at times as oppressive and burdensome. The use of the term "competence" has been criticized as implying technical expertise, drawing attention to the institutionalization of cultural competence as potentially dangerous to the regulation and delivery of mental health services (Kirmayer, 2012). Much of the criticism of existing approaches to cultural competence in professional psychology centers around the complexity of navigating across and within individual, interpersonal, and systemic issues relevant to the client, the therapist, and the therapeutic process, and of addressing the dynamic nature of culture itself. A psychoanalytic perspective can facilitate an understanding of why the implementation of cultural competence requires a deeper examination of social context and identity.

Critique of Psychoanalytic Approaches to Social Context

Among psychoanalytic journal publications, there are no articles that mention attending to the client's and the therapist's social and cultural contexts as a basic value of psychoanalytic approaches. This is also true for the papers that include reviews of empirical evidence for the efficacy of psychoanalytic psychotherapy. There is no mention in these papers (Luborsky & Barrett, 2006; McWilliams, 2003; Shedler, 2010) about the potential influence of social context in clients' lives or in the efficacy of psychoanalytic or psychodynamic psychotherapy.

Watkins (2012) examined reviews and meta-analyses of psychodynamic treatment over the past decade (a total of 104 studies, including over 9000 participants), and found that approximately 75% of the studies did not provide any information about race or ethnicity. The exclusion of information about race and ethnicity is not particular to empirical studies. Such exclusion is also evident in discussions of case studies and case material in clinically oriented scholarship, when the social identity of the client and that of the therapist are either not mentioned at all, or mentioned briefly without connecting social identity factors with clinical presentation or the therapeutic process. Testing instruments further exclude social identity. For example, the Shedler-Westen Assessment Procedure (SWAP; Shedler & Westen, 2007), which aims to assess inner capacities and, more broadly, healthy functioning, does not include any items corresponding to cultural identity or adjustment. In considering issues of social context, we need to understand the history of psychoanalysis.

Aron and Starr (2013) described Freud's self-representation, seated within an anti-Semitic Vienna, as "simultaneously insider and outsider, observer and observed, male scientist and circumcised Jew" (p. 230). Freud's vision was a progressive one that involved the availability of psycho-analysis to the public across lines of culture and social class (Aron & Starr, 2013; Danto, 2005). At the same time, scholars (Akhtar & Tummala-Narra, 2005; Moskowitz, 1995) have described Freud's ambivalence about socio-cultural issues such as race, gender, and religion. Moskowitz (1995), for example, noted that Freud was keenly aware of anti-Semitism directed toward his family and other Jews while growing up, and yet never formally wrote about the effects of this oppression.

Freud and many other analysts lost their homes and were separated from loved ones, and were met with ambivalence in their new adoptive countries (Goggin, Goggin, & Hill, 2004). It became a matter of survival and safety to abandon connections with social and cultural traditions, especially in the face of anti-Semitism and ethnocentrism (Zaretsky, 2006). The traumatic effect of the Nazi Holocaust and anti-Semitism contributed to the neglect of sociocultural factors and social oppression for subsequent generations of psychoanalysts. Although analysts who developed the interpersonal school of psychoanalysis in the United States, such as Sullivan, Fromm, and Horney, presented an alternative psychoanalytic perspective that placed social interaction at the core of individual health and pathology and called attention to psychotherapy as a healing practice reflective of a particular cultural context, their views were not "main-streamed" in American psychoanalysis, in part because of the challenges these perspectives posed to existing dominant economic, social, and political structures. Instead, ego psychology, which explained psychic structures as universal and independent of cultural and political context, emerged as a dominant psychoanalytic tradition in a socially and politically destabilized post-World War I and Great Depression United States (Cushman, 1995). Furthermore, in the early part of the 20th century in the United States, the mental hygiene movement and World War I contributed to a medicalization of psychoanalytic theory and practice, further situating the locus of pathology and health within the individual (Cushman, 1995).

In the post-World War II era, object relations theory and self-psychology shifted the focus of unconscious drive and conflict to the realm of relating between the child and the caregiver, typically the mother. Cushman (1995) has noted that although Winnicott and Kohut elaborated on the construct of the self in relation to significant others (e.g., caregivers), Western, Euro-American historical and cultural context was not considered essential to shaping their conceptions of the nature of the universal self. Ironically, the emphasis on subjectivity that was elaborated in object relations theory and self-psychology, and which influenced the development of relational psychoanalysis, tended not to be reflected in theorizing about sociocultural context.

Over the past several decades, critiques of psychoanalysis have largely centered on the separation of the psychic and the social, the internal and external aspects of experience. Relational psychoanalytic scholars influenced by hermeneutic and social constructivist traditions, however, have begun to place social context at the center of intrapsychic and interpersonal experiences, and have called attention to the inherent dynamics of power and marginalization as they influence the practice of psychotherapy itself (Cushman, 1995; Friedman, 2000; Mitchell, 1988; Hoffman, 1998). Specifically, relational analysts have more actively engaged with sociocultural issues as they are mirrored in the therapeutic relationship. Wachtel (2009) has challenged therapists to move beyond a "session-centric" focus to attending to the individual's daily life, not only how the client experiences life, but what he/she does in his/her life outside the session.

Psychoanalytic Developments in the Study of Diversity

Various psychoanalytic traditions have begun to address issues of social identity, particularly gender, race, immigration, social class, language and bilingualism, religion, sexual orientation, and physical disability. I will briefly highlight a few areas of social context that have received attention in recent years from psychoanalytic scholars. First, psychoanalytic scholars have described the experience of immigration as characterized by cumulative trauma, disorganization, pain, frustration (Grinberg & Grinberg, 1989), regression into earlier stages of development, "culture shock," and discontinuity of identity (Akhtar, 2011). Akhtar has aptly used the term "third individuation" to describe the changes in identity inherent to the immigration process, whereas other theorists have emphasized the interpersonal losses and trauma incurred in immigration and cultural adjustment (Ainslie, 2011; Boulanger, 2004; Foster, 2003).

Second, relational psychoanalytic approaches have challenged Western Eurocentric ideals of human development (Boulanger, 2004; Comas-Díaz, 2011; Layton, 2006; Roland, 1996; Tummala-Narra, 2011). The concepts of healthy attachment, separation–individuation, and good enough mothering are based in Western values of individualism and independence, whereas conceptualizations of healthy attachment in most other cultures emphasize collectivistic values of interdependence and family unity (Tummala-Narra, 2011). Relatedly, psychotherapy has been conceptualized as involving enactments when the therapist and the client are unconsciously drawn to sociocultural norms that are problematic for the client's well-being. As such, cultural conflict is not openly discussed, and aspects of the client's identity remain hidden (Layton, 2006).

Third, when considering issues of race and racism, relational approaches tend not to separate intrapsychic experience from social experience (Aggarwal, 2011; Altman, 2010; Harris, 2012; Leary, 2012; Yi, 1998). The psychoanalytic study of race and racism has also involved an examination of Whiteness, with an emphasis on the processes of introjection and projection among Black and White racial dynamics in the United States (Altman, 2010). Suchet (2007) described Whiteness as "that which is seen and not named. It is present everywhere but absent from discussion. It is a silent norm" (p. 868), suggesting that it is not only those who are oppressed that suffer from melancholia, but also Whites who hold social power. Leary (2006) has further noted that race works along the lines of inclusion and exclusion, and discussions about race open the analyst to scrutiny, and the therapeutic relationship to racial enactments.

Although the study of race and racism in psychoanalysis has focused on racial tensions and dynamics between Whites and African Americans, some scholarship has explored racial dynamics across other cultural groups. For example, the concept of ethnocultural transference developed by Comas-Díaz and Jacobsen (1991) highlighted the ways that sociocultural histories and realities of the client and therapist influence therapeutic dynamics. Comas-Díaz (2000) has further suggested that racism and imperialism systematically deconstruct both individual and collective identities, and as such cause physical and psychological distress. She used the term "postcolonization stress disorder" to describe the psychological experience of colonized people of color, including pervasive identity conflicts, alienation, self-denial, assimilation, and ambivalence resulting from experiences of racism and imperialism. From a perspective that integrates psychoanalytic, feminist, multicultural, and liberation psychologies, Comas-Díaz (2000) challenges the decontextualized approaches to traumatic stress. The concept of "postcolonization disorder" in this integrative view contrasts with post-traumatic stress disorder in that post-traumatic stress disorder as a diagnosis does not reflect the repetitive and ethno-political aspects of racism and imperialism.

Fourth, scholars have addressed the intersection of race and immigration and its relevance to the therapeutic relationship. For example, Eng and Han (2000) coined the term "racial melancholia" to describe the immigrant's wish to preserve a lost ideal of Whiteness in the face of race hierarchies that impose the internalization of stereotypes, contributing to ambivalent identifications with the heritage culture and the new culture. Tummala-Narra (2007) described the ways in which histories of colonialism and slavery have influenced majority and minority groups' perceptions of skin color, related unconscious and conscious associations with ethnic belonging, acculturation, and sense of goodness and badness, and how these associations are mirrored in the therapeutic relationship.

Lastly, areas such as social class, sexual orientation, and physical dis/-ability have received attention from psychoanalytic scholars in recent years (Ainslie, 2011; Brady, 2011; Drescher, 2007; Goodley, 2011; Holmes, 2006; Javier & Herron, 2002). Scholars have drawn attention to the ways in which issues related to social marginalization, such as poverty and racism, influence the mind in a "primary way" (Holmes, 2006, p. 216) and raise anxiety for the therapist, who may or may not recognize the impact of White, middle-class values in which the culture of psychotherapy itself is located (Javier & Herron, 2002). Psychoanalytic theory concerning homosexuality calls attention to the meanings of sexual orientation and identity, and intersectionality in the face of homophobia and heterosexism, rather than etiology of sexual orientation (Burack, 2009; Drescher, 2007; Greene, 2007). With regard to ability status, scholars (Goodley, 2011) have explored defense mechanisms implicated in ableism and the social exclusion of and violence toward people with disabilities. These recent developments in psychoanalytic theory concerning various aspects of diversity have re-energized interest in social and cultural domains in psychoanalytic discourse and have contributed to more complex understandings of the intrapsychic and interpersonal experience in psychotherapy.

Conceptualizing Sociocultural Context from a Psychoanalytic Perspective

In the following sections, I outline several approaches that build on exist-ing psychoanalytic contributions, particularly those from relational theorists, and expand existing conceptualizations of cultural competence. The approaches include the following: (a) expand self-examination to include the exploration of the effects of historical trauma and neglect of sociocultural issues in psychoanalysis on present and future psychoanalytic theory and practice; (b) recognize clients' and therapists' indigenous cultural narratives, and the conscious and unconscious meanings and motivations accompanying these narratives; (c) recognize the role of context in the use of language and the expression of affect in psychotherapy; (d) attend to how clients' and therapists' experiences of social oppression and stereotypes of the other influence the therapist, the client, and the therapeutic process and outcome; and (e) recognize that culture itself is dynamic, and that individuals negotiate complex, intersecting cultural identifications in both creative, adaptive ways, and self-damaging ways, as evidenced in the use of defense. Each of these approaches is detailed below.

Expand Self-Examination

Although psychoanalysts have written extensively about the importance of self-reflection and self-examination, the recognition of historical trauma and cultural context that shaped theory and practice today has not been explicit in much of psychoanalytic literature. Yet this lack of recognition contributes to ongoing separation between the psychic and the social. With respect to technique, the disconnection between historical and cultural influences on the psychotherapy process contributes to therapists' practices such as dismissing or not initiating discussions about social context with clients. Therapists have been socialized to think that they may be disrupting the transference, that they are diluting the therapeutic frame, or might be experienced by the client as a racist or perpetrator if they were to initiate discussions about context. Indeed, these can be difficult discussions to have, with the potential for experiencing feelings of shame, vulnerability, and incompetence. In their study of Jewish women therapists, Greene and Brodbar (2010) discovered that the women's Jewish experience remained invisible despite the Jewish influence on psychoanalysis. Although in recent years a few prominent psychoanalysts have written about their religious and spiritual identities and the influence of these identities on their approach to practice (Aron, 2004; Rizzuto, 2004), in most of this literature, it is clear that the authors have struggled with bringing to their conscious attention the relevance of their social identity, and then publicly discussing their personal experiences within their professional circles. This type of self-examination in theory and practice is critical for developing a sense of authenticity, and for listening to culture, as the therapist's subjectivity influences his/her attention to the clients' experience and what he/she hears in the clients' words (Seeley, 2005; Wheeler, 2006).

Recognize Indigenous Narrative

Although some therapeutic approaches based in multicultural psychology have emphasized using therapeutic approaches with racial minorities that tend to overgeneralize the experiences of racial and ethnic groups (Seeley, 2005), psychoanalytic theory has failed to consider how individual narratives are shaped by their respective cultural groups. The clients' psychic material lies at the core of psychoanalytic theory. Recognizing the indigenous narrative entails listening to what lies beneath these meanings, how and in which context they were formed, the intrapsychic *and* extrapsychic implications these meanings have for the clients' day-to-day life, and the anxiety that is produced in clients' articulation of indigenous narrative for both client and therapist. Harlem (2009) has suggested that this type of listening involves interpreting the client's desires, fears, behaviors, and relationships in the context of a cultural meaning system by "thinking by means of the other" (p. 281). Listening to indigenous narrative necessitates a collaborative relationship in which there is a recognition that the therapist's cultural narrative and the client's cultural narrative differ, and that accompanying motivations interplay unconsciously. As such, it is especially important for the therapist to attend to which narrative (that of the therapist or that of the client) is privileged, and under what circumstances within the therapeutic process. Indigenous cultural narrative allows for a better understanding of resilience and strengths, which are defined in distinct ways across cultures (Comas-Díaz, 2011; Tummala-Narra, 2007). An analysis of the interactions among cultural narratives is also essential to a more accurate understanding of development, pathology and health, and the therapeutic process, from the clients' perspective.

For example, a female immigrant client with limited financial resources may express her belief that her depressed mood is rooted in her inability to fulfill her duty as a daughter to her aging parents who live in her country of origin. She may feel that she has abandoned her responsibilities as a daughter by not taking care of them in old age, and as such, feels responsible for bringing shame to her family's reputation in their community. The therapist's upbringing may incline her to focus more on her conflicted feelings about being a good daughter, or perhaps on her limited ability to travel to her country of origin. A psychoanalytic emphasis on indigenous narrative would involve attention to both how the client experiences the loss of access to visits with her parents, and the client's conflicted feelings about her role as a daughter in the context of physical distance from her parents and her adjustment to living in a new cultural environment. Specifically, the therapist may inquire about how she imagines herself as a daughter if she were still living in the country of origin, and her identification with her culture of origin and her changing cultural identifications since living in a new country. The client is also apt to discuss aspects of her cultural narrative if she experiences the therapist as someone who either implicitly or explicitly conveys that her perspective is valued within their interaction. The therapist, in this case, has to bear his/her own feelings of uncertainty and discomfort that are produced in listening to a narrative that either diverges from or challenges his/her own cultural narrative or preconceived notions of the client's cultural narrative.

Understand the Nuances of Language and Affect in the Psychotherapeutic Relationship

Indigenous narrative and culturally based explanations of development, health, and pathology are closely linked with language and affective experience. Psychoanalytic psychotherapy, similar to other types of therapy, relies heavily on language and verbal expression of affective material. Psychoanalytic perspectives emphasize the ways in which psychotherapy can function as a transitional space (Winnicott, 1971) bridging old and new languages and cultural experiences. Scholars have suggested that the use of native or heritage language in psychotherapy can both facilitate clients' connection with early experiences, and reflect defensive functions in psychotherapy (Akhtar, 2011). Psychoanalytic theory concerning the use of language considers individual meanings of language use, and as such, emphasizes the complex use and interpretation of language. Similarly, the expression of affect should be carefully considered. For example, the experience of silence in psychotherapy can hold different meanings based in sociocultural context. The therapist may assume that the clients' silence is indicative of resistance, and the client may assume that the therapist's silence reflects indifference and lack of understanding. Psychological distress may also be expressed in physical symptomology, such as headaches and gastrointestinal pain, as the direct expression of negative affect may be experienced as conflictual for the client. The therapist in this case is met with the dilemma of whether or not to interpret the physical symptoms of actually reflecting emotional distress, and has to think carefully about how such an interpretation is experienced by a client whose cultural narrative about health and pathology may contrast with that of the therapist. The nuances of both verbal and nonverbal communication and the conscious and unconscious meanings attached to these communications are especially well suited to a psychoanalytic perspective that values the deconstruction of the therapeutic exchange rather than the imposition of one narrative over the other.

Attend to Experiences of Social Oppression

There is strong empirical and clinical evidence that indicates the negative effects of social oppression, such as sexism, racism, homophobia, classism, ableism, and related microaggressions (Altman, 2010; Comas-Díaz, 2011; Greene, 2007; Tummala-Narra, 2007). Discrimination and stereotyping contribute to a powerful "social mirror" (Suárez-Orozco, 2000) and "social unconscious" (Dalal, 2006) that shape self-images and perceptions by others, both of which are re-created both consciously and unconsciously in the therapeutic relationship (Altman, 2010; Holmes, 2006; Leary, 2012). The exploration of oppression in psychoanalytic psychotherapy is not a new idea; however, such exploration has remained circumscribed primarily to experiences of trauma, neglect, and intrapsychic conflict, excluding social and political oppression. The exploration of oppression, social, racial, and political trauma involves an emotional transformation of the client and therapist. The psychoanalytic emphases on transference, countertransference, and the examination of repetitive patterns are especially relevant to the examination of social oppression. The therapist must open him/herself up for scrutiny of his/her own stereotypes and assumptions and that of the client, and recognize that he/she may be complicit in the client's experience of oppression (Leary, 2006). In addition, the therapist should be prepared to recognize and validate the client's lived experiences of oppression in daily life. Therapeutic work involves the movement toward speaking truthfully about and accepting painful realities (McWilliams, 2003). In such a case, the therapist and the client privilege what happens outside of the therapeutic relationship and what happens inside of the therapeutic relationship (Wachtel, 2009). Wachtel (2002) suggested that this approach not only conceptualizes the role of the therapist as someone who helps the client cope with disadvantage, but also addresses the disadvantage itself, implicating the place of social justice in psychoanalytic therapy.

Both therapists who hold a minority status and those who hold majority status with respect to race, ethnicity, immigration, sexual orientation, social class, and dis/ability should consider how their personal experiences of oppression may influence their interactions with clients. Furthermore, psychoanalytic theory can be especially helpful in addressing multiple forms of social oppression experienced by individuals and their families. For example, the therapist can explore how a client may experience racism in one context and sexism in a different context, and how he/she may or may not integrate these competing experiences and how the context may contribute to these experiences.

Recognize the Complex Ways That Intersecting Cultural Identifications Are Negotiated

Individual and social identities develop in the context of dynamic cultural change and transformation. Variations in cultural identity are evident in the heterogeneity of experience within cultural groups and communities. The complexity of cultural identity formation requires multiple psychoanalytic perspectives and an integration of clinical and research knowledge rooted in other traditions (e.g., feminist psychology, feminist psychology, multicultural psychology, social psychology, critical psychology). Hansen (2010) pointed out that the term "identity" assumes a value of unity rather than diversity, and highlights the role of unconscious conflict in "intraindividual diversity" (p. 16). He suggested that the centrality of internal conflict is shared across different psychoanalytic theories, and that postmodern and relational approaches in particular emphasize the importance of multiplicity of subjective experience.

I would argue that theory concerning conflict in cultural identity development has to be situated in the social context, and the cultural narrative of the therapist and the client. For example, a client who experiences conflict about coming out as a gay man to his family has to consider what being openly gay in his family may mean for him and his connection with his family, particularly if his family has strong cultural and religious beliefs that homosexuality is a sin. The therapist's and the client's cultural narratives also influence how cultural identity is approached in psycho-therapy. One particular supervisory example is relevant to this dilemma. I consulted with a White, European American colleague who had been working with a young second-generation Indian American woman who expressed feeling anxious about getting married, particularly after her parents had introduced her to several men with the hope that the client would choose one of these men as her spouse. My colleague expressed her feelings of helplessness in working with this client, and felt that her client was being oppressed by her parents. I asked my colleague whether the client experienced any ambivalence about her parents' involvement, or whether she only experienced negative feelings about meeting potential partners through her parents. My colleague responded by telling me that she could not imagine that her client felt anything except anger and frus-tration, because the idea of arranged marriage was oppressive and out-dated. She did, however, in a following session, ask her client if she ever felt ambivalent about arranged marriages, after which the client stated that there was indeed a part of her that liked meeting someone her parents introduced to her, and that she felt embarrassed to share these feelings with a non-Indian person.

The complexity of identity and its variations across and within cultural groups and generations is also relevant to the issue of intersectionality. The meanings attached to some aspects of identity and where and when they become more salient, and their connections with early life and ongoing interpersonal experiences, can be uniquely addressed through a psycho-analytic lens. The intersectionality of social identities is also relevant to the therapist, who must ask him/herself which aspects of identity feel more salient when working with a client of any particular sociocultural back-ground, and which social identity issues the therapist is more comfortable addressing with a client (Greene, 2007). The therapist's ability not only to engage with the client's internal conflicts concerning social identity, but also to bear the anxiety of not knowing or experiencing difference from the client's cultural identification is critical for a therapeutic relationship that is collaborative and productive. From this perspective, the therapist is required to refrain from the tendency to minimize difference and universalize experience. The therapist's ability to bear anxiety helps to facilitate the client's willingness to negotiate the multiplicity and hybridity of his/her identity and to explore shared fantasies of sameness and the other (Benjamin, 2011). As such, the therapist socializes the client to talk about social context, rather than conveying an implicit or explicit message that this issue is irrelevant or peripheral to the client's internal life.

Concluding Thoughts

A client with whom I worked in psychoanalytic psychotherapy told me during our termination process that the most important thing she gained from psychotherapy was that "someone is able to see who she actually is, which helped her to see herself as she actually is." There are, of course, many qualities of a therapeutic relationship that foster this experience of realness that my client has described, and yet I have been struck with how important it is to listen for contextual issues that interact with and shape psychic experience. The expansion of psychoanalytic theory and practice to consider psychoanalysis within a cultural context is not a stretch, in that psychoanalytic theory has from its inception focused on the relationship between an individual's early experiences with his/her caregiving environment. Considering the context of culture in psychoanalytic theory would entail an extension from the caregiving environment to multiple social contexts that provide important mirroring functions for the individual. This call for inclusion is not meant only for practitioners interested in social issues, but rather for any practitioner whose goal is to help clients with complexity and depth. Within the context of an increasingly pluralistic society and significant disparities in mental health care for marginalized communities, it behooves psychoanalytic practitioners to seriously and consistently practice with deep consideration of the impact of culture considering the intrapsychic *and* extrapsychic implications with psychoanalytic conceptualizations of social identity.

Such a commitment would require changes in theory, research, assessment, practice, and education. For example, diverse psychoanalytic and nonpsychoanalytic theoretical perspectives are necessary for a more thorough understanding of social context and identity. There is a clear need for psychotherapy research that more systematically addresses issues of social and cultural diversity, and includes research participants from diverse backgrounds. Test development and assessment should reflect the consideration of sociocultural factors, and include diverse, representative normative groups.

Responsible psychoanalytic practice would also involve both attending to specific practice approaches detailed in this chapter and addressing institutional and systemic barriers, such as lack of access to interpreters, and lack of ongoing training or access to consultation. Psychoanalytic education and training would need to involve a curriculum that reflects the valuing of sociocultural issues. Typically, there are no standard curricula in psychoanalytic training institutes that formally include educational modules on social context and identity, and few faculty members who are racial, sexual, or other minorities. There are also few academic psychology programs that include psychoanalytic contributions to the study of socio-cultural diversity in their curricula. It is not surprising, then, that psycho-analytic institutes tend to recruit few minority candidates, and that students in graduate training programs in psychology have little access to psycho-analytic ideas. Further, there are gaps between supervisees and supervi-sors (psychoanalytic and nonpsychoanalytic in orientation) with respect to exposure to training in working within our pluralistic culture and social justice issues, contributing to challenges in the supervisory relationship when addressing issues of social identity and context. Trainees and early career professionals are often caught between negotiating contra-dictory messages about the importance and relevance of cultural material in practice.

Adding culture as a core aspect of one's identity formation and insti-tuting it at the training level requires self-examination at individual and institutional levels. Mental health practitioners, especially those with training responsibilities, can either obstruct or facilitate the integration of individual and cultural understanding in education. The issue of access to psychoanalytic knowledge is also an important issue to consider. For example, the financial cost of psychoanalytic training is prohibitive for most individuals, and language that is used in psychoanalytic literature is experienced by many researchers and practitioners as difficult to translate to daily practice. Further, psychoanalytic ideas are typically published in journals that specialize in psychoanalysis, and there is little crossover of these ideas in mainstream academic journals. These issues call attention to a growing disconnection of psychoanalytic thought from academic psychology and professional psychology.

In recent years, several psychoanalytic practitioners have initiated the application of psychoanalytic concepts in community interventions and nonclinical domains, calling attention to the need to both modify existing psychoanalytic theory and create access to psychoanalytic ideas to better address the needs of diverse communities (Hollander, 2010; Liang, Tummala-Narra, & West, 2011; Twemlow & Parens, 2006). The future of psychoanalytic theory and practice and the future of a more robust understanding of the self rely on the active interchange across frameworks. The voices of therapists, clients, students, educators, and communities that experience social marginalization are at the crux of diversity issues, and as such, are likely to be better integrated once these voices are heard and "mainstreamed."

References

Aggarwal, N. K. (2011). Intersubjectivity, transference, and the cultural third. *Contemporary Psychoanalysis, 47*, 204–223.

Ainslie, R. C. (2011). Immigration and the psychodynamics of class. *Psychoanalytic Psychology, 28*, 560–568.

Akhtar, S. (2011). *Immigration and acculturation: Mourning, adaptation, and the next generation.* New York, NY: Jason Aronson.

Akhtar, S., & Tummala-Narra, P. (2005). Psychoanalysis in India. In S. Akhtar (Ed.), *Freud along the Ganges* (pp. 3–25). New York, NY: Other Press.

Altman, N. (2010). *The analyst in the inner city: Race, class, and culture through a psychoanalytic lens* (2nd ed.). New York, NY: Routledge.

American Psychological Association. (2003). Multicultural guidelines: Education, research, and practice. *American Psychologist, 58*, 377–402.

Aron, L. (2004). God's influence on my psychoanalytic vision and values. *Psychoanalytic Psychology, 21*, 442–451.

Aron, L., & Starr, K. (2013). *A psychotherapy for the people: Toward a progressive psychoanalysis.* New York, NY: Routledge.

Arredondo, P., & Perez, P. (2003). Expanding multicultural competence through social justice leadership. *The Counseling Psychologist, 31*, 282–289.

Atkinson, D. R., Morton, G., & Sue, D. W. (Eds.). (1998). *Counseling American minorities* (5th ed.). Boston, MA: McGraw-Hill.

Benjamin, J. (2011). Facing reality together discussion: With culture in mind: The social third. *Studies in Gender and Sexuality, 12*(1), 27–36.

Boulanger, G. (2004). Lot's wife, Cary Grant, and the American dream: Psychoanalysis with immigrants. *Contemporary Psychoanalysis, 40*, 353–372.

Brady, M. T. (2011). "Sometimes we are prejudiced against ourselves": Internalized and external homophobia in the treatment of an adolescent boy. *Contemporary Psychoanalysis, 47*, 458–479.

Brown, L. S. (2010). *Feminist therapy.* Washington, DC: American Psychological Association.

Burack, C. (2009). God, gays and good-enough enemies. *Psychoanalysis, Culture & Society, 14*, 41–48.

Comas-Díaz, L. (2000). An ethnopolitical approach to working with people of color. *American Psychologist*, *55*, 1319–1325.

Comas-Díaz, L. (2011). Multicultural approaches to psychotherapy. In L. Comas-Díaz (Ed.), *History of psychotherapy: Continuity and change* (2nd ed., pp. 243–267). Washington, DC: American Psychological Association.

Comas-Díaz, L., & Jacobsen, F. M. (1991). Ethnocultural transference and countertransference in the therapeutic dyad. *American Journal of Orthopsychiatry*, *61*, 392–402.

Constantine, M. G., & Ladany, N. (2001). New visions for defining and assessing multicultural counseling competence. In M. G. Constantine & N. Ladany (Eds.), *Handbook of multicultural counseling* (2nd ed., pp. 482–498). Thousand Oaks, CA: SAGE.

Cushman, P. (1995). *Constructing the self, constructing America: A cultural history of psychotherapy*. New York, NY: Addison Wesley.

Dalal, F. (2006). Racism: Processes of detachment, dehumanization, and hatred. *Psychoanalytic Quarterly*, *75*(1), 131–161.

Danto, E. A. (2005). *Freud's free clinics: Psychoanalysis and social justice, 1918–1938*. New York, NY: Columbia University Press.

Drescher, J. (2007). Homosexuality and its vicissitudes. In J. C. Muran (Ed.), *Dialogues on difference: Studies of diversity in the therapeutic relationship* (pp. 85–97). Washington, DC: American Psychological Association.

Eng, D. L., & Han, S. (2000). A dialogue on racial melancholia. *Psychoanalytic Dialogues*, *10*, 667–700.

Foster, R. P. (2003). Considering a multicultural perspective for psychoanalysis. In A. Roland, B. Ulanov, & C. Barbre (Eds.), *Creative dissent: Psychoanalysis in evolution* (pp. 173–185). Westport, CT: Praeger.

Friedman, L. (2000). Modern hermeneutics and psychoanalysis. *Psychoanalytic Quarterly*, *69*, 225–264.

Goggin, J. E., Goggin, E. B., & Hill, M. (2004). Emigrant psychoanalysts in the USA and the FBI archives. *Psychoanalysis and History*, *6*(1), 75–92.

Goodley, D. (2011). Social psychoanalytic disability studies. *Disability & Society*, *26*, 715–728.

Greene, B. (2007). How difference makes a difference. In J. C. Muran (Ed.), *Dialogues on difference: Studies of diversity in the therapeutic relationship* (pp. 47–63). Washington, DC: American Psychological Association.

Greene, B., & Brodbar, D. (2010). A minyan of women: Family dynamics, Jewish identity, and psychotherapy practice. *Women & Therapy*, *33*, 155–157.

Grinberg, L., & Grinberg, R. (1989). *Psychoanalytic perspectives on migration and exile*. New Haven, CT: Yale University Press.

Hansen, J. T. (2010). Counseling and psychoanalysis: Advancing the value of diversity. *Journal of Multicultural Counseling and Development*, *38*, 16–26.

Harlem, A. (2009). Thinking through others: Cultural psychology and the psychoanalytic treatment of immigrants. *Psychoanalysis, Culture & Society*, *14*, 273–288.

Harris, A. (2012). The house of difference, or White silence. *Studies in Gender and Sexuality, 13*, 197–216.

Helms, J. E., Nicolas, G., & Green, C. E. (2010). Racism and ethnoviolence as trauma: Enhancing professional training. *Traumatology, 16*(4), 53–62.

Hoffman, I. Z. (1998). *Ritual and spontaneity in the psychoanalytic process: A dialectical-constructivistic view.* Hillsdale, NJ: Analytic Press.

Hollander, N. C. (2010). *Uprooted minds: Surviving the politics of terror in the Americas.* New York, NY: Routledge.

Holmes, D. E. (2006). The wrecking effects of race and social class on self and success. *Psychoanalytic Quarterly, 75*(1), 215–235.

Hurley, E. J., & Gerstein, L. H. (2013). The multiculturally and internationally competent mental health professional. In R. L. Lowman (Ed.), *Internationalizing multiculturalism: Expanding professional competencies in a globalized world* (pp. 227–254). Washington, DC: American Psychological Association.

Javier, R. A., & Herron, W. G. (2002). Psychoanalysis and the disenfranchised: Countertransference issues. *Psychoanalytic Psychology, 19*(1), 149–166.

Kirmayer, L. J. (2012). Rethinking cultural competence. *Transcultural Psychiatry, 49*, 149–164. doi:10.1177/1363461512444673

Layton, L. (2006). Racial identities, racial enactments, and normative unconscious processes. *Psychoanalytic Quarterly, 75*, 237–270.

Leary, K. (2006). In the eye of the storm. *Psychoanalytic Quarterly, 75*(1), 345–363.

Leary, K. (2012). Race as an adaptive challenge: Working with diversity in the clinical consulting room. *Psychoanalytic Psychology, 29*, 271–291.

Liang, B., Tummala-Narra, P., & West, J. (2011). Revisiting community work from a psychodynamic perspective. *Professional Psychology: Research and Practice, 42*, 398–404.

Luborsky, L., & Barrett, M. S. (2006). The history and empirical status of key psychoanalytic concepts. *Annual Review of Clinical Psychology, 2*, 1–19.

McWilliams, N. (2003). The educative aspects of psychoanalysis. *Psychoanalytic Psychology, 20*, 245–260.

Mitchell, S. A. (1988). *Relational concepts in psychoanalysis: An integration.* Cambridge, MA: Harvard University Press.

Moskowitz, M. (1995). Ethnicity and the fantasy of ethnicity. *Psychoanalytic Psychology, 12*, 547–555.

Pedersen, P. B. (1991). Multiculturalism as a generic framework. *Journal of Counseling & Development, 70*, 6–12.

Rizzuto, A. (2004). Roman Catholic background and psychoanalysis. *Psychoanalytic Psychology, 21*, 436–441.

Roland, A. (1996). *Cultural pluralism and psychoanalysis: The Asian and North American experience.* New York, NY: Routledge.

Seeley, K. (2005). The listening cure: Listening for culture in intercultural psychological treatments. *Psychoanalytic Review, 92*, 431–452.

Shedler, J. (2010). The efficacy of psychodynamic psychotherapy. *American Psychologist, 65*(2), 98–109.

Shedler, J., & Westen, D. (2007). The Shedler-Westen Assessment Procedure (SWAP): Making personality diagnosis clinically meaningful. *Journal of Personality Assessment, 89,* 41–55.

Suárez-Orozco, C. (2000). Identities under siege: Immigration stress and social mirroring among the children of immigrants. In A. Robben & M. Suárez-Orozco (Eds.), *Cultures under siege: Social violence and trauma* (pp. 194–226). Cambridge, England: Cambridge University Press.

Suchet, M. (2007). Unraveling whiteness. *Psychoanalytic Dialogues, 17,* 867–886.

Sue, D. W. (2001). Multidimensional facets of cultural competence. *The Counseling Psychologist, 29,* 790–821.

Sue, S. (1998). In search of cultural competence in psychotherapy and counseling. *American Psychologist, 53,* 440–448.

Tummala-Narra, P. (2007). Skin color and the therapeutic relationship. *Psychoanalytic Psychology, 24,* 255–270.

Tummala-Narra, P. (2011). A psychodynamic perspective on the negotiation of prejudice among immigrant women. *Women & Therapy, 34,* 429–446.

Twemlow, S. W., & Parens, H. (2006). Might Freud's legacy lie beyond the couch? *Psychoanalytic Psychology, 23,* 430–451.

Wachtel, P. L. (2002). Psychoanalysis and the disenfranchised: From therapy to justice. *Psychoanalytic Psychology, 19,* 199–215.

Wachtel, P. L. (2009). Knowing oneself from the inside out, knowing oneself from the outside in: The "inner" and "outer" worlds and their link through action. *Psychoanalytic Psychology, 26,* 158–170.

Watkins, C. E. (2012). Race/ethnicity in short-term and long-term psychodynamic psychotherapy treatment research: How "White" are the data? *Psychoanalytic Psychology, 29,* 292–307.

Wheeler, S. (2006). *Difference and diversity in counselling: Contemporary psychodynamic perspectives.* New York, NY: Palgrave Macmillan.

Winnicott, D. W. (1971). *Playing and reality.* New York, NY: Routledge.

Yi, K. Y. (1998). Transference and race: An intersubjective conceptualization. *Psychoanalytic Psychology, 15,* 245–261.

Zaretsky, E. (2006). The place of psychoanalysis in the history of the Jews. *Psychoanalysis and History, 8,* 235–253.

Chapter 16

Self-Care

Staying Connected When Things Fall Apart: The Personal and Professional Life of the Analyst

Roy E. Barsness & Anita Sorenson

As relational psychoanalytic theory has reworked historical models through a perspectival lens, the rules for practice have become less clear. As relational theorists turn from insight as the primary order of change to the reworking of early trauma *within* the therapeutic dyad, new techniques and clinical skills are required. But not only are new techniques and clinical skills necessary, skills in managing and understanding the analyst's own intrapsychic and interpersonal world are imperative. As traditional psychoanalytic thought expands beyond interpretation as the ultimate instrument in psychoanalysis to the self of the analyst as primary instrument, we must pause and ask the question, "What is the impact this shift has on the analyst's self-esteem and capacity for self-regulation?"

We will approach this question by attending to:

- the impact of the patient on the therapist's self-esteem and self-regulation;
- how the therapist's self-esteem is impacted by our external communities;
- the implications of the nature and personality of persons drawn to this work.

We then propose our perspectives on self-care, which offer assistance in holding on when at times we feel as though we are falling apart.

The Impact of the Patient on the Therapist's Self-Esteem and Self-Regulation

A supervisee with tears in her eyes says: "I get so annoyed with myself. I constantly feel that I can't get this. I can't do what you do; I can't get to the metaphors, the underlying meanings, the process instead of the content, the 'What the hell is going on here anyway?' question that you always encourage me to consider. I just can't think quickly enough."

She pauses, "But what keeps coming back to me is that the only way to understand and assist my patient is through immersion into my own affects and experiences of my patient. I have to feel her to know her."

"That is the only way." I respond, "Yes."

We are quiet for a while as we consider the magnitude of what this involves. As we begin to speak, we acknowledge that indeed it is our "selves" that serve as the conduit, the midwife, the window to the deep of the other as we attend to what is being called up through the depth of our own being.

In relational psychoanalysis, it is expected and inevitable "that the treatment will re-evoke aspects of the very experiences that contributed to early developmental difficulties" (Beebe and Lachmann, 2014, p. 68). Slavin and Kriegmann argue that the evocation occurs within both patient and analyst, and therapeutic action is found in a mutual influence process suggesting "that the therapist has to be changed by deepening her awareness of her own struggles that are parallel in some way to those of the patient, [Slavin, refers to this as] 'embodied simulation'" (Beebe and Lachmann, 2014, pp. 73–74).

As you have read the preceding chapters, you have seen that the shibboleth of neutrality has been replaced by the principle of authenticity, privileging a heightened attention to the mutual intersubjectivity of the therapeutic encounter. In these chapters, we have come to see that "the main instrument we have in our efforts to understand . . . is our empathy, the main delivery system of our empathy is our person" (McWilliams, Chapter 5 in this volume), and "in order to find the patient, we must look for him within ourselves" (Bollas, in Chapter 5 in this volume). Pizer (Chapter 6 in this volume) refers to our work as a "tension of tenderness," and "generous involvement," with a "tenacious struggle to bear the patient's rage, hopelessness, dread, or anguish." Aron's treatise on intersubjectivity and thirdness as a means for change (Chapter 7 in this volume) requires an intense emotional involvement with our patients, as does Maroda's invitation to work through projections, ruptures, and enactments (Chapter 9 in this volume). Knoblauch's concepts of improvisation, negotiation, attending to the patterns, rhythms, and linkages (Chapter 8 in this volume) inform the reader of the deep level of concentration required of the analyst. In Barsness and Strawn's chapter on disclosure, we are faced with the challenge of speaking aloud what is aroused within the dyad and to articulate the unspeakable, placing a demand upon the therapist for a particularly high level of transparency (Chapter 10 in this volume). Shaw, in his chapter on love, leaves us with the call to persist in loving as authentically, deeply, respectfully, and responsibly as we can (Chapter 11 in this volume), and Schore (2014) sums it up:

> that the core clinical skills . . . are right brain implicit capacities, including the ability to empathically receive and express bodily based nonverbal communications, the ability to sensitively register very slight changes in another's expression and emotion, an immediate awareness of one's own subjective and intersubjective experience, and the regulation of one's own and the patient's affect. *All techniques sit atop this relational substratum.*
>
> (p. 394, italics added)

We are a long way from the days of abstinence, neutrality, and anonymity, when the self of the analyst was expected to be absent from the encounter. Now the analyst's own personhood, the use of the self, is seen as central to change and transformation for the patient. There is no hiding or dissociating from countertransference reactions. In fact, as Bion has noted, "the patient always knows what the analyst is thinking, and that this is the price the analyst pays for being an analyst" (in Ferro, 2006, p. 661). The subjectivity of the therapist is central to understanding unconscious material, the structure of the intrapsychic and the patient's interpersonal world. We no longer live in the myth of being unseen and unknown as helpful for the patient. Rather, we are required to pay disciplined attention to our thoughts and emotions and to have a keen awareness and acceptance of our deep emotional states and dissociations, in order to situate ourselves non-defensively, when activated by our patient's fragilities and pathologies.

In contrast to treatments which rely heavily on standardized techniques as a filter through which patient behaviors are understood and amended, each new patient from the relational analytic perspective is inimitable. We believe that when technique is developed independent of a deep understanding of the patient's particularity and the therapist can apply the same techniques to multiple patients as they relate to their behaviors (i.e., exposure therapy for phobias; anger management skills for anger; antidepressant medication for depression), we run the risk of foreclosing our understanding and occluding the essential diversity of our patient's story. Behavior from the relational analyst's perspective is influenced by multiple factors related to the patient's personal history and its relentless echoes in their current relational life. Behavior is not general; it is specific, and the means toward change cannot be achieved through impersonal treatment protocols. The analyst's reveries, thought processes, and emotional states are shaped by each individual patient. We are called upon to attend to the vicissitudes of each person's unique narrative, informed by their history, developmental arrests, breaches in attachment, and traumas that interrupt growth and fuel their anxieties and depressions. We do so believing the patient will emerge, not only with changes in behavior, but with a greater degree of confidence, a fuller range of emotional states, and deeper interpersonal relations. This places an emotional and cognitive demand upon the analyst not required of other treatment modalities, requiring "self-analysis as a practice necessary for utilizing the self as a serviceable tool . . . [and to] continually explore the province of our own selves . . . one's own inner availability and receptiveness" (Ferro, 2006, pp. 663–664).

This new expectation is challenging, but it has become the clinical standard requiring us to constantly explore the personal disruptions reverberating within us to best understand the patient's intrapsychic and interpersonal world.

Consider a recent consultation with a therapist who called to seek assistance in terminating with a patient. After two years of treatment, the patient had recently disclosed she had fallen in love with and was sexually attracted to the therapist. The therapist was very clear she was not able to work at this level of intensity and not interested in exploring further countertransference and relational reactions/interactions and their potential usefulness in working with her patient. She felt undone, and wanted to be done. Fortunately, she did not blame the patient, and sought supervision to ethically end the relationship. Although we did find a reasonable path for the treatment to end, we believe both patient and therapist would have benefited from a rich and mutual transformation had the anxieties of the therapist not been so overwhelming. This case is offered to demonstrate the inevitability of deep reactions of unresolved issues from our own past that get evoked, causing us at times to wish to exit rather than to enter further into the treatment. Furthermore, it reminds us that "the cognitive and emotional processes present in an increased cortisol release, creates an elevated state of anxiety and is counterproductive to the reflective vulnerability and surrender needed for accessing self-experience, and is likely to influence countertransference enactments" (Earl Bland, personal communication, 2016). It further illustrates that the impact of working *within* the intersubjective requires far more of the therapist than previous models of psychoanalysis or of any other treatment modality. The use of the self in relational psychoanalysis is demanding.

The Impact of the External Community on the Therapist's Self-Esteem, Self-Worth, and Dignity

In addition to the stirrings our patients evoke, we also function within the community of our training and academic institutes, the clinics in which we work, and the professional guilds to which we belong. These groups of people, in part, evaluate our place within our professional life and hold us accountable. However, these communities can at times be more deregulating than our work with our patients, as members jockey about, establishing their own positions within the community even at the cost of another's.

Perhaps that is why, in the study that formed the basis of this book, an extraneous variable emerged revealing the analysts' insecurities within the analytic community, and the free floating anxiety of not doing things "as they should be done." Although only one interviewee actually used the term, "psychoanalytic police," the preponderance of concern these analysts shared that some of what they did with patients might not meet analytic muster was surprising and perplexing to the research assistants who assisted in analyzing the data. In addressing their concern, it was important for me to first note to them that "policing" has a positive side, and that Tublin's use of the "psychoanalytic third" (see Chapter 4 in this volume) is very helpful in emphasizing our need for accountability. Tublin refers to the importance and relevance of the "psychoanalytic third" as the community of practitioners who essentially serve as the "psychoanalytic unconscious," keeping us on our toes as it "endorses certain theories of mind and interaction, certain 'acceptable' modes of engaging patients, and discourages others." This "psychoanalytic unconscious" is pertinent and essential to understanding and practicing our craft, and holds us responsible.

However, the shadow side of this community is painfully revealed in Sandra Buechler's important text, *Still Practicing* (2012). Referencing the difficulties we share in our communities, Buechler "came to believe that unmet narcissistic needs, on the part of participants at all levels play a significant role" (p. 195). She has particular concern about training and supervision, and quotes Donna Orange (2009), who refers to institutes as "somebody–nobody hierarchies of domination, submission, bullying and humiliation" (p. 354), and Crastnopol (2009), who designates training as a "narcissistic minefield" (p. 359). This domination appears to extend well beyond training, and to continue throughout the analyst's career, where competition, pandering, and grandstanding often form the "essential" community.

Our deepest aches, the hardest blows to our self-esteem, and most painful experiences of shame and self-doubt, though activated in countertransference encounters with our patients, frequently occur most *overwhelmingly* in our professional and social relations. The tools useful in our work with our patients don't translate so easily into our professional lives. Sometimes we may feel as dumb as an ox when our vulnerabilities surface socially or professionally. Within the therapeutic relationship, the splits, projections, idealizations, and devaluations that occur are expected to be worked on, sought out, reflected upon, and transformed. Institutions, on the other hand, are ostensibly set up to avoid or quiet such raw experiences within the system. Consequently, we often feel adrift, and at times incapable of gaining traction in regulating shame, hurt, and anger, and restoring a sense of competence.

Robert Young (2004) wrote a bold article entitled "Vicissitudes of therapists' self-esteem." He begins his paper with: "I think most of us would be embarrassed to speak or write about how insecure we often feel. I'm old and have had some status, so I have decided to risk it" (p. 497). He then refers to the analytic community as no different than the host of other professions in which he had been employed, where he:

> eventually found [himself] fallen among rogues, thieves, and charlatans who get their sense of achievement by competing with the very people with whom they had come together to cooperate. Psychotherapy is no exception . . . yet one imagines that it damn well should be.
>
> (p. 502)

We are hopeful that a shared awareness of this proclivity toward competition and posturing can preserve us at times in navigating the relational difficulties that we face in many of our communities and guilds. And perhaps those who read this text can be persons within our communities who influence robust critique, accountability, and dialogue that further advance the theories and practices of our craft, without damaging the dignity of the other.

The Impact of the Nature of Persons Drawn to This Vocation

Nancy McWilliams (2004) states:

> most people, who are attracted to being psychotherapists like close-ness, dislike separation, fear rejection, and suffer guilt readily. They tend to be self-critical, to be overly responsible and to put people's needs before their own. They feel more unentitled than deserving. They try to avoid feeling greed, anger and other "selfish" states of mind and become disturbed when they notice evidence of their own competitiveness or hostility. They favor the defense of reversal attempting to nourish the child in themselves vicariously by taking care of the child in the client. They identify with victims rather than with oppressors, with children more than with parents.
>
> (p. 105)

We are generally persons who have an innate sense of another's pain, due in part to our receptivity to our own vulnerabilities and woundedness. We are often thin-skinned people, highly intuitive and easily hurt. We tend to overanalyze, take on more responsibility than we should, and overvalue our own analyses of a situation without seeking dialogue with the source of our pain. This vulnerable self is what makes us good at what we do. But our "gift" of vulnerability, receptiveness, and willingness to enter into what is helpful for our patients also evokes our own wounds. Wounded healers we may be, but when wounds are reactivated and we are thrown off kilter, we can be left with feelings of shame, anger, and self-doubt.

Shame, Anger, and Loss

This confluence of the self of the therapist as "primary instrument," our problematic professional communities, and our own wounded nature leaves us vulnerable. We contend these vulnerabilities that hobble our self-esteem tend to appear primarily through shame, anger, and loss.

Shame

Shame is a universal experience occurring repetitively in the life of the therapist, particularly as we risk our vulnerabilities within our therapeutic relations. Shame is subtle, and:

> can seep into the very core of our experience of ourselves and thus constitutes the essential pain, the fundamental disquieting judgment that we make about ourselves as failing, flawed, inferior to someone else, unworthy of the praise or love of another, or falling short of a cherished idea.
>
> (Morrison & Stolorow, 1997, p. 82)

Izard says:

> shame occurs typically, if not always, in the context of an emotional relationship. The sharp increase in self-attention . . . causes the person to feel as though he were naked and exposed to the world. Shame motivates the desire to hide, to disappear. Shame can also produce a feeling of ineptness, incapacity, and a feeling of not belonging.
>
> (in Buechler, 2012, p. 33)

There are four things to consider about shame. First, Buechler (2012) reminds us that shame is an interpersonal event and we have to agree with the "low estimation of us in order to really be ashamed" (p. 205). Second, it is a perception problem. It tends to take on an "an all bad me," attitude (p. 97). Shame seems to take on a life of its own, refusing context and reason. We are only able to emerge from a shaming experience when we are able to see our shame as out of context and out of range of the overall narrative of our lives. Third, although research (Brown, 2014) demonstrates that shame differs by gender—for women, it is about perfection; for men, weakness— we have observed that, regardless of gender, perfection and weakness are common visitors to us all. Fourth, we caution confusing shame with guilt. Shame is "I am bad." Guilt is "I have done badly." Developmentally, shame is more primitive, materializing from an earlier time when a child's essential identity is being consolidated through the primary caregiver's recognitions, or lack thereof, of the child's needs. Guilt is experienced at a later stage, when the child is able to recognize its impact on the other with attempts at negotiating repair. Shame results from fear of rejection and a sense that we don't belong, that we are a sham or inherently bad, and "despair about ever being understood leads to a profound sense of isolation and an inability to express one's feelings" (Richman, 2006, p. 641). The price of shame is to move away and experience disenfranchisement. Guilt, on the other hand, moves us toward repair and reconciliation.

Shame is a frequent and debilitating visitor that requires a regaining of perspective as well as trusted others to assist in navigating us back toward self- acceptance.

Anger

Two emotions that terrify my students more than any other are feelings of the erotic and of aggression within the therapeutic relationship. Consequently, each year I have students write a paper entitled "Conflict and me." The paper requires them to take the Thomas-Kilmann Conflict Mode Instrument (Thomas & Kilmann, 2007) and then reflect upon how they imagine their conflict style may impact the therapeutic relationship. I tell them that psychoanalysis is based on a conflict model that historically emphasized the conflict between id and superego. It was expected that the neutral analyst, through the act of interpreting unconscious material, defensive structures, and resistance to change, facilitated a befriending of sorts, between the id and the superego. The result: a healthy functioning ego. However, within relational psychoanalysis, we now recognize that the battle within is also the battle *between*, and analysts must be prepared to enter the relational conflict that ensues within their work, and in fact, "it is the person of the analyst that actually heals, rather than the use of metapsychology itself" (Bagliacca, in Ferro, 2006, p. 663).

The general result of the "conflict and me" exercise is that 90% of the students are conflict-avoidant. These same 90% were drawn to the field because they had learned they were good listeners, advisors, and caregivers, and that part of their success would be because of their niceness and their non-confrontational nature. Most of us can recognize this trait within ourselves. And considerable shame comes upon us when we are met with difference, unresolvable problems, and negative transferences, and no longer feel so nice and self-sacrificing. However, avoiding conflict is dangerous, not only for the patient, but for us as well. When these feelings become uncomfortable or intolerable, we isolate, and withdraw, licking the wounds of the narcissistic injury of our more kindly version/illusion of ourselves. But withdrawal and isolation have a price. Returning to Richman, she continues: "dissociation can be a merciful defense, but at the same time there is a heavy price to be paid for denying," and suggests we "open the field," and "allow for creativity and imagination to enter the story, the patients, your own and the story being formed" (2006, p. 643).

Loss

In our professional lives as therapists, we go through multiple losses: the loss inherent in having limitations and not being enough; the loss of failing a patient; and the innumerable terminations of treatments following the deep emotional engagement that defines a successful therapy. When a patient says, "enough" and "thank you" and "I will miss you," we of course feel grateful, accomplished, and satisfied. But we also mourn the loss of a relationship that we can no longer have. Jill Salberg reflects: "It is hard to give up feeling needed in the ways in which we feel needed by our patients and to relinquish the pleasure we derive in reparative work" (2010, p. 123). In psychoanalysis, we enter into a close relationship knowing that termination is an inevitable outcome of a good treatment: "loss is imminent to love .... Bonding is fulfilled, and then, it is severed. In all of its iterations, analytic love implicates grief. Every opening of the heart is shadowed by termination" (Grand, 2009, p. 725). Over our professional lifetime, we must bear confidentially the painful impact of numerous anxieties, vicarious trauma, and the loneliness that accompanies private work.

These three—shame, anger, and loss—share commonalities, and can collapse into restricted affect, restricted relationships, restricted imagination, and restricted self-love by the analyst. We may resist vulnerability, establish defensive postures, ward off affective experiences, and foster a practice of stagnation that insulates us from underlying conflicts.

Being able to maintain our emotional balance is a necessary prerequisite to engage in the participant observation that is relational psychoanalysis. Because disciplines of self-care (such as journaling, meditating, writing, exercise, etc.) are specific to the individual, what we offer is more of an attitude or stance allowing for the personal development of individual practices. We trust that an attitude or stance of resilience, along with one's own individual practices, will assist the practitioner in remaining vibrant in this relationally rigorous but highly rewarding work.

What Keeps Us Resilient?

A Growth Mindset

Psychologist Angela Duckworth recently published a popularized version of her research conducted at the University of Pennsylvania on resilience in a book called *Grit* (2016). Grit is about perseverance for long-term goals, passion, and having a growth mindset. In a recent interview, Duckworth said:

> A growth mindset involves understanding failure is not a permanent condition and doing away with the notion that we have ceilings. People with a growth mindset, are people who truly believe that ability itself can be developed, not just that you can get good at something but that your talent might also change. Growth mindset is deep down believing about malleability in people's abilities and their talents.
>
> (in Kapadia, 2016, p. 2)

Gritty, resilient people find an exciting challenge in efforts to exceed their current skill level—grit is the opposite of complacency. This is not unlike Buechler's ideas about resilience, where she writes, "bouncing back from shame, rage, terror and sorrow are not the same, at least for me. But they do have some commonalities. They all prioritize something over something else. Essentially, they all vote for life" (2012, p. 202).

The Internal Chorus

Duckworth also discovered that resilience cannot be achieved in isolation. She learned that to succeed, one had to have a deep sense of belonging to a "culture," an environment of colleagues who expect of each other excellence, coupled with deep commitments to one another. Though we have discussed difficulties in finding supportive communities within our institutions and guilds, collegial and personal support is essential, and it is our challenge to build strong and supportive relationships in order to thrive in this field.

It has been enormously helpful in our own work to consider what Buechler refers to as the "internal chorus," those intellectual, cultural, and spiritual resources needed for a lifetime of clinical practice (Buechler, 2008). This chorus is comprised of persons who have inspired us and given direction in times of disorientation. It may be comprised of teachers, analysts, supervisors, theorists, friends, family, and writers whose words and phrases return to us when we feel lost or conflicted by clinical work. These internalized voices help us to bear the challenges and strains of our intimate profession. We feel backed up and supported by the words of these wise elders who offer us a sense of security and allow us to keep perspective when feeling destabilized, exhausted or overwhelmed clinically. They allow us to mitigate self-recrimination and remain emotionally invested in the analysis.

Applying Our Own Theories to Self-Care

The competencies highlighted in this text are not only useful in our work with patients, but also in the management of our own self-worth and emotional regulation. Just as we discipline ourselves to maintain a stance of radical open-mindedness and curiosity with our patients, we need to also apply this to ourselves. In our attempts to regulate our own emotional states, we borrow from similar reflections we ask in our work with our patients— that is, "What is being triggered?" "What do I need to hear?" "Where is this coming from?" "What am I avoiding?" "What am I trying to protect?" "What else is true?" When we are beset with negative emotions, often around sex, aggression, and shame, we must attempt to hold them without judgment until they are sorted out. In speaking about anger, Buechler says that we must find "a way to use [our] rage rather than worry about having it" (2012, p. 207). This is a good principle with all of our emotions. Winnicott's idea of potential space suggests much the same thing, where we let ourselves play with the experience, permitting emotions to have full sway, as we look for connections and richer variations of who we are. Buechler demonstrates this by allowing herself "the freedom to wander in transitional territory, to graze and to explore . . . [letting] words happen, without subjecting them to judgment or to scrutiny about their origins" (2012, p. 180).

This concept of holding and wandering is further demonstrated in Bion's concept of "alphabetizing." His conceptualization of alpha function as continuously expanding unconscious utilizes a gating mechanism which receives sensory data of emotional experience, processes it, alphabetizes it, and transforms it into alpha elements for further mental digestion, to be thought about or to become dream elements for postponement and storage. He addresses our predilection towards what he calls "disasterism," defined as an unrealistic fantasy "about my need to anticipate any unexpected event, concerned as I was that I did not have sufficient resources or presence to help me in difficult times . . . ." Upon reflection, we might be able to see that "disasterism" shields "oneself from some feared, catastrophic change where instead of *elaborating* the contents, there is rather an attempt to set up *cordon sanitaria* that isolates them preventively" (in Ferro, 2006, p. 669, italics added). Bion's concept of elaboration invites us to reflect upon patterns and links within our past, and revisit and make peace with the origins of our shame and self-doubt.

Lying Fallow

Masud Khan (1983) thought that a mental state of lying fallow was essential to any creative endeavor. He recommended to analysts the restorative potential of withdrawal.

Lying fallow is not to be confused with laziness, but is a recognition that the unimaginative path we are currently on needs rejuvenation As fields must be plowed but left unseeded seasonally to allow nourishment of the soil, so we too must lie fallow in a wider sense. We may need to step away from our practices through vacations, clinical retraining, and for immersion in our personal lives and other emotional pursuits in order to remain vibrant, engaged, and resilient. Burnout is an ever-present possibility in our clinical practices. Developing rhythms of renewal and personal formation help us to guard against this dramatic emotional depletion.

Healing from Our Patients

Martin Buber distinguished genuine dialogue from *technical* dialogue (a dialogue prompted by the need for objective understanding) and *monologue disguised as dialogue* (dialogue referring to speaking in a circuitous, pseudo manner), both forms parading as sincere forms of dialogue to escape mutuality and genuineness (see Buber, 1923/1970). When our work descends into technical dialogue or meaningless chatter, when we discover the work to be insufferable, and when we find our patients annoying and objectify them, we have most likely lost our way, and need to consult. Because, when two persons *turn* towards the other, even in the many desperate moments involved in the analytic journey, we most often will discover our work vitalizing and life-giving.

In contrast to technical and monological dialogue, Buber spoke of *genuine dialogue*—a dialogue with the intention of establishing a living mutual relationship between two persons. It is Buber's "genuine dialogue" that best frames the relational approach to psychoanalysis, where our patient is not seen as an object, but as subject, as are we, and where change occurs through the negotiating of the relationship—both the highs and the lows—where "both analyst and patient emerge to a new awareness of the unique subjectivity of each other" (Hoffman, 2011, p. 103). This does not come easily. Our vocation is one that requires suffering on behalf of the other, but if we approach our task with humility and with "surrender . . . the work is immensely fulfilling and the analyst grows with his patients" (Ghent, 1990, p. 133). Ghent's idea of surrender does not seek suffering, but understands suffering as a "suffering without ego, without intention, with sincerity . . . it simply suffers it for the sake of the other" (Orange, 2016, p. 58). Relational psychoanalysis' unique relational stance of situating ourselves intersubjectively with an attitude of curiosity, genuineness, confirmation, mutuality, and surrender "engenders in us a sense of worth or personal dignity of having a special part to play within the whole" (Shabad, quoted in Hoffman, 2011, p. 127).

What we have discovered in our own analytic practices over the years is that our clinical work, depleting at times, more often rejuvenates. This is an area of resilience that we do not want eclipsed. Even as we have talked of disciplines and practices of self-care outside the routines of our practices and our patients, we hope to remind the reader of the very gift who sits or reclines in our offices, session after session: the people, our patients, who courageously open their lives to us and bring healing and transformation to us hourly. Perhaps one of the hidden gifts to the relational analyst who has moved out from behind the screen is the discovery that in meeting the other face to face, both persons—analyst and patient—are transformed.

In this chapter, we have presented what we might call an attitude toward self-care. We have offered ways of being that respect the individual person and invite the reader to consider specific disciplines that align with their own spirit and personality.

We end with words of encouragement for any young professional accepted into an institute as a candidate for psychoanalytic training or any early career student enamored with relational psychoanalysis:

> Remember who you are, that you are valued, that you are unique, and it is you, the person, not your theory that is transformative. Be careful

of dogmatism, and let your heart and mind be open to the discovery of the theories and practices that resonate with you. Sharpen these theories and practices the rest of your career. And never forget that it is your presence and your authenticity, more than your theories, that serve as the primary agent of change. Therefore, you must remain open to all of your thoughts and emotions, and consider them to be windows into your own soul and the souls of those with whom you work. The more at home you are in your body, mind, and soul, the more your patients will thrive under your care. When conflict arises with colleagues or demons from your past, address these irksome feelings of shame, anger, and self-doubt by calling upon your internal chorus—those witnesses to your life and your profession who ground you and give you a compass. Never stop seeking, and wrestling. Psychoanalysis is not about "getting it," it is about living it together.

References

Beebe, B., & Lachmann, F. M. (2014). *The origins of attachment: Infant research and adult treatment*. New York, NY. Routledge

Brown, B. (2014). *Men, women and worthiness*. Louisville, CO: Sounds True.

Buber, M. (1923). *I and Thou* (W. Kaufman, Trans.). New York, NY: Touchstone, 1970.

Buechler, S. (2008). *Making a difference in patients' lives*. New York, NY: Routledge.

Buechler, S. (2012). *Still practicing*. New York, NY: Routledge.

Crastnopol, M. (2009). Institute life beyond graduation. *Contemporary Psychoanalysis*, *45*, 358–363.

Duckworth, A. (2016). *Grit*. New York: NY: Scribner Press.

Ferro, A. (2006). The psychoanalyst as individual: Self-analysis and gradients of functioning. *Psychoanalytic Quarterly*, *73*, 659–683.

Ghent, E. (1990). Masochism, submission, surrender: Masochism as a perversion of surrender. *Contemporary Psychoanalysis*, *26*, 108–136.

Grand, S. (2009). Termination as necessary madness. *Psychoanalytic Dialogues*, *19*(6), 725–735.

Hoffman, M. (2011). *Towards mutual recognition*. New York, NY: Routledge.

Kapadia, S. (2016, January 14). Renowned psychologist impressed with Seahawks' "culture of grit" [Blog post]. Retrieved from www.espn.com/blog/seattle-seahawks/post/_/id/17555/renowned-psychologist-impressed-with-seahawks-culture-of-grit

Khan, M. (1983). *Hidden selves*. London, England: Karnac.

McWilliams, N. (2004). *Psychoanalytic sensibility*. New York, NY: Guilford Press.

Morrison, A. P., & Stolorow, R. D. (1997). Shame, narcissism, and intersubjectivity. In M. R. Lansky & A. P. Morrison (Eds.), *The widening scope of shame* (pp. 63–99). Hillsdale, NJ: Analytic Press

Orange, D. (2009). A psychoanalytic colloquium. *Contemporary Psychoanalysis, 45*, 353–358.

Orange, D. (2016). *Nourishing the inner lives of clinicians and humanitarians.* New York, NY: Routledge.

Richman, S. (2006). Finding one's voice: Transforming trauma into autobiographical narrative. *Contemporary Psychoanalysis, 42*, 639–651.

Salberg, J. (2010). *Good enough endings.* New York, NY: Routledge.

Schore, A. N. (2014). The right brain is dominant in psychotherapy. *Psychotherapy, 3*, 388–397.

Thomas, K. W., & Kilmann, R. H. (2007). *Thomas-Kilmann Conflict Mode Instrument.* Mountain View, CA: CPP.

Young, R. (2004). Vicissitudes of therapists' self-esteem. *Free Associations, 4*, 407–519.

Part IV

A Critique

Chapter 17

Critique of Relational Psychoanalysis

Jon Mills

Introduction by Roy E. Barsness

In this final chapter, Jon Mills, psychoanalyst and philosopher, offers us a valuable critique of the contemporary perspective. It is both insightful and controversial. Many relational analysts feel that his critique is overstated and even misrepresents primary relational constructs such as intersubjectivity; multiplicity, the role of the individual self; the interpersonal over the intrapsychic; the primacy of relatedness over drive theory; the role of the unconscious and self-disclosure. Nonetheless, Mills' critique vitalizes the conversation, sharpens our theories, prompts further debate and dialogue, and invites counter-critique and further analysis. Any theory worth its weight requires critique. This chapter offers the reader a reflection on these theoretical constructs that continue to need revision, conversation, thoughtfulness, and thoroughness in order to continue to advance our field. A Postscript to the critique is provided by psychoanalyst Steven Kuchuck.

This chapter offers a sustained series of arguments to systematically evaluate the philosophical premises that justify relational theory and to give some form, coherency, and voice to a plurality of ideas within relational psychoanalysis. Because the relational movement has become such a progressive and indispensable presence within the history of the psychoanalytic terrain, it deserves our serious attention, along with a rigorous evaluation of the philosophical foundations on which it stands. It is my hope that through such crucial dialogue, psychoanalysis can avail itself to further understanding.

The scope of this chapter is largely preoccupied with tracing:

- the philosophical underpinnings of contemporary relational theory;
- the problem with postmodernism;
- illegitimate attacks on Classical Psychoanalysis;
- consilence.

The Philosophical Underpinnings of Contemporary Relational Theory

The Primacy of Relatedness

When Greenberg and Mitchell (1983) inaugurated the relational turn by privileging relatedness with other human beings as the central motive behind mental life, they displaced Freud's drive model in one stroke of the pen. Although Greenberg (1991) later tried to fashion a theoretical bridge between drive theory and a relational model, he still remained largely critical. Mitchell (1988, 2002), however, had continued to steadfastly position relationality in antithetical juxtaposition to Freud's metapsychology until his untimely death. From his early work, Mitchell (1988) states that the relational model is "an alternative perspective which considers relations with others, *not drives*, as the basic stuff of mental life" (p. 2, italics added), thus declaring the cardinal premise of all relational theorists.

Intersubjective Ontology

Relational psychoanalysis privileges intersubjectivity over subjectivity and objectivity, although most theorists would generally concede that their position does not refute the existence of individual subjects nor the external objective world. Yet this is still a topic of considerable debate in philosophy, let alone the field of psychoanalysis, which remains relatively naive to formal metaphysics.

Robert Stolorow and his colleagues (Stolorow, Brandchaft, & Atwood, 1987), as well as Jessica Benjamin (1988), are often identified as introducing intersubjective thinking to psychoanalysis, although this concept has a 200-year history dating back to German Idealism. Intersubjectivity was most prominently elaborated by Hegel (1807) as an emergent process describing the unequal power distributions between servitude and lordship, culminating in a developmental, historical, and ethical transformation of recognizing the subjectivity of the other. Two forms of intersubjectivity dominate the analytic literature—the *developmental* view, and the *systems* view—each of which may be operative at different parallel process levels.

Like Hegel, D. N. Stern (1985), Benjamin (1988), and Mitchell (2002) view intersubjectivity as a developmental achievement of coming to acknowledge the existence and value of the internalized other, a dynamic that readily applies to the maternal–infant dyad and the therapeutic encounter. Daniel N. Stern (1985) has focused repeatedly on the internal experience of the infant's burgeoning sense of self as an agentic organization of somatic, perceptual, affective, and linguistic processes that unfold within the interpersonal presence of dyadic interactions with the mother. In his view, intersubjectivity is like Hegel's, where there is a gradual recognition of the subjectivity of the m/other as an independent entity with similar and competing needs of her own.

Beebe and Lachmann's (2003) dyadic systems theory is predicated on intersubjectivity and the mutuality of dyadic interactions whereby each partner within the relational matrix affects each other, thus giving rise to a dynamic systems view of self-regulation based on bidirectional, coordinated interactional attunement and cybernetic interpersonal assimilations resulting in mutual modifications made from within the system.

Stolorow, Atwood, and their colleagues (Stolorow et al., 1987; Stolorow & Atwood, 1992; Orange, Atwood, & Stolorow, 1997) cast intersubjectivity as a more basic, ontological category of interdependent, intertwining subjectivities that give rise to a "field" or "world," similar to general references to an intersubjective "system" or an "analytic third" (Ogden, 1994).

These absolutist overstatements lend themselves to decentering intrapsychic activity over relational interaction, and draws into question:

- the separateness of the self;
- the pre-existent developmental history of the patient prior to treatment;
- the prehistory of unconscious processes independent of one's relatedness to others;
- a priori mental organization that precedes engagement with the social world.

These *statements* irrefutably replace psychoanalysis as a science of the unconscious with an intersubjective ontology that gives priority to conscious experience. To privilege consciousness over unconsciousness to me appears to subordinate the value of psychoanalysis as an original contribution to understanding human experience. Even if we as analysts are divided by competing theoretical identifications, it seems difficult at best to relegate the primordial nature of unconscious dynamics to a trivialized backseat position that is implicit in much of the relational literature. For Freud (1900), the "unconscious is the true psychical reality" (p. 613), which by definition is the necessary condition for intersubjectivity to materialize and thrive.

What is clearly privileged in the relational platform over and above the unique internal experiences of an individual's intrapsychic configurations is the intersubjective field or dyadic system that interlocks, emerges, and becomes contextually organized as a distinct entity of its own. Following key propositions from the relational literature, the intersubjective system must *exist*, for it is predicated on being, hence on actuality; therefore, we may assume that it encompasses its own attributes, properties, and spatiotemporal dialectical processes.

In fact, the intersubjective system is a process-oriented entity that derives from the interactional union of two concretely existing subjective entities, thus making it an *emergent property* of the multiple (often bidirectional) interactions that form the intersubjective field. This ontological commitment immediately introduces the problem of agency, a topic I will repeatedly address throughout this critique. So we must ask:

- How can a system acquire an agency of its own?
- How can the interpersonal field become its own autonomous agent?
- What happens to the agency of the individual subjects that constitute the system?
- How can a "third" agency materialize and have determinate choice and action over the separately existing human beings that constitute the field to begin with?
- What becomes of individual freedom, independence, and personal identity with competing needs, intentions, wishes, and agendas that define individuality if the "system" regulates individual thought, affect, and behavior?
- What happens to the system if one participant decides to no longer participate?
- Does the system die, is it suspended, does it reconstitute later?

- What becomes of the system if one participant exerts more will or power over that of the other subject?
- Is not the system merely a temporal play of events rather than an entity?

If these experiences were possible, it would render the system impotent, acausal, and non-regulatory, which directly opposes the relational view that the intersubjective field, dyadic system, relational matrix, or analytic third has causal influence and supremacy over the individual autonomy of its constituents. These conundrums have led Peter Giovacchini (2005) to conclude that for the intersubjectivists, the individual mind becomes this ephemeral ether that evaporates the moment one enters into dialogue or social relations with anyone. While intersubjectivists do not claim that the individual mind vanishes, they do unequivocally concede that it becomes subordinated to the intersubjective system or relational matrix that regulates it.

Psychoanalytic Hermeneutics

The relational turn has largely embraced a constructivist epistemology and method of interpretation, what Hoffman (1998) refers to as "critical" or "dialectical" constructivism based on "mutual influence and constructed meaning" (p. xii). As Stolorow (1998) puts it, "the analyst has no privileged access" to the patient's mind or what truly transpires between the analyst and analysand, for "objective reality is unknowable by the psychoanalytic method" (p. 425). Drawing on Kant's Idealism, claiming we cannot have true knowledge of things in themselves, these epistemological positions are largely gathered from postmodern sensibilities that loosely fall under the umbrella of what may not be inappropriately called psychoanalytic hermeneutics: namely, methods of interpretation derived from subjective experience and participation in social relations that constitute meaning and knowledge.

Constructivist positions—and there are many kinds, social, ethical, feminist, empirical, mathematical—hold a variety of views with points of similarity, and divergence depending upon their agenda or mode of inquiry. Generally, we may say that many relational analysts have adopted a variant of social constructivism by claiming that knowledge is the product of our linguistic practices and social institutions that are specifically instantiated in the interactions and negotiations between others. This readily applies to the consulting room, where knowledge emerges from dialogic relational involvement wedded to context. This is why Hoffman and others rightfully state that meaning is not only discovered, but also created, including the therapeutic encounter and the way we come to understand and view our lives. In fact, analysis is a creative self-discovery and process of becoming, and despite the generic use of the terms "construction" and "co-construction," relational analysts have largely avoided specifically delineating their methodology. With the exception of Donnel B. Stern (1997), who largely aligns with Gadamer's hermeneutic displacement of scientific conceptions of truth and method, Donna Orange's (1995) perspectival epistemology, which is a version of James' and Peirce's pragmatic theories of truth, and Hoffman's brand of dialectical constructivism—the term "dialectic" lacking any clear definition or methodological employment—Relational Psychoanalysis lacks a solid philosophical foundation, one it claims to use to justify its theories and practices. Perhaps with the exception of Stolorow and his collaborators' numerous attempts, none of the relational analysts I've mentioned provide their own detailed theoretical system that guides analytic method, hence falling short of offering a formal framework based on the systematically elaborated, logical rigor we would properly expect from philosophical paradigms. Of course, psychoanalysis can claim that it is not philosophy, so placing such demands on the field is illegitimate; but contemporary frameworks are basing their purported innovations on justifications that derive from established philosophical traditions. Therefore, it is incumbent upon these "new view" theorists (Eagle, Wolitzky, & Wakefield, 2001) to precisely define their positions. Without doing so, relational analysts will continue to invite misinterpretation. Moreover, the psychoanalytic community may continue to misinterpret their frequent use of arcane and abstruse philosophical language, but they may be quite inaccurate when they are dislocated from the tradition in which they originally emerged.

A coherent framework of psychoanalytic hermeneutics has not been attempted since Ricoeur's (1970) critique of Freud's metapsychology, and there has been nothing written, to my knowledge, that hermeneutically critiques contemporary theory. What appears is a pluralistic mosaic—perhaps even a cacophony—of different amalgamated postmodern, hermeneutic traditions derived from constructivism, critical theory, post-structuralism, feminist philosophy, sociology, linguistics, narrative literary criticism, deconstructionism, and—believe it or not—analytic philosophy that have shared visions and collective identifications, but with misaligned projects and competing agendas. For these reasons alone, I doubt we will ever see one coherent comparative-integrative contemporary psycho-analytic paradigm. These disparate groups of theories exist because human knowledge and explanation radically resist being reduced to a common denominator, and here the relationalist position is well taken. There is too much diversity, complexity, difference, particularity, and plurality to warrant such an onerous undertaking. While I have emphasized the recent upsurge of attention on constructivist epistemology in relational circles, it may be said that a general consensus exists for most practicing analysts that absolute truth, knowledge, and certainty do not rest on the crown of the analyst's epistemic authority, and that insight, meaning, and explanation are an ongoing, emerging developmental aspect of any analytic work subject to the unique intersubjective contingencies of the analytic dyad.

The Problem with Postmodernism

I now wish to turn our attention to what may perhaps be the most controversial theoretical debate between the relational traditions and previous analytic schools: namely, the subject–object divide.

Contemporary Relational Psychoanalysis claims to have transcended the theoretical ailments that plague classical analysis by emphasizing the irreducible subjectivity of the analyst (Renik, 1993) over objective certainty, the fallacy of the analyst's epistemological authority, the primacy of context and perspective over universality and essentialism, and the adoption of a "two-person psychology" that is thoroughly intersubjective. But these premises are not without problems. The questions we must ask are:

- Does the analyst's subjectivity foreclose the question of objecti-vity?
- Does epistemically limited access to knowledge necessarily delimit our understanding of truth and reality?
- Does particularity and pluralism negate the notion of universals and collectivity?
- Does a nominalist view of subjectivity necessarily annul the notion of essence?
- Does a two-person model of intersubjectivity minimize or cancel the force and value of intrapsychic reality and lived individual experience?

What Do We Mean by the Term "Postmodernism"?

Although postmodernism has no unified body of theory, thus making it unsystematized, one unanimous implication is the demise of the individual subject. Postmodernism may be generally said to be a cross-disciplinary movement largely comprising linguistic, post-structural, constructivist, historical, narrative, deconstructivist, and feminist social critiques that oppose most Western philosophical traditions. As a result, postmodern doctrines are anti-metaphysical, anti-epistemological, and anti-colonial, thus opposing realism, foundationalism, essentialism, neutrality, and the ideal sovereignty of reason. In this respect, they may be most simply characterized by negation—No! Moreover, erasure—~~Know~~.

Consequently, the transcendental notions of freedom, liberation, individuality, personal independence, authenticity, and reflective deliberate choice that comprise the essential activities of personal agency are altogether disassembled. In other words, the self is anaesthetized.

Meaning is merely a social construction, and all analytic discourse that transpires within the consulting room is dialogical, then meaning and interpretation are conditioned on linguistic social factors then language and culture are causally determinative.

What perhaps appears to be the most widely shared claim in the relational tradition is the assault on the analyst's epistemological authority to objective knowledge. Stolorow (1998) tells us that "objective reality is unknowable by the psychoanalytic method, which investigates only subjective reality . . . there are no neutral or objective analysts, no immaculate perceptions, no God's-eye views of anything" (p. 425). What exactly does this mean? If my patient is suicidal and he communicates this to me, providing he is not malingering, lying, or manipulating me for some reason, does this not constitute some form of objective judgment independent of his subjective verbalizations? Do we not have some capacities to form objective appraisals, here the term "objective" being used to denote making reasonably correct judgments about objects or events outside of our unique subjective experience? Is not Stolorow making an absolute claim despite arguing against absolutism when he says that "reality is unknowable"? Why not say that knowledge is proportional or incremental rather than totalistic, thus subject to modification, alteration, and interpretation, rather than categorically negate the category of an objective epistemology?

In doing so, he reifies intersubjectivity at the expense of subjective life, subordinates the role, scope, and influence of the unconscious, and favors a relational focus on treatment rather than on the intrapsychic dynamics of the analysand.

For all practical purposes, the epistemic emphasis on subjectivity that opposes objectivity is a bankrupt claim because this devolves into untenability where everything potentially becomes relative. I once had a student who was an ardent champion of relativism until I asked him to stand up and turn around. When he did, I lifted his wallet from his back pocket and said: "If everything is relative, then I think I am entitled to your wallet because the university does not pay me enough." Needless to say, he wanted it back. Relativism collapses into contradiction, inexactitude, nihilism, and ultimately absurdity, because no one person's opinion is any more valid than another's, especially including value judgments and ethical behavior, despite qualifications that some opinions are superior to others. When one takes relativism to the extreme, constructivism becomes creationism, which is simply a grandiose fantasy of omnipotence.

Although postmodern psychoanalytic thought is attractive for its emphasis on contextuality, linguistic, gender, and cultural specificity, political reform, postcolonial anti-patriarchy, the displacement of pure reason and phallocentrism, and the epistemic refutation of positivistic science, it does so at the expense of eclipsing metaphysical inquiry, which was the basis of Freud's foray into understanding the ontology of the unconscious and establishing psychoanalysis as a science of subjectivity.

The Separateness of the Self?

Most relational analysts would not deny the existence of an independent, separate subject or self, and in fact have gone to great lengths to account for individuality and authenticity within intersubjective space. A problematic is introduced, however, when a relational or intersubjective ontology is defined in opposition to separateness, singularity, distinction, and individual identity.

Following from these premises, there is no such thing as separate human beings, which is tantamount to the claim we are all identical because we are ontologically indistinguishable. If there is no distinction between two subjects that form the relational encounter, then only the dyadic intersubjective system can claim to have any proper identity. Jon Frederickson (2005) perspicaciously argues that despite the relational emphasis on subjectivity over objectivity, relational analysis inadvertently removes the subject from the subjective processes that constitute relational exchange to begin with, hence contradicting the very premise it seeks to uphold.

While some relational analysts advocate for a singular, cohesive self that is subject to change yet endures over time (Fosshage, 2003; Lichenberg, Lachmann, & Fosshage, 2002), others prefer to characterize selfhood as existing in multiplicity: rather than one self, there are "multiple selves" (Bromberg, 1994; Mitchell, 1993). But how is that possible? To envision multiple "selves" is philosophically problematic on ontological grounds, introduces a plurality of contradictory essences, obfuscates the nature of agency, and undermines the notion of freedom. Here we have the exact opposite position of indistinguishability: multiple selves are posited to exist as separate, distinct entities that presumably have the capacity to interact and communicate with one another and the analyst.

But this is problematic, and we are left with such questions as:

- What becomes of the self in the system?
- Is it free from the causal efficacy of the relational encounter, or is it determined by the encounter?
- Does the self evaporate, or is it merely dislocated, hence demoted in ontological importance?
- And what about the locus of agency?
- How can an interactional process acquire any agency at all?

I believe the relational turn would be better served to indubitably acknowledge that the intersubjective system, field, or matrix is not an agentic subject, being (*Sein*), or entity (*ens*), but rather a "space" forged through transactional psychic temporal processes. By conceiving the relational matrix as intersubjective space instantiated through temporal dynamic mediacy generated by separate subjective agencies in dialogue, the ontological problematic of an emergent, systemically constituted (hence created) entity or analytic third is ameliorated. From my account, there is no third subjectivity or agency, only experiential space punctuated by embodied, transactional temporal processes that belong to the unique contingencies of the human beings participating in such interaction, whether this from the developmental perspective of the mother–infant dyad to the therapeutic encounter. This is what I believe the best-intentioned writers are thinking of when they speak of a relational field theory not as an entity, but as a complex succession of temporal processes This is not a third subject or agency, only the product of enriched, complex interactional transmutations, partially co-constructed, but ultimately conditioned on the unique contingencies (unconscious, historical, developmental, etc.) and teleological (purposeful) trajectories that inform each participant's inner experience, choice, and actions within any interpersonal encounter.

Illegitimate Attacks on Classical Psychoanalysis

What is perhaps the most salient transgression repeatedly made by relational psychoanalysis is its unrelenting misinterpretation of Freudian theory. Richards (1999) argues that the relational school has constructed a false dichotomy between drive theory and relational theory, when in fact Freud's mature theoretical system clearly accounts for relational concepts (Reisner, 1992)—a position Frank (1998) cogently reveals began in Freud's early career. Furthermore, Lothane (2003) recently and persuasively argued that Freud was an interpersonalist, while Roazen (1995) and Lohser and Newton (1996) show that Freud was at times quite relational in his therapeutic actions, as evinced by testimonials acquired from firsthand accounts of his patients.

Let us first examine the exaggerated polarization the relational turn has created between the concepts of relation and drive—an antithesis it has capitalized on to serve as a launching-pad for its "new" theory. Mitchell (1988) specifically tells us that his approach is "a purely *relational* mode perspective, unmixed with drive-model premises" (p. 54). Here Mitchell clearly wants to create a fissure between his relational matrix theory and drive theory Unlike Greenberg (1991), who was concerned with reconciling classical drive theory with contemporary relational perspectives, Mitchell was not only not interested in attempting to account for drive theory, he wanted to debunk it entirely. In doing so, he jettisons the primacy of embodiment.

What becomes of our corporeality in a relational field theory if drives are no longer acknowledged as basic constituents of psychic activity? Mitchell's denunciation of the drives is tantamount to a fundamental denial of our embodied facticity.

Freudian drive theory is an ontological treatise on unconscious organization, human motivation, and psychic development. Unlike Mitchell, Freud was deeply engaged in the problem of nature, hence the empirical *and* speculative investigation of our embodiment. It is not enough (let alone sufficient) to claim that everything is relational or intersubjective without attempting to explain how relationality is constituted. For this reason alone, the relational school can hardly claim to have a sophisticated metaphysical position on the matter. In fact, it was Freud who first explained how relationality was made possible through the transformation of the drives (Mills, 2002).

Drives are the initial impetus underlying the evolution and sublimation of the human soul (*Seele*) and civilization (*Kultur*). What is most interesting about Freud's notion of drive is that he ostensibly introduces the presence of otherness within the very fabric of libidinal and aggressive motivation. A drive has a *telos*, hence an aim (*Zeal*)—It (*Es*) seeks, yearns, pines for satisfaction, for fulfillment—which may only be sated through an object (*Object*). Freud says that an object is the "most variable" aspect to drive activity, but he ultimately privileges human connection. The force or impetus of a drive is to seek human contact and relatedness in order to fulfill its aims. What Freud meant by a human object was in fact a subject— namely, another individual who was separate from the self. Yet Mitchell (1988) avers that "Freud . . . eschew[ed] any role for primary relatedness in his theory and reli[ed] instead solely on drive economies" (p. 54). This tenet is naively fallacious: let us examine why.

Not only is Freud's object relations theory predicated on his seminal paper, "Drives and their fate" (*Triebe und Triebschicksale*; Freud, 1915b), thus making a conceptual clearing for "primary relatedness," he specifically elevates the process of identification, hence an interpersonal dynamic, to the status of a relational phenomenon. Freud (1921) specifically tells us that identification is "the earliest expression of an emotional tie with *another person*" (p. 105, italics added). Later he reiterates this point more clearly: "Identification [*Identifizierung*] . . . [is] the assimilation of one ego [*Ich*] to another one, as a result of which the first ego behaves like the second in certain respects, imitates it and in a sense takes it up into itself" (Freud, 1932–1933, p. 63). Freud goes on to say that it is "a very important form of *attachment* to someone else, probably the very first, and not the same thing as the choice of an object" (p. 63, italics added). Here he deliberately wants to differentiate the psychic importance and affective value of internalizing a parent or dependency figure, rather than merely coveting any arbitrary object for libidinal gratification. And Freud (1931) specifically concedes that for each gender, the mother becomes the original and most important object of identification (see p. 225), "established unalterably for a whole lifetime as the first and strongest love-object and as the prototype of all later love-relations—for both sexes" (Freud, 1938, p. 188). Here Freud ostensibly says that "love from these passages, Freud is clearly describing an intrapsychic process of incorporating the attributes and qualities of another subject (in German, *Person*) encountered through ongoing intersubjective, relational exchange.

It may be argued that relational concepts were implicit in Freud's early work all along: Oedipalization is based on coveting one's parents, to possess him or her, to extract their desired attributes, to *be* them. Despite the fact that Freud did not use terms such as "interpersonal" or "intersubjective," Lothane (2003) rightfully points out that therapy was always characterized in terms of dyadic, interpersonal terms manifesting in all aspects of the treatment, including resistance, transference, working through, and the free-associative method. Freud (1912) defines one facet of technique as the analyst's ability to "turn his own unconscious like a receptive organ towards the transmitting unconscious of the patient (p. 115), hence arguably a dynamic that is accomplished by the analyst's attunement of his own subjectivity to the subjectivity of the patient. Yet Mitchell (1988, p. 297) and others (Hoffman, 1998, pp. 97–102) still misrepresent Freud's depiction of the analytic encounter by referring to the analyst as a "blank screen," when Freud (1912) actually said that the analyst should be "opaque" (*undurchsichtig*) to his patients, hence invoking the metaphor of a "mirror" (*Spiegelplatte*) (p. 118). There is nothing blank about opacity, and a reflective surface is hardly a screen. Take another example: transference is the reiteration of the internalized presence of another person, hence a relational enterprise, which Freud (1915–1917) flatly tells us depends upon "the personal relation between the two people involved" (p. 441), namely the analyst and analysand. We *relate* to our internal objects—that is, the internalized subjectivity of another. It should be irrefutably clear that from Freud's own writings, he establishes relatedness as a primary role in personality development and the clinical encounter.

These invented schisms between classical and relational viewpoints, which only serve to differentiate contemporary approaches from previous schools under the guise of betterment and novelty, create more polarization and tension rather than unity and collective identification, despite having many shared affinities based upon a common calling.

Therapeutic Excess

Frank (1998) argues that the relational tradition has overstated its claim to providing an original contribution to the field, instead giving the "appearance" of a unique position when it is merely the re-appropriation of old paradigms with a make-over, what Giovacchini (1999) calls "old wine in murky bottles." I would say that this is not entirely the case. From the standpoint of redefining therapeutic intervention, analytic posturing, and technical priority, relational analysis is a breath of fresh air. Having questioned, disassembled, and revamped the classical take on neutrality, anonymity, and abstinence, analysts now behave in ways that are more personable, authentic, humane, and reciprocal rather than reserved, clinically detached, and withholding. While it is indeed difficult to make generalizations about all relational clinicians, which is neither desirable nor possible, one gets the impression that within the consulting room, there is generally more dialogue rather than monologue, less interpretation and more active attunement to the process within the dyad, more emphasis on affective experience over conceptual insight, and more interpersonal warmth conveyed by the analyst, thus creating a more emotionally satisfying climate for both involved.

And here is what I believe is the relational position's greatest contribution—the way they practice. There is malleability in the treatment frame, selectivity in interventions that are tailored to the unique needs and qualities of each patient, and a proper burial of the prototypic solemn analyst who is fundamentally removed from relating as one human being to another in the service of a withholding, frustrating, and ungratified methodology designed to provoke transference enactments, deprivation, and unnecessary feelings of rejection, shame, guilt, and rage. Today's relational analyst is more adept at customizing technique to fit each unique dyad (Beebe & Lachmann, 2003; Greenberg, 2001), what Bacal (1998) refers to as a specificity of intervention choice, and rallies against a blanket standardization or manualization of practice. Because of these important modifications to methodology, one may not inappropriately say that a relational approach can be a superior form of treatment for many patients because it enriches the scope of human experience in relation to another's and validates their wish for understanding, meaning, recognition, and love, what may very well be the most coveted and exalted ideals that make psychoanalysis effectively transformative and healing.

Self-Disclosure

Despite these noted strengths, relational analysis has generated a great deal of controversy with regard to the question and procedural role of analyst self-disclosure. On one hand, relational approaches break down barriers of difference by emphasizing dyadic reciprocal involvement, which naturally includes the analyst having more liberty to talk about his/her own internal experiences within the session. However, the question arises: "Where do we draw the line?" This question has led many critics of the relational turn to wonder about the level of what Jay Greenberg (2001) refers to as "psychoanalytic excess," or what Freud (1912) called "therapeutic ambition." Equally, we may be legitimately concerned about the undisciplined use of self-disclosure, countertransference enactments, uninhibited risk-taking, and flagrant boundary violations that have the potential to materialize within this evolving framework of analytic practice. While I believe that most relational analysts are very sound clinicians, it is incumbent upon us to flag potentially questionable or experimental practices in order to bring them into a frank and open discussion on exactly what constitutes a legitimate execution of analytic method. On the one hand, relational analysts are commendably brave to report case studies where their own internal processes and intimate experiences are discussed openly in professional space. On the other hand, we are introduced to material that evokes questions of potential misuse. There is always a danger with the over-expression of personal communications, countertransference disclosures, and the insistence on providing reciprocal revelations that may reveal more about the needs of the analyst rather than the patient's.

Mutuality

The acceptance of mutuality within relational discourse is often un-questioned due to the systemic emphasis on dyadic reciprocal relations, dialogic exchange, and the value of the analyst's presence and participation in the therapeutic process. But we may ask: "What do we mean by mutual?" Is everything mutual, or are there independent forces, pressures, and operations at play that are defined in opposition to difference? When relational analysts employ the notion of mutuality, do they really mean equality, such as having the same relationship, or are they merely inferring that something is shared between them? Modell (1991) refers to mutuality as a form of "egalitarianism," specifically canceling the notion of difference in favor of equality. In fact, relational analysts often equate mutuality with equality, when I believe this is misguided.

Equality implies that there is no difference between each subject in the dyad, that they are identical, and that they have the same value. This position seems to ignore the substantial individual differences that exist between the analyst and the analysand, not to mention the power differentials, role asymmetry, and purported purpose of forming a working relationship to begin with. This is why I prefer to refer to analytic mutuality as defined through proportional exchange, whereby a patient, namely one who suffers, seeks out my professional assistance as an identified authority and pays me a large fee to help. There is nothing equal about it: I'm not the one being analyzed. We must be mindful that we need to be sensitive to the patient's unique needs, and not foist or superimpose our own for the sake of our desires for gratification despite identifying with a certain therapeutic ideal.

Malleability

Relationalists demand malleability in the treatment frame, rather than applying a rigid, orthodox, or authoritarian procedure, because malleability is necessary in order to cater to the unique contingencies of each dyad; and this necessitates abolishing any illusory fixed notions of practice that can be formulaically applied to all situations. I believe most analysts can buy into this premise, but regardless of its pragmatic value, it still begs the question of method. If every intervention is contextually based, then it is relative and subjectively determined, hence not open to universal applications. The question of uniform technique becomes an illegitimate question because context determines everything. The best we can aim for is to have an eclectic skill set (under the direction of clinical judgment, experience, self-reflectivity, and wisdom) to apply to whatever possible clinical realities we may encounter. Hoffman (1994) tells us to "throw away the book" once we have mastered it. Fair enough. But what if a neophyte were reading the relational literature and took such a statement literally? What about reliability and treatment efficacy if there is no proper method to which we can claim allegiance? Could this not lead to an "anything goes" approach conducted by a bunch of loose cannons justifying interventions under the rubric of relationality? Yet the same potential for abuse exists when applying any approach rigidly, whether it is a formal procedure, orienting principle, or general technical considerations; thus the question of method will always remain an indeterminate question with some approaches being more justifiable than others.

As I have stated elsewhere (Mills, 2004), psychoanalysis is ultimately about process over anything else—perhaps even above technical principles, theory, and interventions—for it relies on the indeterminate unfolding of inner experience within intersubjective space. The analyst has the challenging task of attending to the patient's associations within particular contexts of content and form, perpetuity versus discontinuity, sequence and coherence, thus noting repetitions of themes and patterns, and the convergence of such themes within a teleological dynamic trajectory of conceptual meaning. The clinician has to be vigilant for competing, overlapping, and/or parallel processes that are potentially operative at once, thus requiring shifts in focal attention and process. Observation becomes a way of being that requires listening on multiple levels of experiential complexity—from manifest to latent content, detecting unconscious communications, recognizing resistance, defense, drive derivatives, transference manifestations, and differential elements of each compromise, tracking the dialectical tensions between competing wishes, fantasies, and conflicts with close attention to their affective reverberations, listening at different levels of abstraction, ferreting out one's countertransference from ordinary subjective peculiarities—to tracing the multifarious interpersonal components of therapeutic exchange. Given such complexity and the overdetermination of multiple competing processes, I hardly think psychoanalytic technique is capable of being manualized by following a step-by-step method.

Consilence

The conception of psychoanalysis as a science was as much a criticism of Freud's time as it is today. Even Freud (1915a) himself recognized the limits to the so-called "scientific method," and stated: "We have often heard it maintained that sciences should be built up on clear and sharply defined basic concepts. In actual fact no science, not even the most exact, begins with such definitions" (p. 117). For anyone actually working in empirical research, we all know how easy it is to statistically manipulate data; "scientific'" reports are primarily based on the theoretical beliefs of the researcher who is attempting to advocate a specific line of argument under the guise of "objectivity." Freud (1912) saw through this game:

> Cases which are devoted from the first to scientific purposes and treated accordingly suffer in their outcome; while the most successful cases are those in which one proceeds, as it were, without any purpose in view, allows oneself to be taken by surprise by any new turn in them, and always meets them with an open mind, free from any presuppositions.
>
> (p. 114)

Hence he alerted us to the potential interference of the analyst's subjectivity.

Because psychoanalysis has historically always fought prejudice against its scientific achievements—a phenomenon that dominates mainstream academic psychology and psychiatry—perhaps the relational tradition is finding new momentum in the field because of the felt dissatisfactions inherent in an epistemological scientific framework. And with so many generations of analysts having to labor continually to justify their trade to an increasingly cynical public that wants only quick symptom relief rather than insight, it comes as no surprise that the rejuvenation of subjectivity needs to vanquish objective science by making it the contemporary whipping boy. The problem comes when radical adherents for each side attempt to ground their positions through the negation of the other, rather through seeking the fruitful unification that science and hermeneutics have to offer one another as a complex holism. Can the two identificatory bodies of knowledge co-exist in some type of comparative-integrative harmony or dialectical order? This I cannot answer. Yet I believe it remains an important task to pursue this possibility in order for psychoanalysis to prosper and reclaim its cultural value.

Following Bowman's work, I believe it is important to reiterate the point that psychoanalysis is a behavioral science, and not a natural (hard) science, which consequently elevates the role of subjectivity, negotiation, consensus, and relational exchange when making any observation, interpretation, or epistemological assertion. The implication of this thesis is that any form of science by definition simultaneously becomes intimately conjoined with the humanities. Yet at the same time, any true scientist would not make dogmatic metaphysical statements of irrefutable objective certainty, because science (in theory) is always open to the possibility that any theoretical system or methodological framework is an evolving avenue or medium for procuring knowledge, not as fixed, irrefutable determined fact, but as a process of becoming. Given that Relational Psychoanalysis is enjoying adventures of change by re-appropriating philosophy and incorporating the empirical findings of infant observation research, cognitive neuroscience, and attachment theory, this seems to me to be an auspicious sign for our profession.

References

Bacal, H. (Ed.). (1998). *How therapists heal their patients*. Northvale, NJ: Aronson.

Beebe, B., & Lachmann, F. (2003). The relational turn in psychoanalysis: A dyadic systems view from infant research. *Contemporary Psychoanalysis, 39*, 379–409.

Benjamin, J. (1988). *The bonds of love*. New York, NY: Pantheon Books.

Bromberg, P. (1994). "Speak!, that I may see you": Some reflections on dissociation, reality, and psychoanalytic listening. *Psychoanalytic Dialogues, 4*, 517–547.

Eagle, M., Wolitzky, D. L., & Wakefield, J. C. (2001). The analyst's knowledge and authority: A critique of the "new view" in psychoanalysis. *Journal of the American Psychoanalytic Association, 49*, 457–488.

Fosshage, J. L. (2003). Contextualizing self psychology and relational psychoanalysis: Bi-directional influence and proposed syntheses. *Contemporary Psychoanalysis, 39*(3), 411–448.

Frank, G. (1998). On the relational school of psychoanalysis: Some additional thoughts. *Psychoanalytic Psychology, 15*(1), 141–153.

Frederickson, J. (2005). The problem of relationality. In J. Mills (Ed.), *relational and intersubjective perspectives in psychoanalysis: A critique*. Northvale, NJ: Jason Aronson.

Freud, S. (1900). The interpretation of dreams. In J. Strachey (Ed. & Trans.), *The standard edition of the complete psychological works of Sigmund Freud* (Vols. 4–5). London, England: Hogarth Press.

Freud, S. (1912). Recommendations to physicians practicing psycho-analysis. In J. Strachey (Ed. & Trans.), *The standard edition of the complete psychological works of Sigmund Freud* (Vol. 12). London, England: Hogarth Press.

Freud, S. (1915a). Instincts and their vicissitudes. In J. Strachey (Ed. & Trans.), *The standard edition of the complete psychological works of Sigmund Freud* (Vol. 14). London, England: Hogarth Press.

Freud, S. (1915b). *Triebe und Triebschicksale*, Book X, *Werke aus den Jahren, 1913–1917*. In A. Freud, E. Bibring, W. Hoffer, E. Kris, & O. Isakower (Eds.), in collaboration with M. Bonaparte, *Gesammelte Werke, chronologisch geordnet* (pp. 210–232). London, England: Hogarth Press, 1940–1952; Frankfurt am Main, Germany: S. Fischer, 1968.

Freud, S. (1915–1917). Introductory lectures on psycho-analysis. In J. Strachey (Ed. & Trans.), *The standard edition of the complete psychological works of Sigmund Freud* (Vols. 15–16). London, England: Hogarth Press, 1916–1917.

Freud, S. (1921). Group psychology and the analysis of the ego. In J. Strachey (Ed. & Trans.), *The standard edition of the complete psychological works of Sigmund Freud* (Vol. 18). London, England: Hogarth Press.

Freud, S. (1931). Female sexuality. In J. Strachey (Ed. & Trans.), *The standard edition of the complete psychological works of Sigmund Freud* (Vol. 21., pp. 225–243). London, England: Hogarth Press.

Freud, S. (1932–1933). New introductory lectures on psycho-analysis. In J. Strachey (Ed. & Trans.), *The standard edition of the complete psychological works of Sigmund Freud* (Vol. 22). London, England: Hogarth Press.

Freud, S. (1938). An outline of psycho-analysis. In J. Strachey (Ed. & Trans.), *The standard edition of the complete psychological works of Sigmund Freud* (Vol. 23, pp. 144–207). London, England: Hogarth Press, 1940.

Giovacchini, P. (1999). *Impact of narcissism: The errant therapist on a chaotic quest*. Northvale, NJ: Jason Aronson.

Giovacchini, P. (2005). Subjectivity and the ephemeral mind. In J. Mills (Ed.), *relational and intersubjective perspectives in psychoanalysis: A critique*. Northvale, NJ: Jason Aronson.

Greenberg, J. (1991). *Oedipus and beyond: A clinical theory*. Cambridge, MA: Harvard University Press.

Greenberg, J. (2001). The analyst's participation: A new look. *Journal of the American Psychoanalytic Association, 49*(2), 359–381.

Greenberg, J., & Mitchell, S. (1983). *Object relations in psychoanalytic theory*. Cambridge, MA: Harvard University Press.

Hegel, G. F. W. (1807). *Phenomenology of spirit* (A. V. Miller, Trans.). Oxford, England: Oxford University Press, 1977.

Hoffman, I. Z. (1994). Dialectical thinking and therapeutic action in the psychoanalytic process. *Psychoanalytic Quarterly, 63,* 187–218.

Hoffman, I. Z. (1998). *Ritual and spontaneity in the psychoanalytic process*. Hillsdale, NJ: Analytic Press.

Lichtenberg, J. D., Lachmann, F. M., & Fosshage, J. (2002). *A spirit of inquiry: Communication in psychoanalysis*. Hillsdale, NJ: Analytic Press.

Lohser, B., & Newton, P. (1996). *Unorthodox Freud: A view from the couch*. New York, NY: Guilford Press.

Lothane, Z. (2003). What did Freud say about persons and relations? *Psychoanalytic Psychology, 20*(4), 609–617.

Mills, J. (2002). Deciphering the "Genesis problem": On the dialectical origins of psychic reality. *Psychoanalytic Review, 89*(6), 763–809.

Mills, J. (2004). *Treating attachment pathology*. Northvale, NJ: Jason Aronson.

Mitchell, S. A. (1988). *Relational concepts in psychoanalysis: Integration*. Cambridge, MA: Harvard University Press.

Mitchell, S. A. (1993). *Hope and dread in psychoanalysis*. New York, NY: Basic Books.

Mitchell, S. A. (2002). *Relationality: From attachment to intersubjectivity.* Hillsdale, NJ: Analytic Press.

Modell, A. H. (1991). The therapeutic relationship as a paradoxical experience. *Psychoanalytic Dialogues, 1,* 13–28.

Ogden, T. H. (1994). The analytic third: Working with intersubjective clinical facts. *International Journal of Psycho-Analysis, 75,* 3–19.

Orange. D. (1995). *Emotional understanding.* New York, NY: Guilford Press.

Orange, D. M., Atwood, G. & Stolorow, R. D. (1997). *Working intersubjectively: Contextualism in psychoanalytic practice.* Hillsdale, NJ: Analytic Press.

Reisner, S. (1992). Eros reclaimed: Recovering Freud's relational theory. In N. J. Skolnick & S. C. Warshaw (Eds.), *relational perspectives in psycho-analysis* (pp. 281–312). Hillsdale, NJ: Analytic Press.

Renik, O. (1993). Analytic interaction: Conceptualizing technique in light of the analyst's irreducible subjectivity. *Psychoanalytic Quarterly, 62,* 553–571.

Richards, A. D. (1999). Book review of *Ritual and spontaneity in the psychoanalytic process: A dialectical constructivist point of view. Psychoanalytic Psychology, 16*(2), 288–302.

Ricoeur, P. (1970). *Freud and philosophy.* New Haven, CT: Yale University Press.

Roazen, P. (1995). *How Freud worked.* Hillsdale, NJ: Jason Aronson.

Stern, D. B. (1997). *Unformulated experience: From dissociation to imagination in psychoanalysis.* Hillsdale, NJ: Analytic Press.

Stern, D. N. (1985). *The interpersonal world of the infant.* New York, NY: Basic Books.

Stolorow, R. D. (1998). Clarifying the intersubjective perspective: A reply to George Frank. *Psychoanalytic Psychology, 15*(3), 424–427.

Stolorow, R. D., & Atwood, G. (1992). *Contexts of being: The intersubjective foundations of psychological life.* Hillsdale, NJ: Analytic Press.

Stolorow, R. D., Brandchaft, B., & Atwood, G. (1987). *Psychoanalytic treatment: An intersubjective approach.* Hillsdale, NJ: Analytic Press.

Postscript to Chapter 17

Steven Kuchuck

There is much to appreciate in Jon Mills' latest writing. His expansive knowledge of philosophy and psychoanalysis, and critical, analytical approach to evaluating theory, serve him well in Chapter 17 and his previous writing on this and other subjects (2005, 2012a, 2012b). I am glad for this opportunity to respond to his critique.

It seems important to first situate myself theoretically as a way of contextualizing my comments on Dr. Mills' critique. My initial background was as a student of classical theory, later expanding to include what has sometimes been referred to as the "small r" relational interpersonalist theories of Harry Stack Sullivan, the British object relations theorists, the self-psychology theories influenced by Heinz Kohut, and Robert Stolorow and his intersubjective theory associates, before going on to discover Relational Psychoanalysis (see below for a definition of Relational Psychoanalysis[1] as it differs from "small r" relational theory) as introduced by Stephen Mitchell and his colleagues. Relational psychoanalysis has become a theoretical home for me, offering a broader amalgam of psychoanalytic theories that attend to both the intrapsychic and the interpersonal. I continue to advance Relational ideas by serving as a board member, and at the time of publication, President-Elect of the International Association for Relational Psychoanalysis and Psychotherapy, Editor of the relational journal *Psychoanalytic Perspectives*, and Associate Editor of Routledge's *Relational Perspectives Book Series*. In the spirit of full disclosure, I served as series consultant for this volume. My response to Mills emerges from this theoretical and professional background. I will approach this brief commentary by addressing each of the author's points individually.

Conflating Theoretical Differences

Many of the criticisms that Mills launches against relational psychoanalysis are the very same ones that Jay Greenberg and Stephen Mitchell (1983) sought to correct for in differentiating between object relations theory— what they saw as an intrapsychic theory—and interpersonal psychoanalysis, which de-emphasized the internal world. Greenberg and Mitchell (1983) first coined the term "relational" (small r) as a way of identifying a common theme among a diverse group of theories that had not previously been considered connected or unified in any way. Each of the schools that appeared under the new umbrella of "relational" (which are primarily—as Mills mentions—interpersonal, object relations, self-psychology, and intersubjective theory) emphasized a person's embeddedness in the social context (rather than the isolated individual) as the primary unit of study. But it wasn't until his first solo-authored book that Mitchell (1988) began using the term "relational" to *also* refer to a newly developing perspective— in some ways overlapping with, but also distinct from, the earlier theories that he and Greenberg had included under the heading of "relational psychoanalysis." Mitchell's new thinking arose from a melding of Fairbairn's object relations theory with interpersonal psychoanalysis, feminist, queer, gender, and other social theories, and is now sometimes referred to as the New York School, or North American Relational Psychoanalysis. This new and expanded perspective also became referred to as "big R" Relational Psychoanalysis, in order to distinguish it from Mitchell's original use of the term "relational." Among the theorists Mills references who identify as "big R" Relational Psychoanalysts are Mitchell, Lewis Aron, Jessica Benjamin, Virginia Goldner, Adrienne Harris, and Irwin Hoffman. Mills moves in and out of discussions of "small r" and "big R" relational models, usually without noting which of the two frameworks he is referring to.

Further complicating the field Mills is critiquing, there is no singular "school" of "big R" Relational Psychoanalysis. For that reason, this way of thinking that Mitchell first identifies in 1988 has often been referred to as a perspective rather than a theoretical school. Although there are a number of universal characteristics, including dialectical movement between intrapsychic and interpersonal, acknowledgment of intersubjectivity and the inevitable impact of the analyst's subjectivity, multiplicity, and many other variables (Harris, 2011; Aron, 1996), each Relational analyst defines and practices the perspective in his/her own particular way. Given the numerous stances that Mills is collapsing into one or two categories without any differentiation, and his further conflation of relational and Relational Psychoanalysis, it becomes difficult to fully track and respond to his work. But the difficulty doesn't end there.

Intersubjectivity and the Unconscious

There is an additional problem with terminology. Although Mills correctly notes that different theorists have different understandings of the term "intersubjectivity" (i.e., Benjamin, and Stolorow, Atwood & Orange), he uses the word freely without noting how he is defining the term or whose definition he is adhering to. At some points, he even seems to be using the *term* "intersubjectivity" (by which I believe he sometimes means intersubjectivity—sometimes called intersubjective— theory, which assumes no two people can be seen as separate, disembedded objects or subjects) and the *phenomena* of intersubjectivity, generally speaking: the study of experience that does not focus on either subject or object exclusively, and takes into account both conscious and unconscious experience, interchangeably.

For Mills, relational psychoanalysis privileges intersubjectivity over subjectivity and objectivity; he believes that relational psychoanalysis favors conscious experience over the primacy of the unconscious. I agree that most relational analysts challenge a positivistic notion of objectivity: the ability of the analyst to be the holder of absolute, objective truth. But other than perhaps Stolorow and his colleagues (intersubjectivity/intersubjective theorists—relational but not Relational), who, as described above, note that all dynamic formulations must assume intersubjectivity because there is no such thing as a separate, disembedded object or subject, I don't understand the basis for Mills' assertion. The Relational analysts that I know all dialectically move between exploring the patient's and analyst's subjectivity and mutual, intersubjective impact. Relational analysts, in speaking of a "two-person psychology," have never intended to deny that there are two distinct individuals with their own minds and inner worlds. Rather, the purpose of a "two-person psychology" is to recognize the emergence of what Ogden calls "the intersubjective analytic third": "These emergent properties of the dyad exist in dialectical relation to the individual subjectivities of the patient and the analyst" (Mitchell & Aron, 1999, p. xv).

As for conscious versus unconscious work, Mills may be accurately describing some early versions of interpersonal psychoanalysis (as mentioned above, here again is yet another category error—the conflation of interpersonal psychoanalysis and other schools of relational and/or Relational Psychoanalysis) and interpersonal theorist Merton Gill's (1979) ideas about the necessity of focusing exclusively on the here and now. This is an inaccurate interpretation of both contemporary interpersonal theory and relational/Relational Psychoanalysis, though probably not an uncommon misperception of what relationalists do. While I can't speak for the entire community of relational analysts of any ilk, it is difficult to imagine that any of us work only with here and now, secondary process material, or that it's even possible to practice any form of psychotherapy or psychoanalysis that doesn't involve some amount of unconscious-to-unconscious communication. I am perplexed by this split, and find myself asking where the misperception comes from. Many, or more likely all, of us in the relational world move between here and now, which is usually both conscious and unconscious, and deeper unconscious-to-unconscious communications and interpretations. One doesn't have to abandon notions of intersubjectivity or go back to Freud for that level of depth. But more critically, why would focusing on the here and now necessarily be contrasted with exploring the unconscious? Certainly, there are unconscious dynamics operating in regard to content that is about the here and now and that might be explored without referring back to the past or to other objects. When we explore a patient's unconscious perceptions of us, let alone fantasies about our subjectivity, there is much about these perceptions that is out of awareness, some of which is preconscious, but much of which is dynamically unconscious, maintained out of awareness by unconscious defenses which themselves need exploration. Why, then, would a here and now focus necessarily imply any disregard for or de-emphasis of unconscious material?

The Authority of the Analyst and His/Her Objectivity

Mills believes that "the most widely shared claim in the relational tradition is the assault on the analyst's epistemological authority to objective knowledge," quoting Stolorow that "there are no neutral or objective analysts . . . ." Mills is correct that Relational (and some "small r") analysts do adhere to a newer model for clinical technique and attitude in which the remote, "neutral," "objective" analyst is now replaced with a creative, interactive, human who is willing to recognize his/her part in things. It's not just that relationalists simply believe analysts need to be warmer, more "human," and less remote. The fact is, a major change brought about by both relational (including, but not limited to, intersubjective theorists) and Relational thinking is that we no longer believe patients and analysts have isolated minds. Our relational understanding of a two-person psychology assumes a significant theoretical difference from the classical perspective that Mills seems to prefer. The relational move beyond the "neutral" emerges from a significant rethinking of Freud's metapsychology, and drive theory/metapsychology has been re-evaluated based on newer thinking about patients' minds as intersubjective, rather than isolated.

Mills goes on to claim that Stolorow "reifies intersubjectivity at the expense of subjective life, subordinates the role, scope, and influence of the unconscious, and favors a relational focus on treatment rather than on the intrapsychic dynamics of the analysand." I think that he is correctly describing Stolorow's privileging of intersubjectivity over subjectivity, but Mills also creates what relationalists would see as a false binary between "relational focus" and "intrapsychic dynamics," as I state above.

Multiplicity

Mills asks how it is possible to adhere to a theory of multiple selves without introducing a "plurality of contradictory essences," which is "philosophically problematic on ontological grounds." I agree that multiplicity does in fact assume contradiction. As we know, even anecdotally, different aspects of oneself are by nature often in opposition. By example, think about the fact that on certain days and under particular circumstances, the very same person might feel shy, outgoing, and eager for social contact, or longing for solitude. The examples of differing and often contradictory self-states are likely endless. At least in practice, I don't see a (philosophical or other) problem with this concept.

Although Mills makes a number of assertions that seem not to be mutually exclusive from an assumption of multiplicity and therefore able to be held in tension with multiplicity, he also asks a series of questions that some may find helpful in understanding this central tenet of relational psychoanalysis. Though it is beyond the scope of this brief Postscript to address each of his queries, it is particularly important to respond to his question, *"Is the self free from the causal efficacy of the relational encounter, or is it determined by the encounter?"* Self-states are not necessarily caused by the relational encounter as much as they may be stirred and assume lesser or greater dominance in the here and now. One goal of a Relational analysis is to increase a patient's access to various self-states, and as Philip Bromberg writes, to help patients develop the capacity to remember and be aware of a multitude of other self-states even while inhabiting one specific set of such states; what Bromberg calls "standing in the spaces" (1996). And as to his question, *"Does the self evaporate, or is it merely dislocated, hence demoted in ontological importance?"*, the answer is that various self-states move in and out of foreground and background.

Drive Theory

Mills notes that "the relational school has constructed a false dichotomy between drive theory and relational theory." Although initially founded on the premise that object-seeking rather than drive discharge is what motivates us and therefore needs to be central to any relational theory, and while this is still a significant component of the relational zeitgeist, Greenberg (1993) later suggested that relationalists (including Relational analysts) might need to consider retaining some form of a drive theory model. Other relationalists have since adapted that view as well, and from the very beginning, Mitchell was clear that his new vision of psychoanalysis was not to be hegemony. There is much less of a dichotomy between these metapsychologies than Mills seems to recognize. He goes on to note that Mitchell's rejection of the drives is equal to wholesale renunciation of our embodied selves. On the contrary, there is a large and growing Relational literature on embodiment (Sletvold, 2014; Knoblauch, 1996; Katz & Kelly, 2016).

One need not assume that our primary motivations are for the gratification of bodily based drives in order to argue that our bodies are central to our sense of self and relatedness with others and with the world around us.

Privileging Freud

The author contends that "Freud's mature theoretical system clearly accounts for relational concepts . . . ." He declares that, from the onset, psychoanalysis was always intersubjective and inclusive of object relations. The only problem, he mentions, is that these aspects of classical psycho-analysis, though already there and even referred to, had not yet been adequately theorized, articulated, and emphasized. I've heard this said by classical psychoanalysts numerous times about object relations and other post-Freudian theories (Schwartz, 2012; Carmeli & Blass, 2010; Bachant, Lynch, & Richards, 1995). In fact, there seems to be a tradition of declaring that nothing significantly new has occurred since Freud that dates back to Freud himself. In a letter to Eva Rosenfeld, a patient, colleague, and family friend, Sigmund Freud writes:

> You know my attitude to the teachings of Melanie Klein. I too believe that she has discovered something new, but I do not know whether it means as much as she thinks, and I am sure that it grants no right to put theory and technique on a new basis.
>
> (August 15, 1937, in Heller, 1992, p. 45)

While I have no reason to believe that this is Mills' intent, by saying that relational theories only differ from classical theory in emphasis, and therefore have nothing theoretically new to add, he allows critics of the newer theories to justify maintaining the status quo, and gives support to the theoretical, political, and institutional powerbase, to diminish the important contributions of the relational schools. This stance rationalizes not having to learn new theory or deal with the threatening, possibly disorienting experiences of changing how one might think about theory, prior personal and professional treatments, and current ways of practicing. Freud once told the following joke:

> A. borrowed a copper kettle from B. and after he had returned it was sued by B. because the kettle now had a big hole in it which made it unusable. A.'s defense was: "First, I never borrowed a kettle from B. at all; secondly, the kettle had a hole in it already when I got it from him; and thirdly, I gave him back the kettle undamaged."
>
> (1905/1960, p. 62)

Each one of these defenses is valid in itself, but taken together, they exclude one another. In my view, the mainstream response to innovation in psychoanalysis is structured very much along the lines of this joke. First, what you are saying is wrong or partial. Second, we have already known it, and have always maintained this to be the case; third, whatever is good in what you are saying, we have now learned from you and incorporated, but with the advantage of putting it into its proper place within the whole comprehensive theory of psychoanalysis, while you have merely substituted the part for the whole.[2]

Self-Disclosure

As for the author's concerns about misuse and overuse of self-disclosure, I don't know a single relational/Relational analyst who would disagree with the necessity for vigilance in this area (Aron, 1996; Kuchuck, 2009, Barsness & Strawn, Chapter 12 of this volume). Likewise, Mills tells us that relational analysts mistake mutuality for equality, and strive for both in ways that are harmful to patients. I'm not aware of relational/Relational writing that suggests this, but I can point the reader to Lewis Aron's frequently cited writing about the importance of mutuality in a two-person psychology, and the necessary differentiation between mutuality and symmetry. In his seminal text on relational psychoanalysis, Aron writes that the analyst–analysand relationship is mutual, but asymmetrical (1996). This stands in direct contrast to what strikes me as Mills' possible misunderstanding about this area of relational thinking and practice.

Wild Psychoanalysis

Chapter 17 closes with Mills' observation that relational analysts advocate for flexibility in the therapeutic frame in order to cater to the unique needs of each dyad. I agree, and would go so far as to remind the reader that Thomas Ogden suggests "it is the analyst's responsibility to reinvent psychoanalysis for each patient and continue to reinvent it throughout the course of the analysis" (2004, p. 861). Mills doesn't seem to dispute this assertion, and even quotes Irwin Hoffman's (1994) contention that we must "throw away the book" (p. 188), and makes what most relationalists would agree is a valid claim:

> the best we can aim for is to have an eclectic skill set (under the direction of clinical judgment, experience, self-reflectivity, and wisdom) to apply to whatever possible clinical realities we may encounter . . . . But what if a neophyte were reading the relational literature and took [Hoffman's] statement literally? What about reliability and treatment efficacy if there is no proper method to which

we can claim allegiance? Could this not lead to an "anything goes" approach conducted by a bunch of loose cannons justifying interventions under the rubric of relationality?

(p. 336)

I would answer that indeed, this could and does happen whenever someone—of any theoretical background—is undertrained or otherwise enacting something. Earlier versions of such irresponsible behavior were practiced by our classical ancestors and colleagues, and called "wild analysis" (Shafer, 1985). Perhaps Mills agrees with me on this, because he seems to contradict himself, or at least removes the specificity of his concern from the confines of relational theory, when he adds: "Yet the same potential for abuse exists when applying any approach rigidly . . . thus the question of method will always remain an indeterminate question . . . ." On this we can agree, as is also the case when he credits the relational perspective for advancing numerous treatment techniques and necessary changes in older, more rigid and inhibiting analytic attitudes.

Moving Forward

I will close as I began, by expressing my appreciation for the opportunity to respond to Mills' thoughtful, erudite essay. This is just the latest iteration of an ongoing dialogue that can help to clarify and expand readers' understanding of the often complex and overlapping meanings of relational theories and perspectives. I thank Jon Mills for moving the conversation forward. And I want to point readers to three upcoming publications that will expand the debate: "The relational approach and its critics—a conference with Dr. Jon Mills," which will be published in the journal *Psychoanalytic Perspectives*; Aron, L., Grand, S., & Slochower, J. (Eds.) (in press), *De-Idealizing Relational Theory: A Critique from Within* (London, England: Routledge); and Aron, L., Grand, S., & Slochower, J. (Eds.) (in press), *Decentering Relational Theory: A Comparative Critique* (London, England: Routledge).

Notes

1   Parts of this Postscript are based on an unpublished manuscript by the author and Lewis Aron. I am grateful for Aron's permission to include that material here, and for his generous contributions to this Postscript.

2　I am grateful to Lewis Aron for bringing this joke and its relevance to this Postscript to my attention.

References

Aron, L. (1996). *A meeting of minds: Mutuality in psychoanalysis*. New York, NY: Routledge.

Bachant, J. L., Lynch, A. A., & Richards, A. D. (1995). Relational models in psychoanalytic theory. *Psychoanalytic Psychology, 12*, 71–87.

Bromberg, P. (1996). Standing in the spaces: The multiplicity of self and the psychoanalytic relationship. *Contemporary Psychoanalysis, 32*, 509–535.

Carmeli, Z., & Blass, R. (2010). The relational turn in psychoanalysis: Revolution or regression? *European Journal of Psychotherapy and Counselling, 12*, 217–224.

Freud, S. (1905). Jokes and their relation to the unconscious. In J. Strachey (Ed. & Trans.), *The standard edition of the complete psychological works of Sigmund Freud* (Vol. 8, pp. 9–236). London, England: Hogarth Press, 1960.

Gill, M. (1979). The analysis of the transference. *Journal of the American Psychoanalytic Association, 27*, 263–288.

Greenberg, J. (1993). *Oedipus and beyond: A clinical theory.* Cambridge, MA: Harvard University Press.

Greenberg, J., & Mitchell, S. (1983). *Object relations in psychoanalytic theory.* Cambridge, MA: Harvard University Press.

Harris, A. E. (2011). The relational tradition: Landscape and canon. *Journal of the American Psychoanalytic Association, 59*, 701–735.

Heller, P. (1992). *Anna Freud's letters to Eva Rosenfeld.* Madison, CT: International Universities Press.

Hoffman, I. (1994). Dialectical thinking and therapeutic action in psychoanalytic process. *Psychoanalytic Quarterly, 63*, 187–218.

Katz, A., & Kelly, J. (Eds.). (2016). *The analyst's body in the consulting room* (special issue). *Psychoanalytic Perspectives, 13*(2).

Knoblauch, S. (1996). The play and interplay of passionate experience: Multiple organizations of desire. *Gender & Psychoanalysis, 1*, 323–344.

Kuchuck, S. (2009). Do ask, do tell? Narcissistic need as a determinant of analyst self-disclosure. *Psychoanalytic Review, 96*, 1007–1024.

Mills, J. (2005). A critique of relational psychoanalysis. *Psychoanalytic Psychology, 22*(2), 155–188.

Mills, J. (2012a). *Conundrums: A critique of contemporary psychoanalysis.* New York, NY: Routledge.

Mills, J. (2012b). *The unconscious abyss: Hegel's anticipation of psychoanalysis.* New York, NY: State University of New York Press.

Mitchell, S. (1988). *Relational concepts in psychoanalysis.* Cambridge, MA: Harvard University Press.

Mitchell, S., & Aron, L. (1999). *Relational psychoanalysis: The emergence of a tradition*. Hillsdale, NJ: Analytic Press.

Ogden, T. H. (2004). This art of psychoanalysis: Dreaming undreamt dreams and interrupted cries. *International Journal of Psycho-Analysis, 85*, 857–877.

Schafer, R. (1985). Wild analysis. *Journal of American Psychoanalytic Association, 33*(2), 275–299.

Schwartz, H. P. (2012). Intersubjectivity and dialecticism. *International Journal of Psycho-Analysis, 93*, 401–425.

Sletvold, J. (2014). *The embodied analyst: From Freud and Reich to relationality*. New York, NY: Routledge.

Coda

Roy E. Barsness

I began this book in Chapter 1 with a reference to Freud, who acknowledged that:

> the plasticity of all mental processes, and the great number of the determining factors involved prevent the formulation of a stereotyped technique . . . and yet these circumstances do not prevent us from establishing a procedure for the physician which will be found most generally efficient.
>
> (1912, p. 342)

With that in mind, I sought to provide a structure or a set of Core Competencies that ground and serve the practitioner in the practice of an effective psychotherapy. Core Competencies are not a set of applied techniques, but more a way of situating ourselves within the therapeutic relationship. We hold to a particular stance, we listen in a particular way, and we work within the relationship by linking past and present. We courageously enter and address the relationship that "speaks" to us from within the therapeutic dyad itself. The relational model holds to the idea that change and transformation happens through a genuine encounter with the other. To that end, our "technique" is always evolving, and reconsidered anew in each relational dyad. These competencies demand a great deal of us, as they cannot function effectively in isolation, but are effective only in relation to the authenticity of the practitioner. Martin Buber (1951) effectively states our situation in this way:

> On this paradoxical foundation, laid with great wisdom and art, the psychotherapist now practices with skill and also with success. Until . . . a therapist is terrified because he begins to suspect that at least in

some cases, but finally, perhaps in all, something entirely other is demanded of him. Something incompatible with the economics of his profession, dangerously threatening . . . . What is demanded of him is . . . a call not to his confidently functioning security of action, but to the abyss, that is to the self of the doctor, that selfhood that is hidden under the structures erected through training and practice, that is itself encompassed by chaos, itself familiar with demons, but is graced with the humble power of wrestling and overcoming, and thus is ready to wrestle and overcome anew.

(Buber, 1951, p. 19)

It is my hope that this text will guide and help you in your "wrestling" as you continue to commit to the very important and sacred call of psychoanalysis/psychotherapy, assisting others through their pain and their trauma towards a full and meaningful life.

References

Buber, M. (1951). Healing through meeting. In J. Agassi (Ed.), *Martin Buber on psychology and psychotherapy: Essays, letters, and dialogues* (pp. 17–21). Syracuse, NY: Syracuse University Press.

Freud, S. (1912). Recommendations to physicians practicing psycho-analysis. In J. Strachey (Ed. & Trans.), *The standard edition of the complete psychological works of Sigmund Freud* (Vol. 31, pp. 342–343). London, England: Hogarth Press.

Permissions

Chapter 3 first published as Harris, A. (2011). The relational tradition: Landscape and canon. *Journal of American Psychoanalytic Association*, *59*, 701–734. Reprinted by permission of SAGE Publications Ltd.

Chapter 4 first published as Tublin, S. (2011). Discipline and freedom in psychoanalytic technique. *Contemporary Psychoanalysis*, *47*, 519–545. Reprinted by permission of Taylor & Francis, LLC.

Chapter 5 first published as McWilliams, N. (2004). The psychoanalytic sensibility. In *Psychoanalytic sensibility in psychoanalytic psychotherapy: A practitioner's guide* (pp. 27–45). New York, NY: Guilford Press. Reprinted by permission of Guilford Press.

Chapter 6 first published as Pizer, S. A. (2014). The analyst's generous involvement: Recognition and the "tension of tenderness." *Psychoanalytic Dialogues*, *24*, 1–13. Reprinted by permission of Taylor & Francis, LLC.

Chapter 7 first published as Aron, L. (2006). Analytic impasse and the third: Clinical implications of intersubjectivity theory. *International Journal of Psychoanalysis*, *87*, 349–368. Reprinted by permission of John Wiley & Sons, Inc.

Index

Abbass, A. 36
abstinence 186
acceptance 107, 111
affect 96–7, 292–3
affective attunement 104–19, *105*
affective communications of traumatized self-states 252
affective intensity 82
affective sharing (communion) 106
affect regulation 245, 253
agency 323–4
Age of Certainty (postwar period) 50
aggressive countertransferences 204
Ahlin, Goran 34
Akhtar, S. 287
"alphabetizing" (Bion) 313
Althusser, L. 48
Altman, N. 57
American Psychological Association (APA) 241, 255, 284
analysands *see* patients
analysts/therapists: Classical analytic role 165; countertransferential responses 251; double-mindedness 135; emotional balance 311; emotional closeness 155; expressing feelings 171; external community 306–8; father figures 146, 190–1, 194–5; identifying with clients 93–4; insecurities in analytic community 306; loss 311; masochistic self-effacement 208; motivations for becoming analysts 163; myth of surrogate parent 170–1; narcissistic self-regulation 197–8; passive aggressive 164; patient's perspective 133–4; *personal role* 165; revealing conflicts in functioning 134; self-care 302–16; self-disclosure and thirdness 132; self-esteem 302–6; self-regulation 302–6; sexual feelings 187; shame 309–10; subjectivity 55, 304, 338; use of the self 304
analytic love 202–10, 211–12, 215 *see also* love (*agape/amae*); therapeutic love
analytic neutrality 183, 303, 345
analytic reverie 56
analytic symbolization 139
analytic third 122
analytic vulnerability 56
androphiles 270, 271
anger 173–4, 310–11
anorexia 92
antidepressants 24, 25, 28, 30–1, 32 *see also* cognitive behavioral therapy (CBT)
anti-Semitism 286
APA Presidential Task Force on Evidence-Based Practice 241
Apprey, M. 57
archaic selfobject (Teicholz) 209–10
Archives of Sexual Behavior (online journal) 264
Ari (patient) 202–3, 212–14
Aron, Lewis: dialectical relations 344; Freud's self-representation 285–6; impasse 55; intersubjectivity 303; mutuality 54, 349; psychotherapy and psychoanalysis 57; reactive push-and-pull cooperation 138; relational practices 16–18; technique 198; third/thirdness 79, 303
arranged marriages 295
Aspland, H. 252
Association for Behavioral and Cognitive Therapies 25
Atlas, G. 277
attachment 50–1, 58–9, 97–9, 107, 109–10

Taylor & Francis eBooks

Helping you to choose the right eBooks for your Library

Add Routledge titles to your library's digital collection today. Taylor and Francis ebooks contains over 50,000 titles in the Humanities, Social Sciences, Behavioural Sciences, Built Environment and Law.

Choose from a range of subject packages or create your own!

Benefits for you

>> Free MARC records
>> COUNTER-compliant usage statistics
>> Flexible purchase and pricing options
>> All titles DRM-free.

Benefits for your user

>> Off-site, anytime access via Athens or referring URL
>> Print or copy pages or chapters
>> Full content search
>> Bookmark, highlight and annotate text
>> Access to thousands of pages of quality research at the click of a button.

REQUEST YOUR **FREE** INSTITUTIONAL TRIAL TODAY

Free Trials Available
We offer free trials to qualifying academic, corporate and government customers.

eCollections – Choose from over 30 subject eCollections, including:

Archaeology	Language Learning
Architecture	Law
Asian Studies	Literature
Business & Management	Media & Communication
Classical Studies	Middle East Studies
Construction	Music
Creative & Media Arts	Philosophy
Criminology & Criminal Justice	Planning
Economics	Politics
Education	Psychology & Mental Health
Energy	Religion
Engineering	Security
English Language & Linguistics	Social Work
Environment & Sustainability	Sociology
Geography	Sport
Health Studies	Theatre & Performance
History	Tourism, Hospitality & Events

For more information, pricing enquiries or to order a free trial, please contact your local sales team:
www.tandfebooks.com/page/sales

 Routledge
Taylor & Francis Group

The home of
Routledge books

www.tandfebooks.com